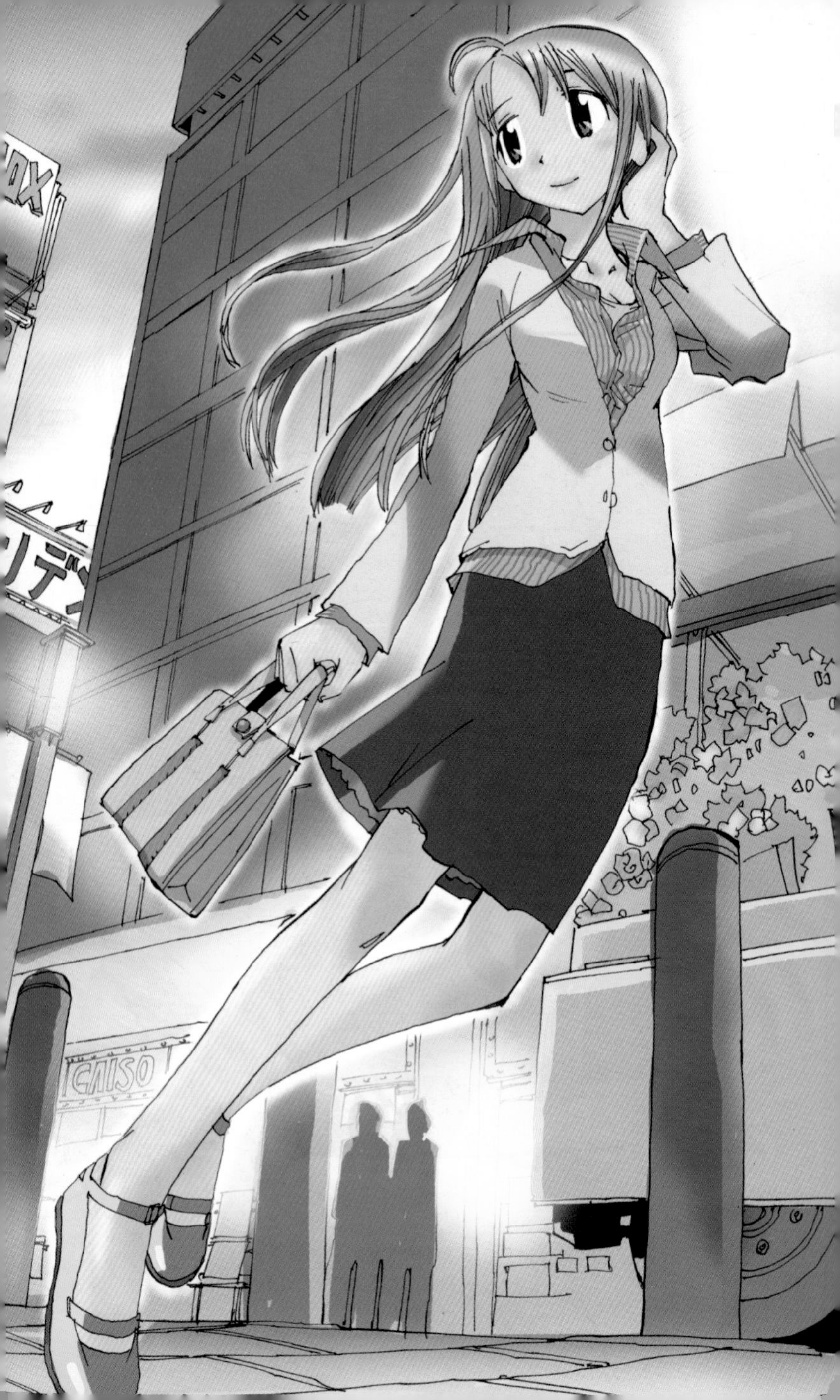

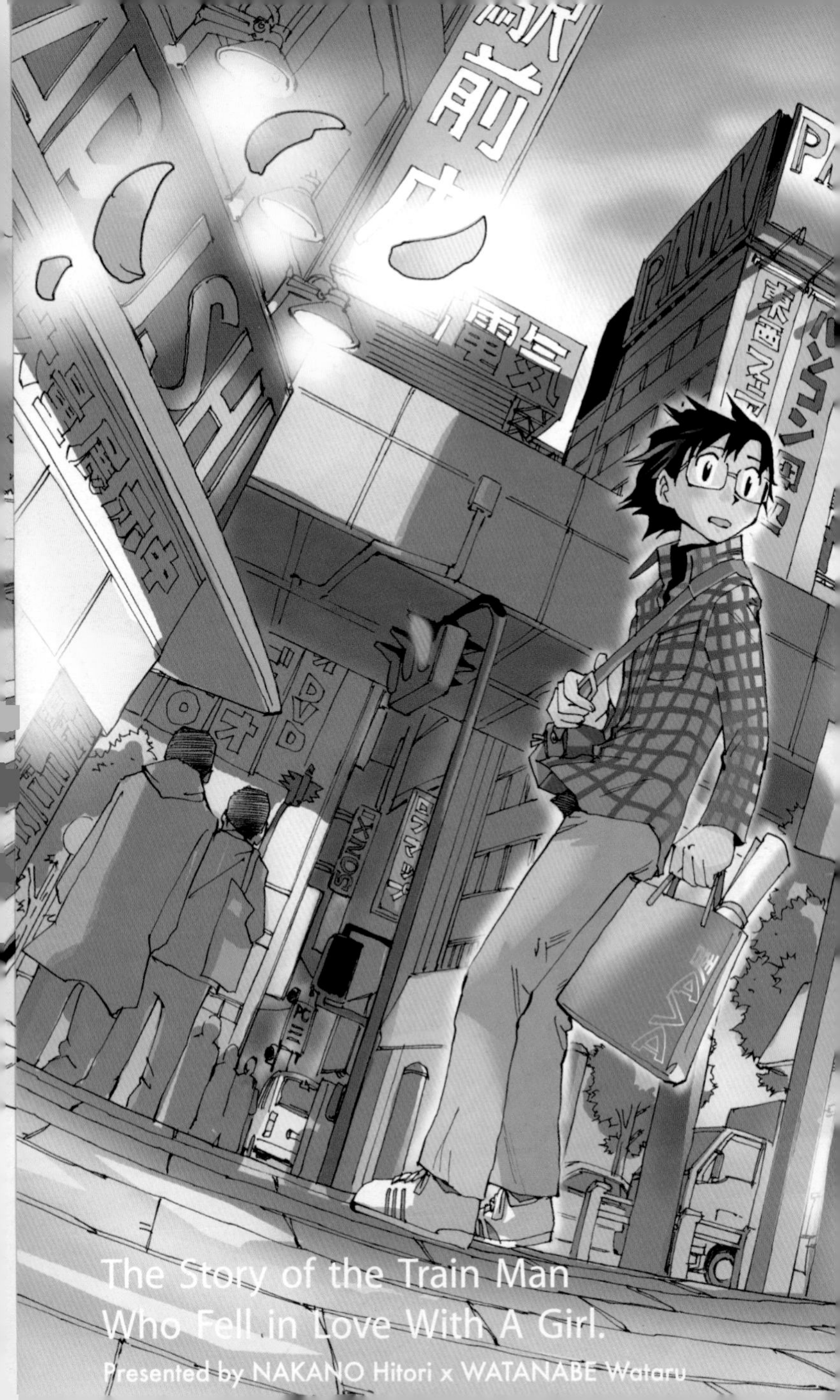
The Story of the Train Man
Who Fell in Love With A Girl.
Presented by NAKANO Hitori x WATANABE Wataru

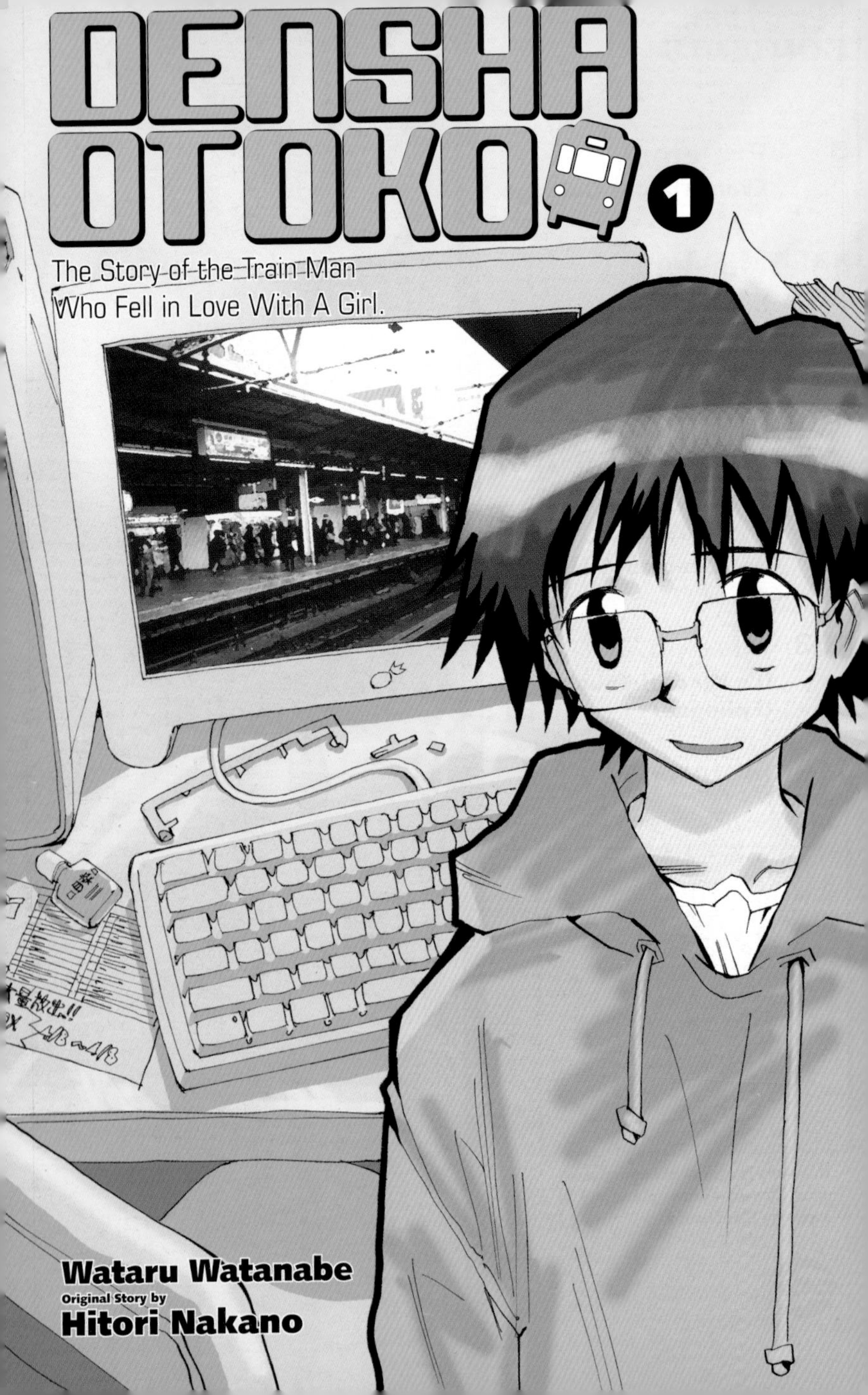
DENSHA OTOKO
1
The Story of the Train Man
Who Fell in Love With A Girl.
Wataru Watanabe
Original Story by
Hitori Nakano

CONTENTS

3 **Prologue:**
Even Without Courage

14 **Mission.1:**
I...I...

53 **Mission.2:**
Muri-Po ("I Can't Do This!")...

93 **Mission.3:**
Be Tenacious? How?...

133 **Mission.4:**
It's Kind of Tough...
(Epilogue)

179 **Editorial**

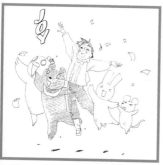

This story is a work of fiction based upon *Densha-Otoko*, published in Japan by Shinchosha

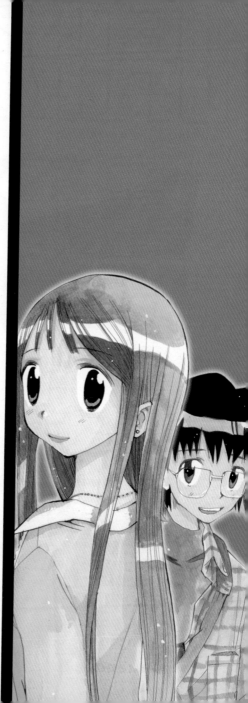

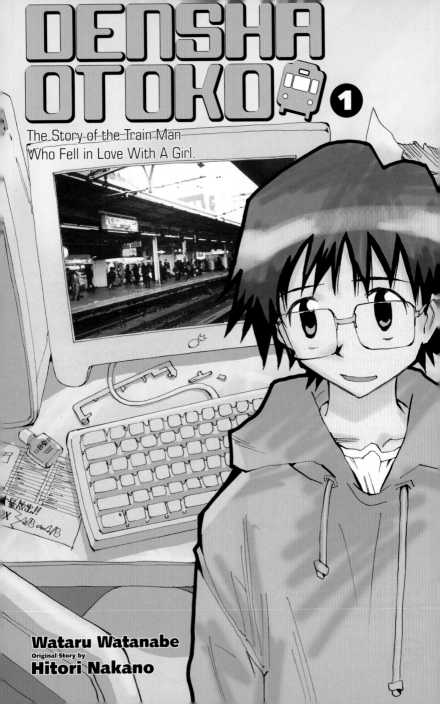

CONTENTS

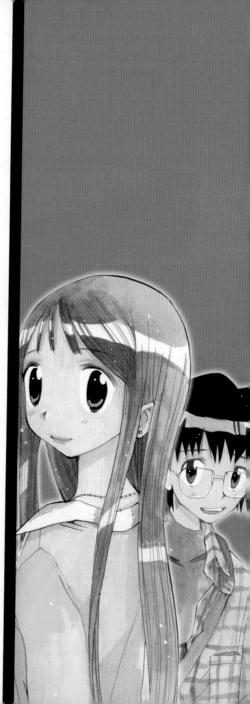

3   **Prologue:**
Even Without Courage

14   **Mission.1:**
I...I...

53   **Mission.2:**
Muri-Po ("I Can't Do This!")...

93   **Mission.3:**
Be Tenacious? How?...

133   **Mission.4:**
It's Kind of Tough... (Epilogue)

179   **Editorial**

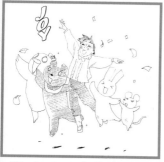

This story is a work of fiction based upon *Densha-Otoko*, published in Japan by Shinchosha

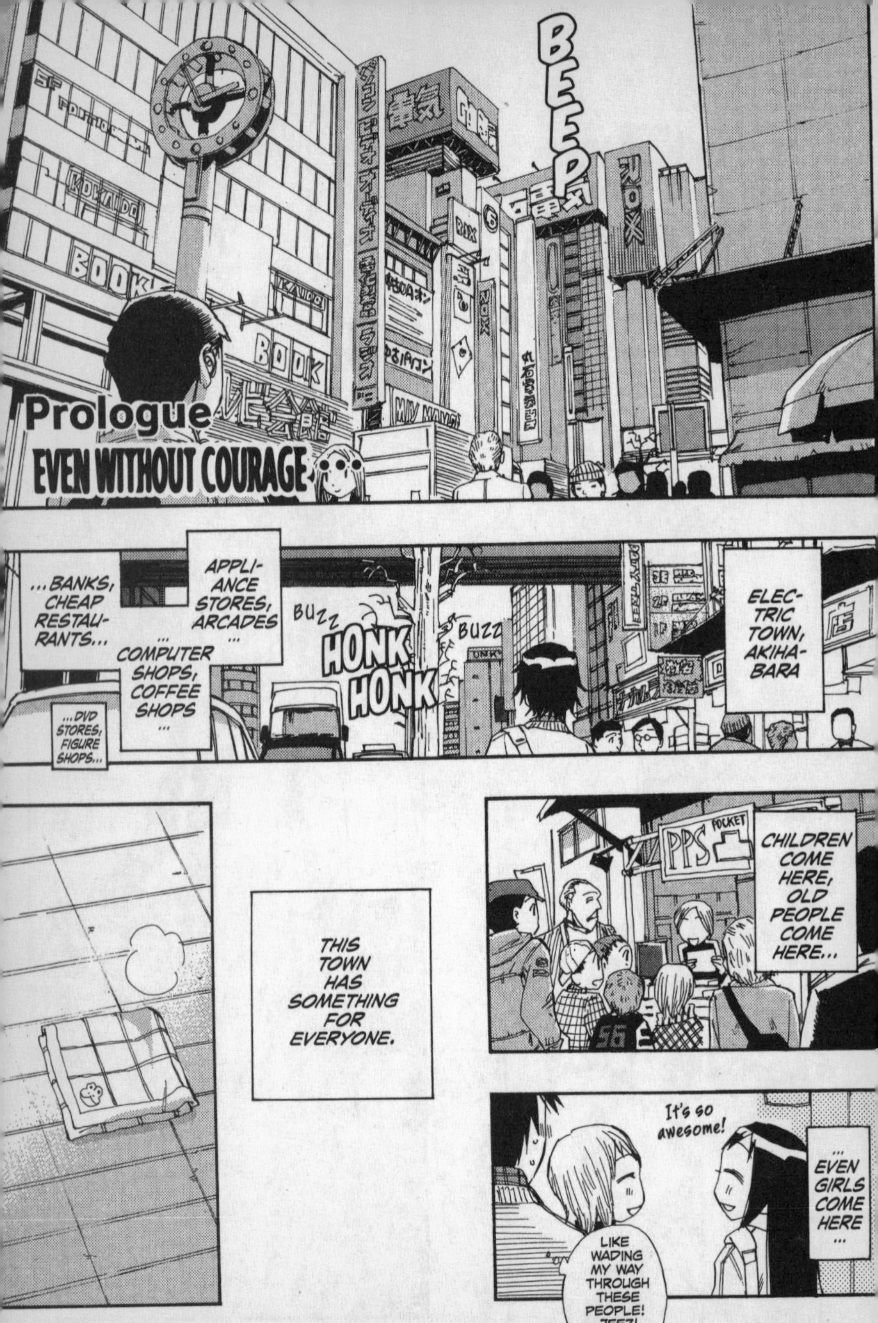
BEEP
Prologue
EVEN WITHOUT COURAGE
ELECTRIC TOWN, AKIHABARA
BUZZ
HONK HONK
BUZZ
APPLIANCE STORES, ARCADES ...
...BANKS, CHEAP RESTAURANTS...
...COMPUTER SHOPS, COFFEE SHOPS ...
...DVD STORES, FIGURE SHOPS...
CHILDREN COME HERE, OLD PEOPLE COME HERE...
...EVEN GIRLS COME HERE ...
It's so awesome!
LIKE WADING MY WAY THROUGH THESE PEOPLE! JEEZ!
THIS TOWN HAS SOMETHING FOR EVERYONE.

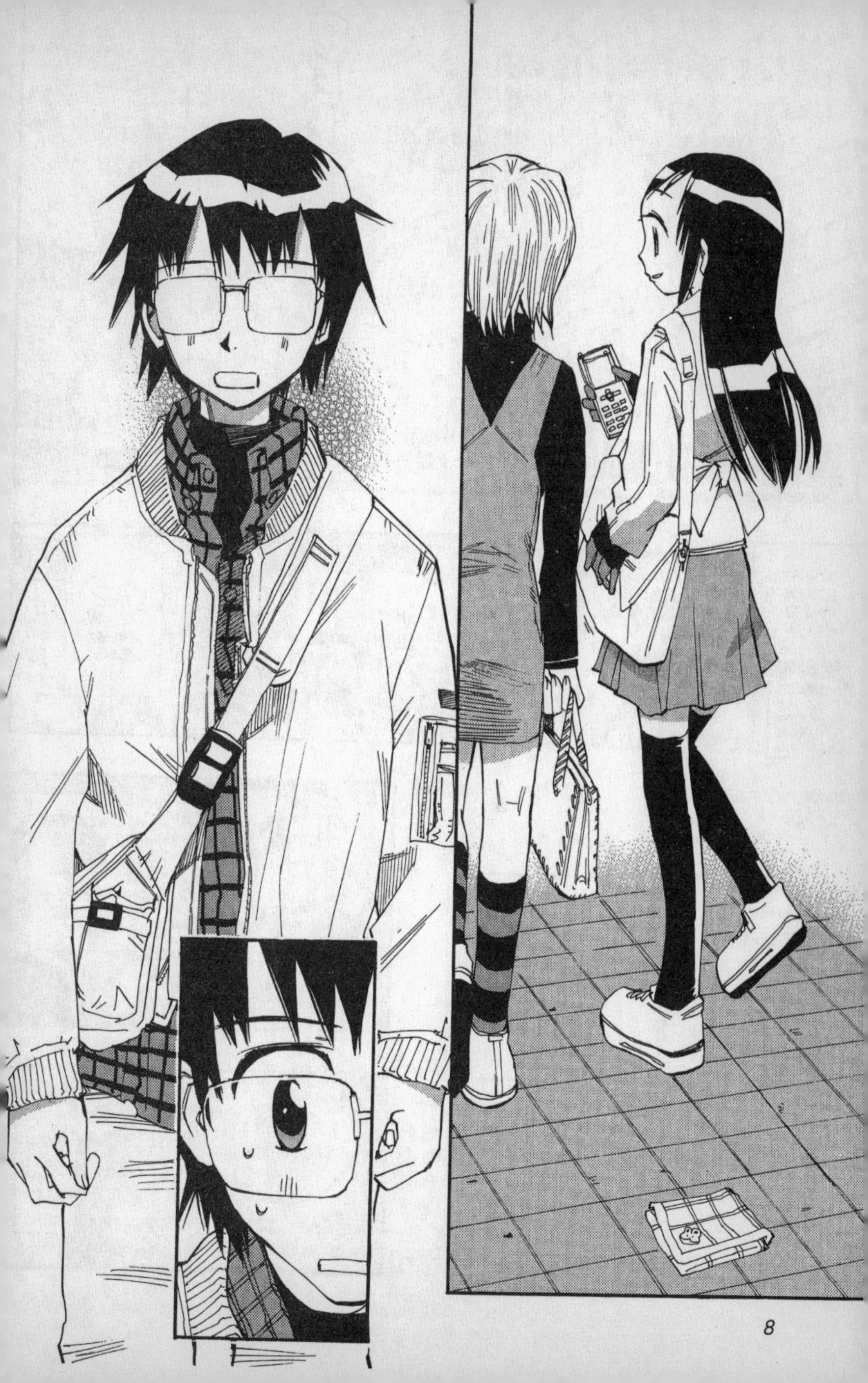

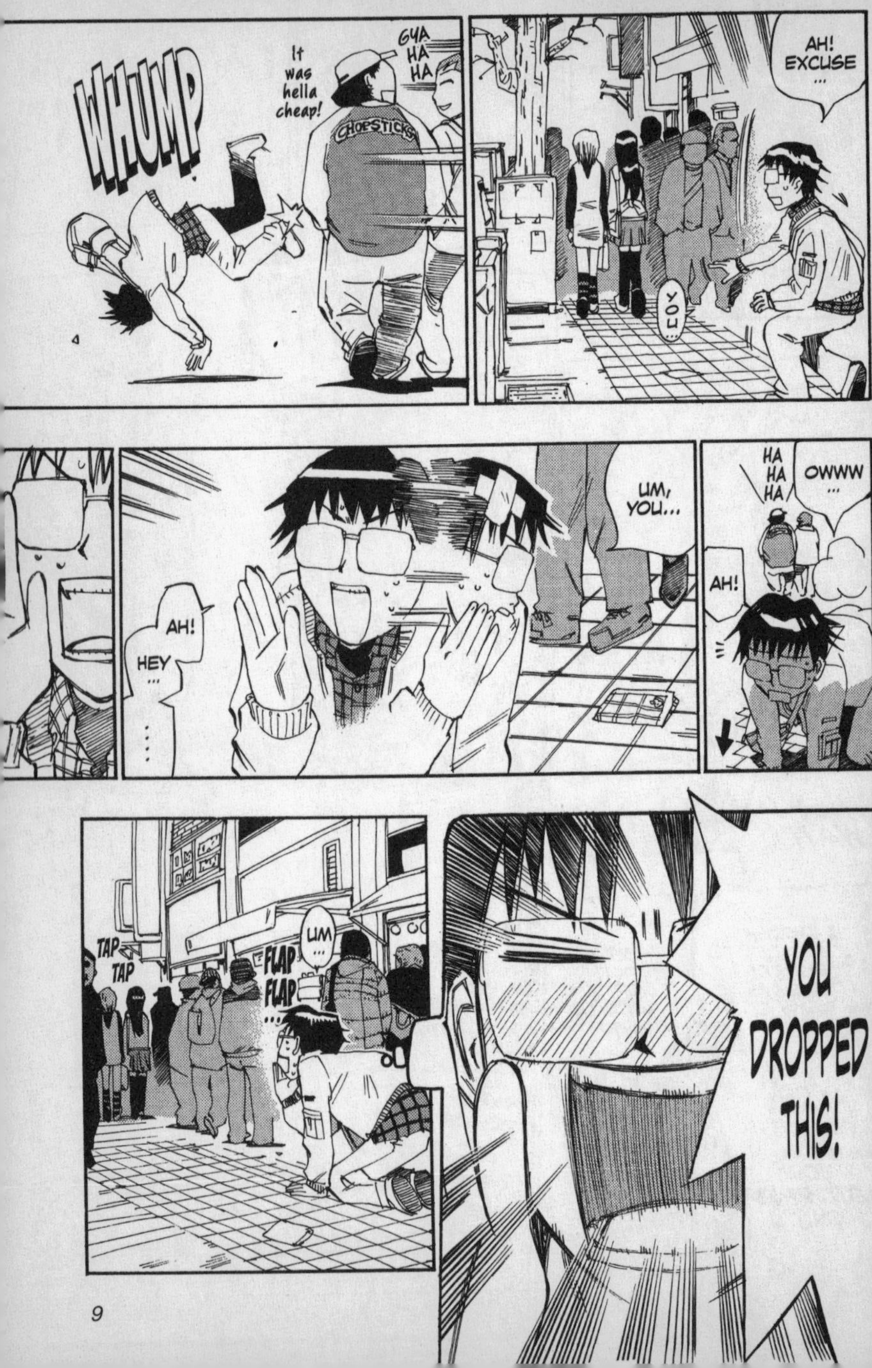
AH! EXCUSE ...
YOU...
GYA HA HA
It was hella cheap!
CHOPSTICKS
WHUMP
OWWW ...
HA HA HA
AH!
UM, YOU...
AH! HEY ...
....
YOU DROPPED THIS!
UM ...
FLAP FLAP ...
TAP TAP

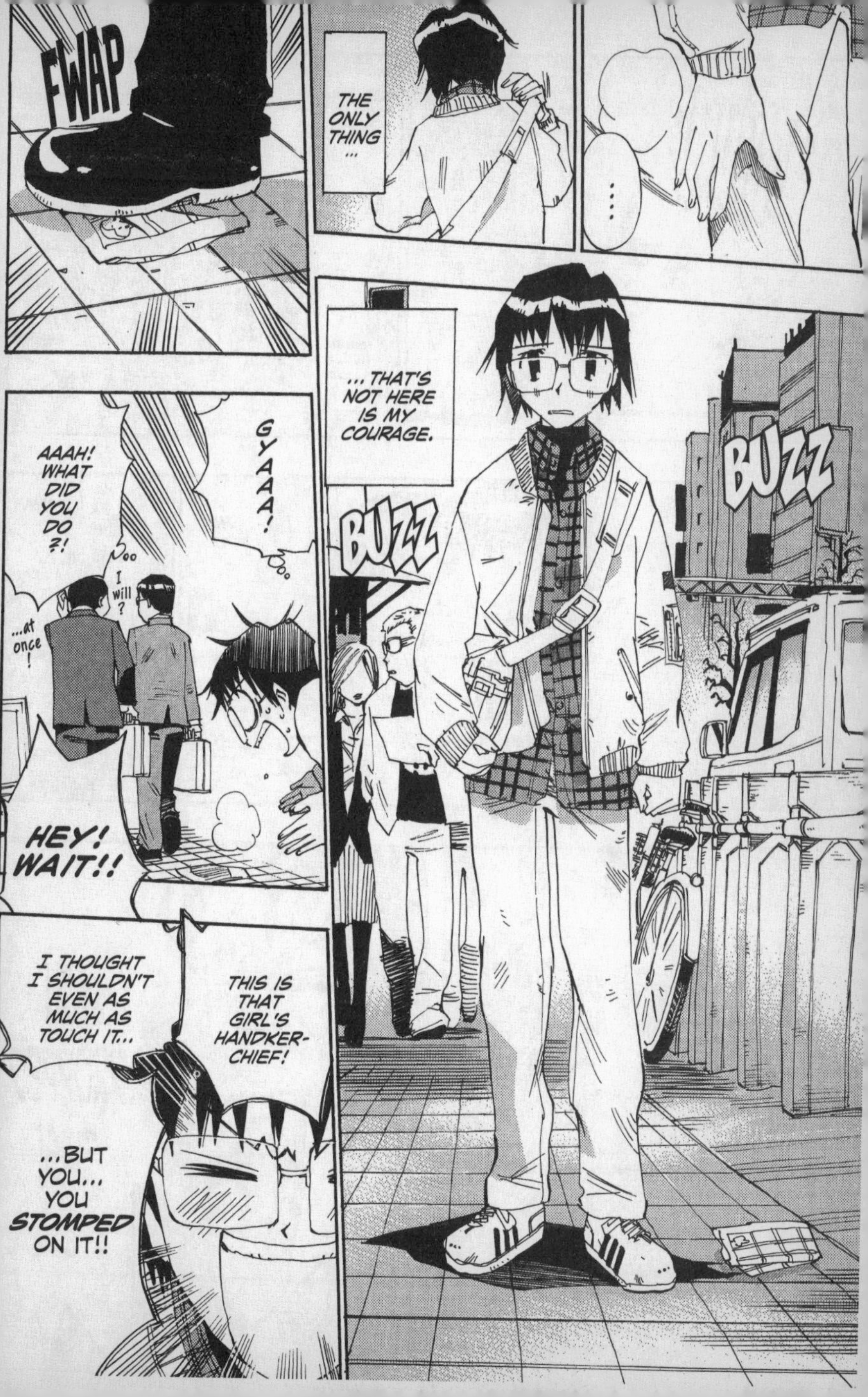
....
THE ONLY THING...
FWAP
...THAT'S NOT HERE IS MY COURAGE.
BUZZ
BUZZ
GYAAA!
AAAH! WHAT DID YOU DO?!
I will?
...at once!
HEY! WAIT!!
THIS IS THAT GIRL'S HANDKER-CHIEF!
I THOUGHT I SHOULDN'T EVEN AS MUCH AS TOUCH IT...
...BUT YOU... YOU STOMPED ON IT!!

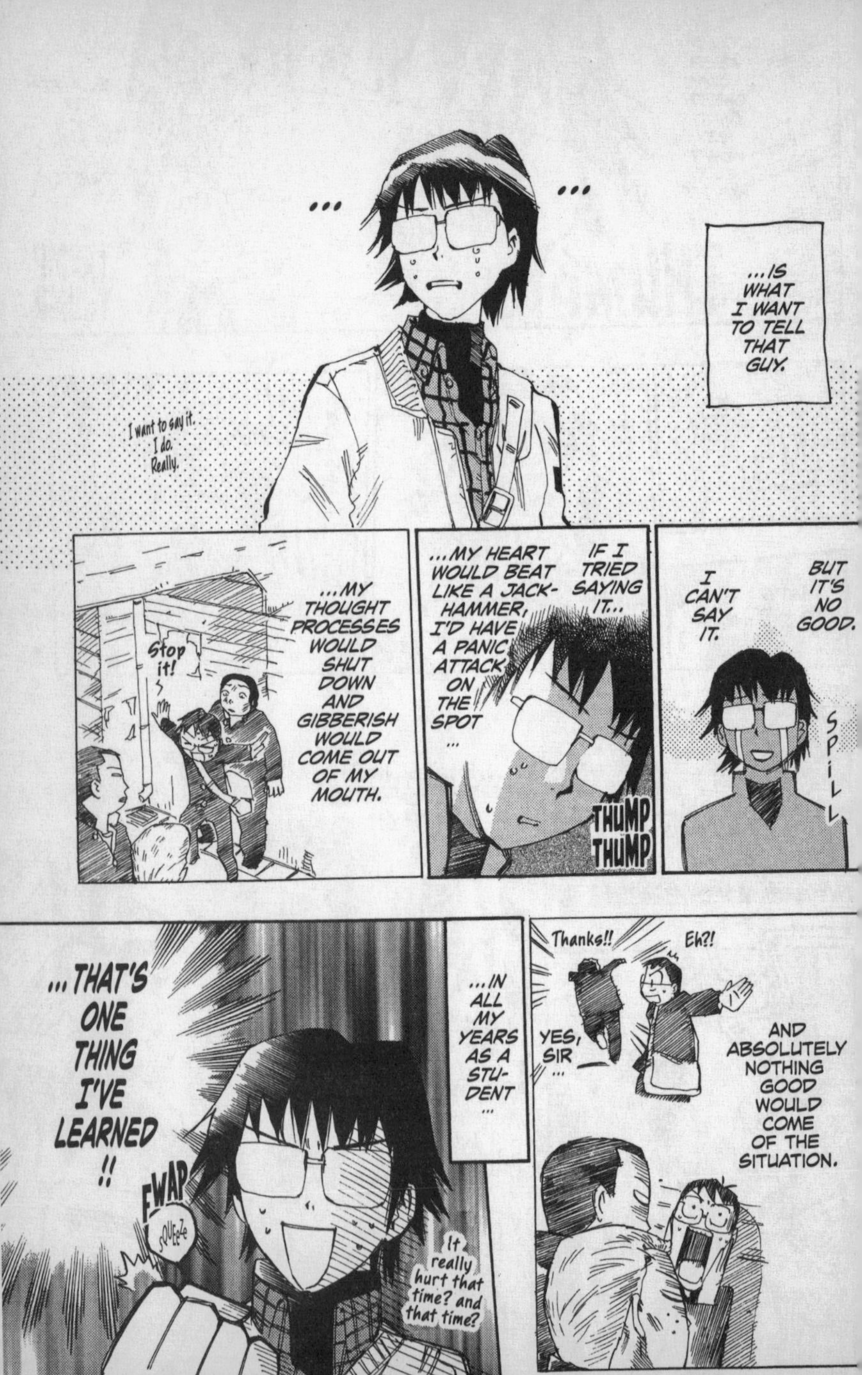
...IS WHAT I WANT TO TELL THAT GUY.
...
...
I want to say it. I do. Really.
BUT IT'S NO GOOD.
I CAN'T SAY IT.
SPILL
IF I TRIED SAYING IT...
...MY HEART WOULD BEAT LIKE A JACK-HAMMER, I'D HAVE A PANIC ATTACK ON THE SPOT ...
THUMP THUMP
...MY THOUGHT PROCESSES WOULD SHUT DOWN AND GIBBERISH WOULD COME OUT OF MY MOUTH.
Stop it!
Eh?!
Thanks!!
AND ABSOLUTELY NOTHING GOOD WOULD COME OF THE SITUATION.
YES, SIR ...
...IN ALL MY YEARS AS A STU-DENT ...
...THAT'S ONE THING I'VE LEARNED !!
FWAP
SQUEEZE
It really hurt that time? and that time?

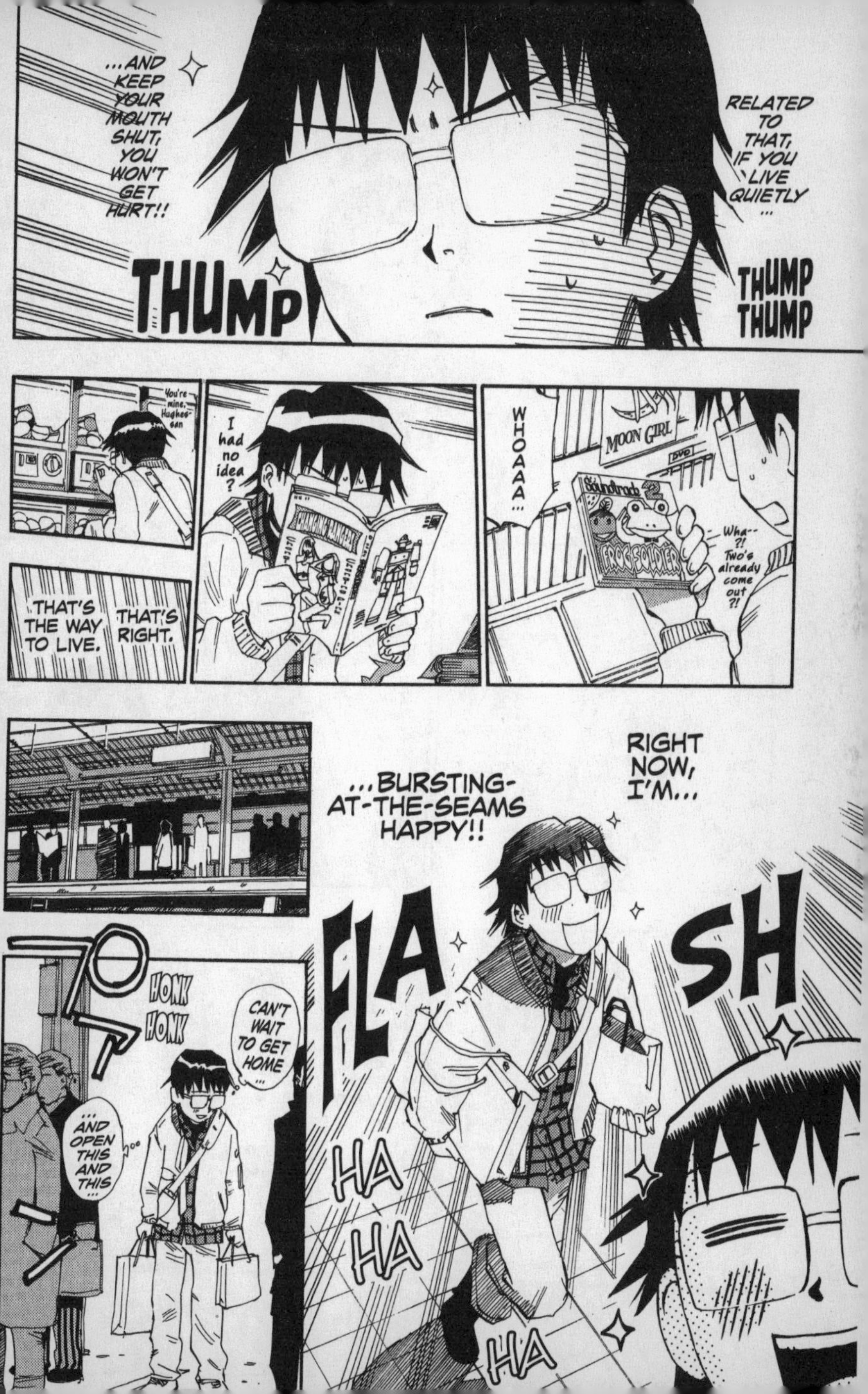
RELATED TO THAT, IF YOU LIVE QUIETLY ...
THUMP THUMP
...AND KEEP YOUR MOUTH SHUT, YOU WON'T GET HURT!!
THUMP
WHOAAA...
MOON GIRL
DVD
Soundtrack 2
FROG SOLDIER
Wha-- ?! Two's already come out ?!
I had no idea ?
CHANGING RANGER
You're mine, Hughes-san
THAT'S RIGHT.
THAT'S THE WAY TO LIVE.
RIGHT NOW, I'M...
...BURSTING-AT-THE-SEAMS HAPPY!!
FLASH
HA
HA
HA
HONK HONK
CAN'T WAIT TO GET HOME ...
... AND OPEN THIS AND THIS ...

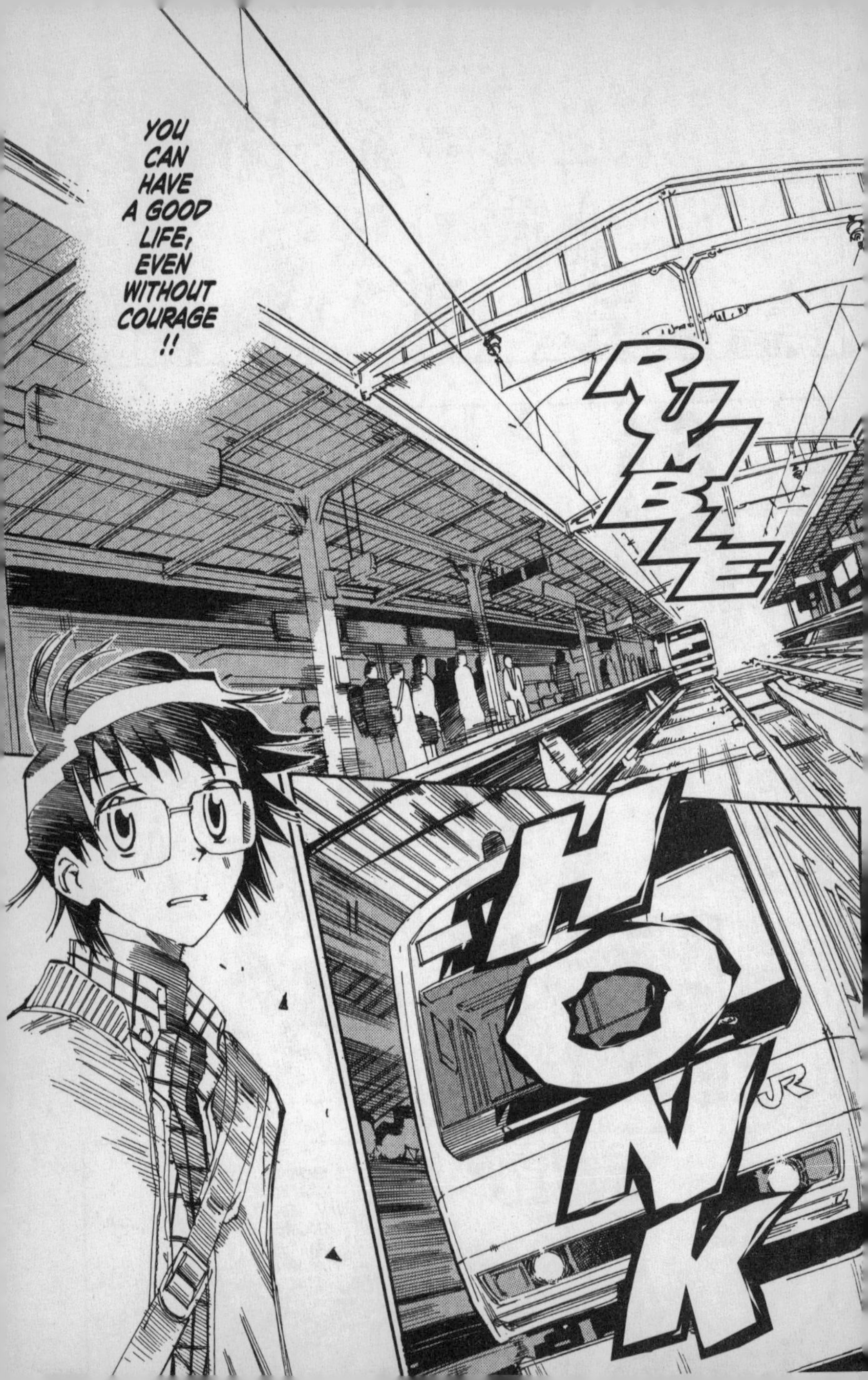
YOU CAN HAVE A GOOD LIFE, EVEN WITHOUT COURAGE !!
RUMBLE
HONK
JR

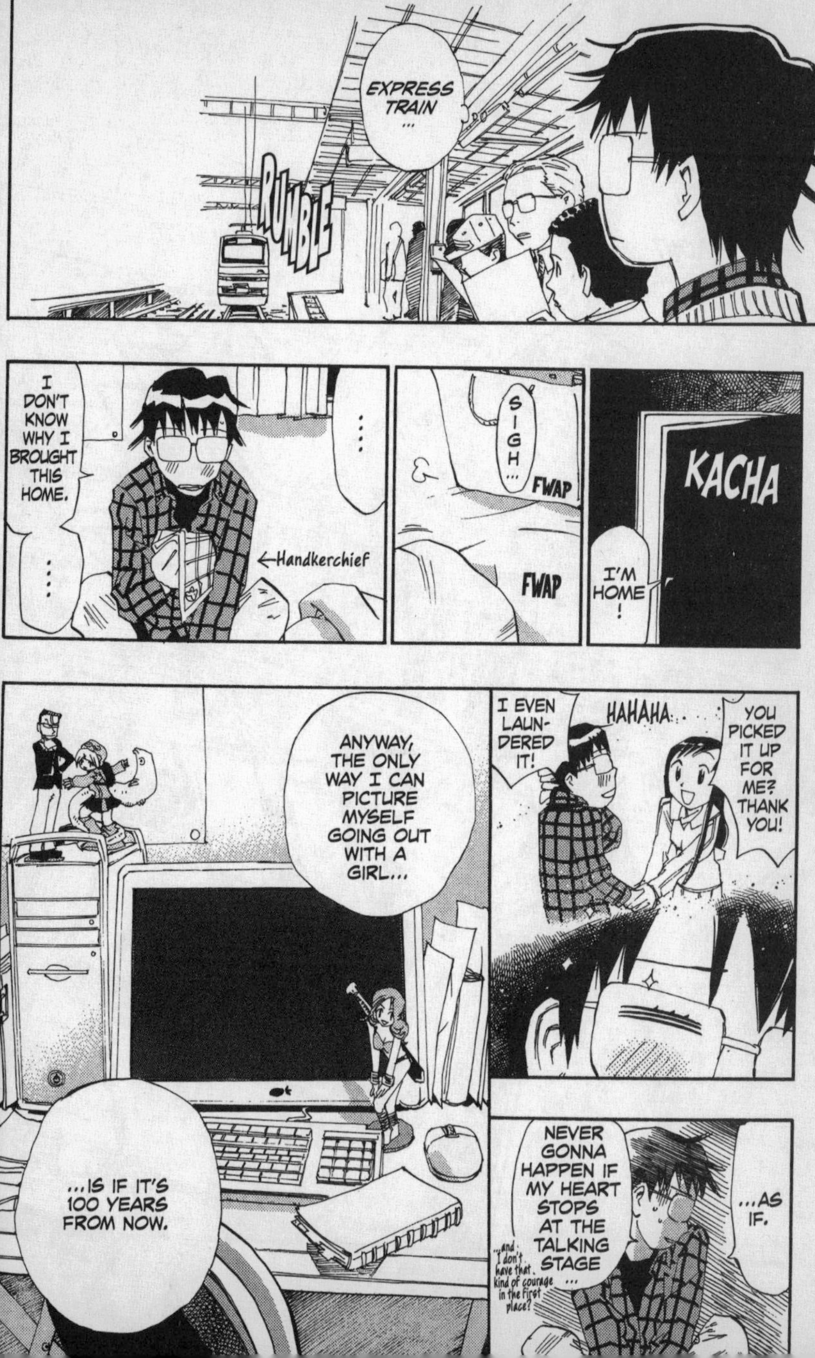
EXPRESS TRAIN ...
RUMBLE
KACHA
I'M HOME!
SIGH...
FWAP
FWAP
....
I DON'T KNOW WHY I BROUGHT THIS HOME.
....
←Handkerchief
YOU PICKED IT UP FOR ME? THANK YOU!
HAHAHA
I EVEN LAUNDERED IT!
...AS IF.
NEVER GONNA HAPPEN IF MY HEART STOPS AT THE TALKING STAGE ...
...and I don't have that kind of courage in the first place?
ANYWAY, THE ONLY WAY I CAN PICTURE MYSELF GOING OUT WITH A GIRL...
...IS IF IT'S 100 YEARS FROM NOW.

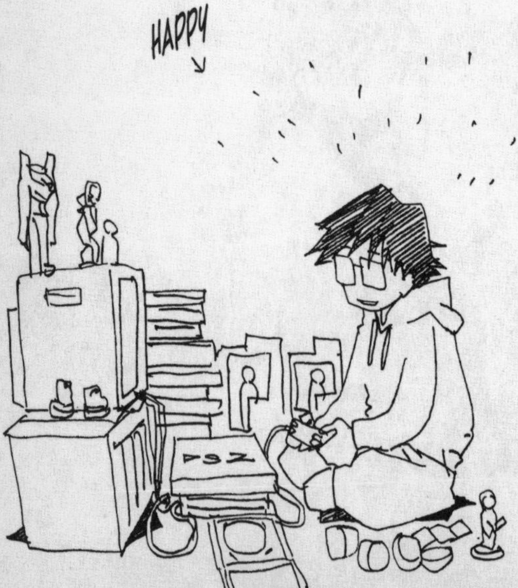
HAPPY
PS2

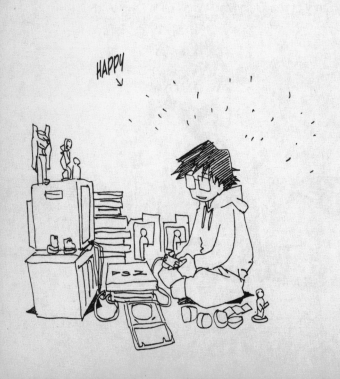

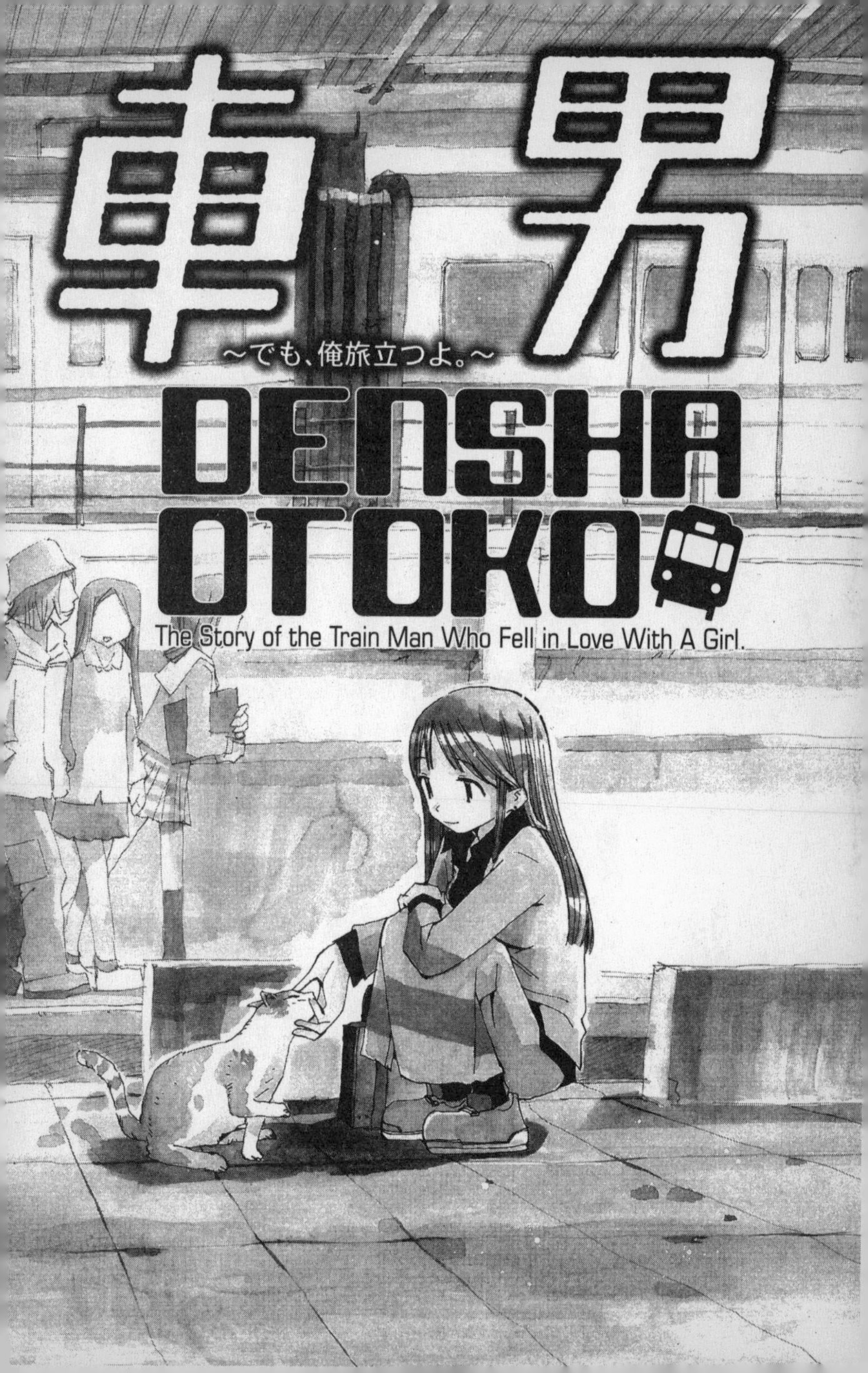
車
男
～でも、俺旅立つよ。～
DENSHA
OTOKO
The Story of the Train Man Who Fell in Love With A Girl.

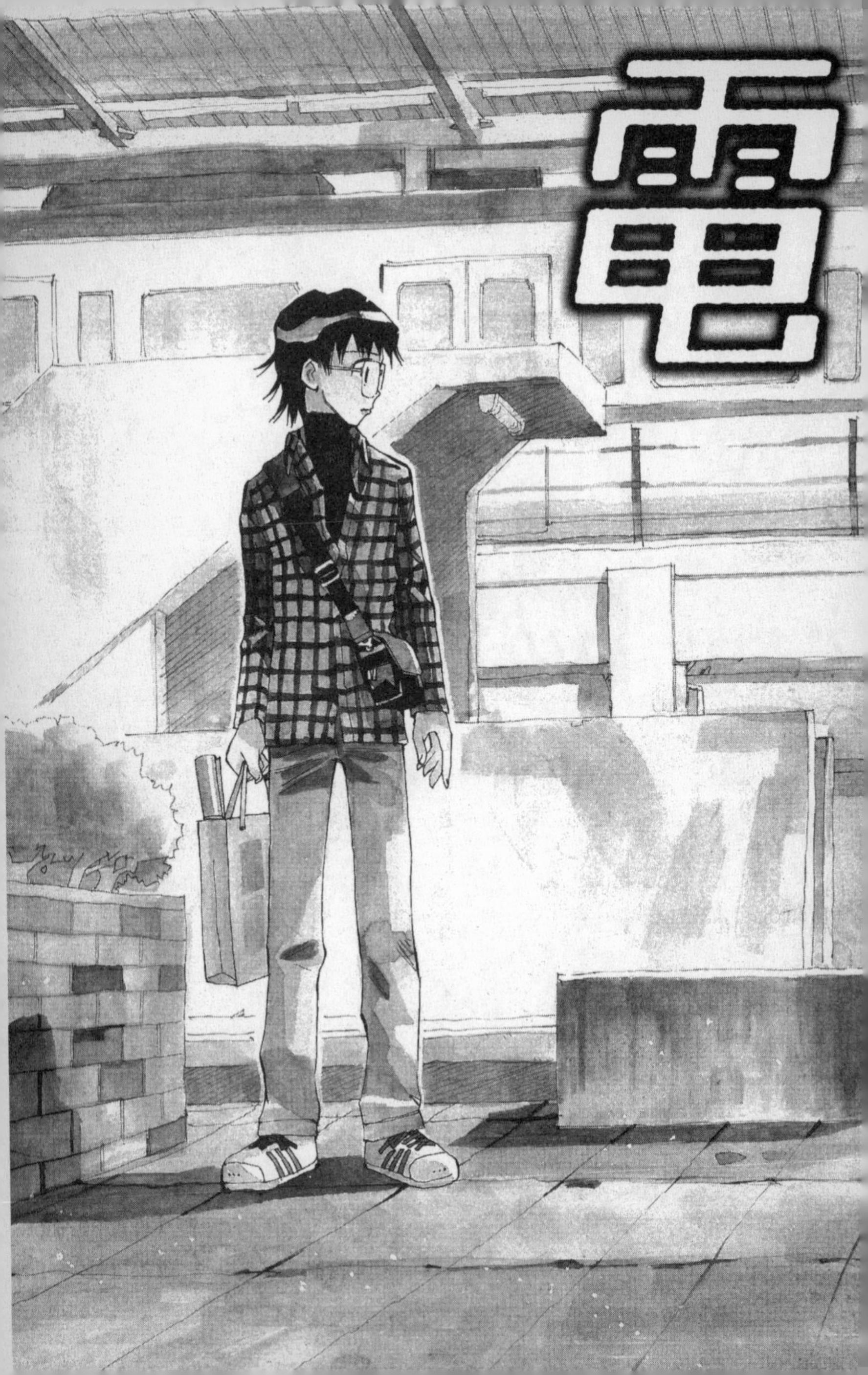
電車

Mission 1

I... I...

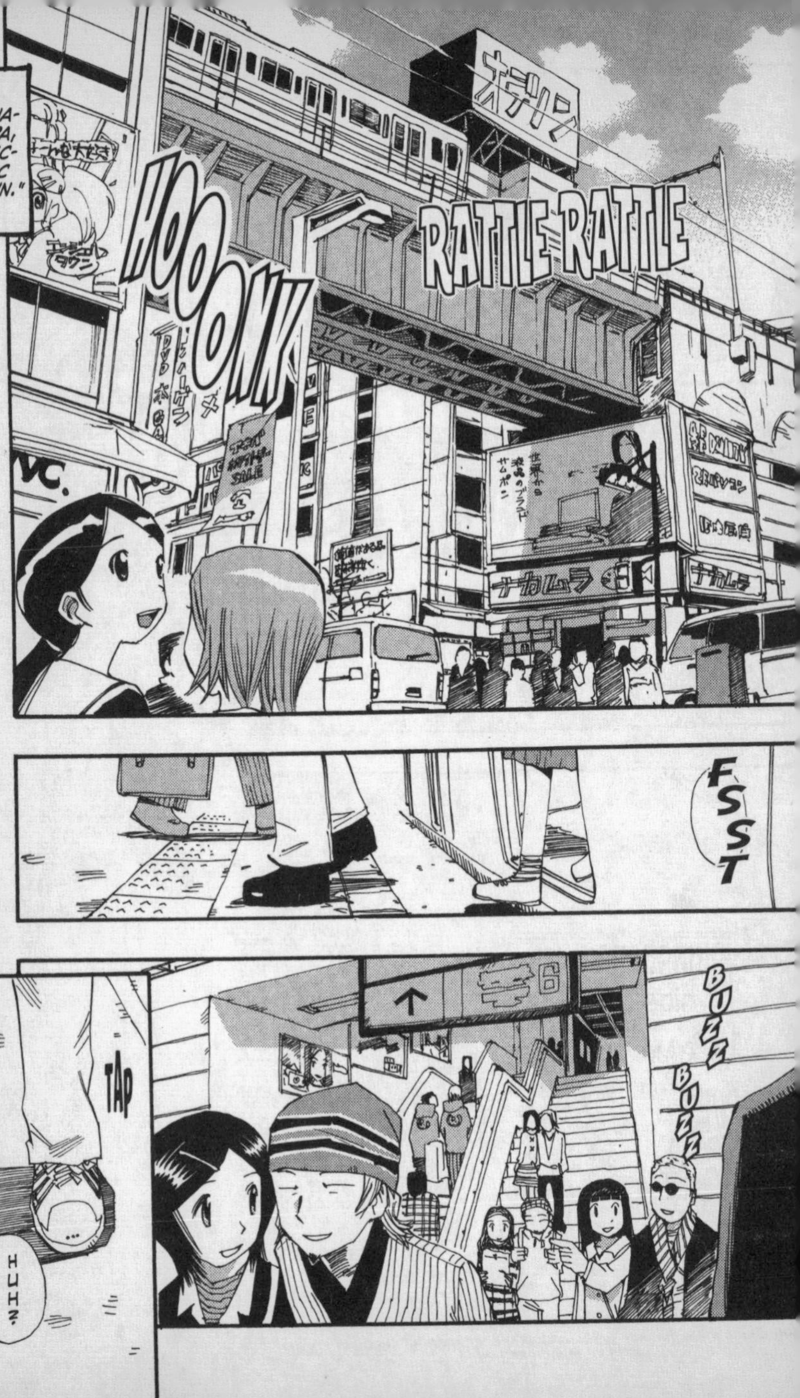
RATTLE RATTLE
HOOONK
AKIHABARA, "ELECTRIC TOWN."
FSST
BUZZ BUZZ
TAP
...
HUH?

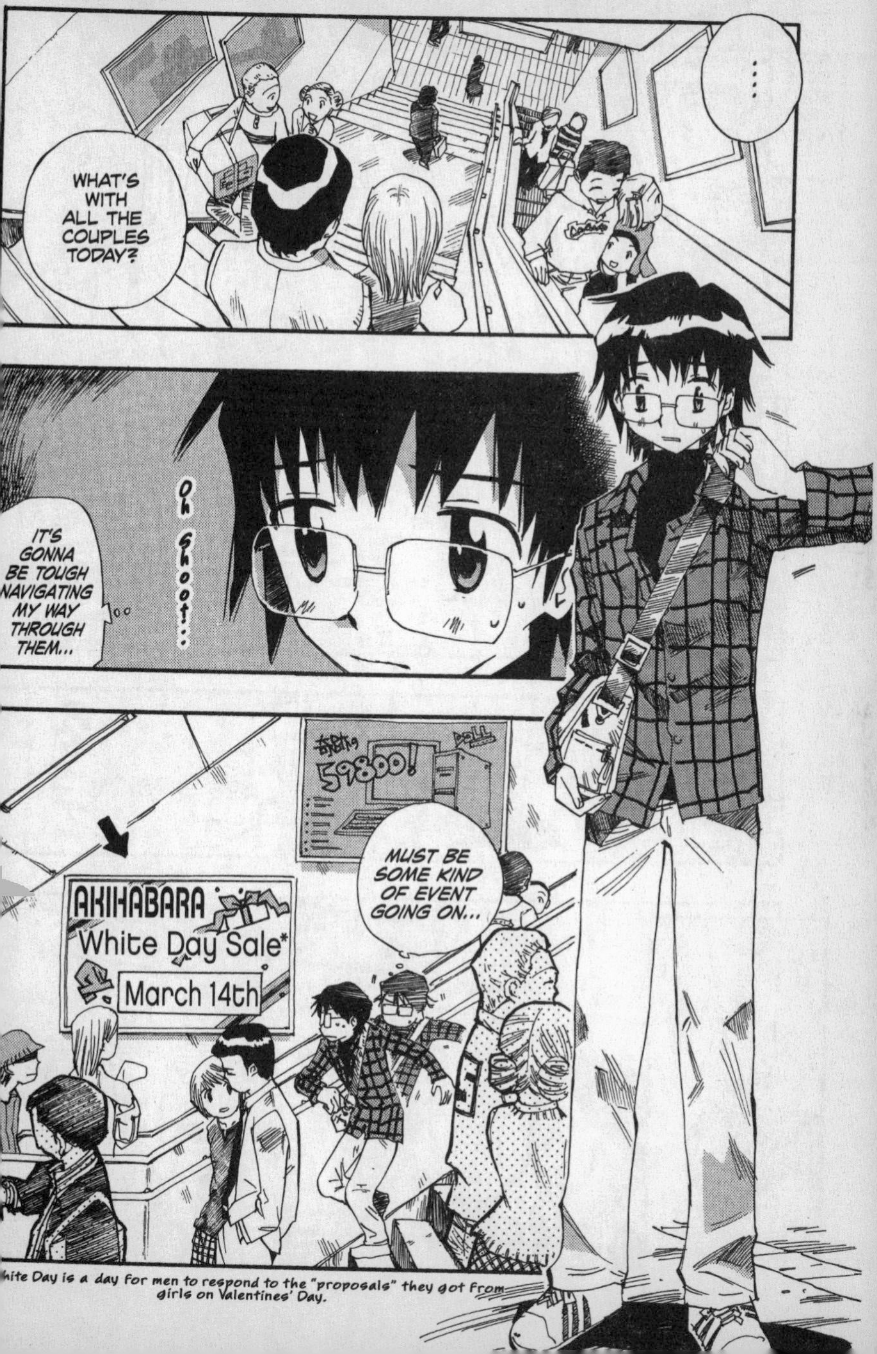
....
WHAT'S WITH ALL THE COUPLES TODAY?
Oh Shoot...
IT'S GONNA BE TOUGH NAVIGATING MY WAY THROUGH THEM...
59800!
MUST BE SOME KIND OF EVENT GOING ON...
AKIHABARA
White Day Sale*
March 14th

hite Day is a day for men to respond to the "proposals" they got from girls on Valentines' Day.

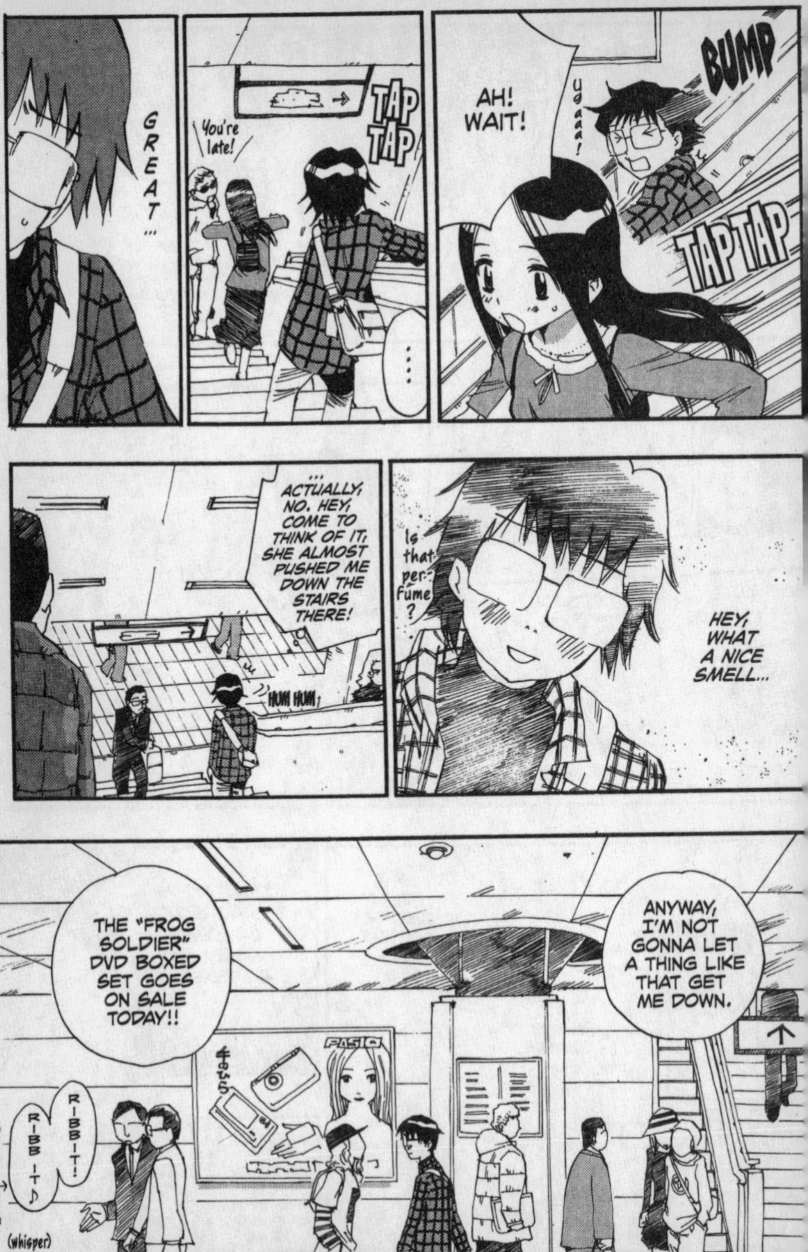
BUMP
Ugaaa!
AH! WAIT!
TAPTAP
TAP TAP
You're late!
...
GREAT...
HEY, WHAT A NICE SMELL...
Is that perfume?
...ACTUALLY, NO. HEY, COME TO THINK OF IT, SHE ALMOST PUSHED ME DOWN THE STAIRS THERE!
HUM HUM
ANYWAY, I'M NOT GONNA LET A THING LIKE THAT GET ME DOWN.
THE "FROG SOLDIER" DVD BOXED SET GOES ON SALE TODAY!!
FASIO
RIBBIT!
RIBB IT♪
Opening theme
(whisper)

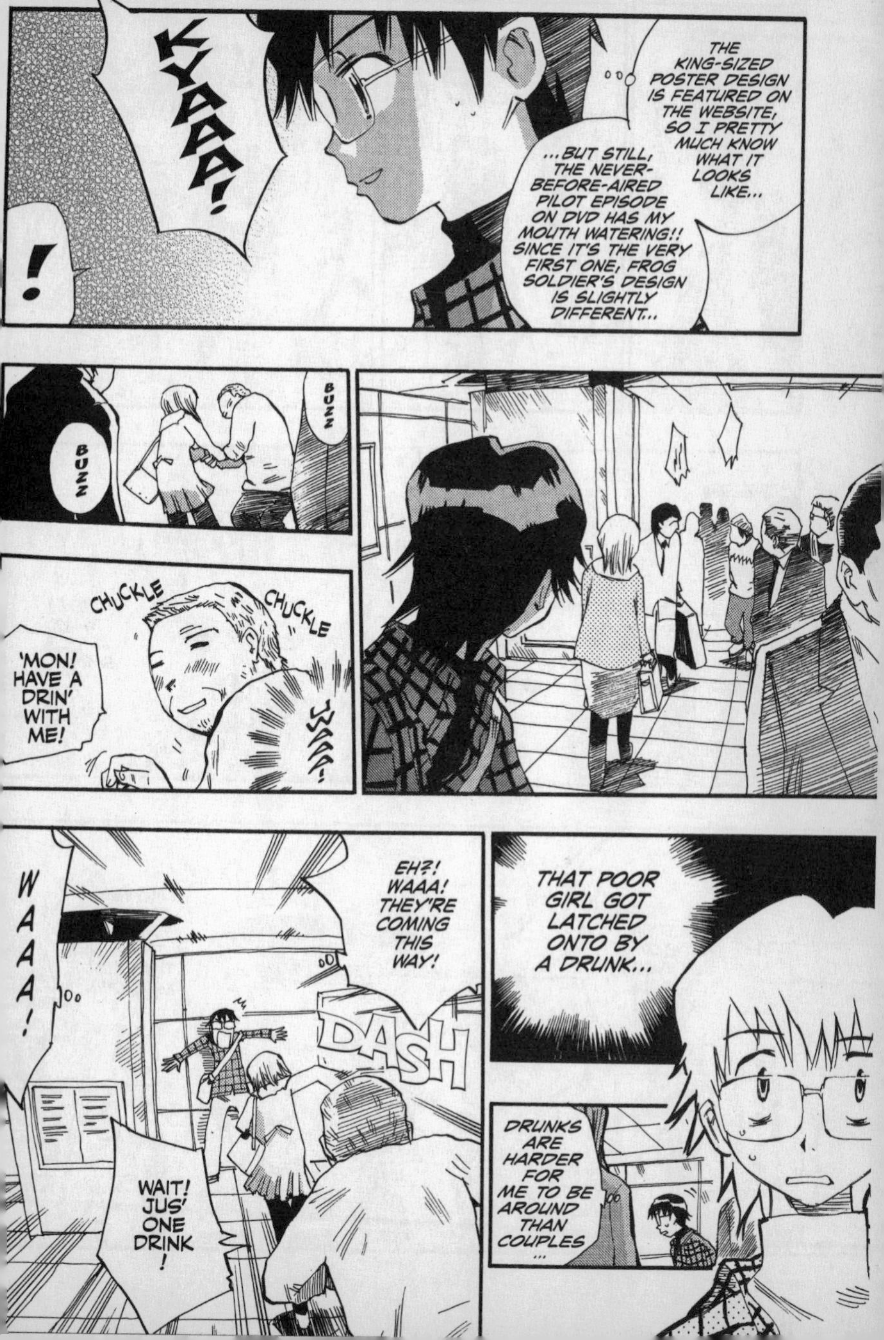
THE KING-SIZED POSTER DESIGN IS FEATURED ON THE WEBSITE, SO I PRETTY MUCH KNOW WHAT IT LOOKS LIKE...
...BUT STILL, THE NEVER-BEFORE-AIRED PILOT EPISODE ON DVD HAS MY MOUTH WATERING!! SINCE IT'S THE VERY FIRST ONE, FROG SOLDIER'S DESIGN IS SLIGHTLY DIFFERENT...
KYAAA!
!
BUZZ
BUZZ
CHUCKLE
CHUCKLE
'MON! HAVE A DRIN' WITH ME!
WAAA!
THAT POOR GIRL GOT LATCHED ONTO BY A DRUNK...
DRUNKS ARE HARDER FOR ME TO BE AROUND THAN COUPLES...
EH?! WAAA! THEY'RE COMING THIS WAY!
DASH
WAAAA!
WAIT! JUS' ONE DRINK!

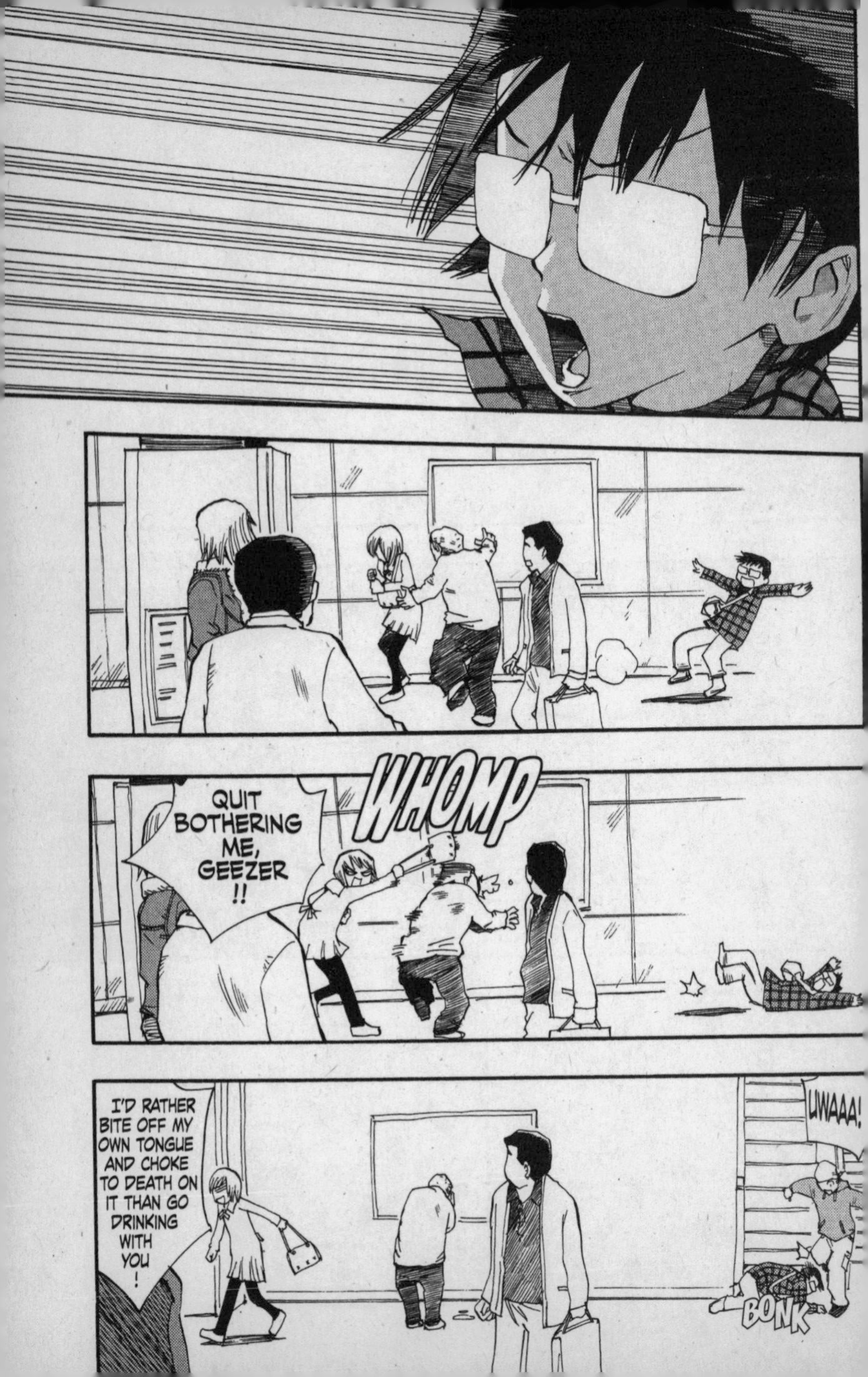
WHOMP
QUIT BOTHERING ME, GEEZER !!
UWAAA!
I'D RATHER BITE OFF MY OWN TONGUE AND CHOKE TO DEATH ON IT THAN GO DRINKING WITH YOU !
BONK

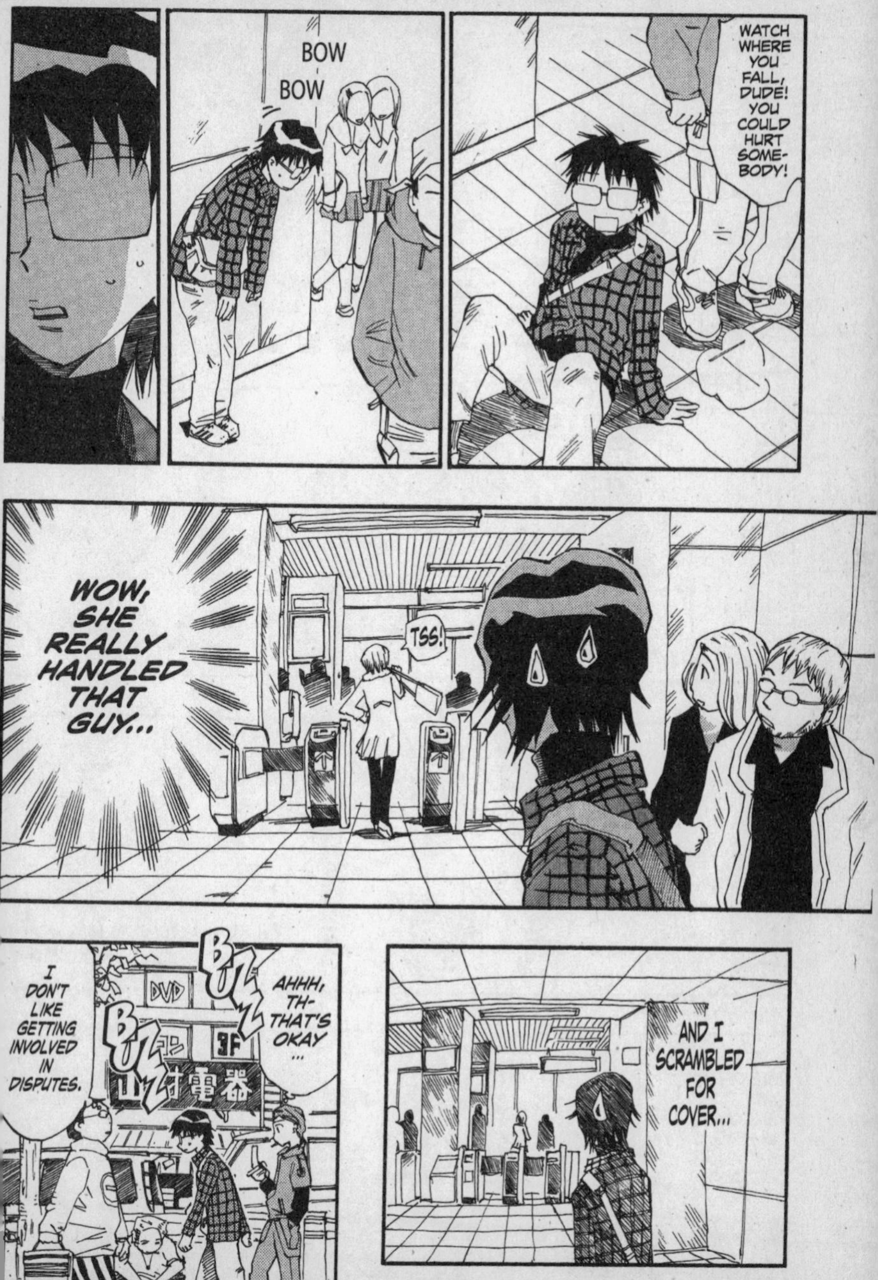
WATCH WHERE YOU FALL, DUDE! YOU COULD HURT SOMEBODY!
BOW
BOW
TSS!
WOW, SHE REALLY HANDLED THAT GUY...
AND I SCRAMBLED FOR COVER...
AHHH, TH-THAT'S OKAY ...
BUZZ
BUZZ
DVD
3F
I DON'T LIKE GETTING INVOLVED IN DISPUTES.

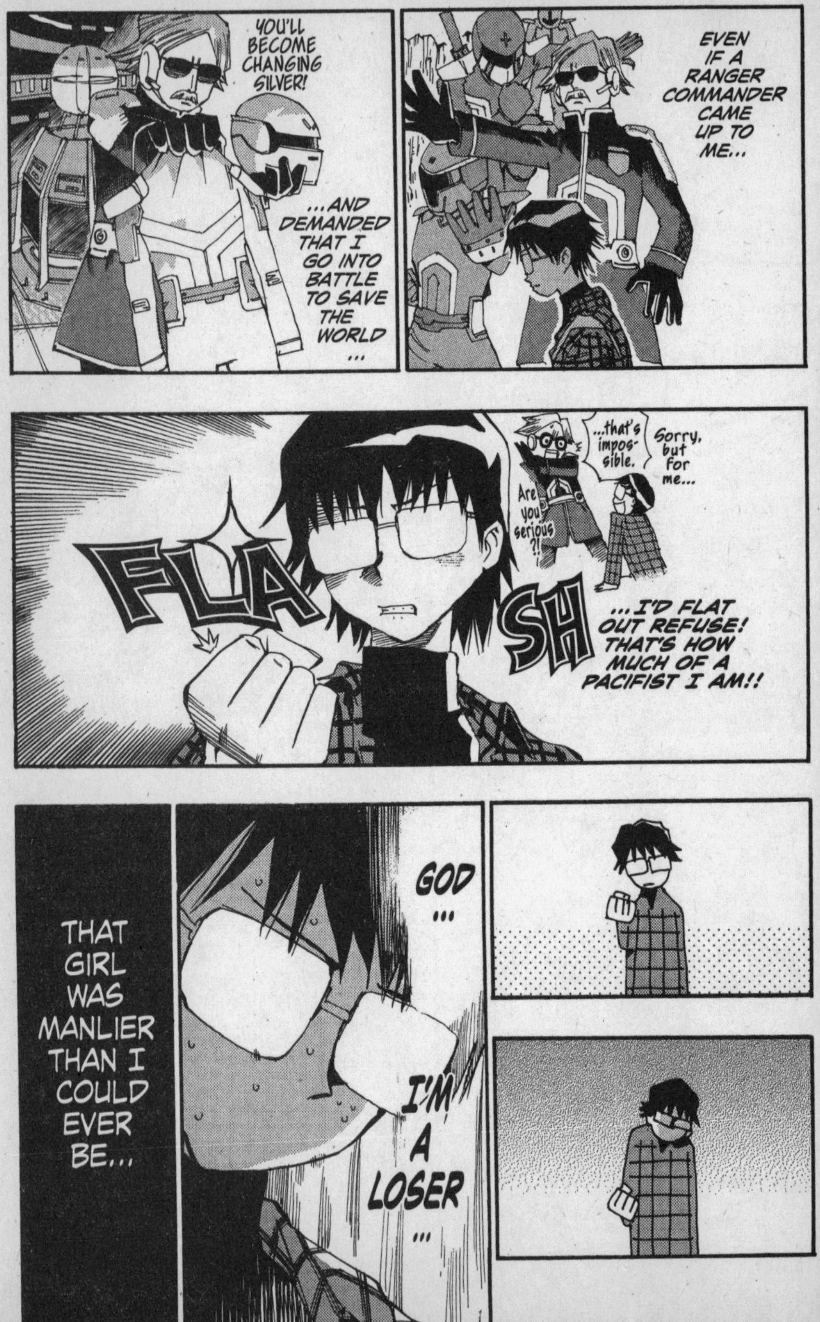
EVEN IF A RANGER COMMANDER CAME UP TO ME...
YOU'LL BECOME CHANGING SILVER!
...AND DEMANDED THAT I GO INTO BATTLE TO SAVE THE WORLD...
Sorry, but for me...
...that's impossible.
Are you serious?!
FLASH
...I'D FLAT OUT REFUSE! THAT'S HOW MUCH OF A PACIFIST I AM!!
GOD...
I'M A LOSER...
THAT GIRL WAS MANLIER THAN I COULD EVER BE...

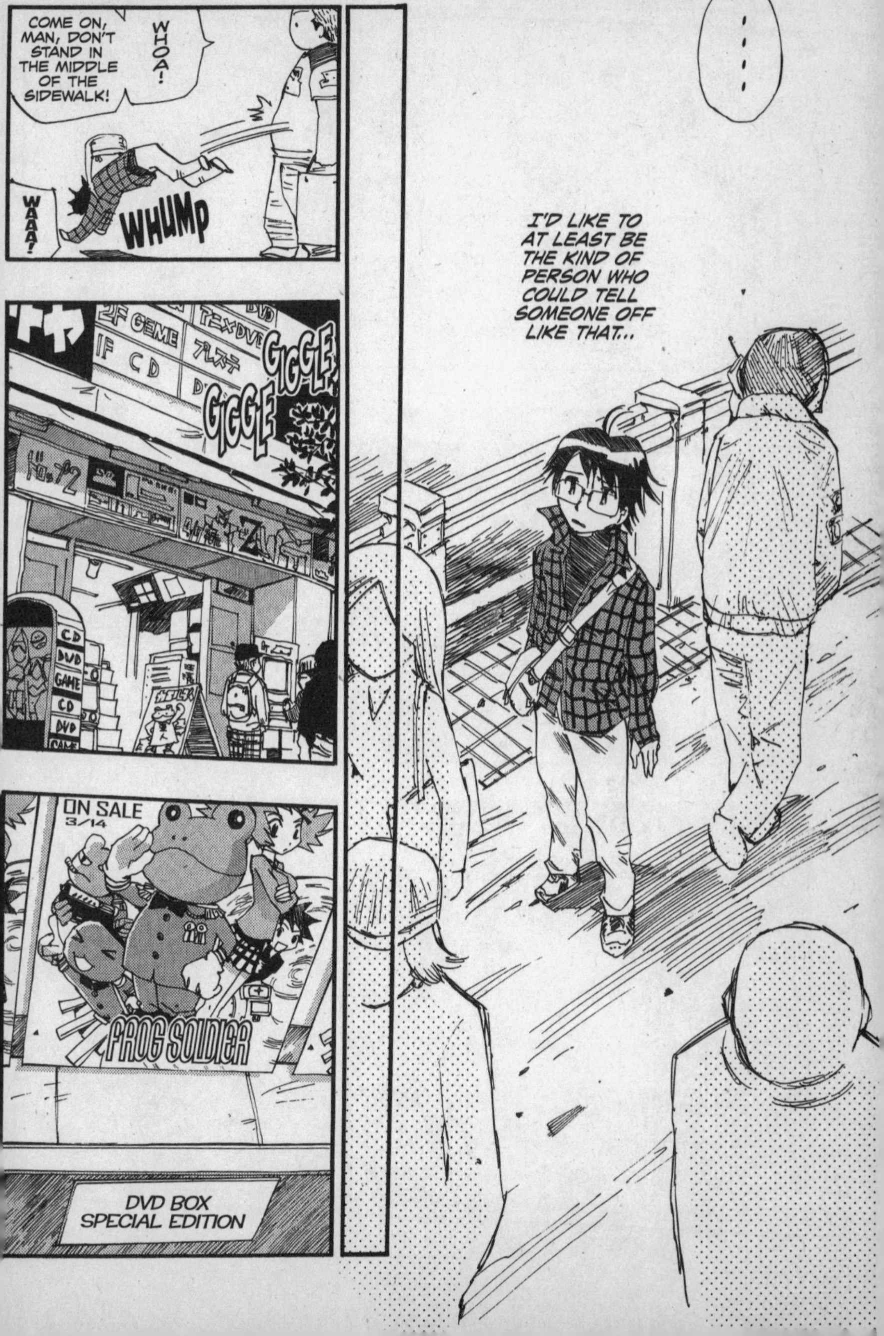
...
I'D LIKE TO AT LEAST BE THE KIND OF PERSON WHO COULD TELL SOMEONE OFF LIKE THAT...
WHOA!
COME ON, MAN, DON'T STAND IN THE MIDDLE OF THE SIDEWALK!
WHUMP
WAAA!
GIGGLE
GIGGLE
ON SALE 3/14
FROG SOLDIER
DVD BOX SPECIAL EDITION

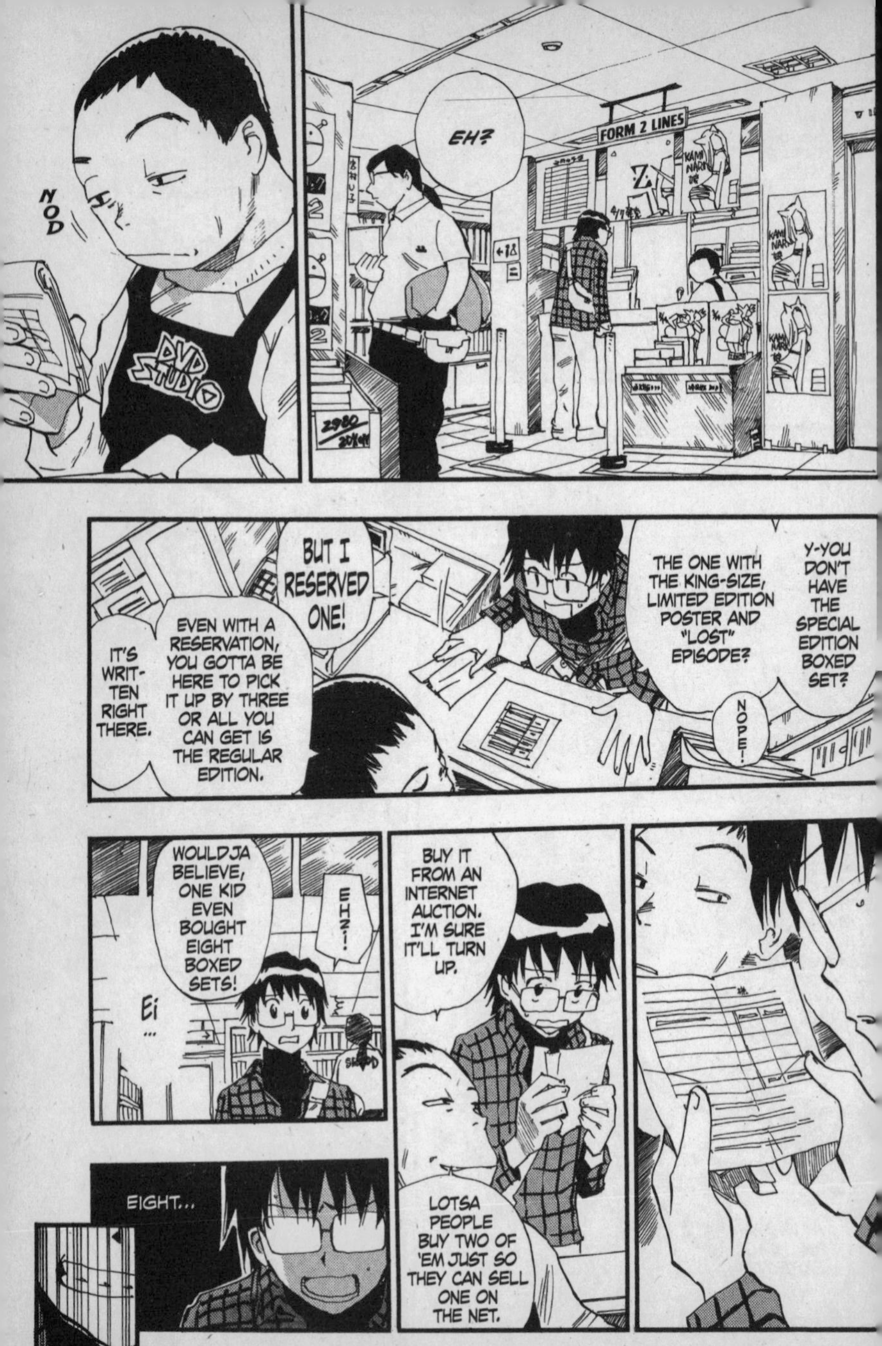
EH?
FORM 2 LINES
KAMI NARI
NOD
DVD STUDIO
Y-YOU DON'T HAVE THE SPECIAL EDITION BOXED SET?
THE ONE WITH THE KING-SIZE, LIMITED EDITION POSTER AND "LOST" EPISODE?
NOPE!
BUT I RESERVED ONE!
EVEN WITH A RESERVATION, YOU GOTTA BE HERE TO PICK IT UP BY THREE OR ALL YOU CAN GET IS THE REGULAR EDITION.
IT'S WRIT-TEN RIGHT THERE.
BUY IT FROM AN INTERNET AUCTION. I'M SURE IT'LL TURN UP.
LOTSA PEOPLE BUY TWO OF 'EM JUST SO THEY CAN SELL ONE ON THE NET.
WOULDJA BELIEVE, ONE KID EVEN BOUGHT EIGHT BOXED SETS!
EHZ!
Ei ...
EIGHT...

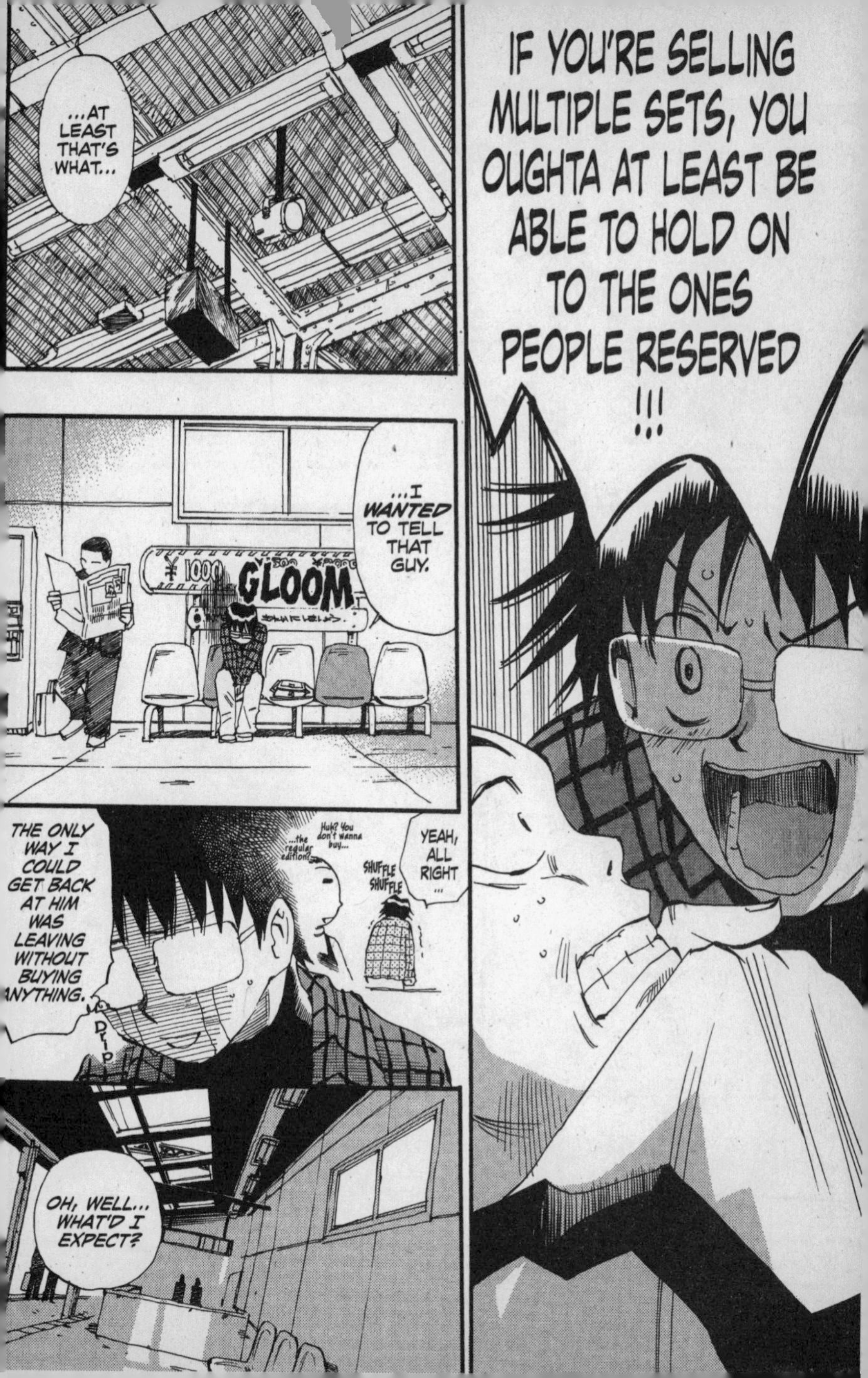
IF YOU'RE SELLING MULTIPLE SETS, YOU OUGHTA AT LEAST BE ABLE TO HOLD ON TO THE ONES PEOPLE RESERVED !!!
...AT LEAST THAT'S WHAT...
...I WANTED TO TELL THAT GUY.
GLOOM
Huh? You don't wanna buy...
...the regular edition!?
YEAH, ALL RIGHT ...
SHUFFLE SHUFFLE
THE ONLY WAY I COULD GET BACK AT HIM WAS LEAVING WITHOUT BUYING ANYTHING.
DRIP
OH, WELL... WHAT'D I EXPECT?

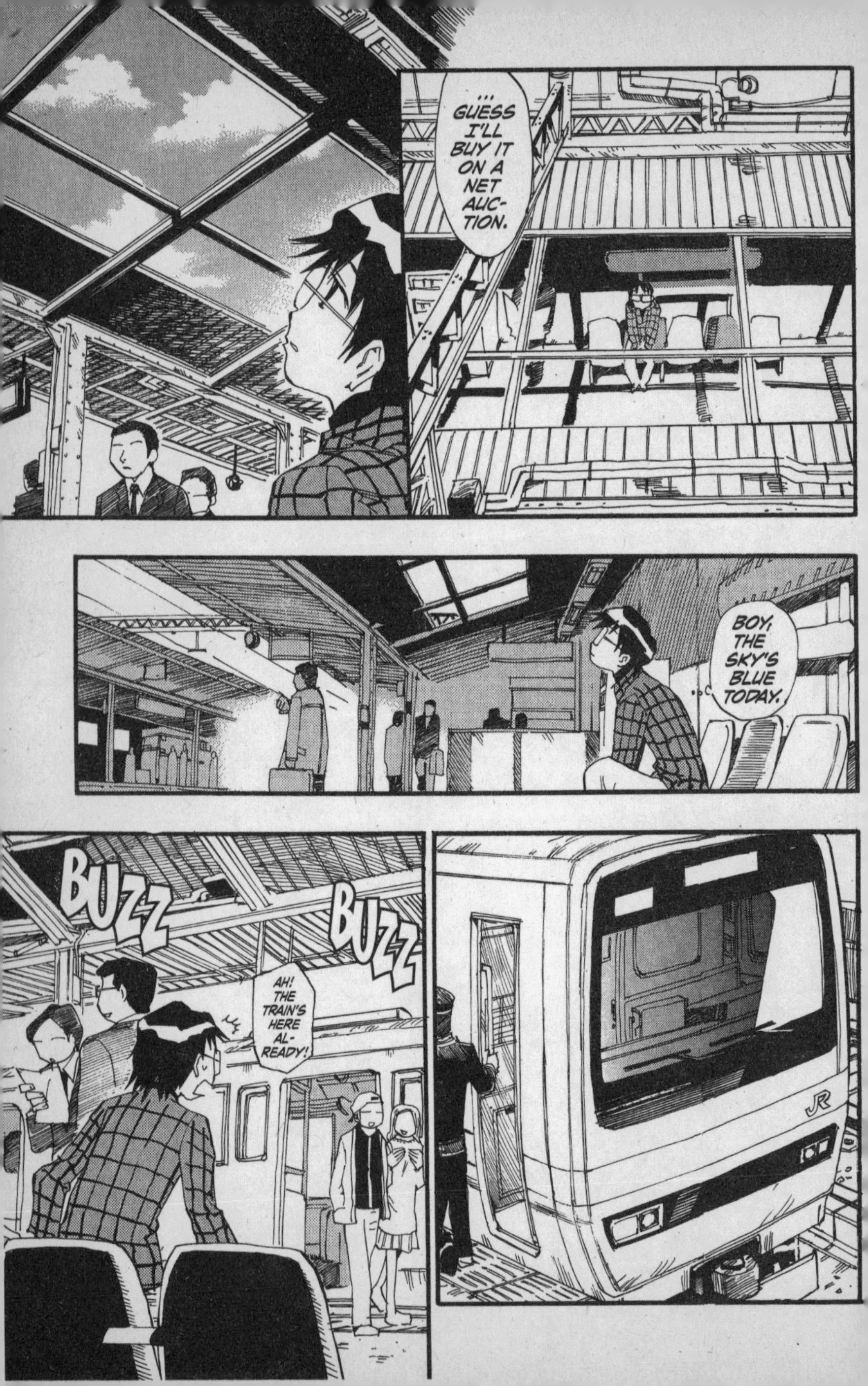
...GUESS I'LL BUY IT ON A NET AUC-TION.
BOY, THE SKY'S BLUE TODAY.
BUZZ
BUZZ
AH! THE TRAIN'S HERE AL-READY!

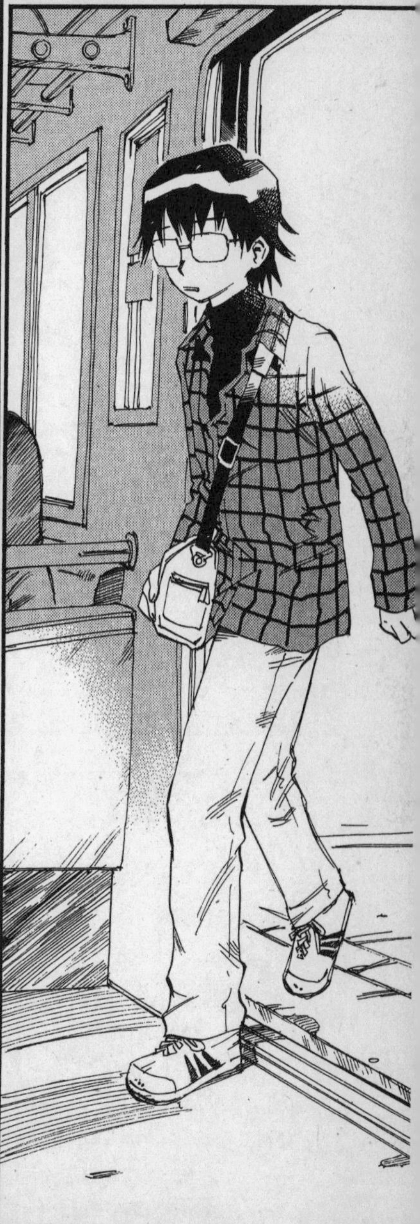

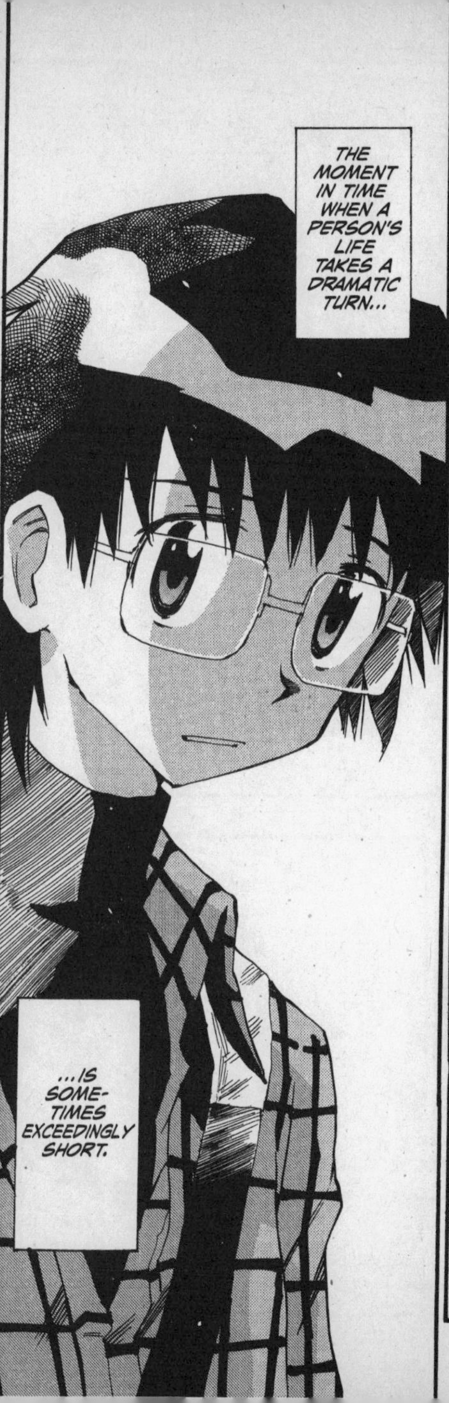
THE MOMENT IN TIME WHEN A PERSON'S LIFE TAKES A DRAMATIC TURN...
...IS SOMETIMES EXCEEDINGLY SHORT.

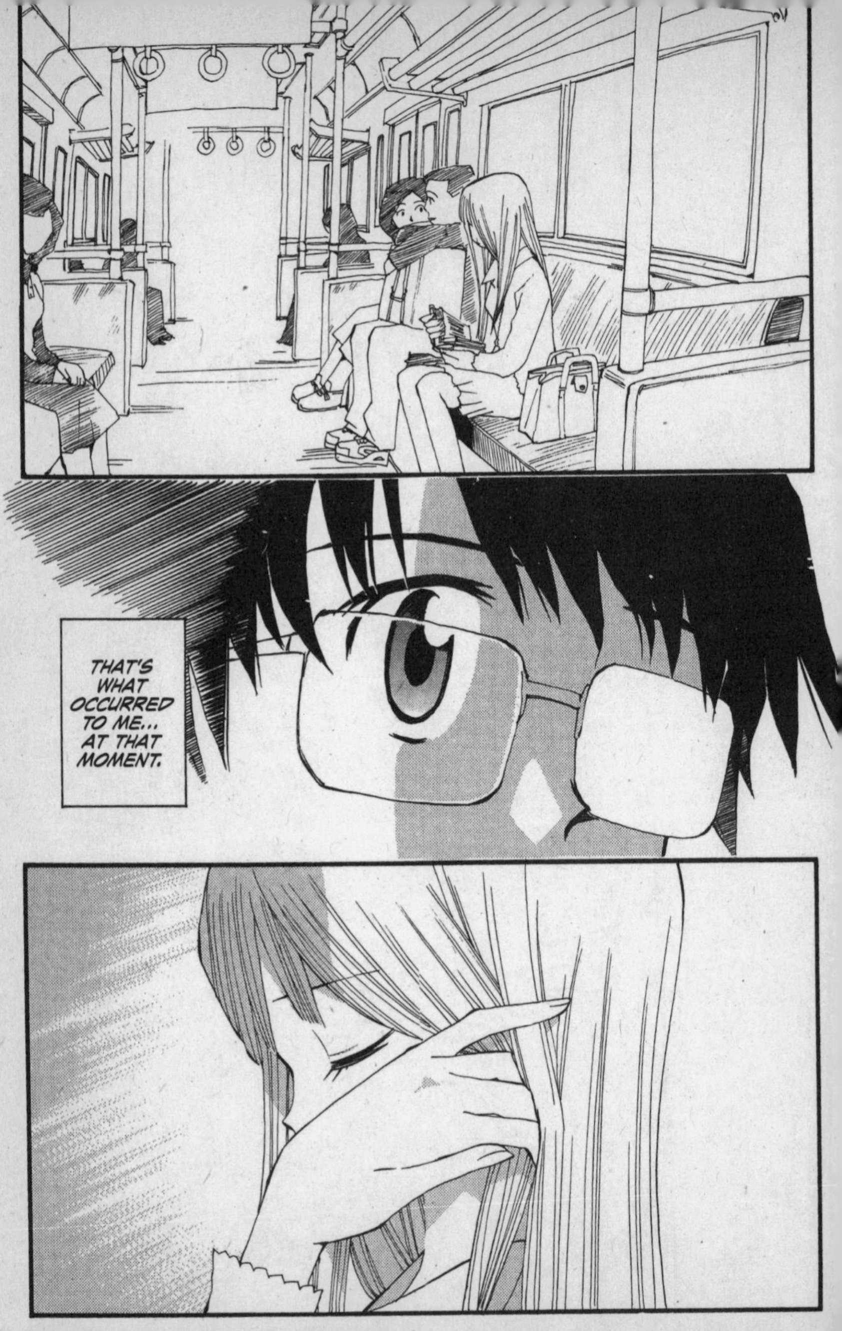
THAT'S WHAT OCCURRED TO ME... AT THAT MOMENT.

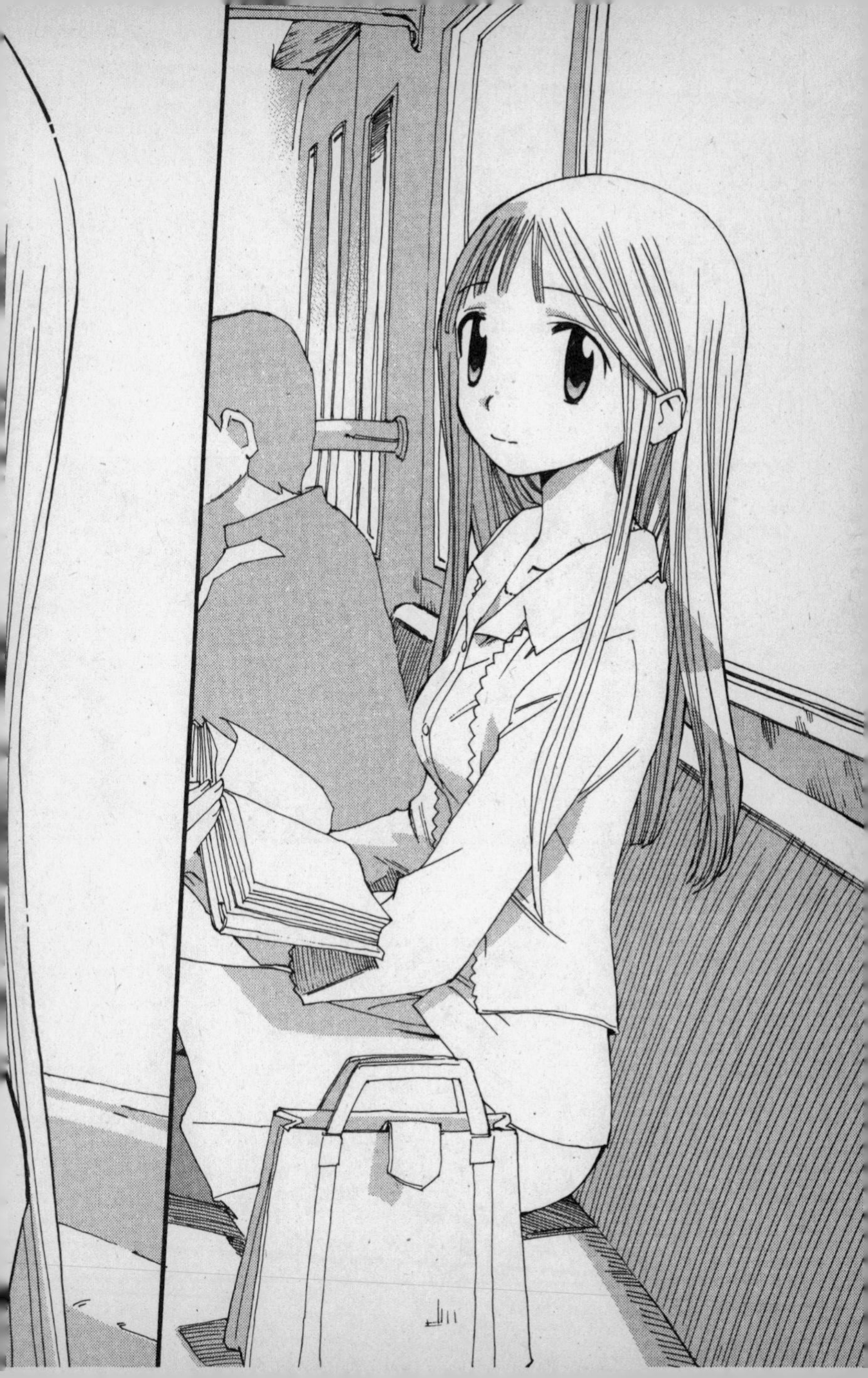

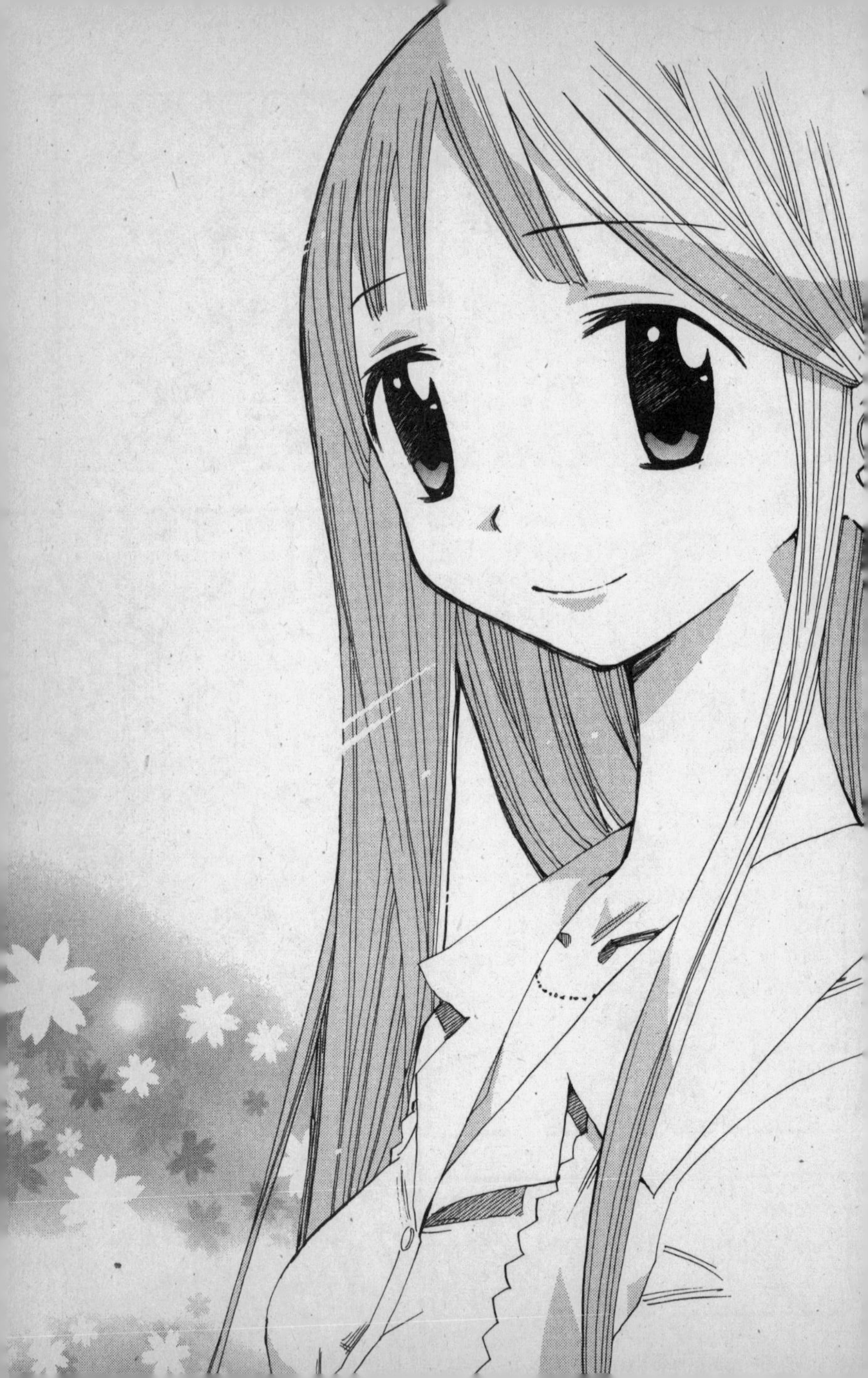

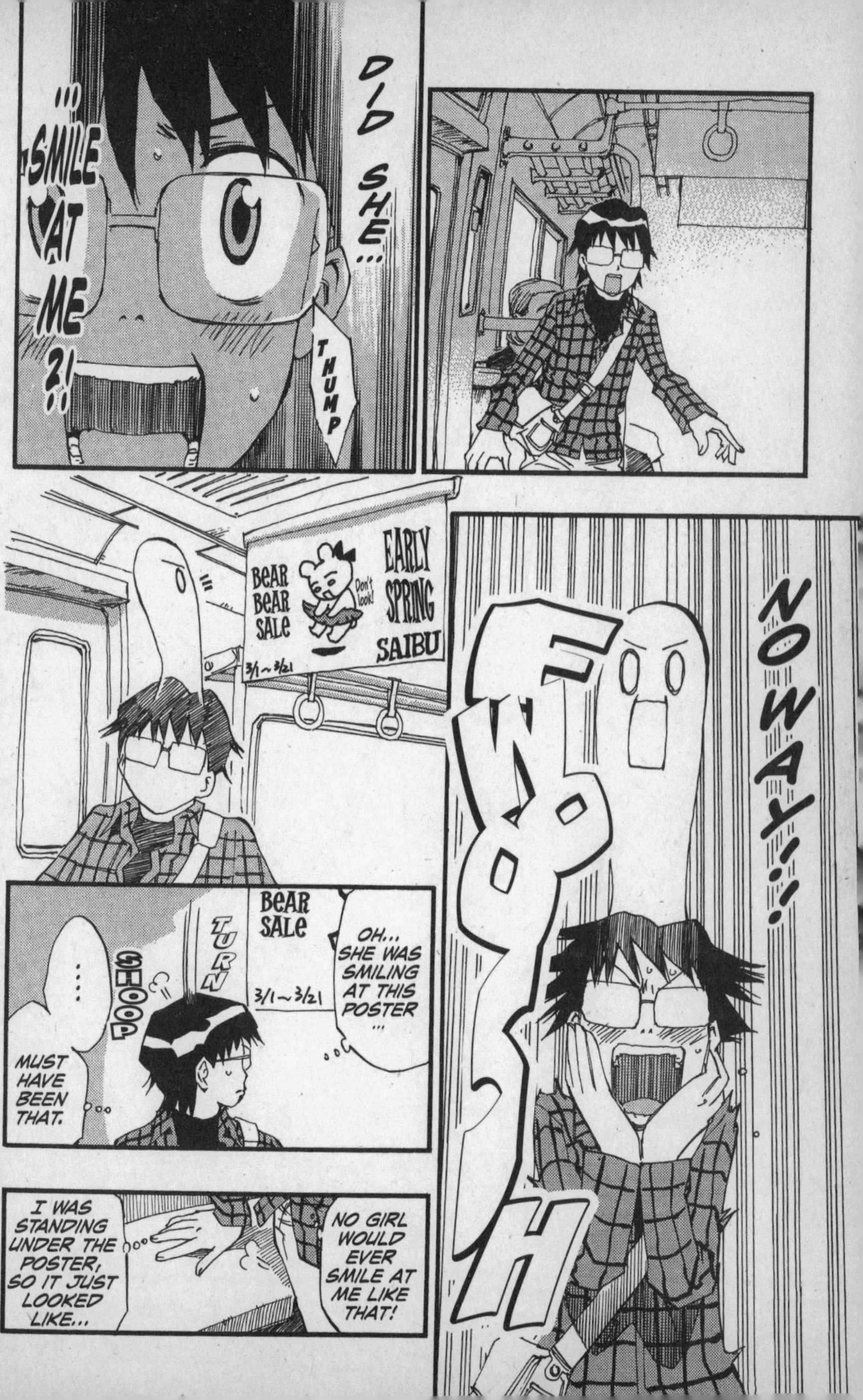
DID SHE...
...SMILE AT ME?!
THUMP
NO WAY!!!
BeAR BeAR SALE
Don't look!
EARLY SPRING
SAIBU
3/1~3/21
OH... SHE WAS SMILING AT THIS POSTER...
BeAR SALE
3/1~3/21
TURN
SHOOP
....
MUST HAVE BEEN THAT.
NO GIRL WOULD EVER SMILE AT ME LIKE THAT!
I WAS STANDING UNDER THE POSTER, SO IT JUST LOOKED LIKE...

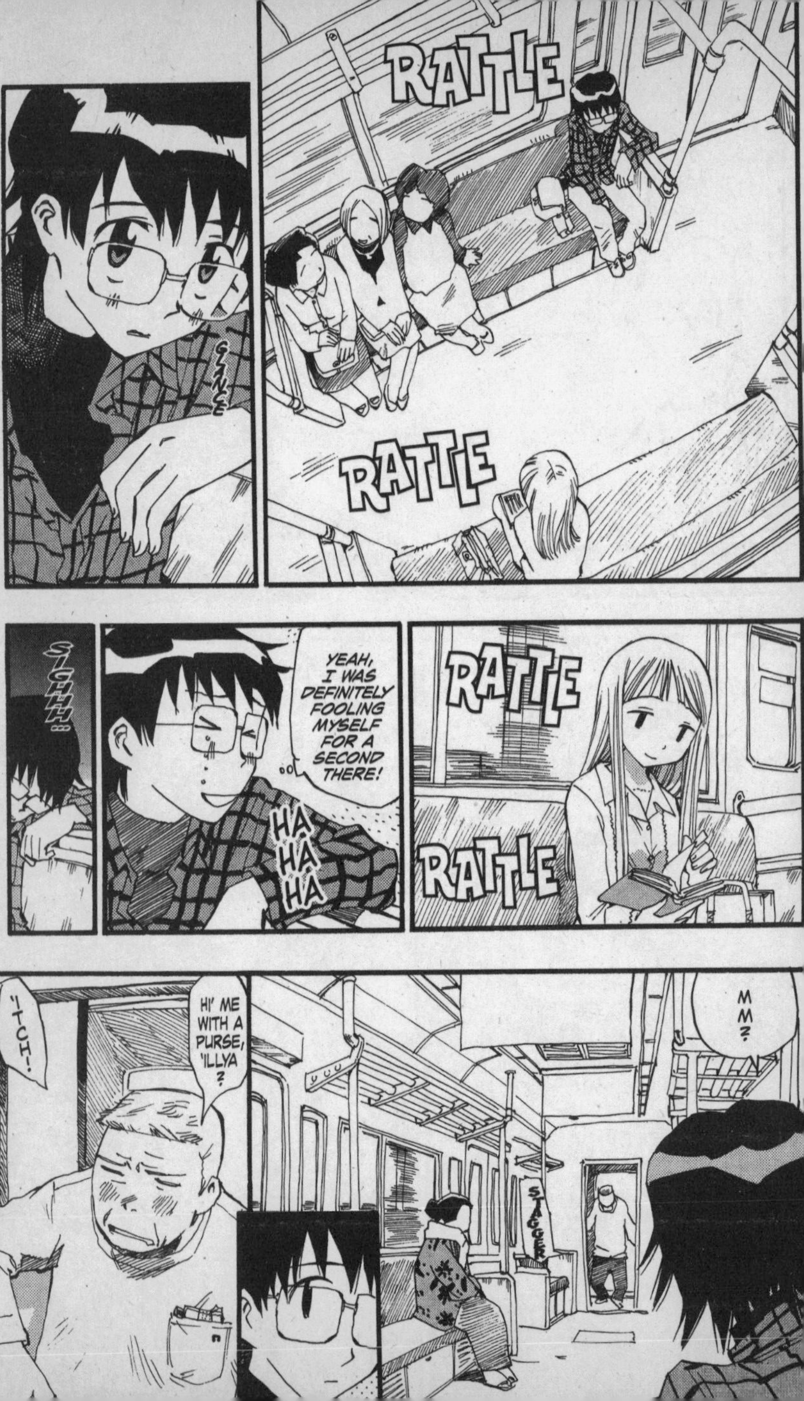
RATTLE
RATTLE
GLANCE
RATTLE
RATTLE
YEAH, I WAS DEFINITELY FOOLING MYSELF FOR A SECOND THERE!
HA HA HA
SIGHHH..
MMM?
STAGGER
HI' ME WITH A PURSE, 'ILLYA?
'ITCH!

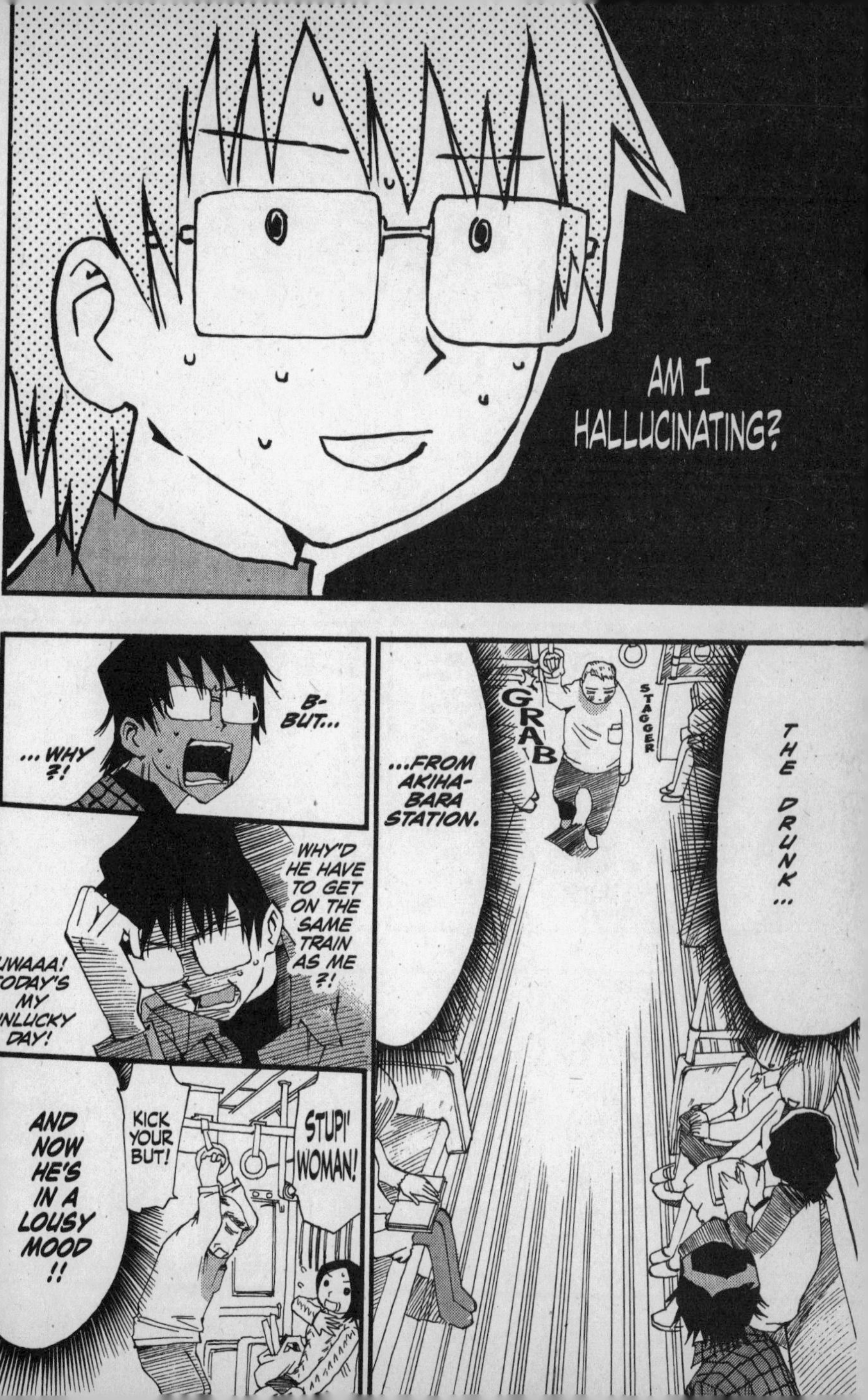
AM I HALLUCINATING?
THE DRUNK...
GRAB
STAGGER
...FROM AKIHA-BARA STATION.
B-BUT...
...WHY?!
WHY'D HE HAVE TO GET ON THE SAME TRAIN AS ME?!
UWAAA! TODAY'S MY UNLUCKY DAY!
STUPI' WOMAN!
KICK YOUR BUT!
AND NOW HE'S IN A LOUSY MOOD!!

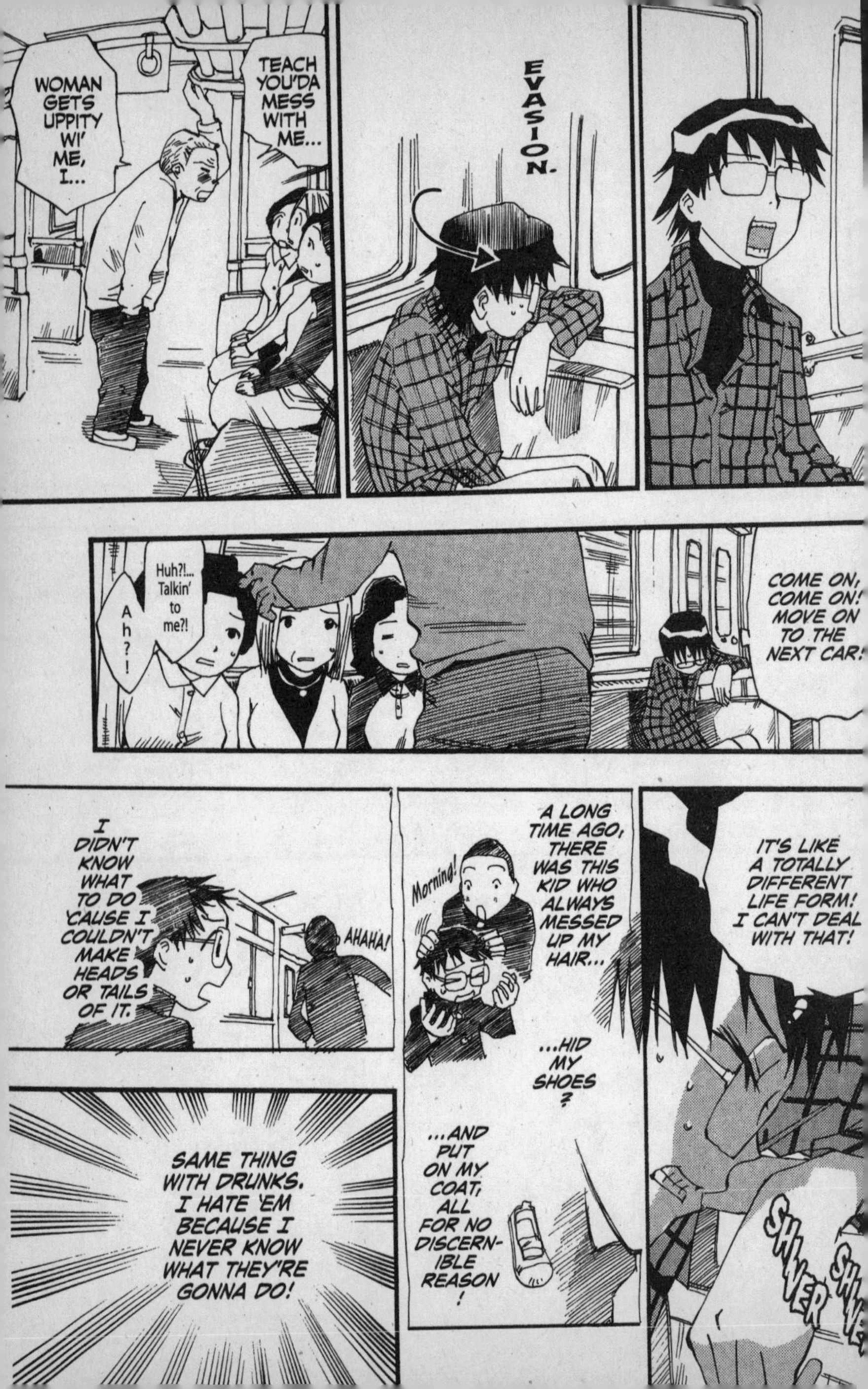
EVASION.
TEACH YOU'DA MESS WITH ME...
WOMAN GETS UPPITY WI' ME, I...
COME ON, COME ON! MOVE ON TO THE NEXT CAR!
Huh?!... Talkin' to me?!
Ah?!
IT'S LIKE A TOTALLY DIFFERENT LIFE FORM! I CAN'T DEAL WITH THAT!
SHIVER
SHIVER
A LONG TIME AGO, THERE WAS THIS KID WHO ALWAYS MESSED UP MY HAIR...
Morning!
...HID MY SHOES?
...AND PUT ON MY COAT, ALL FOR NO DISCERNIBLE REASON!
I DIDN'T KNOW WHAT TO DO 'CAUSE I COULDN'T MAKE HEADS OR TAILS OF IT.
AHAHA!
SAME THING WITH DRUNKS. I HATE 'EM BECAUSE I NEVER KNOW WHAT THEY'RE GONNA DO!

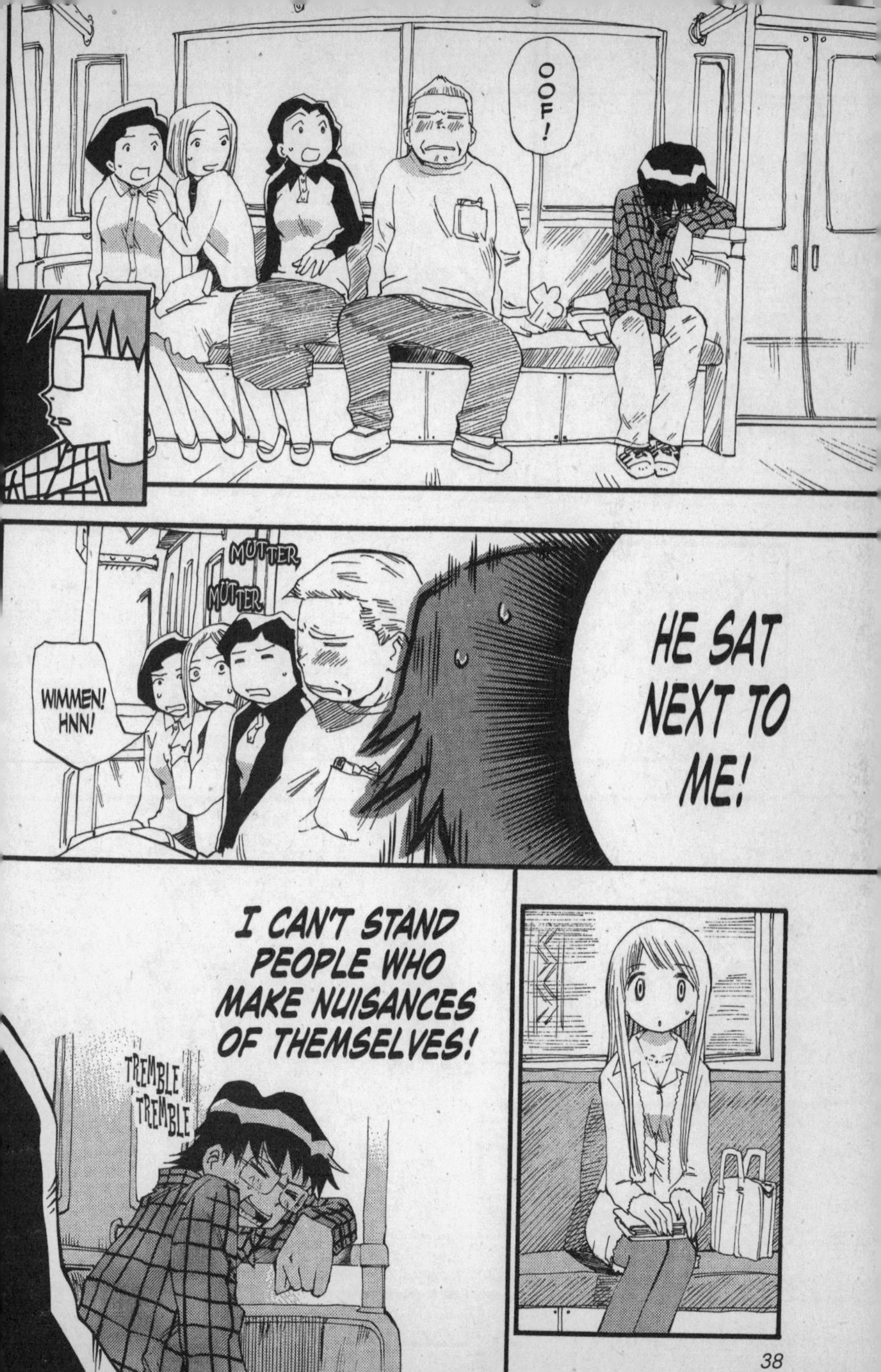
OOF!
HE SAT NEXT TO ME!
MUTTER
MUTTER
WIMMEN! HNN!
I CAN'T STAND PEOPLE WHO MAKE NUISANCES OF THEMSELVES!
TREMBLE TREMBLE

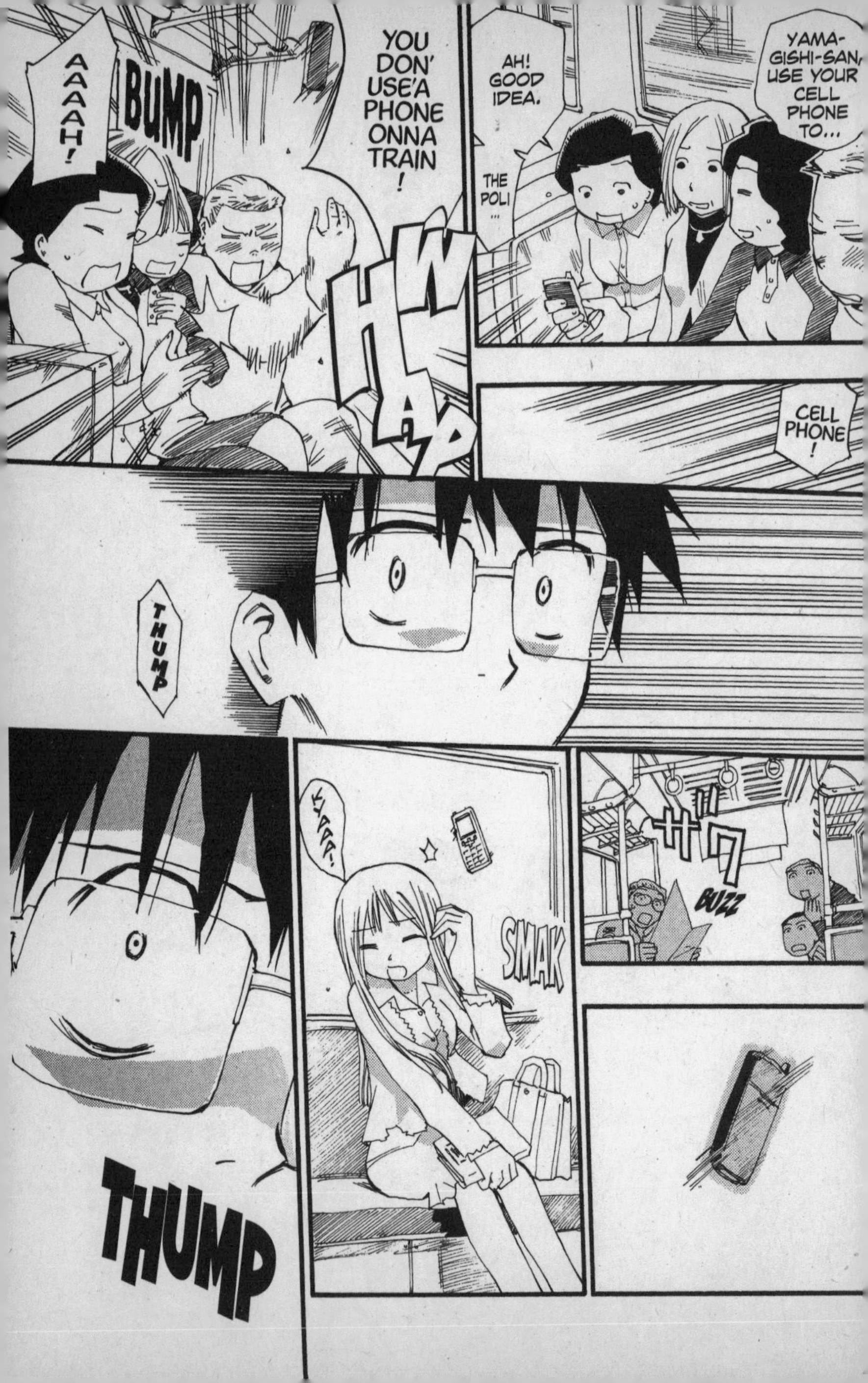
YAMA-GISHI-SAN, USE YOUR CELL PHONE TO...
AH! GOOD IDEA.
THE POLI...
CELL PHONE!
YOU DON' USE'A PHONE ONNA TRAIN!
AAAAH!
BUMP
HWAP
THUMP
ザク
BUZZ
KYAAA!
SMAK
THUMP

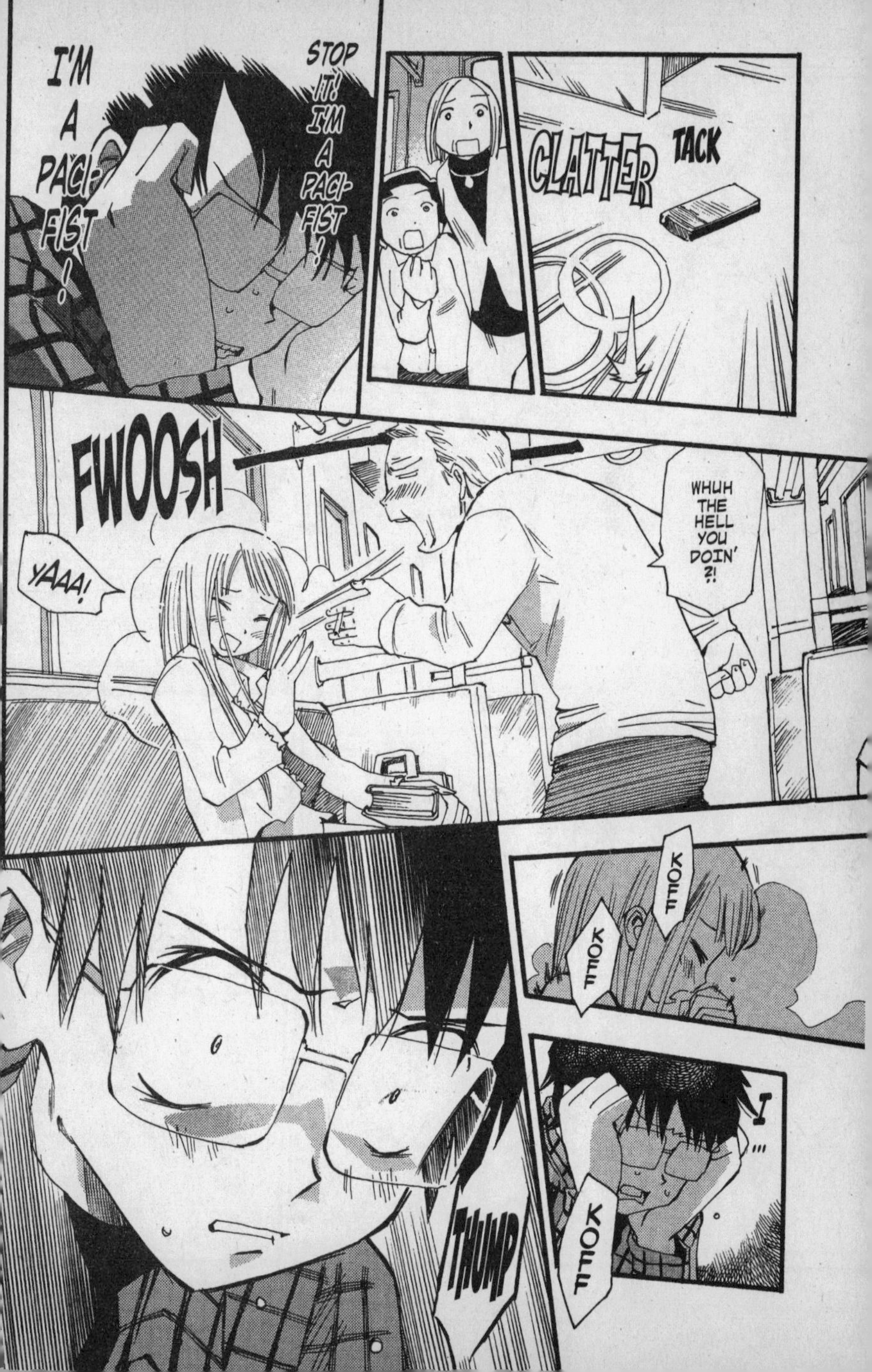

CLATTER
TACK
STOP IT! I'M A PACI-FIST!
I'M A PACI-FIST!
WHUH THE HELL YOU DOIN'?!
FWOOSH
YAAA!
KOFF
KOFF
I...
KOFF
THUMP

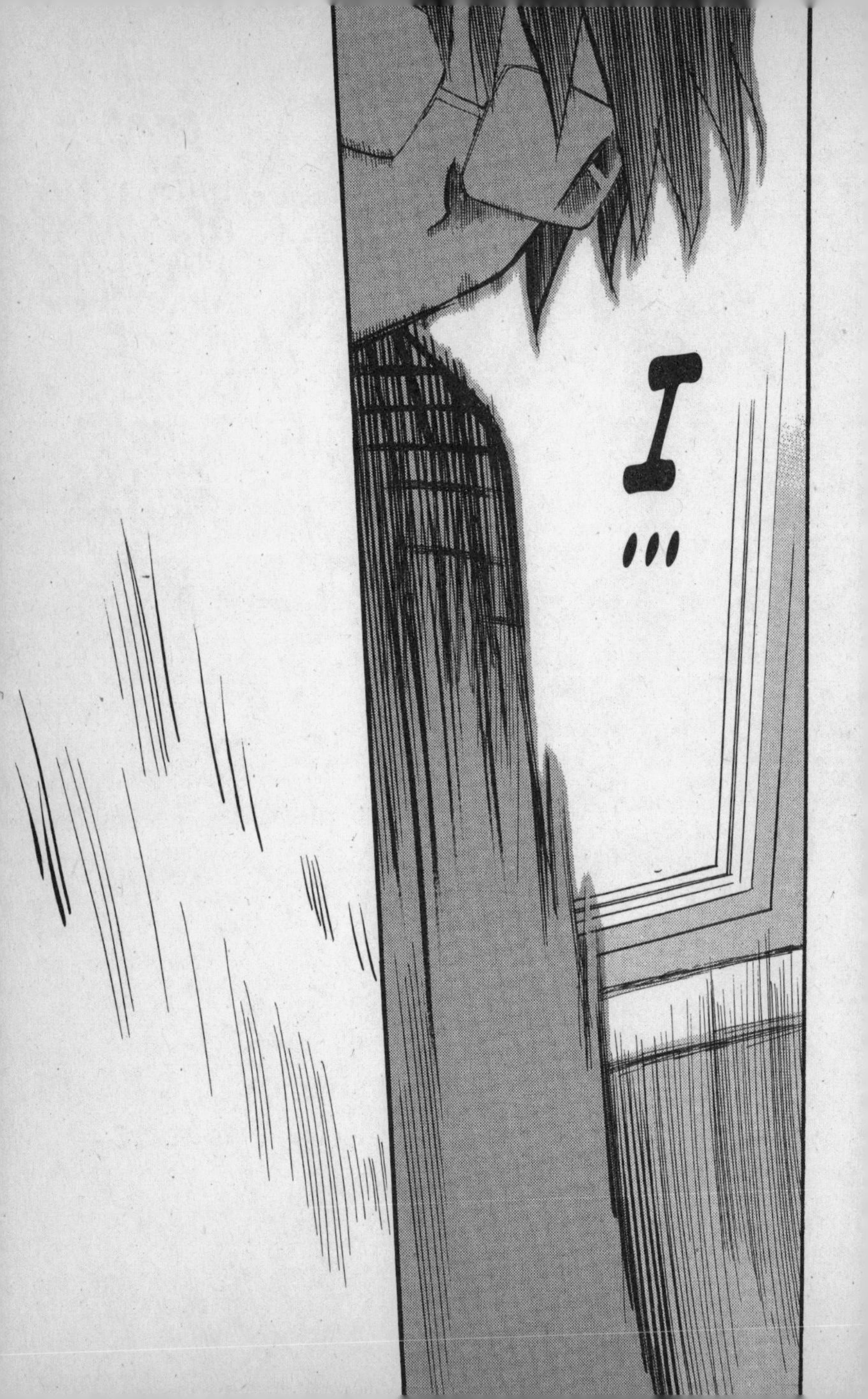
I...

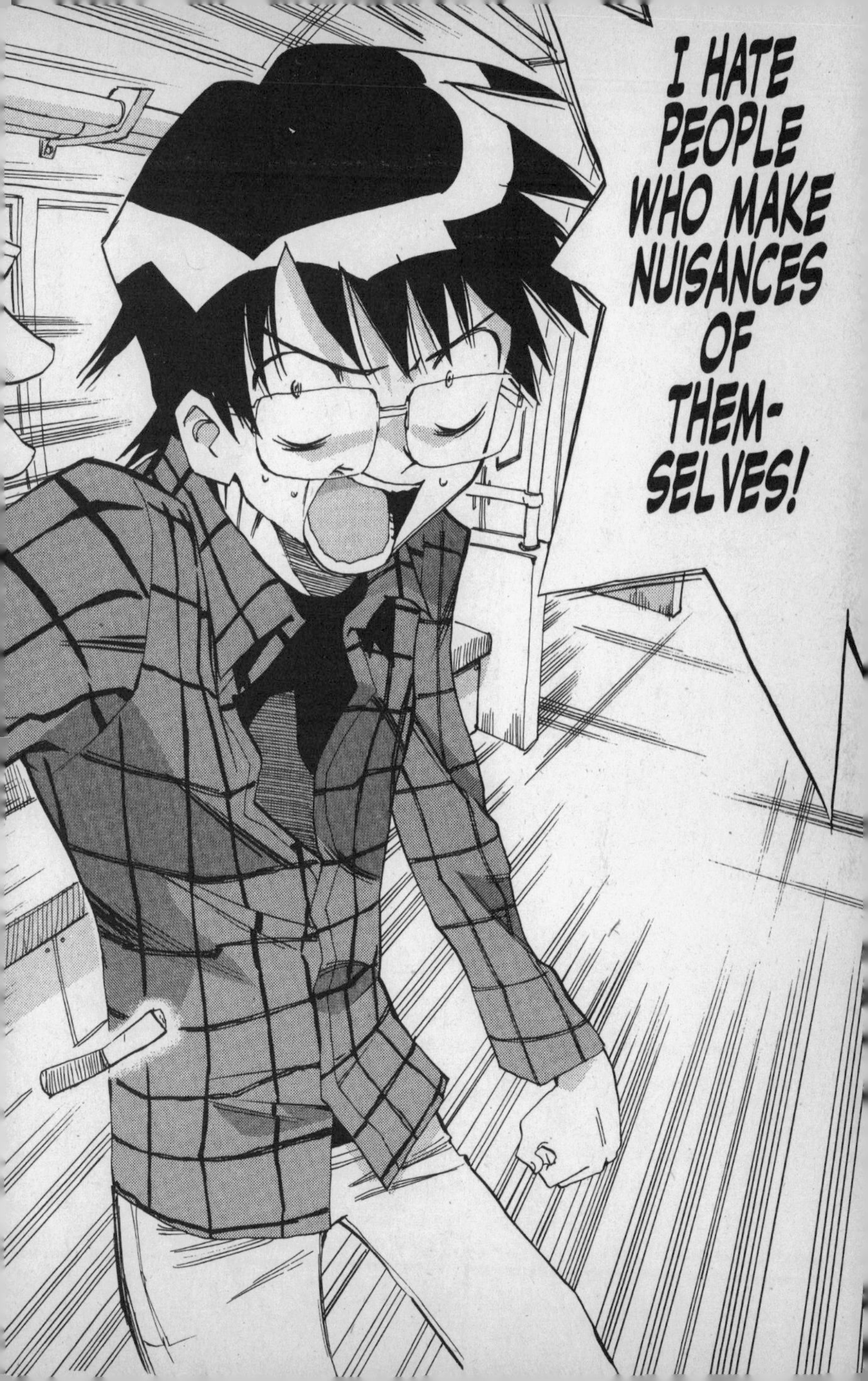
I HATE PEOPLE WHO MAKE NUISANCES OF THEM-SELVES!

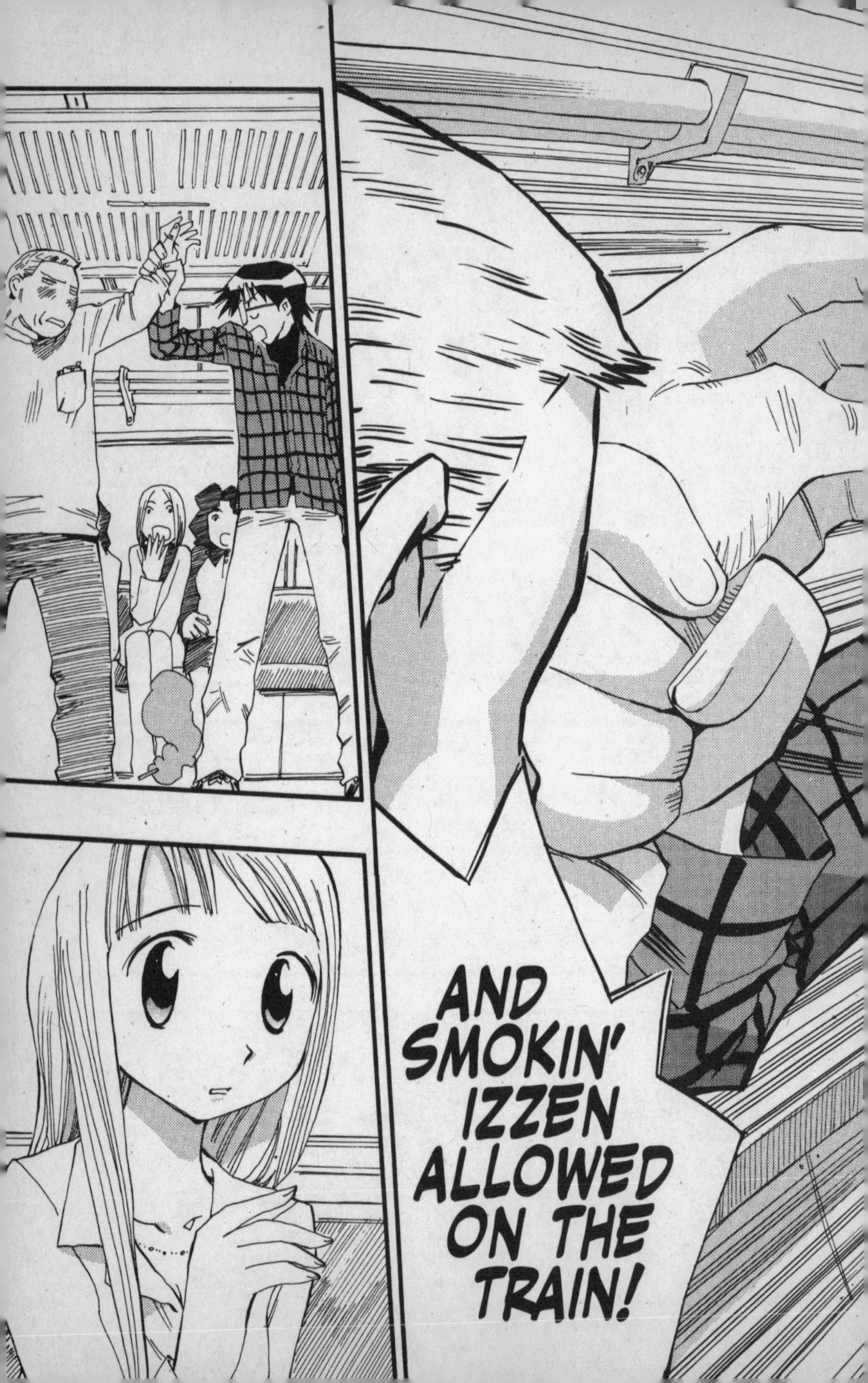
AND SMOKIN' IZZEN ALLOWED ON THE TRAIN!

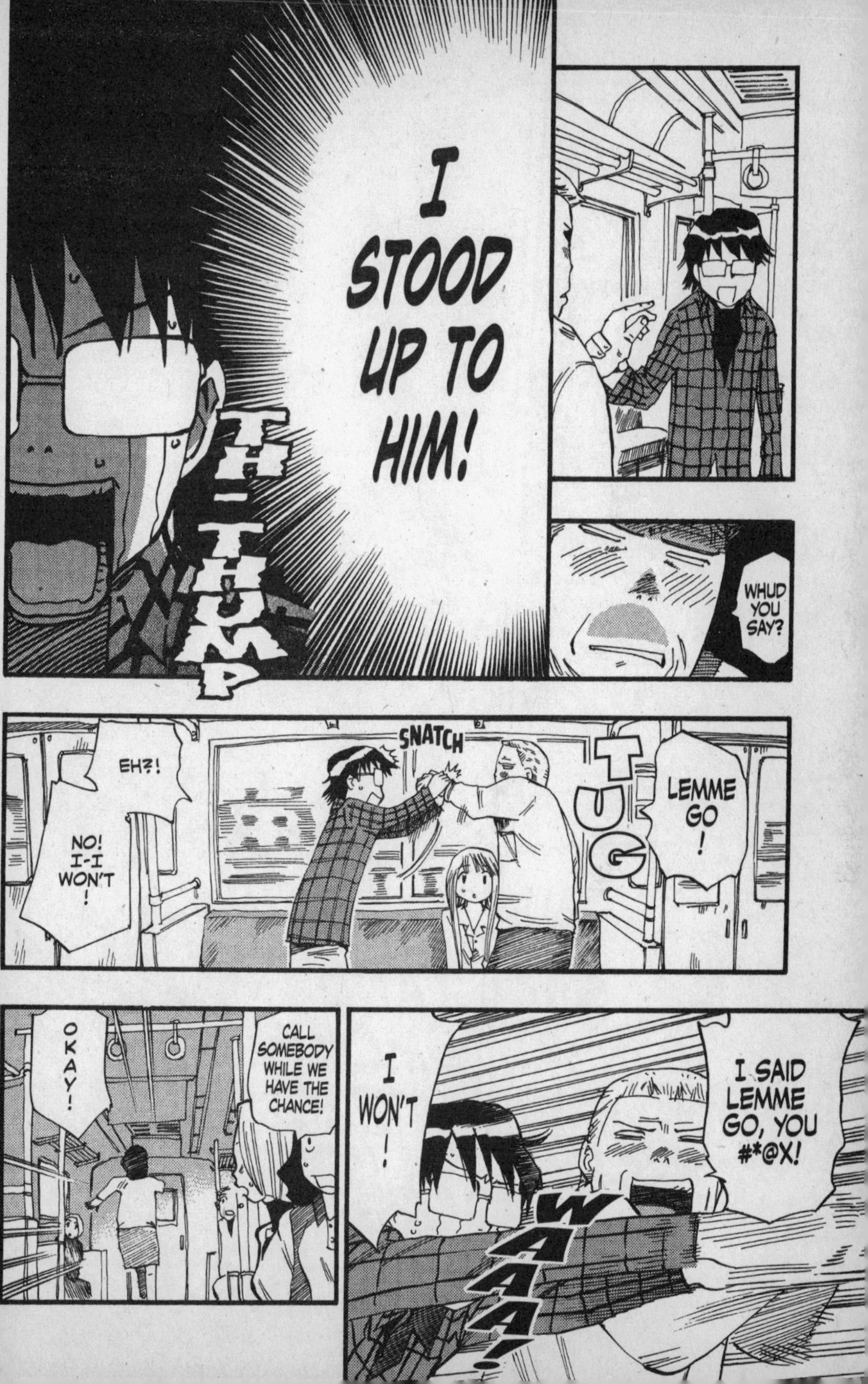
WHUD YOU SAY?
I STOOD UP TO HIM!
TH-THUMP
LEMME GO!
TUG
SNATCH
EH?!
NO! I-I WON'T!
I SAID LEMME GO, YOU #*@X!
I WON'T!
WAAAA!
CALL SOMEBODY WHILE WE HAVE THE CHANCE!
OKAY!

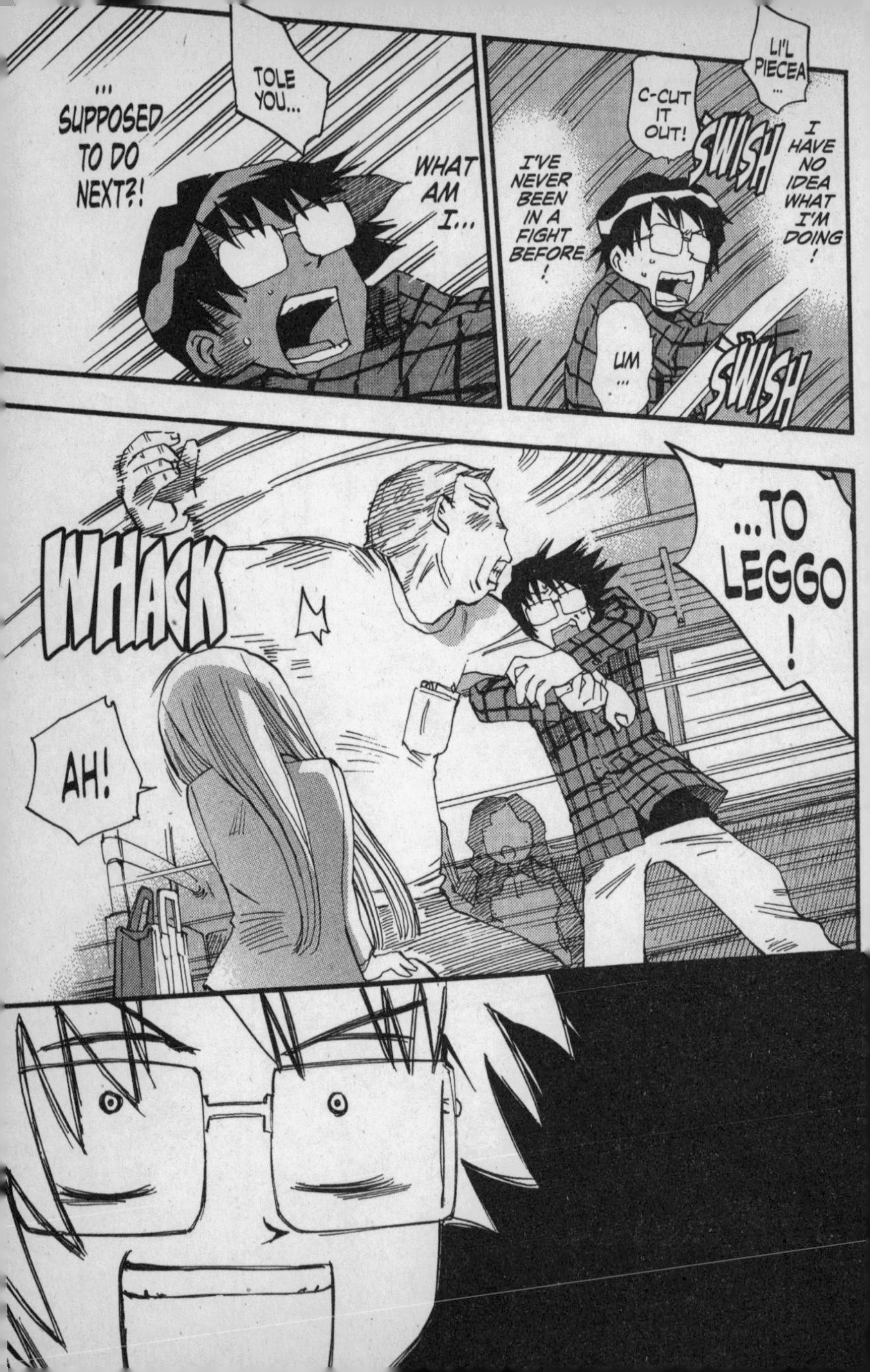
LI'L PIECEA ...
C-CUT IT OUT!
SWISH
I HAVE NO IDEA WHAT I'M DOING!
I'VE NEVER BEEN IN A FIGHT BEFORE!
UM ...
SWISH
TOLE YOU...
WHAT AM I...
... SUPPOSED TO DO NEXT?!
...TO LEGGO!
WHACK
AH!

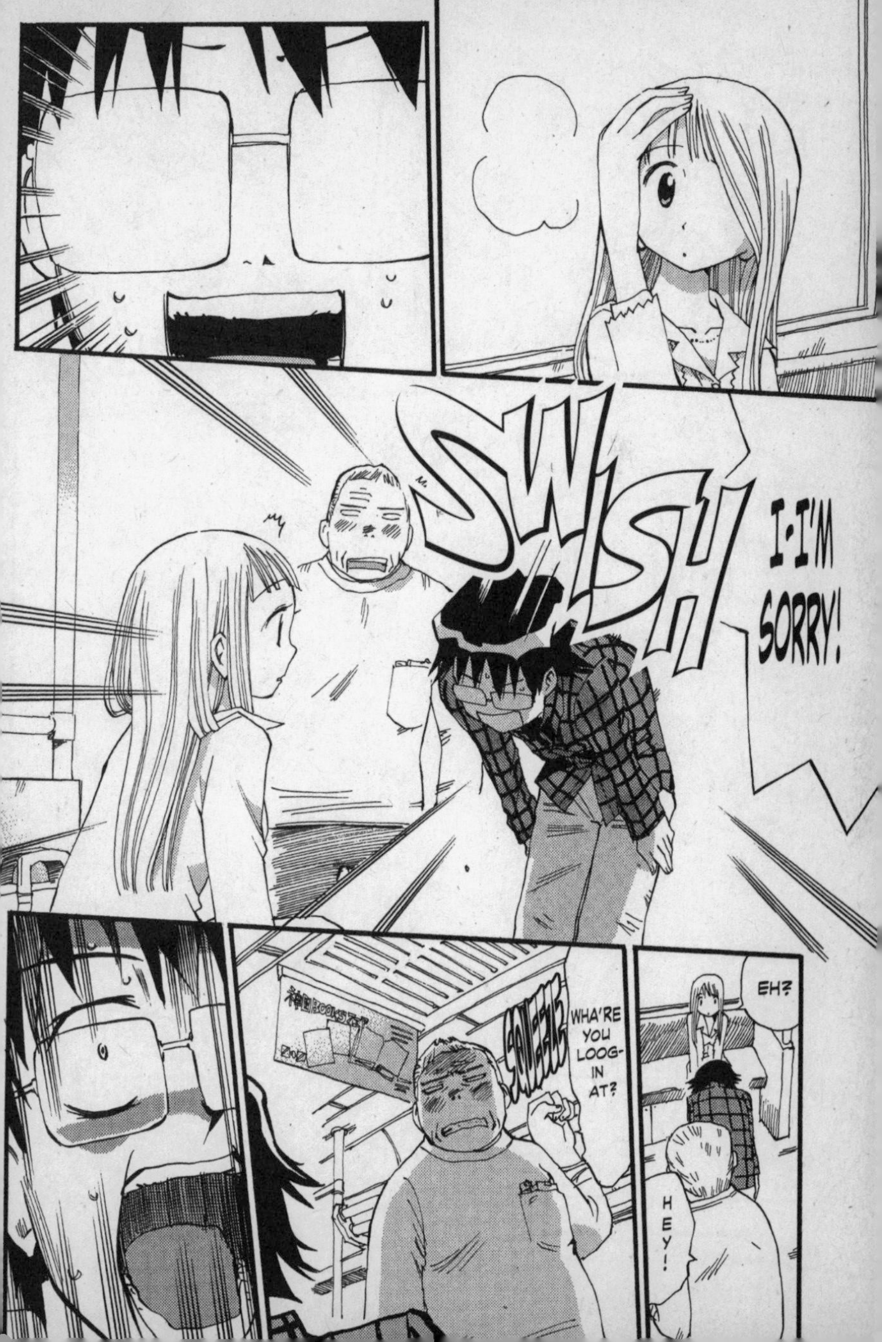
SWISH
I-I'M SORRY!
EH?
HEY!
WHA'RE YOU LOOG-IN AT?

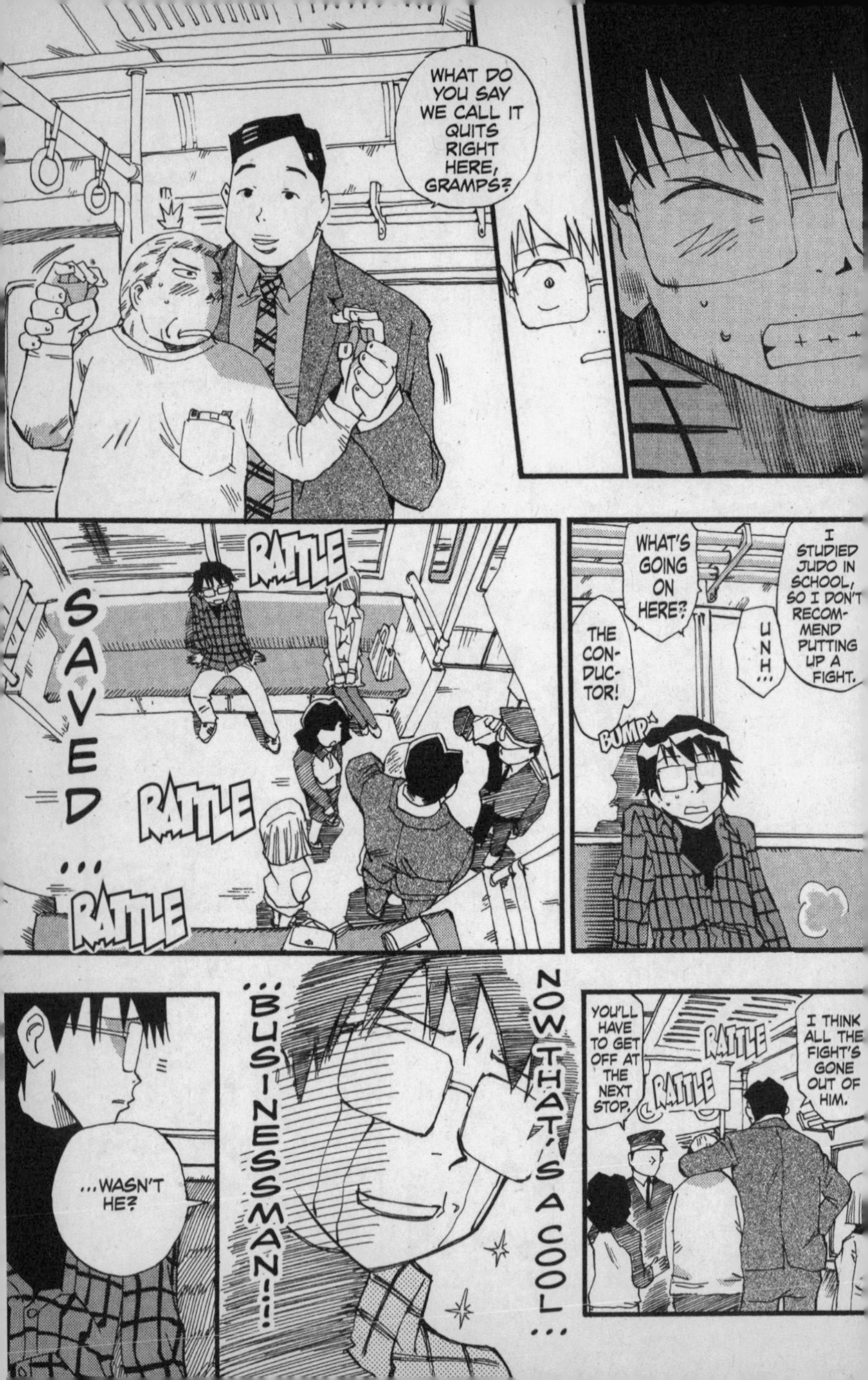
WHAT DO YOU SAY WE CALL IT QUITS RIGHT HERE, GRAMPS?
I STUDIED JUDO IN SCHOOL, SO I DON'T RECOMMEND PUTTING UP A FIGHT.
UNH...
WHAT'S GOING ON HERE?
THE CONDUCTOR!
BUMP
RATTLE
SAVED...
RATTLE
RATTLE
I THINK ALL THE FIGHT'S GONE OUT OF HIM.
RATTLE
RATTLE
YOU'LL HAVE TO GET OFF AT THE NEXT STOP.
NOW THAT'S A COOL...
...BUSINESSMAN!!
...WASN'T HE?

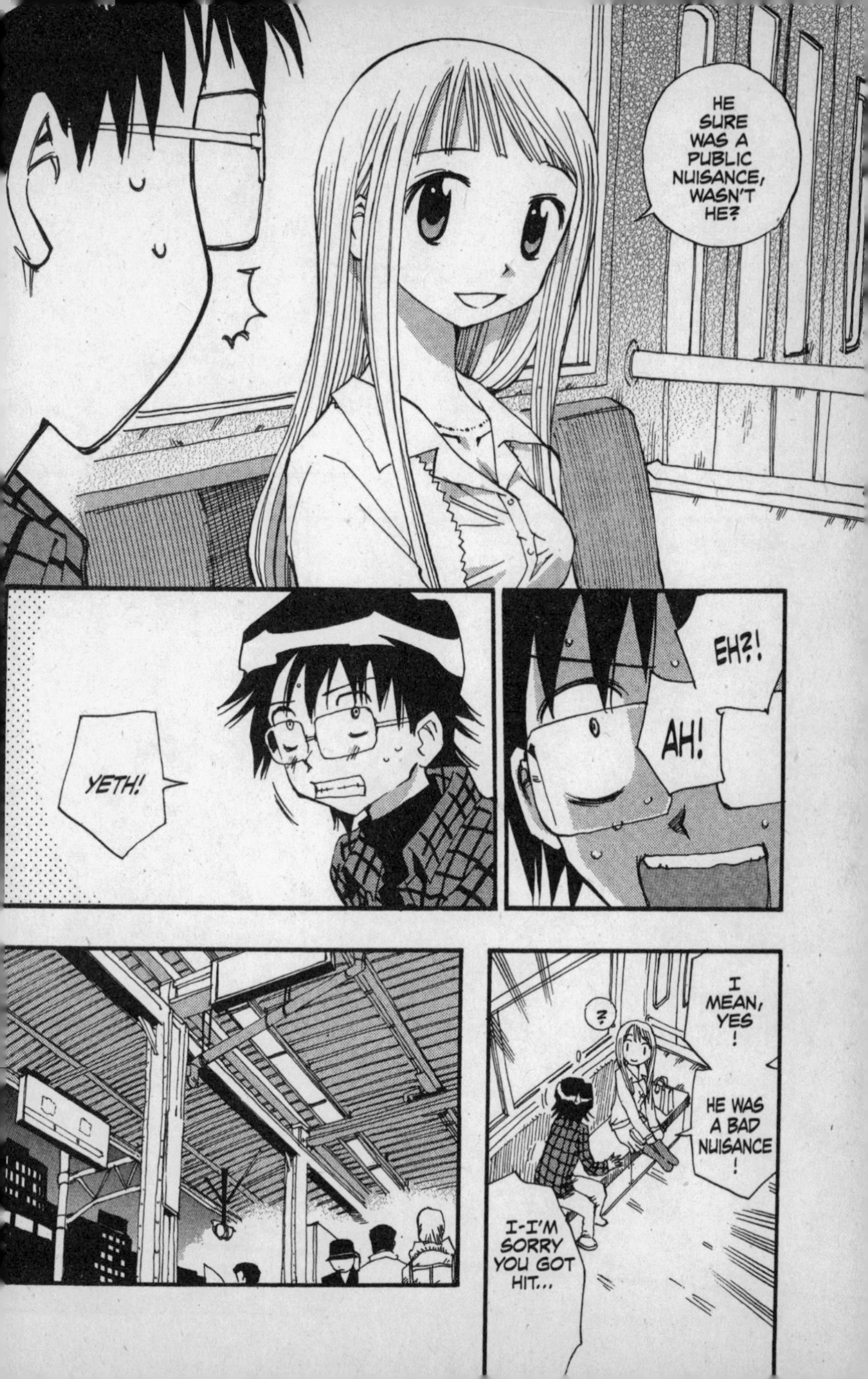
HE SURE WAS A PUBLIC NUISANCE, WASN'T HE?
EH?!
AH!
YETH!
I MEAN, YES!
HE WAS A BAD NUISANCE!
I-I'M SORRY YOU GOT HIT...

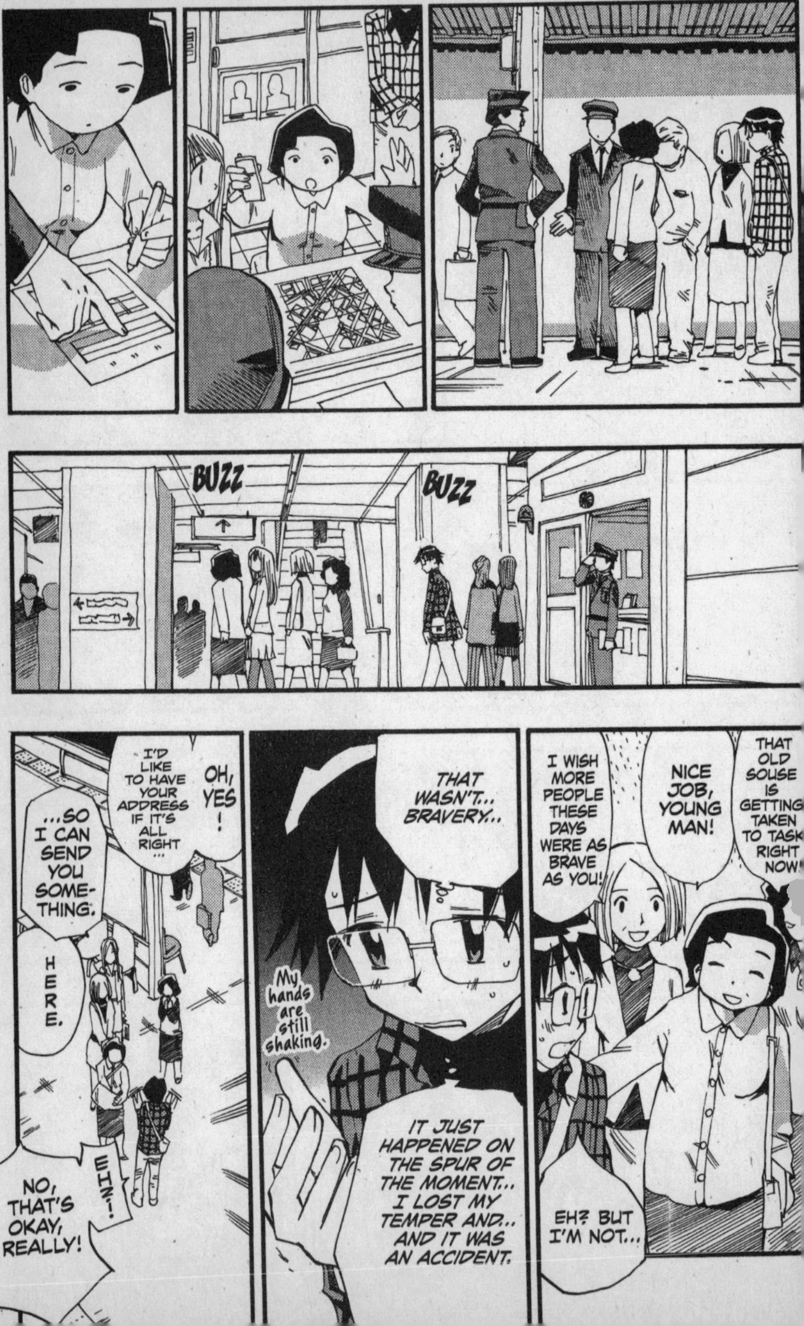
BUZZ
BUZZ
THAT OLD SOUSE IS GETTING TAKEN TO TASK RIGHT NOW!
NICE JOB, YOUNG MAN!
I WISH MORE PEOPLE THESE DAYS WERE AS BRAVE AS YOU!
EH? BUT I'M NOT...
THAT WASN'T... BRAVERY...
My hands are still shaking.
IT JUST HAPPENED ON THE SPUR OF THE MOMENT... I LOST MY TEMPER AND... AND IT WAS AN ACCIDENT.
OH, YES!
I'D LIKE TO HAVE YOUR ADDRESS IF IT'S ALL RIGHT...
...SO I CAN SEND YOU SOMETHING.
HERE.
EH?!
NO, THAT'S OKAY, REALLY!

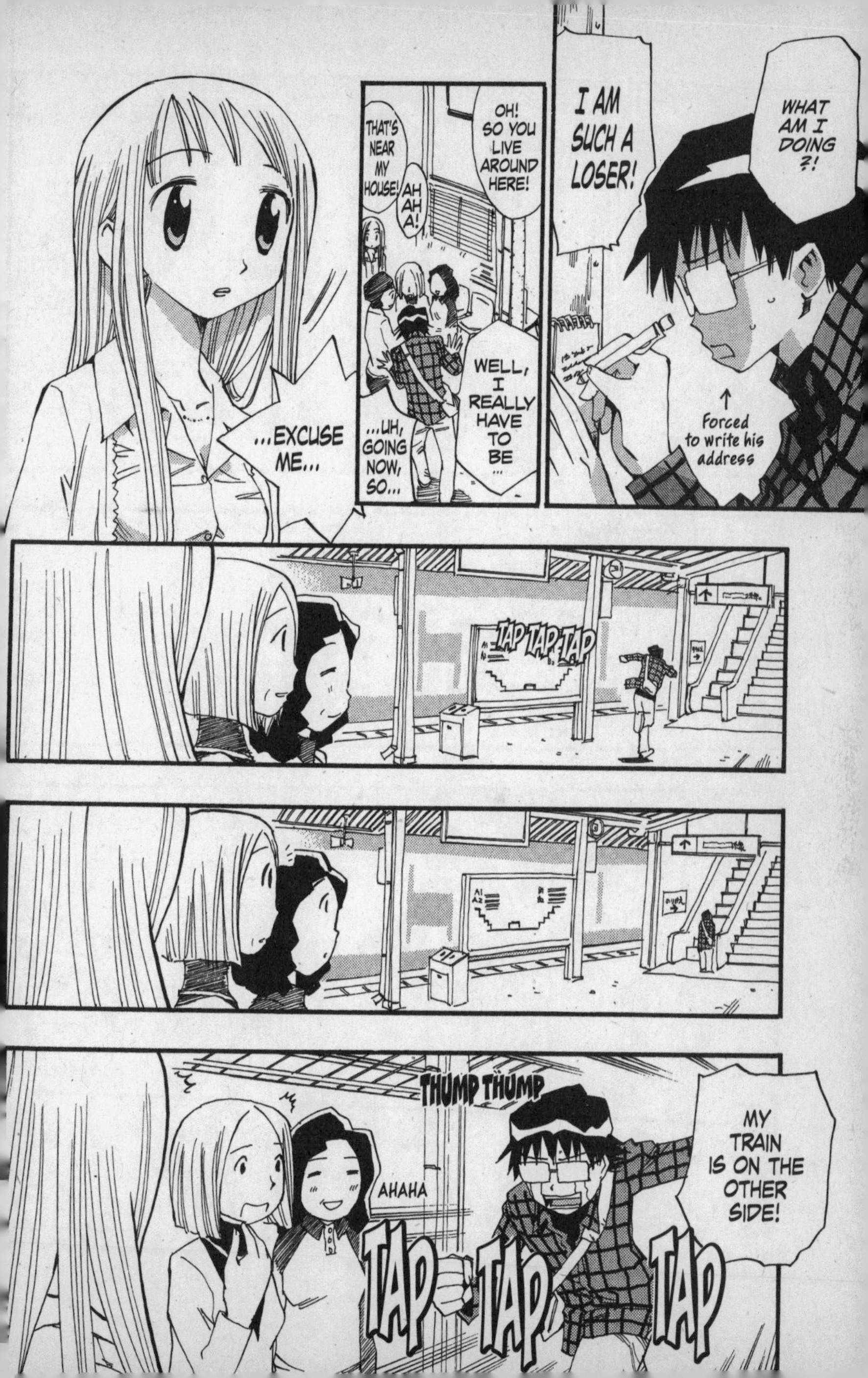
WHAT AM I DOING ?!
I AM SUCH A LOSER!
↑ Forced to write his address
OH! SO YOU LIVE AROUND HERE!
THAT'S NEAR MY HOUSE!
AH AH A!
WELL, I REALLY HAVE TO BE ...
...UH, GOING NOW, SO...
...EXCUSE ME...
TAP TAP TAP
MY TRAIN IS ON THE OTHER SIDE!
THUMP THUMP
AHAHA
TAP TAP TAP

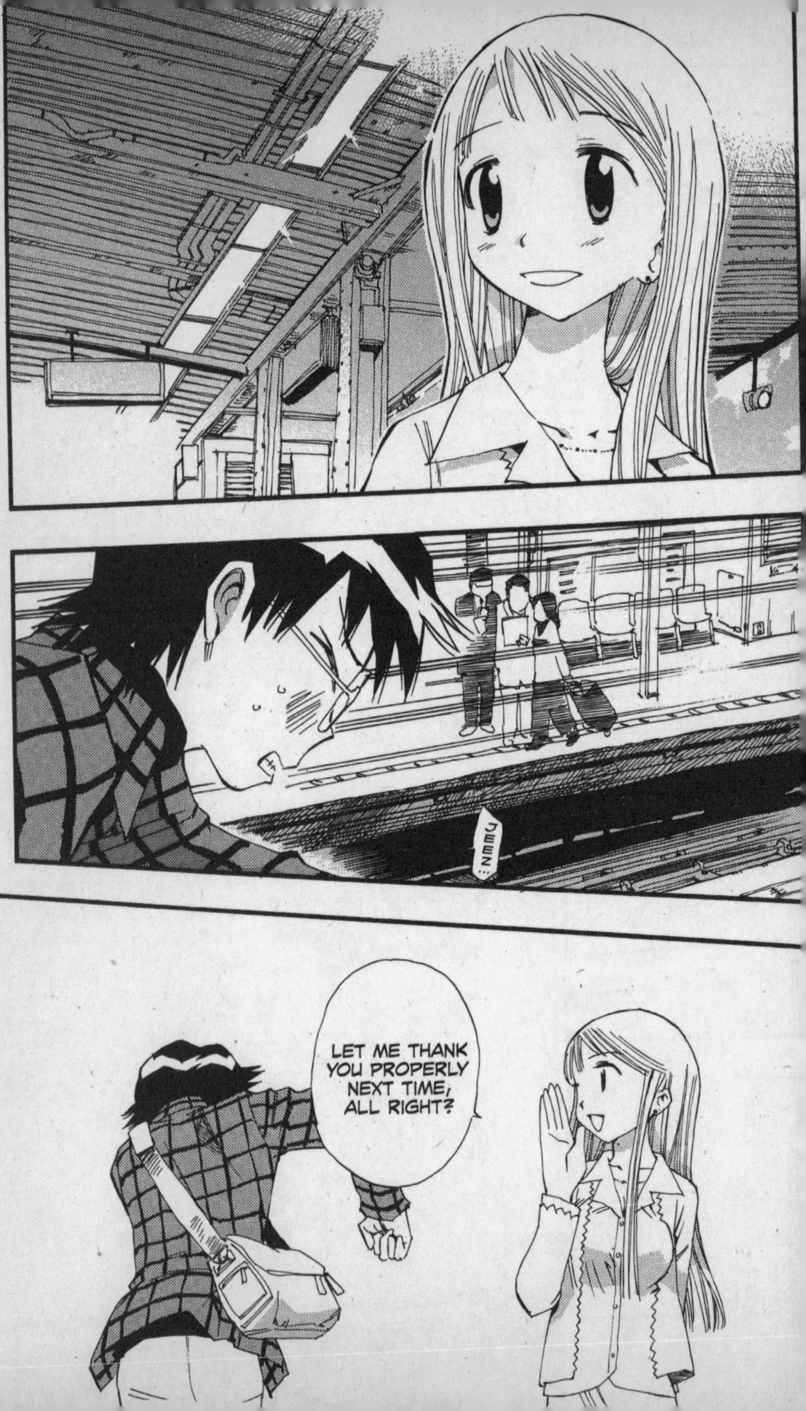
JEEZ...
LET ME THANK YOU PROPERLY NEXT TIME, ALL RIGHT?

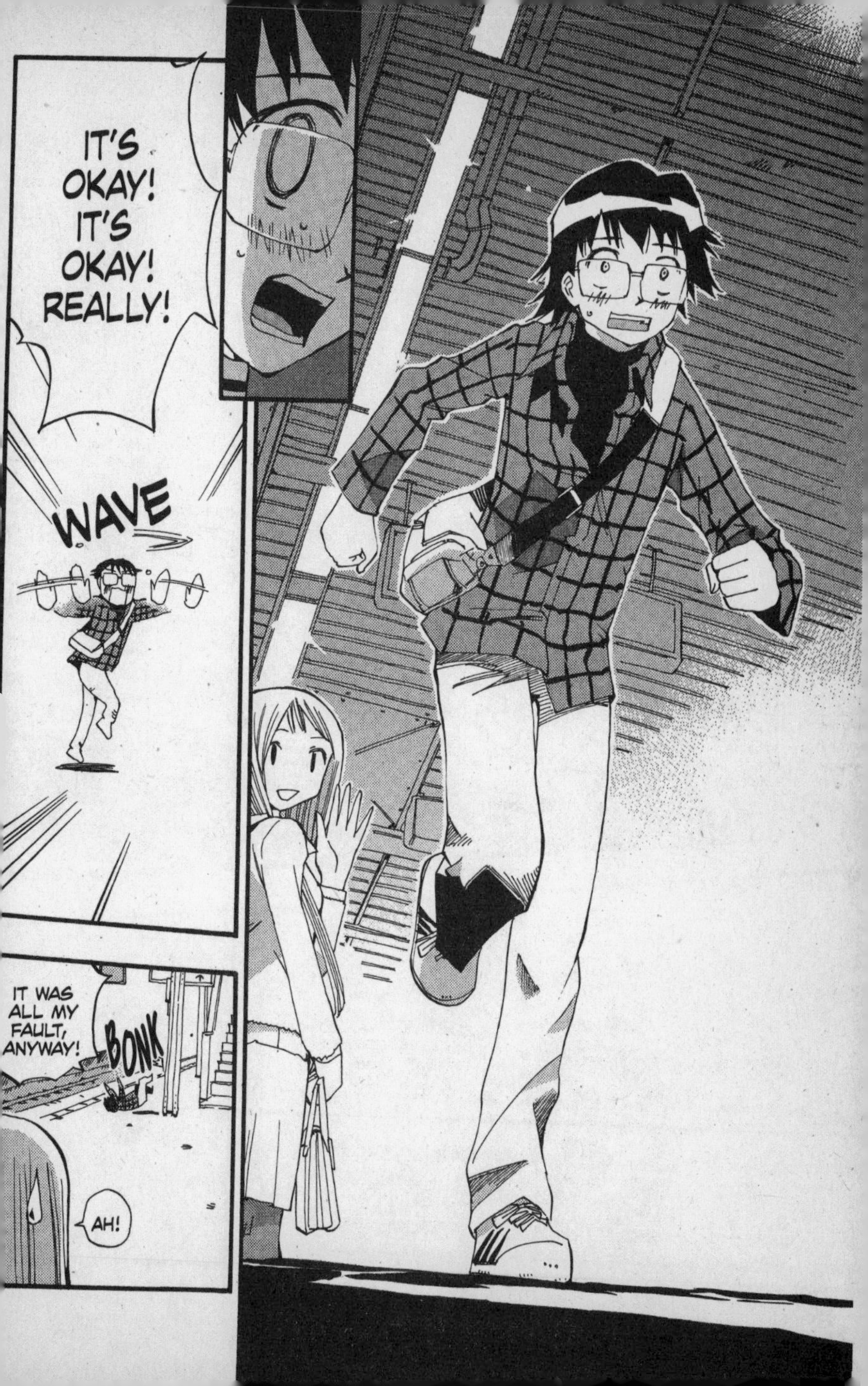
IT'S OKAY! IT'S OKAY! REALLY!
WAVE
IT WAS ALL MY FAULT, ANYWAY!
BONK
AH!

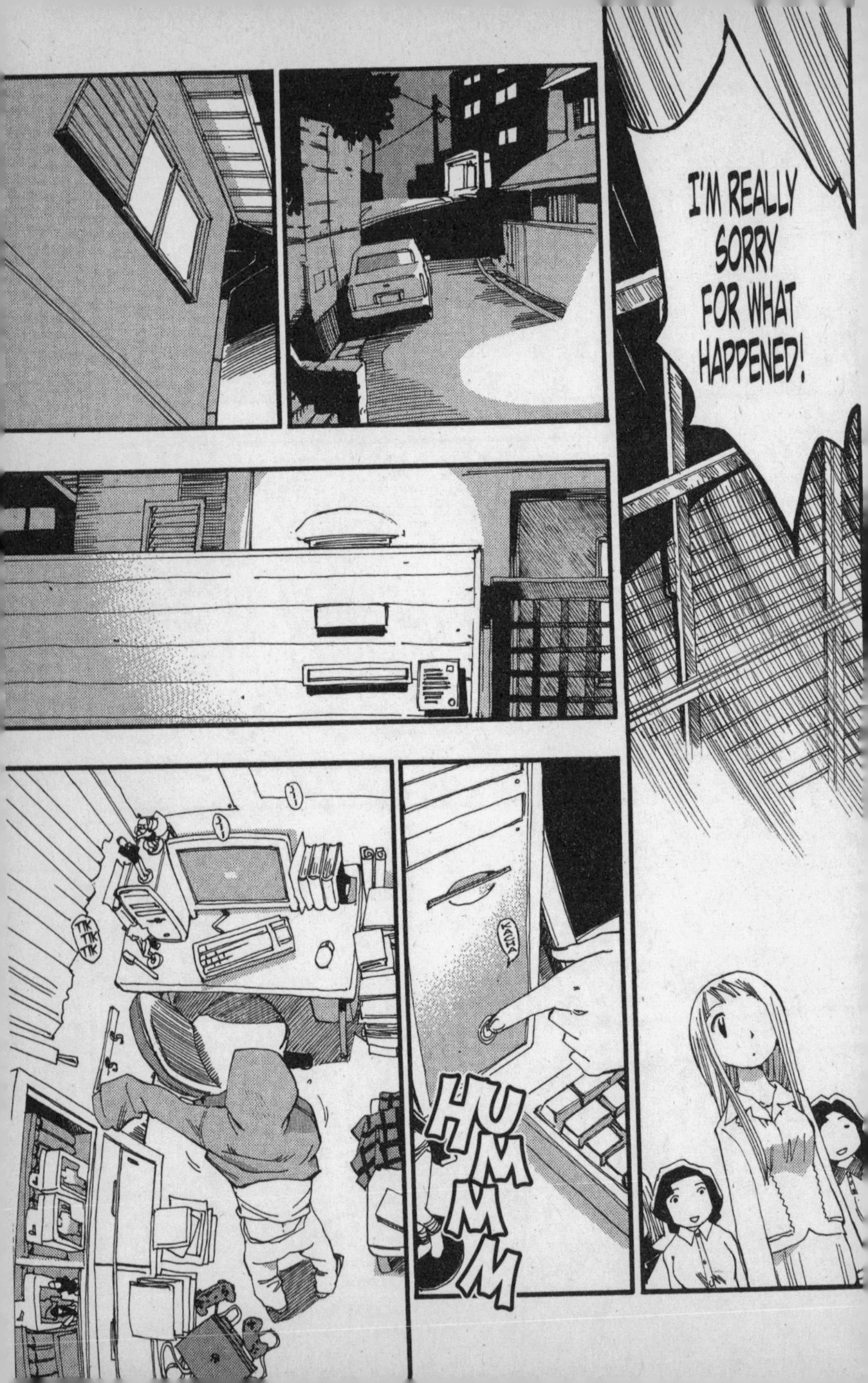
I'M REALLY SORRY FOR WHAT HAPPENED!
KACHA
HUMMM
TIK TIK TIK

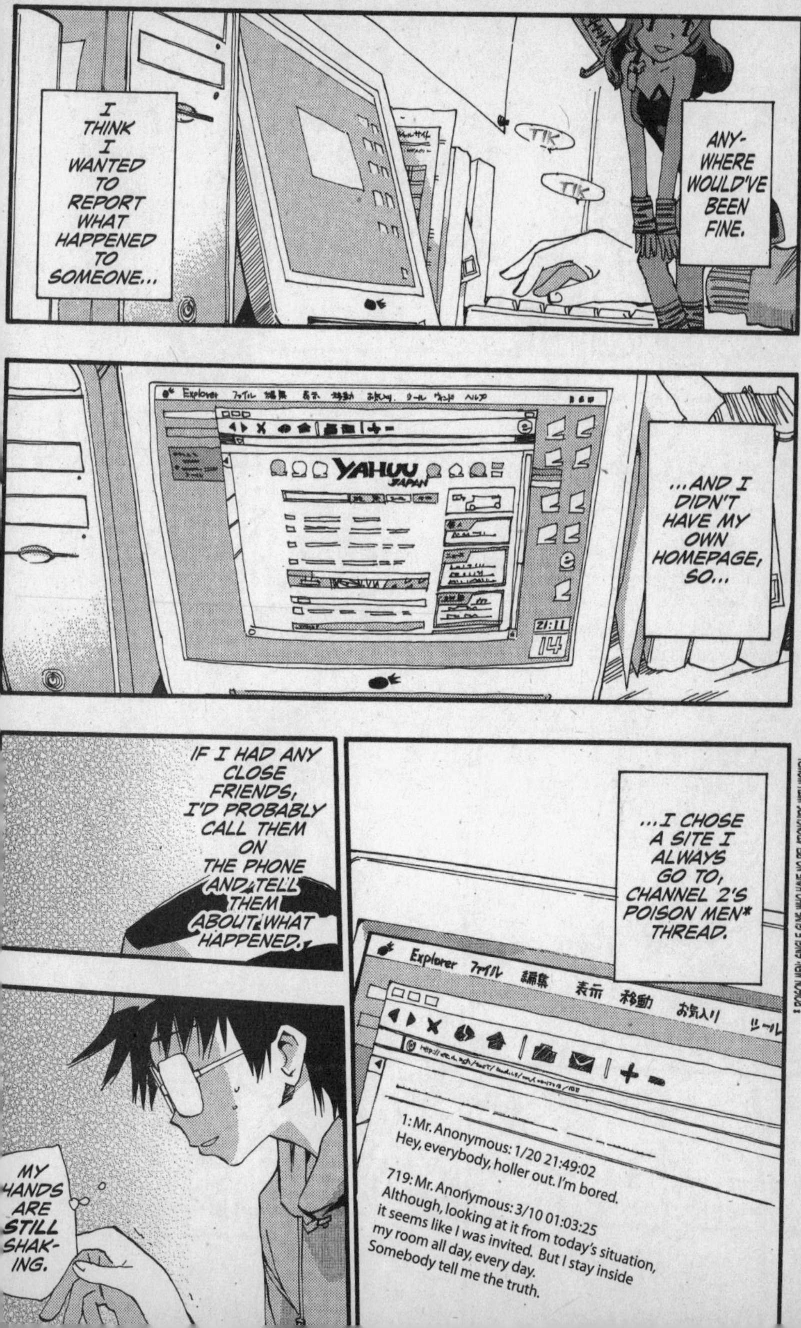
ANY-WHERE WOULD'VE BEEN FINE.
TIK
TIK
I THINK I WANTED TO REPORT WHAT HAPPENED TO SOMEONE...
...AND I DIDN'T HAVE MY OWN HOMEPAGE, SO...
Explorer
YAHUU JAPAN
21:11
14
...I CHOSE A SITE I ALWAYS GO TO, CHANNEL 2'S POISON MEN* THREAD.
Explorer ファイル 編集 表示 移動 お気入り ツール
1: Mr. Anonymous: 1/20 21:49:02
Hey, everybody, holler out. I'm bored.
719: Mr. Anonymous: 3/10 01:03:25
Although, looking at it from today's situation, it seems like I was invited. But I stay inside my room all day, every day. Somebody tell me the truth.
IF I HAD ANY CLOSE FRIENDS, I'D PROBABLY CALL THEM ON THE PHONE AND TELL THEM ABOUT WHAT HAPPENED.
MY HANDS ARE STILL SHAK-ING.

* POISON MEN: SINGLE GUYS WHO HAVE NO RELATIONSHIPS WITH WOMEN

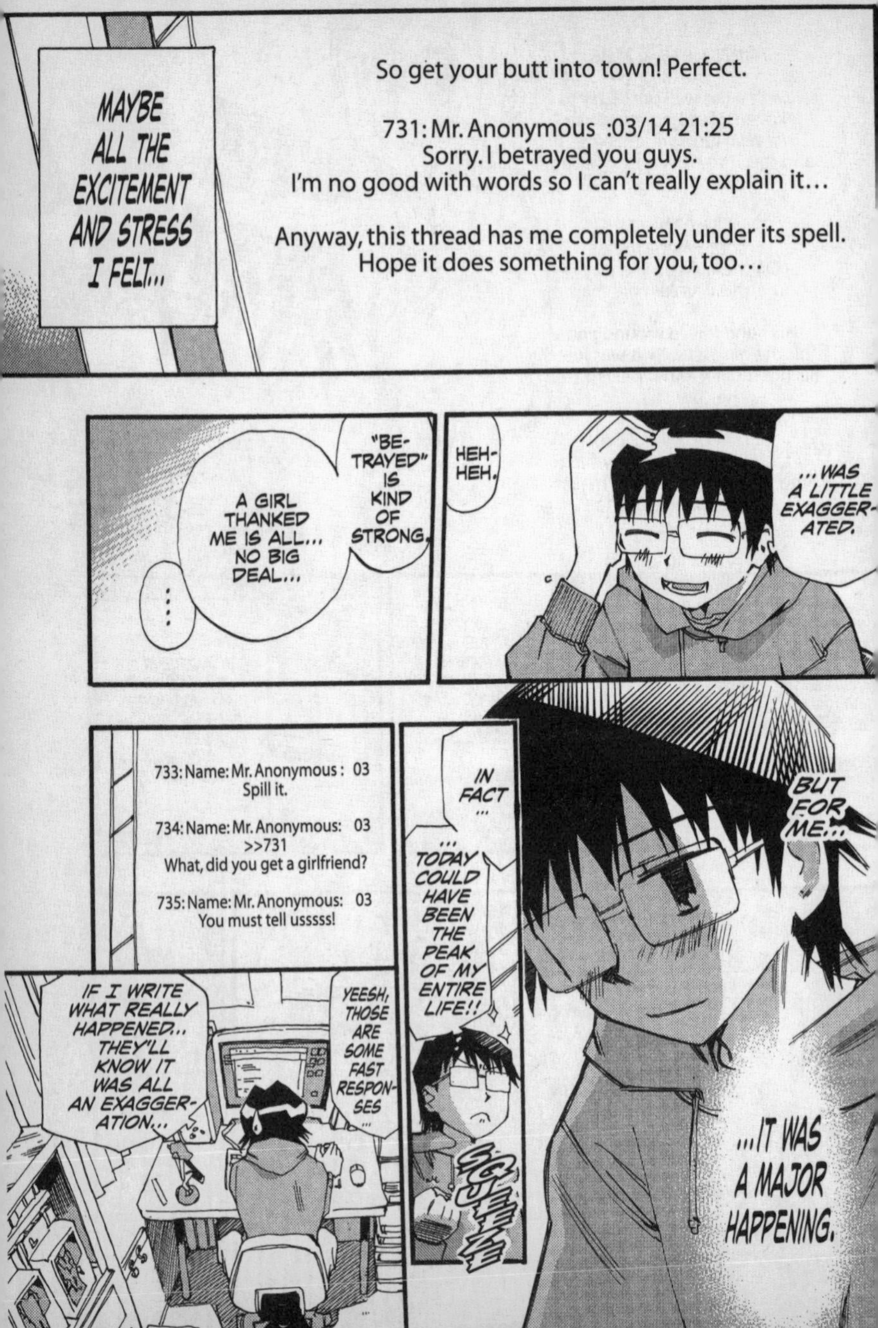
So get your butt into town! Perfect.
731: Mr. Anonymous :03/14 21:25
Sorry. I betrayed you guys.
I'm no good with words so I can't really explain it…
Anyway, this thread has me completely under its spell.
Hope it does something for you, too…
MAYBE ALL THE EXCITEMENT AND STRESS I FELT...
...WAS A LITTLE EXAGGER-ATED.
HEH-HEH.
"BE-TRAYED" IS KIND OF STRONG.
A GIRL THANKED ME IS ALL... NO BIG DEAL...
....
BUT FOR ME...
...IT WAS A MAJOR HAPPENING.
IN FACT...
...TODAY COULD HAVE BEEN THE PEAK OF MY ENTIRE LIFE!!
733: Name: Mr. Anonymous : 03
Spill it.
734: Name: Mr. Anonymous: 03
>>731
What, did you get a girlfriend?
735: Name: Mr. Anonymous: 03
You must tell ussssss!
YEESH, THOSE ARE SOME FAST RESPON-SES...
IF I WRITE WHAT REALLY HAPPENED... THEY'LL KNOW IT WAS ALL AN EXAGGER-ATION...

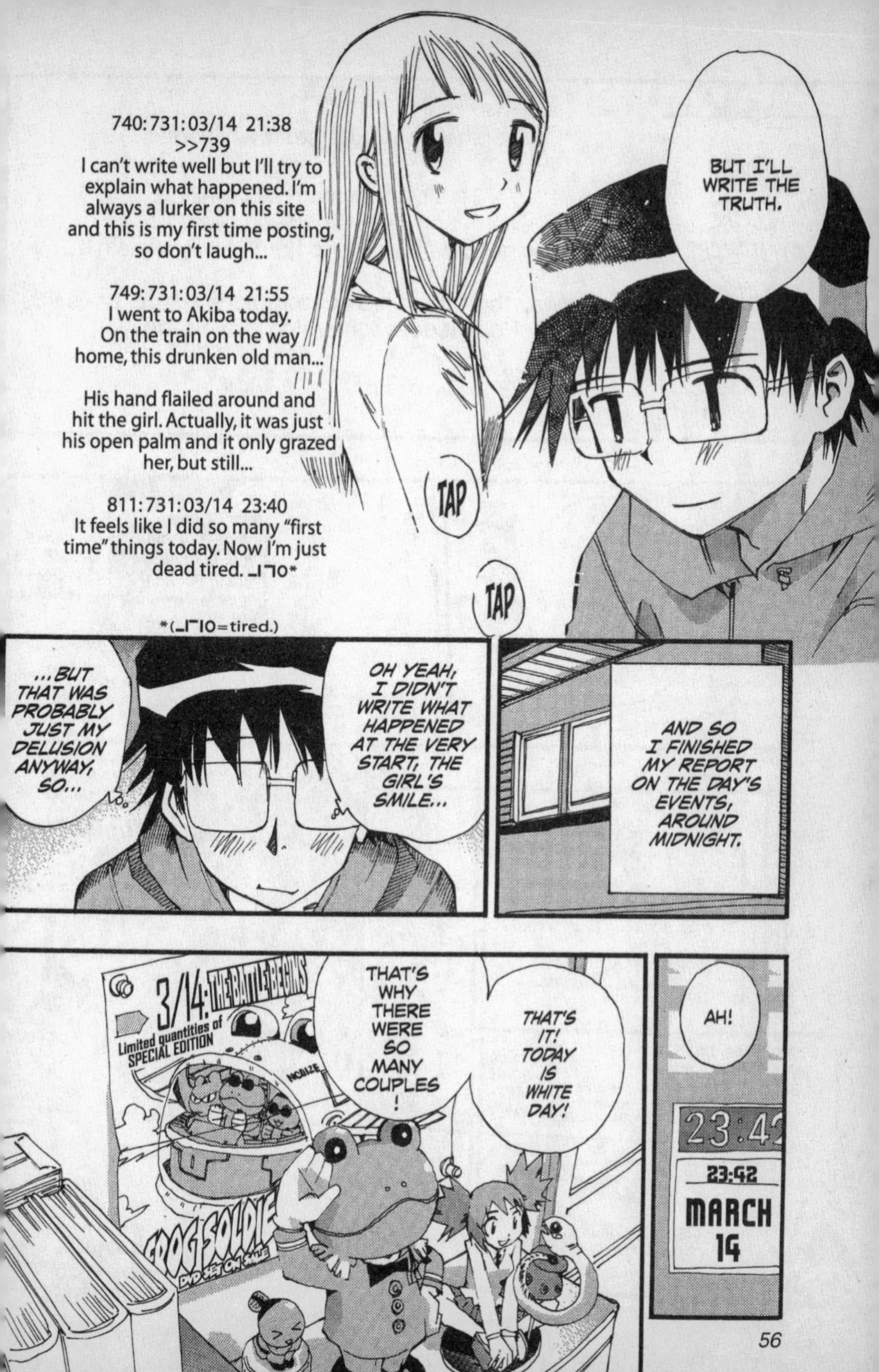
BUT I'LL WRITE THE TRUTH.
740: 731: 03/14 21:38
>>739
I can't write well but I'll try to explain what happened. I'm always a lurker on this site and this is my first time posting, so don't laugh...
749: 731: 03/14 21:55
I went to Akiba today. On the train on the way home, this drunken old man...
His hand flailed around and hit the girl. Actually, it was just his open palm and it only grazed her, but still...
811: 731: 03/14 23:40
It feels like I did so many "first time" things today. Now I'm just dead tired. _l¯lo*
TAP
TAP
*(_l¯lo=tired.)
AND SO I FINISHED MY REPORT ON THE DAY'S EVENTS, AROUND MIDNIGHT.
OH YEAH, I DIDN'T WRITE WHAT HAPPENED AT THE VERY START, THE GIRL'S SMILE...
...BUT THAT WAS PROBABLY JUST MY DELUSION ANYWAY, SO...
AH!
23:42
MARCH 14
THAT'S IT! TODAY IS WHITE DAY!
THAT'S WHY THERE WERE SO MANY COUPLES!
3/14: THE BATTLE BEGINS
Limited quantities of SPECIAL EDITION
DVD SET ON SALE

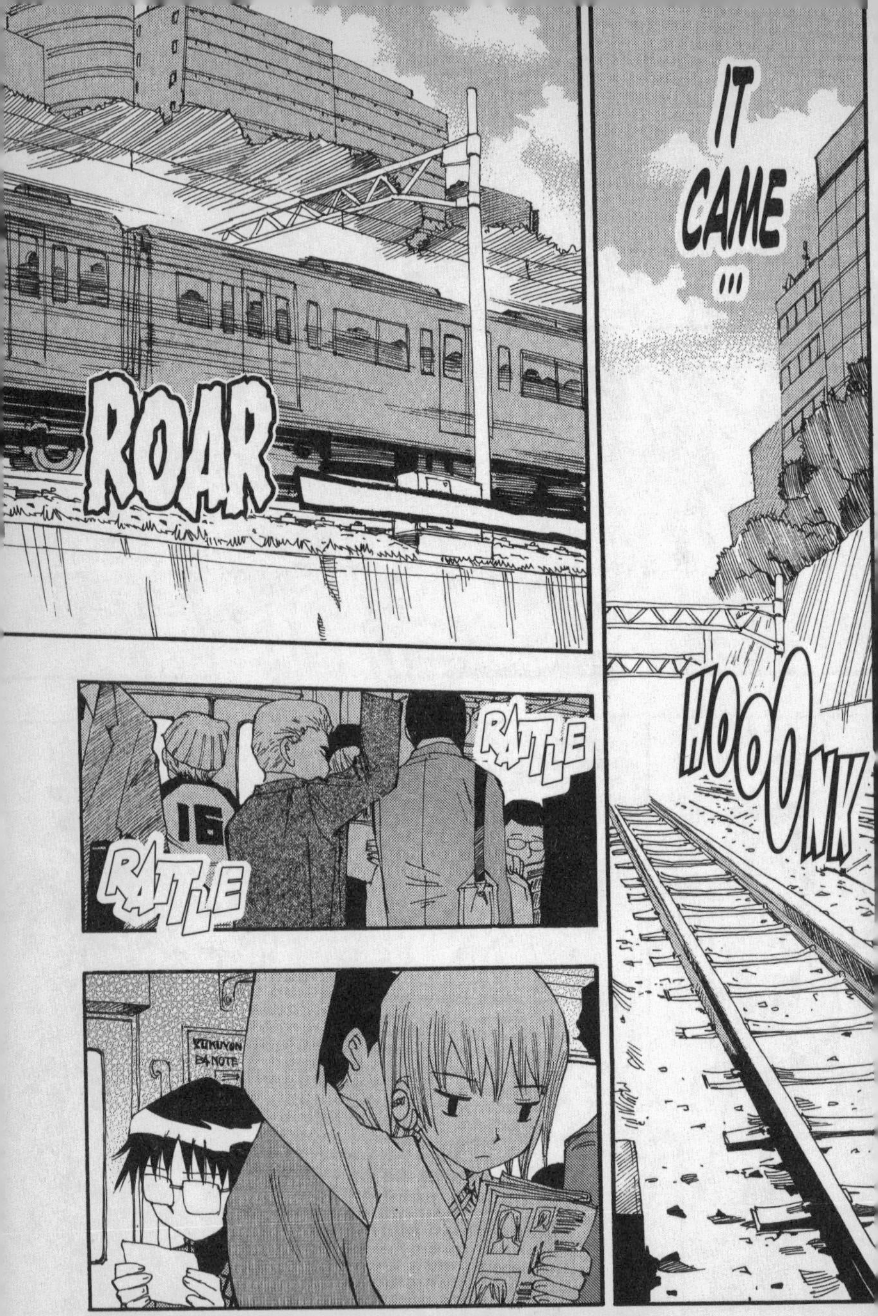
IT CAME ...
HOOONK
ROAR
RATTLE
RATTLE

Mission 2 : Muri-Po: I Can't Do This...

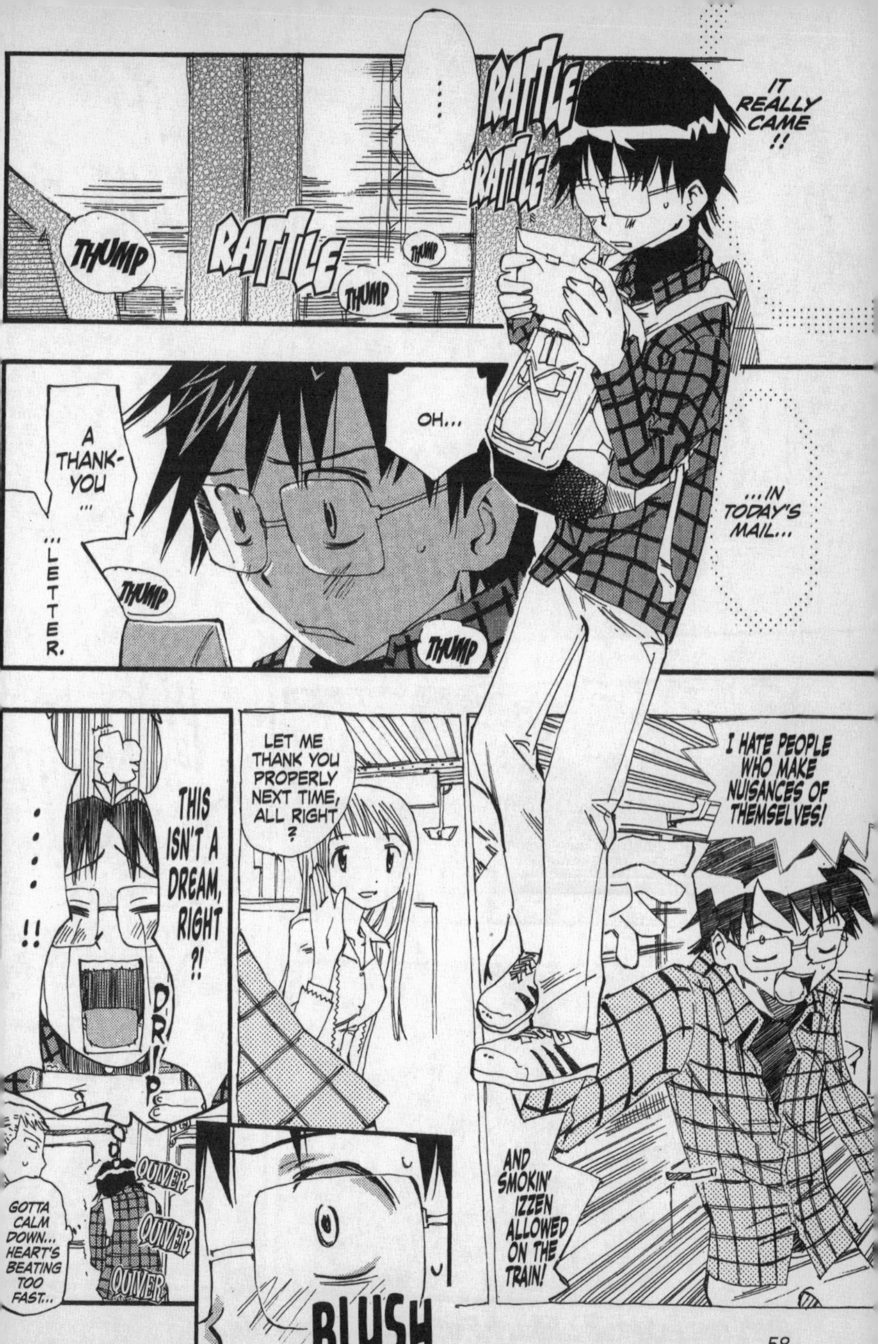
IT REALLY CAME!!
RATTLE
RATTLE
....
RATTLE
THUMP
THUMP
THUMP
...IN TODAY'S MAIL...
OH...
A THANK-YOU...
...LETTER.
THUMP
THUMP
I HATE PEOPLE WHO MAKE NUISANCES OF THEMSELVES!
AND SMOKIN' IZZEN ALLOWED ON THE TRAIN!
LET ME THANK YOU PROPERLY NEXT TIME, ALL RIGHT?
THIS ISN'T A DREAM, RIGHT?!
....!!
DRIP
BLUSH
QUIVER
QUIVER
QUIVER
GOTTA CALM DOWN... HEART'S BEATING TOO FAST...

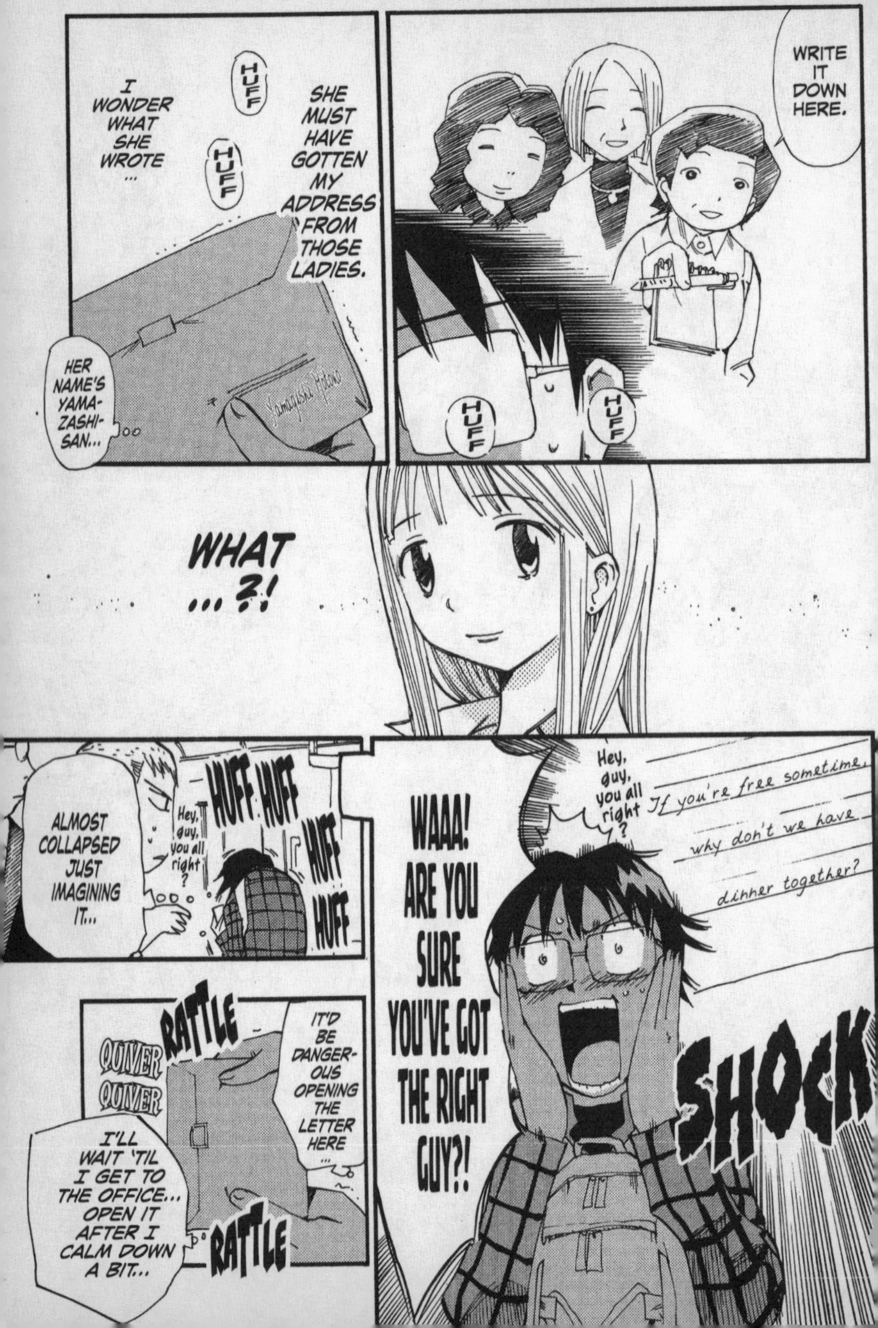
WRITE IT DOWN HERE.
HUFF
HUFF
SHE MUST HAVE GOTTEN MY ADDRESS FROM THOSE LADIES.
HUFF
HUFF
I WONDER WHAT SHE WROTE ...
HER NAME'S YAMAZASHI-SAN...
WHAT ...?!
If you're free sometime, why don't we have dinner together?
Hey, guy, you all right?
WAAA! ARE YOU SURE YOU'VE GOT THE RIGHT GUY?!
SHOCK
HUFF HUFF
HUFF HUFF
Hey, guy, you all right?
ALMOST COLLAPSED JUST IMAGINING IT...
IT'D BE DANGEROUS OPENING THE LETTER HERE ...
RATTLE
QUIVER QUIVER
I'LL WAIT 'TIL I GET TO THE OFFICE... OPEN IT AFTER I CALM DOWN A BIT...
RATTLE

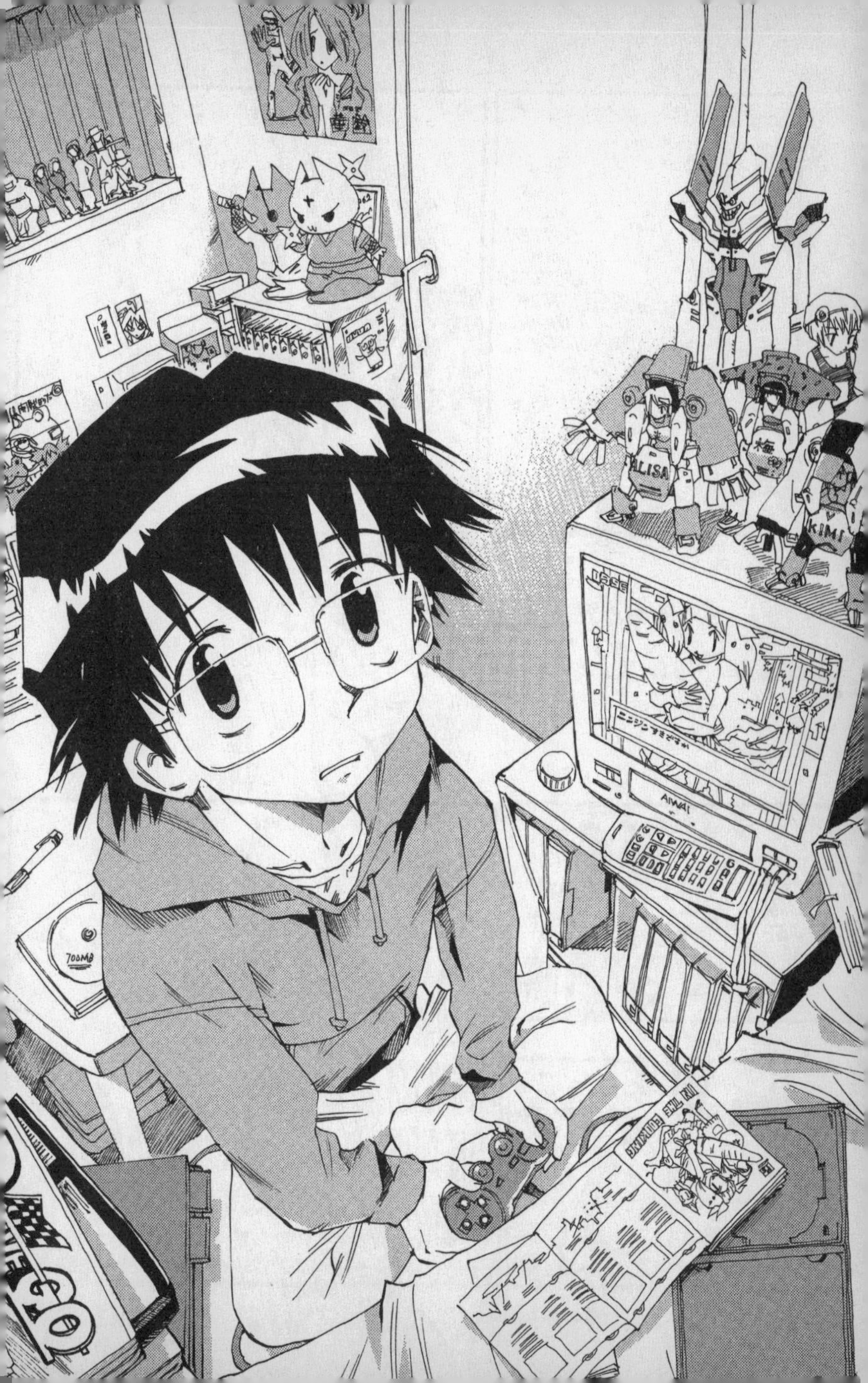
ALISA
KIMI
ニンジンすきですか
AIWA
700MB

Mission 2:

"Muri-Po: I Can't Do This..."

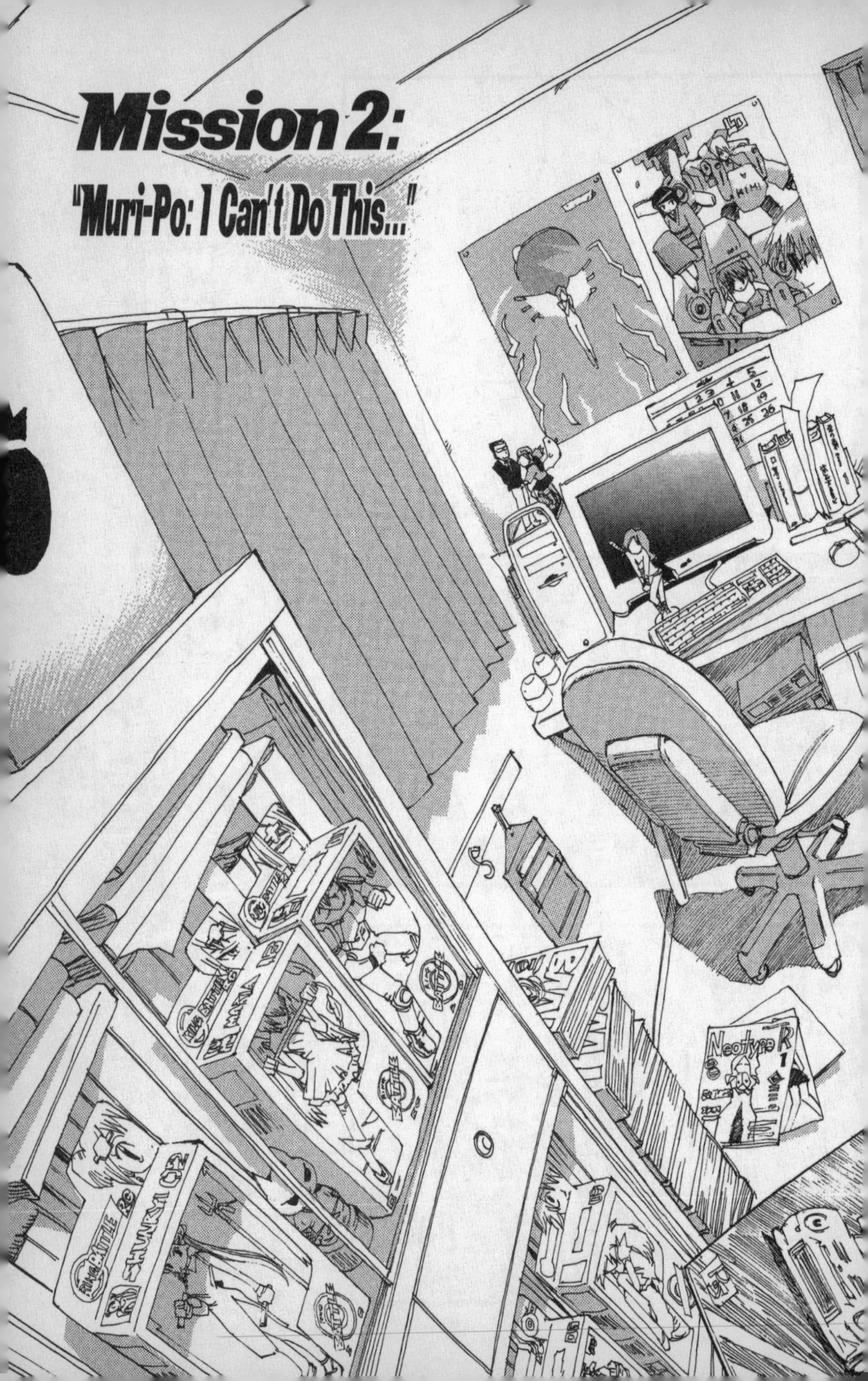

Neotype R

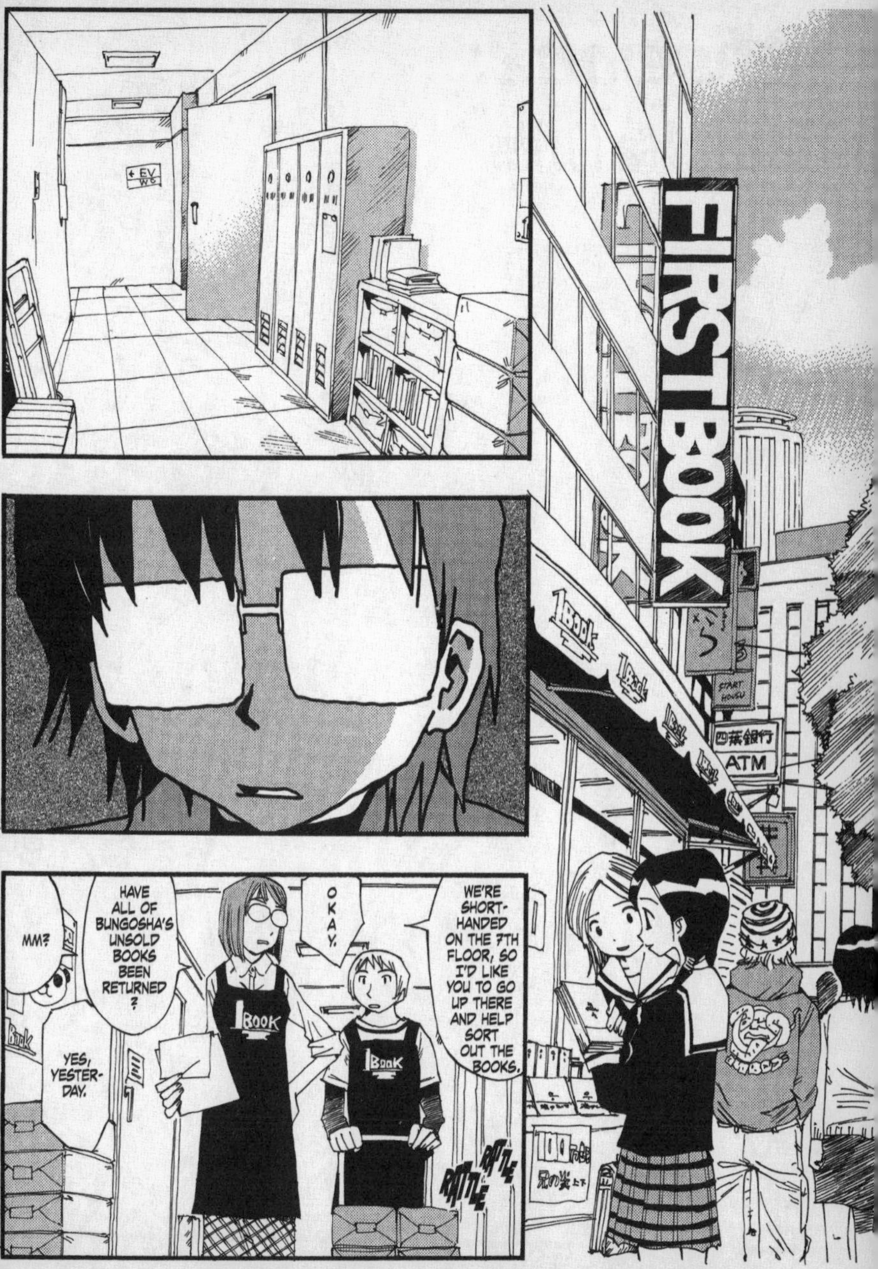
FIRST BOOK
1Book
START HOUSU
四葉銀行
ATM
EV
WC
WE'RE SHORT-HANDED ON THE 7TH FLOOR, SO I'D LIKE YOU TO GO UP THERE AND HELP SORT OUT THE BOOKS.
OKAY.
HAVE ALL OF BUNGOSHA'S UNSOLD BOOKS BEEN RETURNED?
MM?
YES, YESTER-DAY.
1BOOK
RATTLE RATTLE

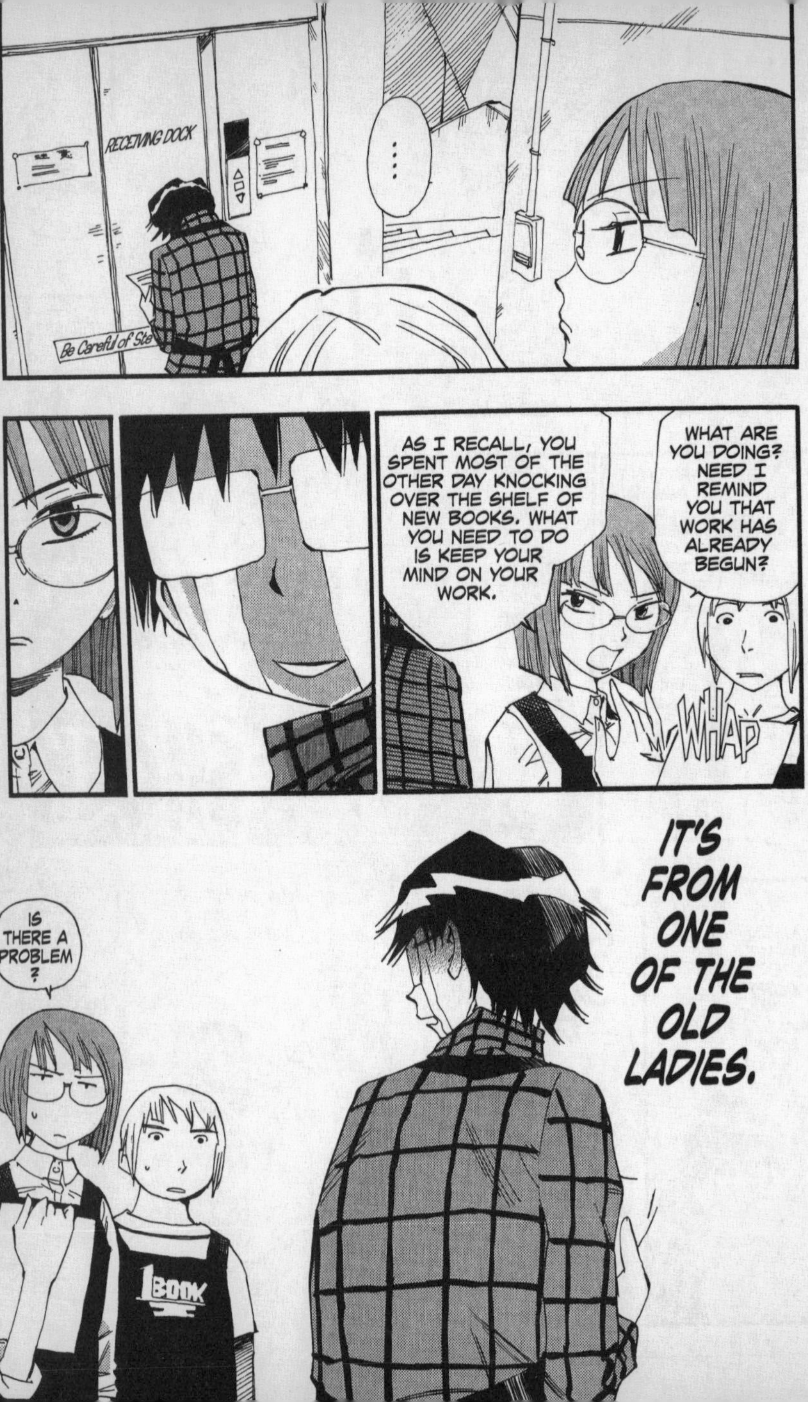
....
RECEIVING DOCK
Be Careful of Ste
WHAT ARE YOU DOING? NEED I REMIND YOU THAT WORK HAS ALREADY BEGUN?
AS I RECALL, YOU SPENT MOST OF THE OTHER DAY KNOCKING OVER THE SHELF OF NEW BOOKS. WHAT YOU NEED TO DO IS KEEP YOUR MIND ON YOUR WORK.
WHAP
IT'S FROM ONE OF THE OLD LADIES.
IS THERE A PROBLEM?
1BOOK

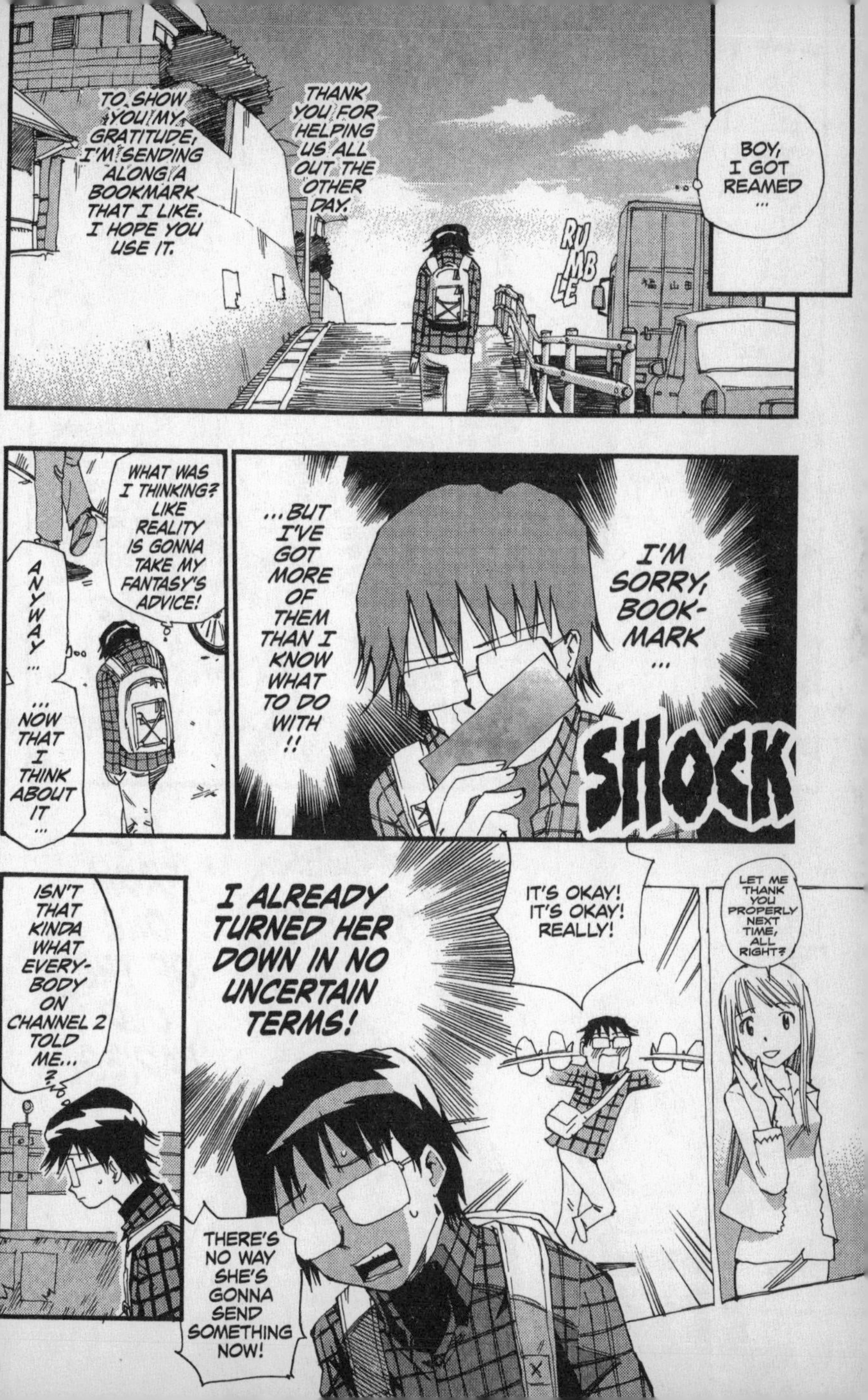
BOY, I GOT REAMED ...
RUMBLE
THANK YOU FOR HELPING US ALL OUT THE OTHER DAY.
TO SHOW YOU MY GRATITUDE, I'M SENDING ALONG A BOOKMARK THAT I LIKE. I HOPE YOU USE IT.
I'M SORRY, BOOKMARK ...
SHOCK
...BUT I'VE GOT MORE OF THEM THAN I KNOW WHAT TO DO WITH !!
WHAT WAS I THINKING? LIKE REALITY IS GONNA TAKE MY FANTASY'S ADVICE!
ANYWAY ...
... NOW THAT I THINK ABOUT IT ...
LET ME THANK YOU PROPERLY NEXT TIME, ALL RIGHT?
IT'S OKAY! IT'S OKAY! REALLY!
I ALREADY TURNED HER DOWN IN NO UNCERTAIN TERMS!
THERE'S NO WAY SHE'S GONNA SEND SOMETHING NOW!
ISN'T THAT KINDA WHAT EVERYBODY ON CHANNEL 2 TOLD ME...?

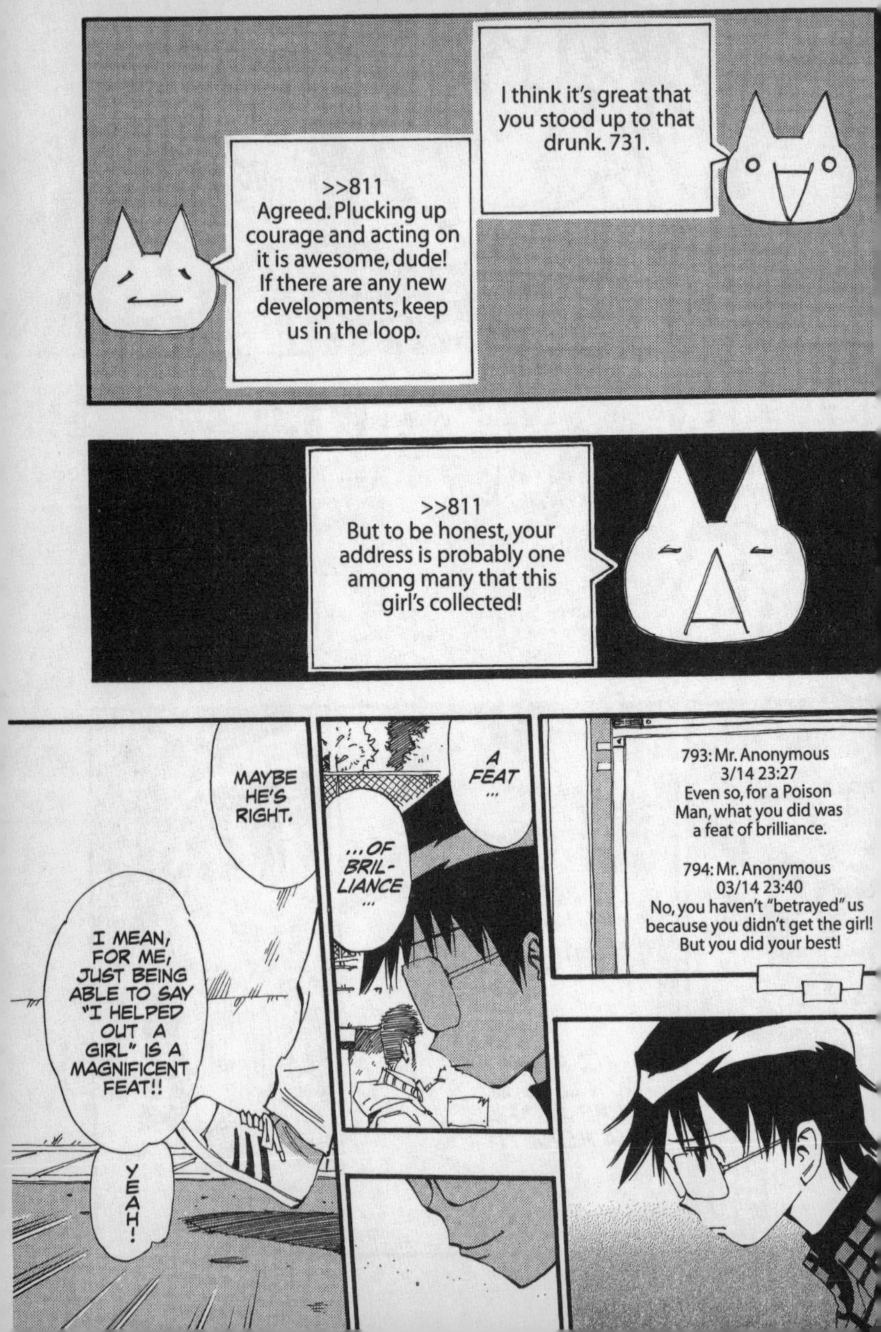
I think it's great that you stood up to that drunk. 731.
>>811 Agreed. Plucking up courage and acting on it is awesome, dude! If there are any new developments, keep us in the loop.
>>811 But to be honest, your address is probably one among many that this girl's collected!
793: Mr. Anonymous 3/14 23:27 Even so, for a Poison Man, what you did was a feat of brilliance.
794: Mr. Anonymous 03/14 23:40 No, you haven't "betrayed" us because you didn't get the girl! But you did your best!
A FEAT...
...OF BRIL-LIANCE...
MAYBE HE'S RIGHT.
I MEAN, FOR ME, JUST BEING ABLE TO SAY "I HELPED OUT A GIRL" IS A MAGNIFICENT FEAT!!
YEAH!

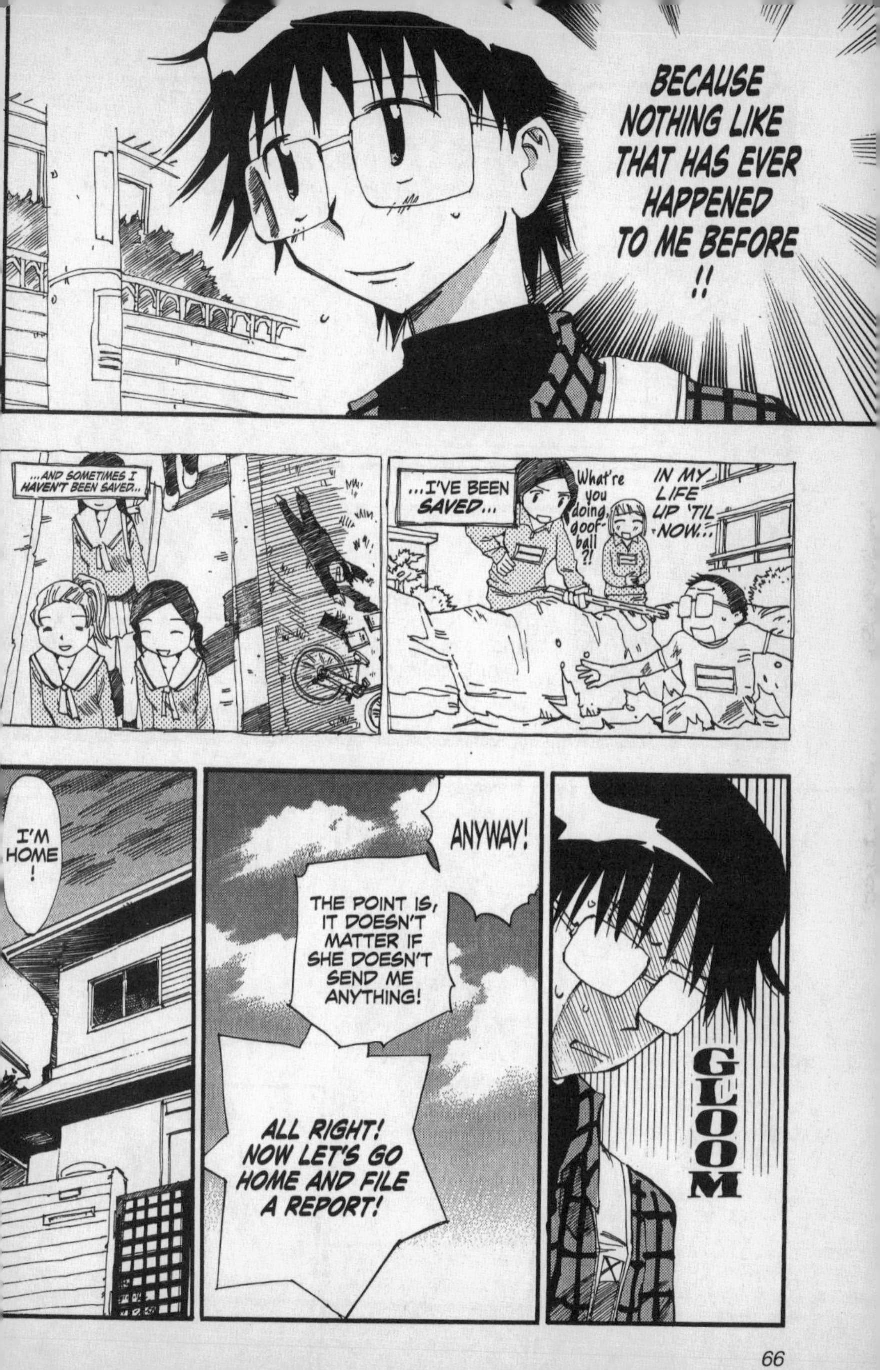
BECAUSE NOTHING LIKE THAT HAS EVER HAPPENED TO ME BEFORE !!
IN MY LIFE UP 'TIL NOW...
What're you doing, goofball?!
...I'VE BEEN SAVED...
...AND SOMETIMES I HAVEN'T BEEN SAVED...
GLOOM
ANYWAY!
THE POINT IS, IT DOESN'T MATTER IF SHE DOESN'T SEND ME ANYTHING!
ALL RIGHT! NOW LET'S GO HOME AND FILE A REPORT!
I'M HOME !

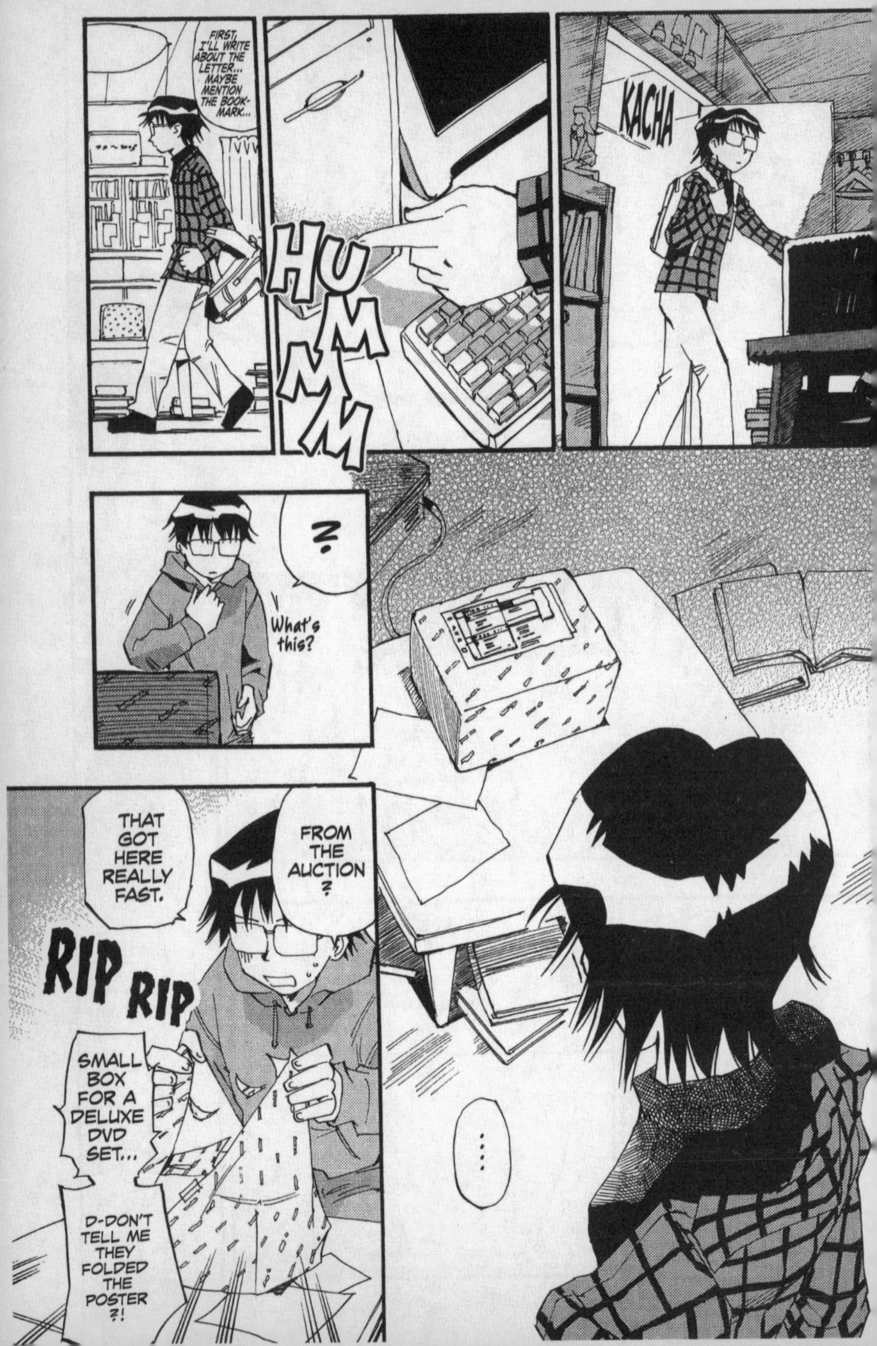
KACHA
HUMMMM
FIRST, I'LL WRITE ABOUT THE LETTER... MAYBE MENTION THE BOOK-MARK...
....
?
What's this?
FROM THE AUCTION?
THAT GOT HERE REALLY FAST.
RIP RIP
SMALL BOX FOR A DELUXE DVD SET...
D-DON'T TELL ME THEY FOLDED THE POSTER?!

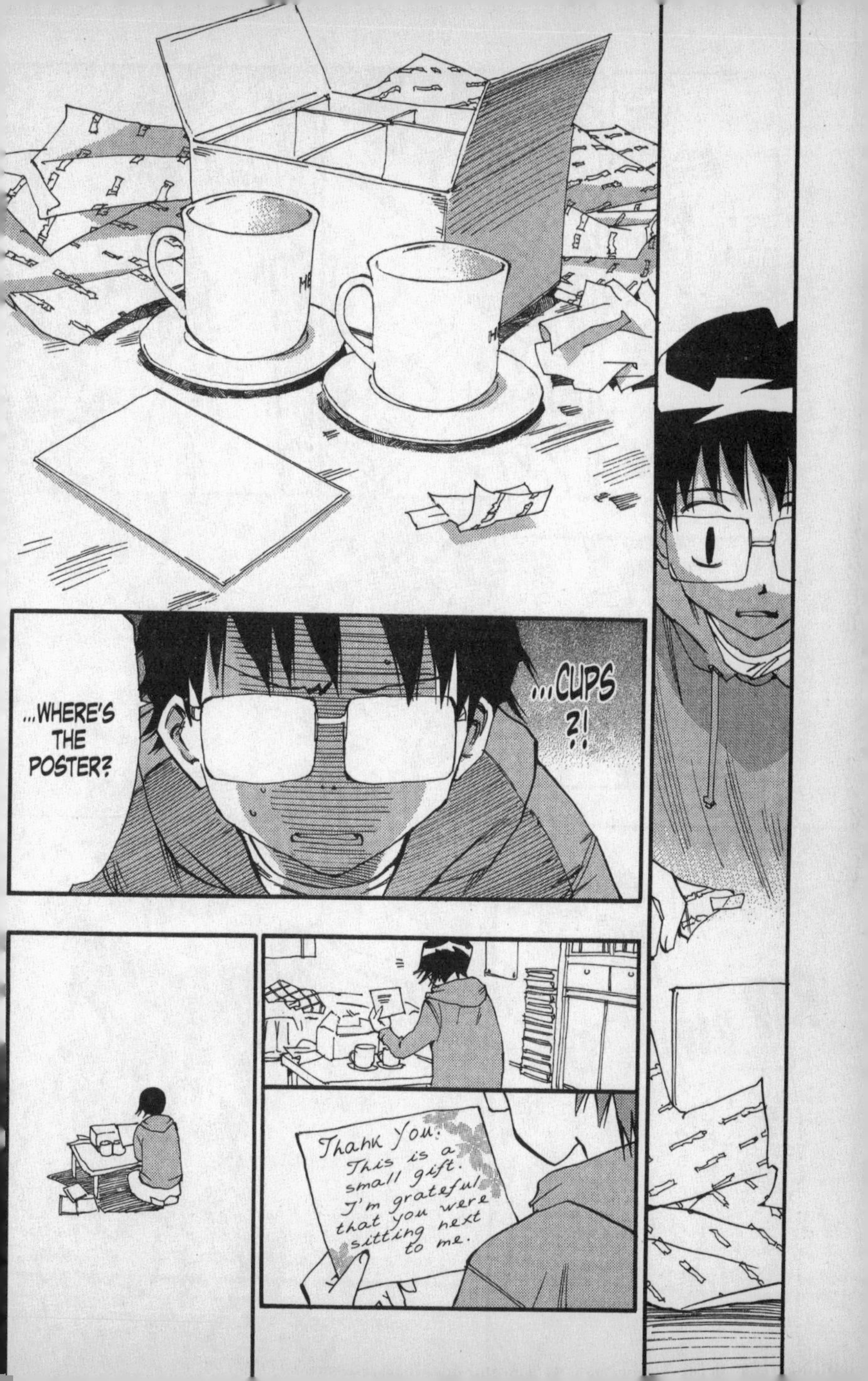
...CUPS ?!
...WHERE'S THE POSTER?
Thank You: This is a small gift. I'm grateful that you were sitting next to me.

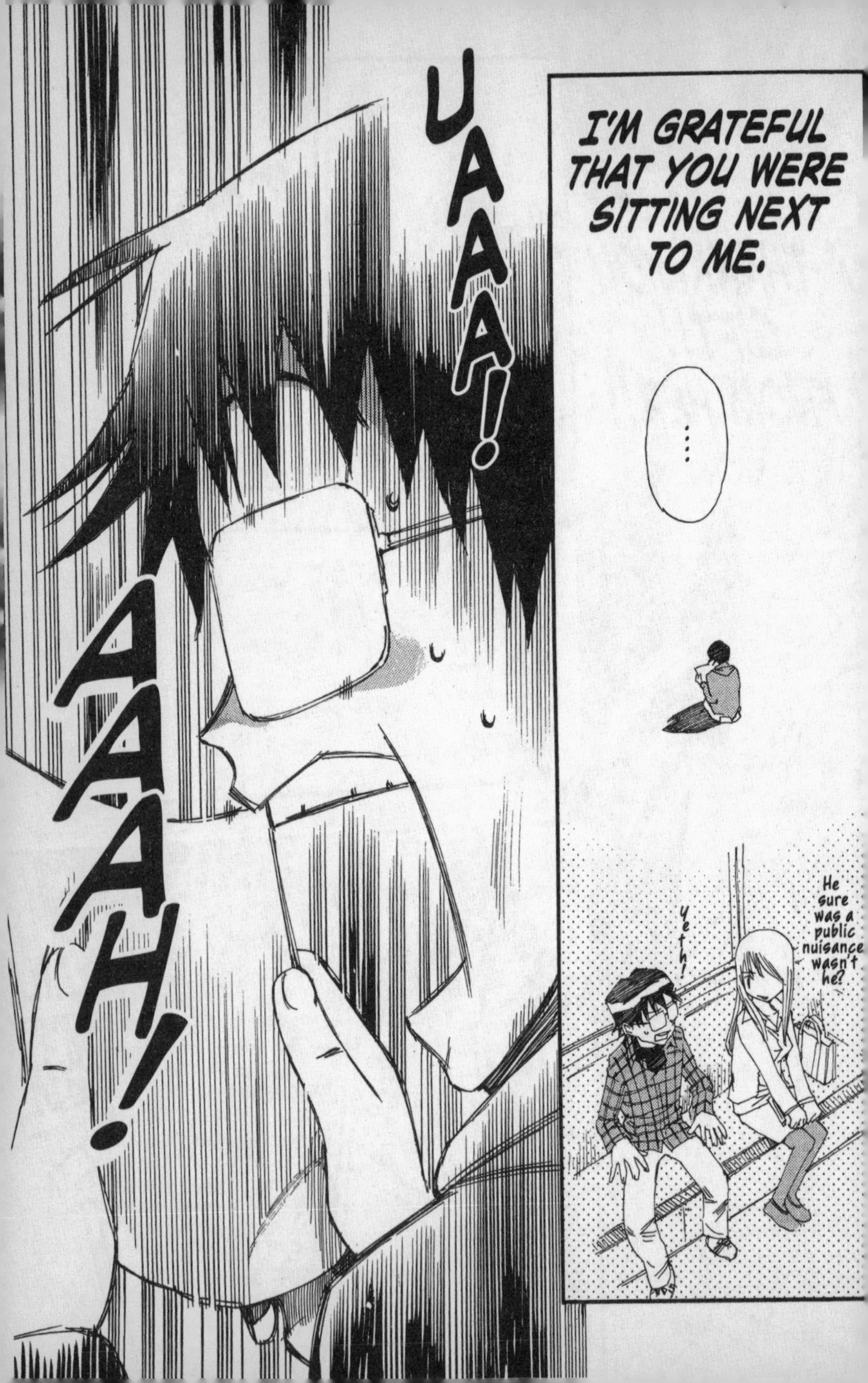
I'M GRATEFUL THAT YOU WERE SITTING NEXT TO ME.
....
He sure was a public nuisance wasn't he?
Yeth!
UAAA!
AAAAH!

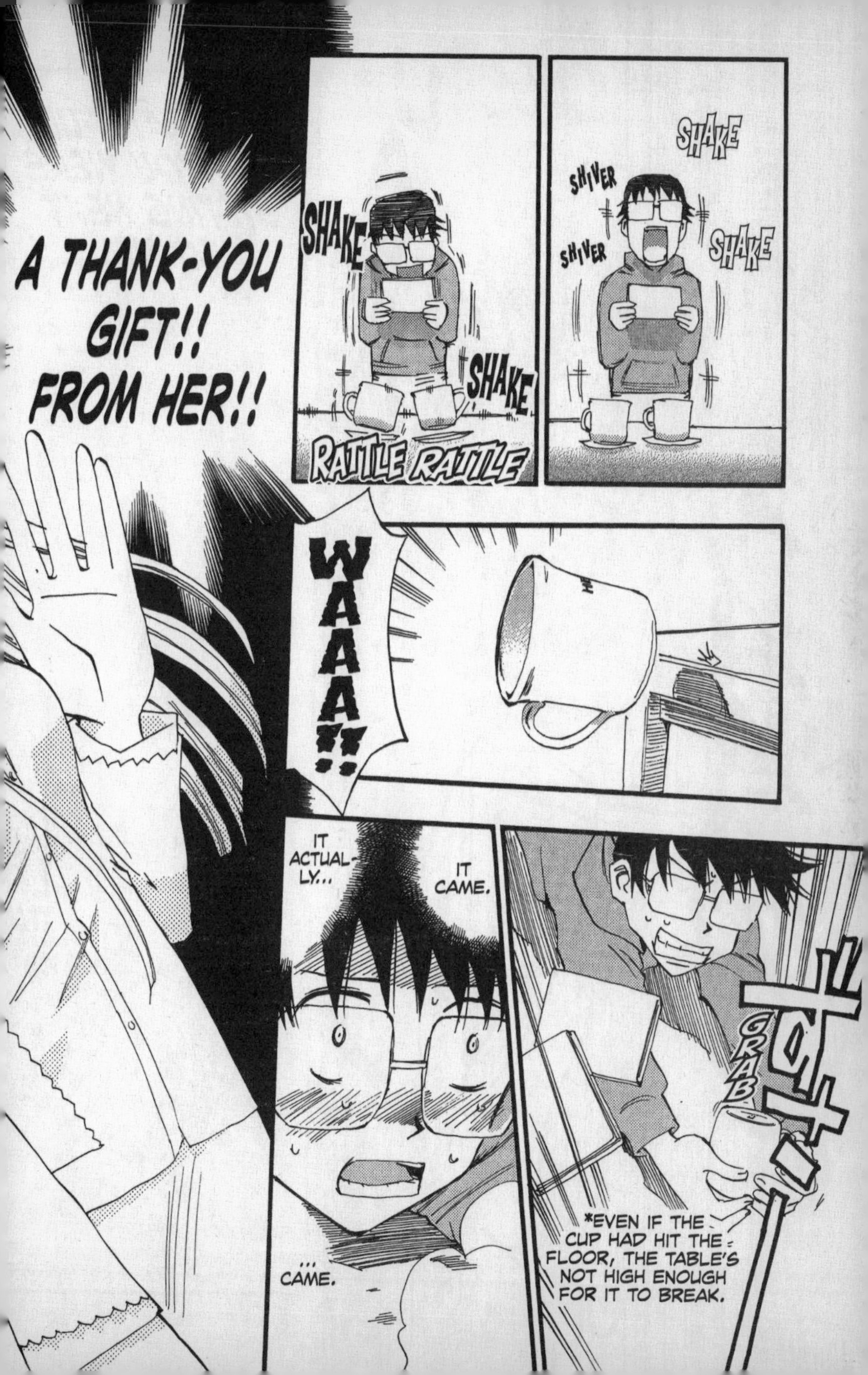
SHAKE
SHIVER
SHIVER
SHAKE
SHAKE
SHAKE
RATTLE RATTLE
WAAAA!!
GRAB
*EVEN IF THE CUP HAD HIT THE FLOOR, THE TABLE'S NOT HIGH ENOUGH FOR IT TO BREAK.
IT ACTUAL-LY...
IT CAME.
...CAME.
A THANK-YOU GIFT!! FROM HER!!

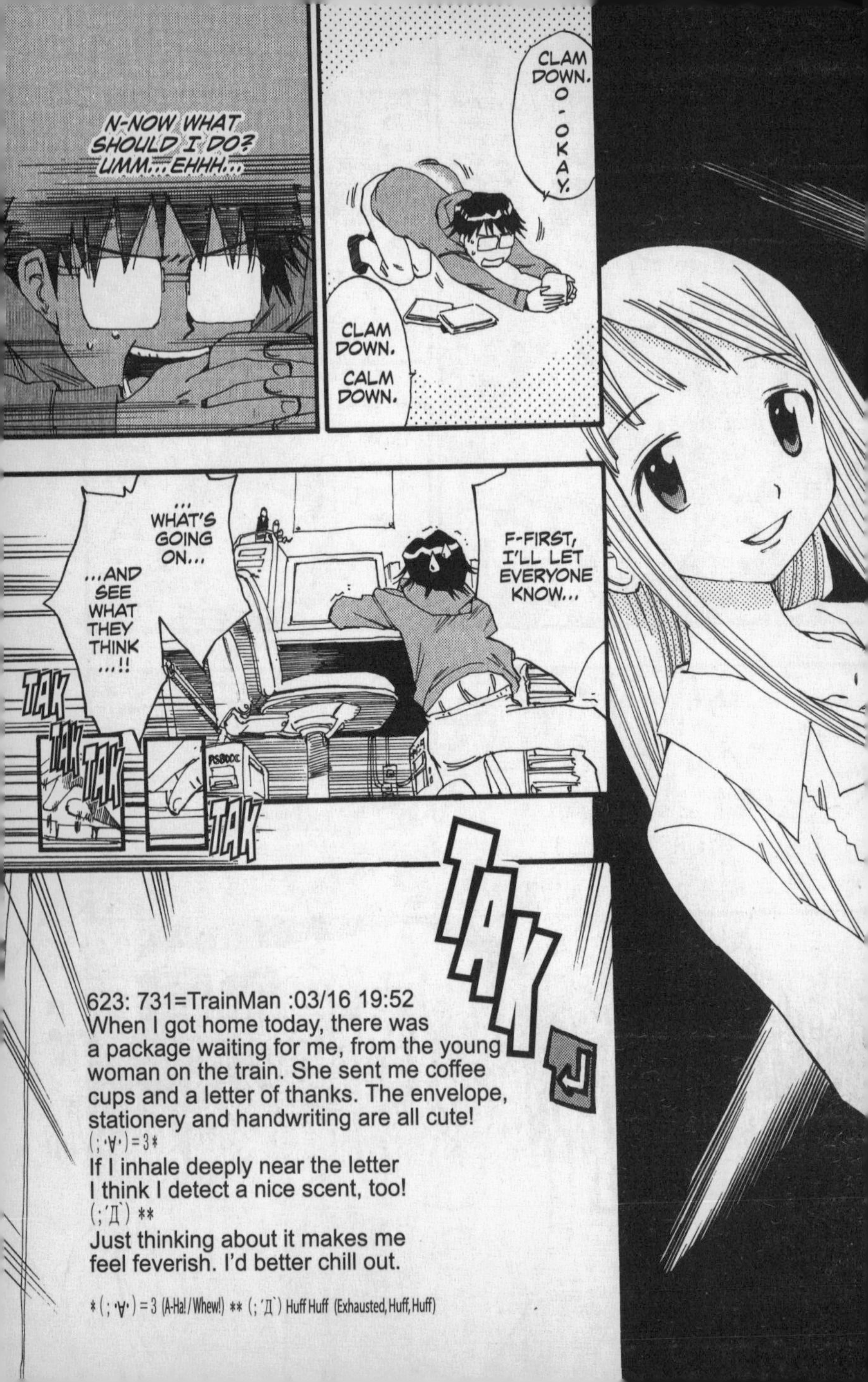
CLAM DOWN.
O-OKAY.
CLAM DOWN.
CALM DOWN.
N-NOW WHAT SHOULD I DO? UMM... EHHH...
F-FIRST, I'LL LET EVERYONE KNOW...
...WHAT'S GOING ON...
...AND SEE WHAT THEY THINK ...!!
TAK
TAK
TAK
TAK
TAK
623: 731=TrainMan :03/16 19:52
When I got home today, there was a package waiting for me, from the young woman on the train. She sent me coffee cups and a letter of thanks. The envelope, stationery and handwriting are all cute!
(;·∀·)=3*
If I inhale deeply near the letter I think I detect a nice scent, too!
(;´Д`)**
Just thinking about it makes me feel feverish. I'd better chill out.

*(;·∀·)=3 (A-Ha!/Whew!) **(;´Д`) Huff Huff (Exhausted, Huff, Huff)

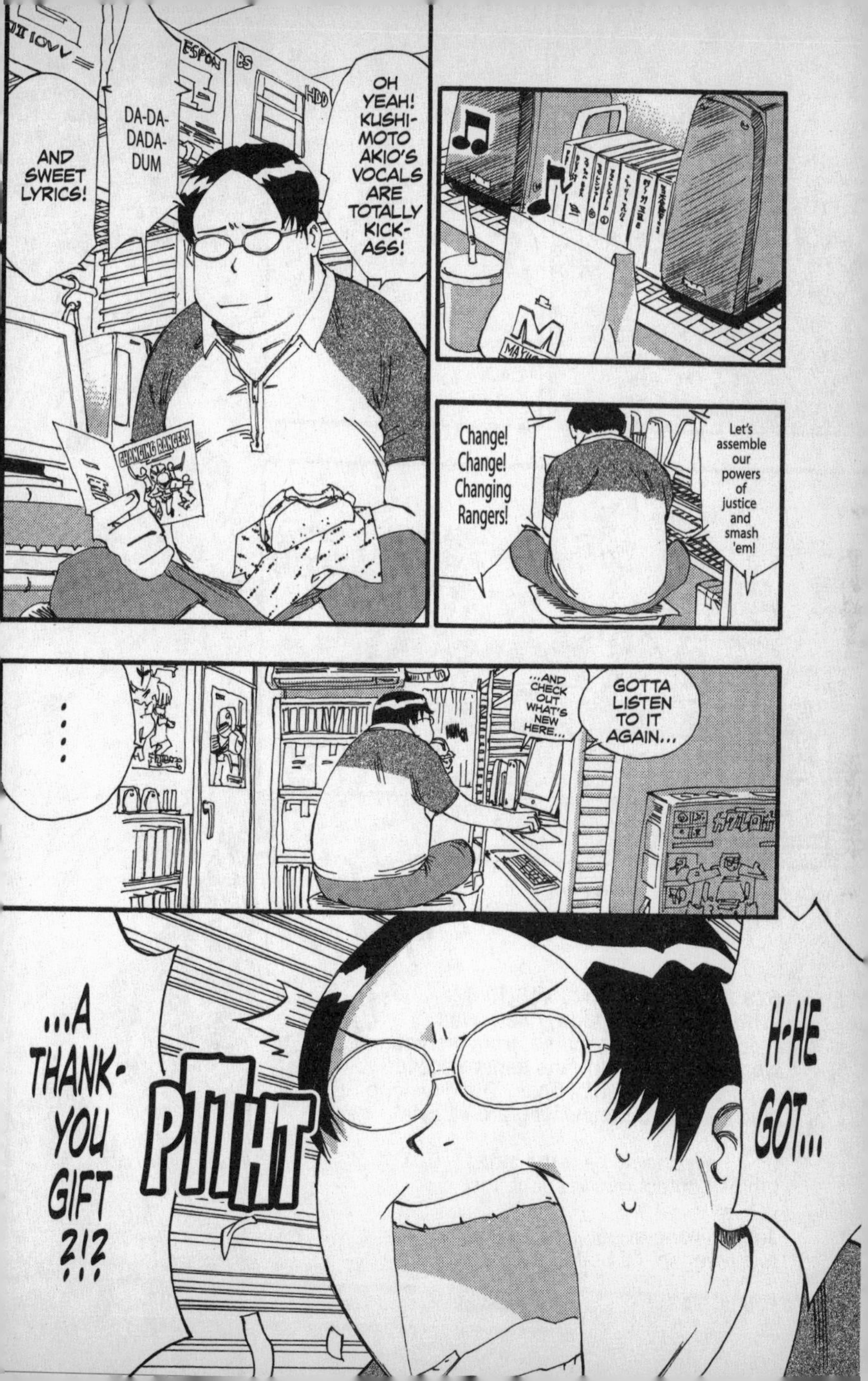
Let's assemble our powers of justice and smash 'em!
Change! Change! Changing Rangers!
OH YEAH! KUSHIMOTO AKIO'S VOCALS ARE TOTALLY KICK-ASS!
DA-DA-DADA-DUM
AND SWEET LYRICS!
CHANGING RANGERS
GOTTA LISTEN TO IT AGAIN...
...AND CHECK OUT WHAT'S NEW HERE...
....
H-HE GOT...
PTIHT
...A THANK-YOU GIFT ?!?

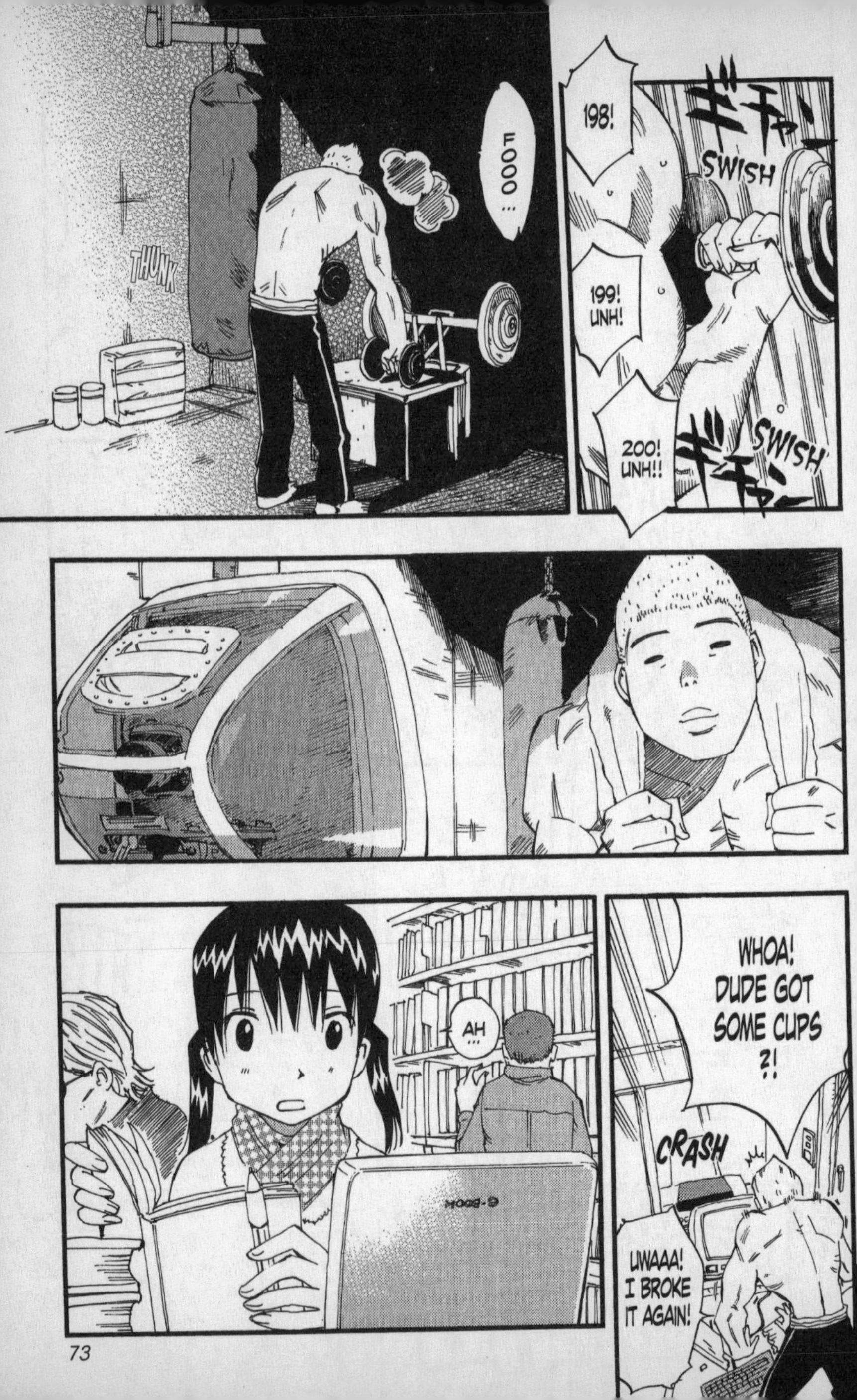
198!
SWISH
199! UNH!
200! UNH!!
SWISH
FOOO...
THUNK
WHOA! DUDE GOT SOME CUPS?!
CRASH
UWAAA! I BROKE IT AGAIN!
AH...

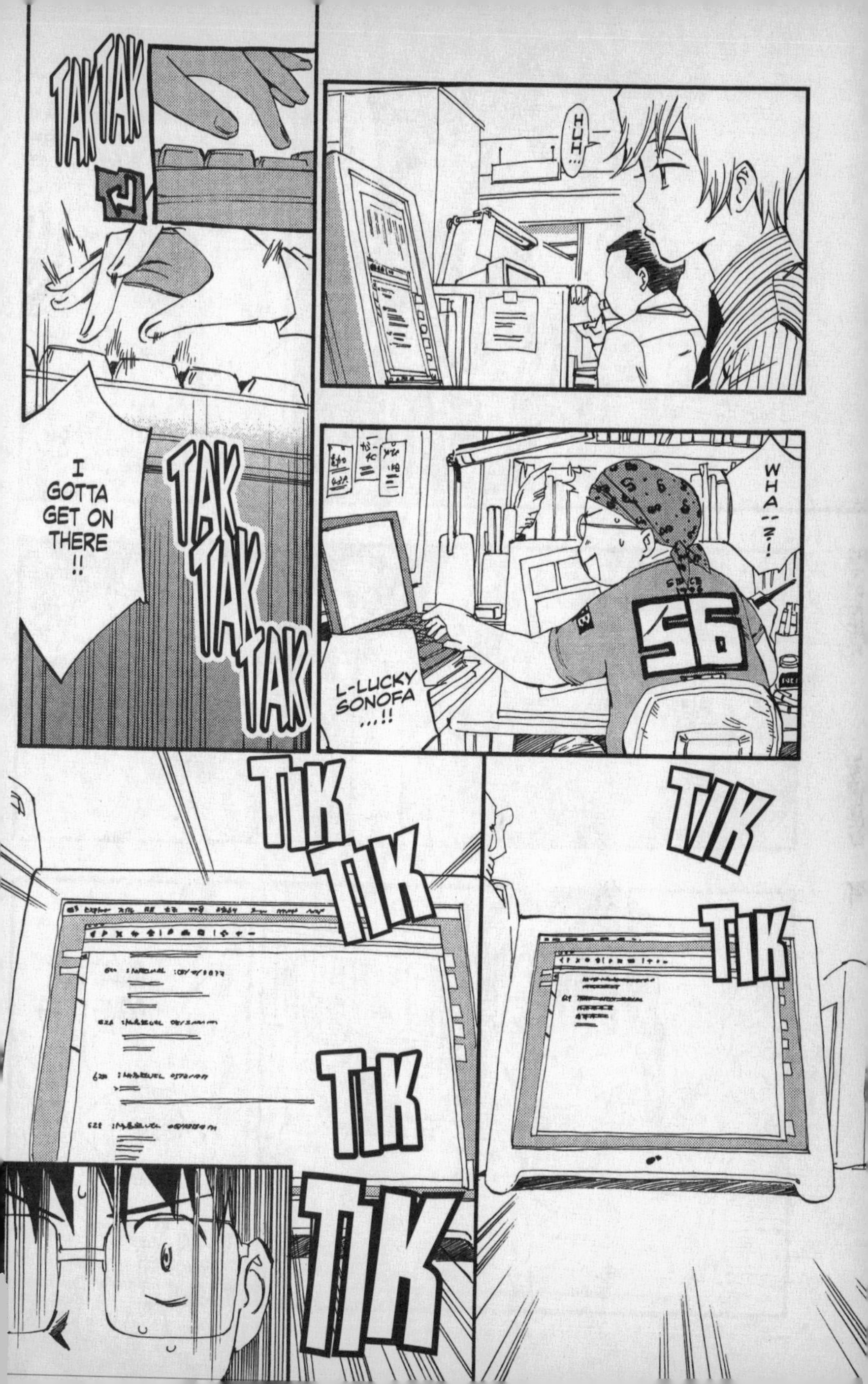
HUH...
TAKTAK
WHA--?!
L-LUCKY SONOFA...!!
I GOTTA GET ON THERE!!
TAK TAK TAK
TIK
TIK
TIK
TIK
TIK

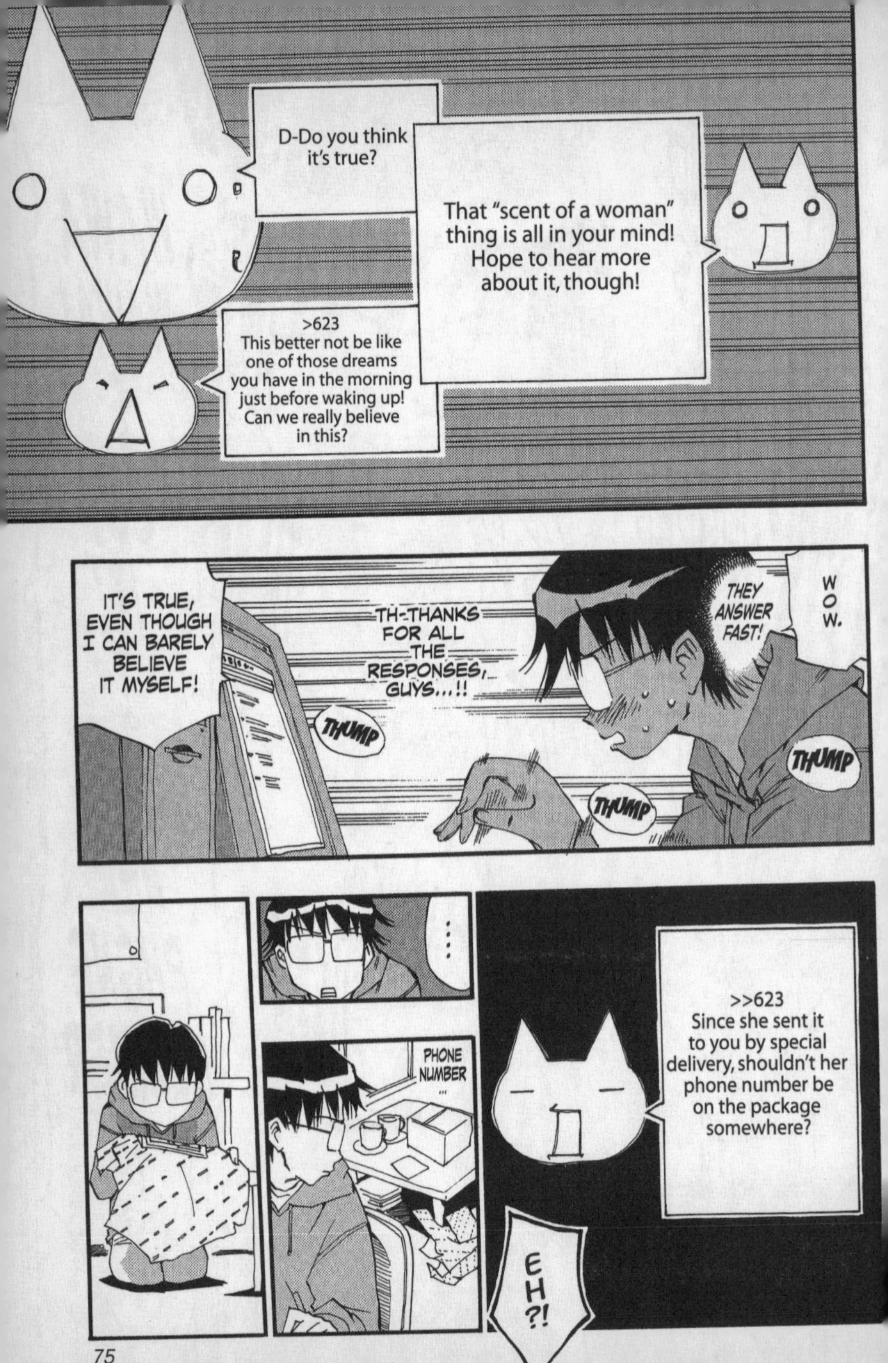
D-Do you think it's true?
That "scent of a woman" thing is all in your mind! Hope to hear more about it, though!
>623 This better not be like one of those dreams you have in the morning just before waking up! Can we really believe in this?
WOW.
THEY ANSWER FAST!
THUMP
THUMP
TH-THANKS FOR ALL THE RESPONSES, GUYS...!!
THUMP
IT'S TRUE, EVEN THOUGH I CAN BARELY BELIEVE IT MYSELF!
>>623 Since she sent it to you by special delivery, shouldn't her phone number be on the package somewhere?
EH?!
....
PHONE NUMBER ...

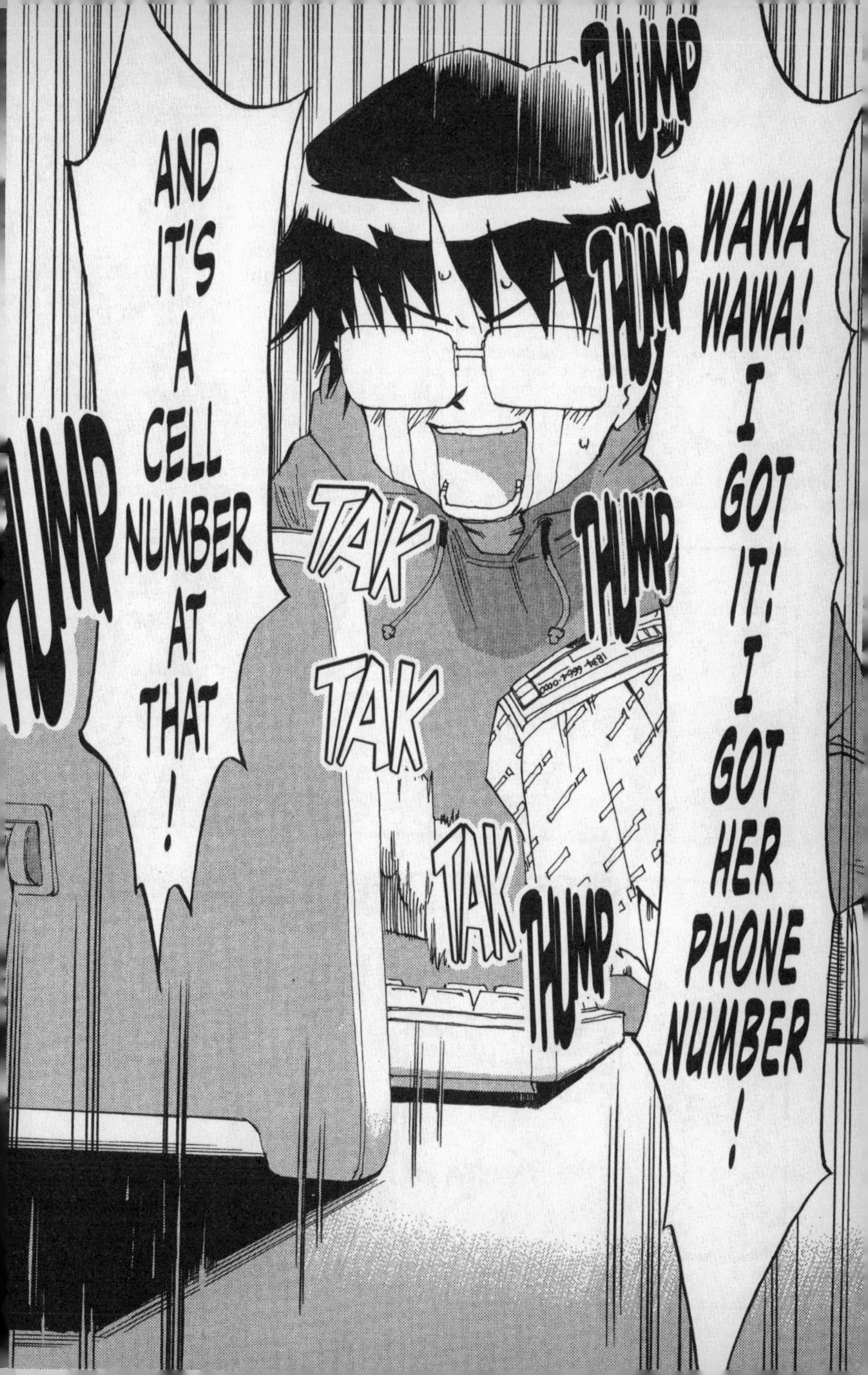
WAWA WAWA! I GOT IT! I GOT HER PHONE NUMBER!
THUMP
THUMP
THUMP
THUMP
TAK
TAK
TAK
AND IT'S A CELL NUMBER AT THAT!
THUMP

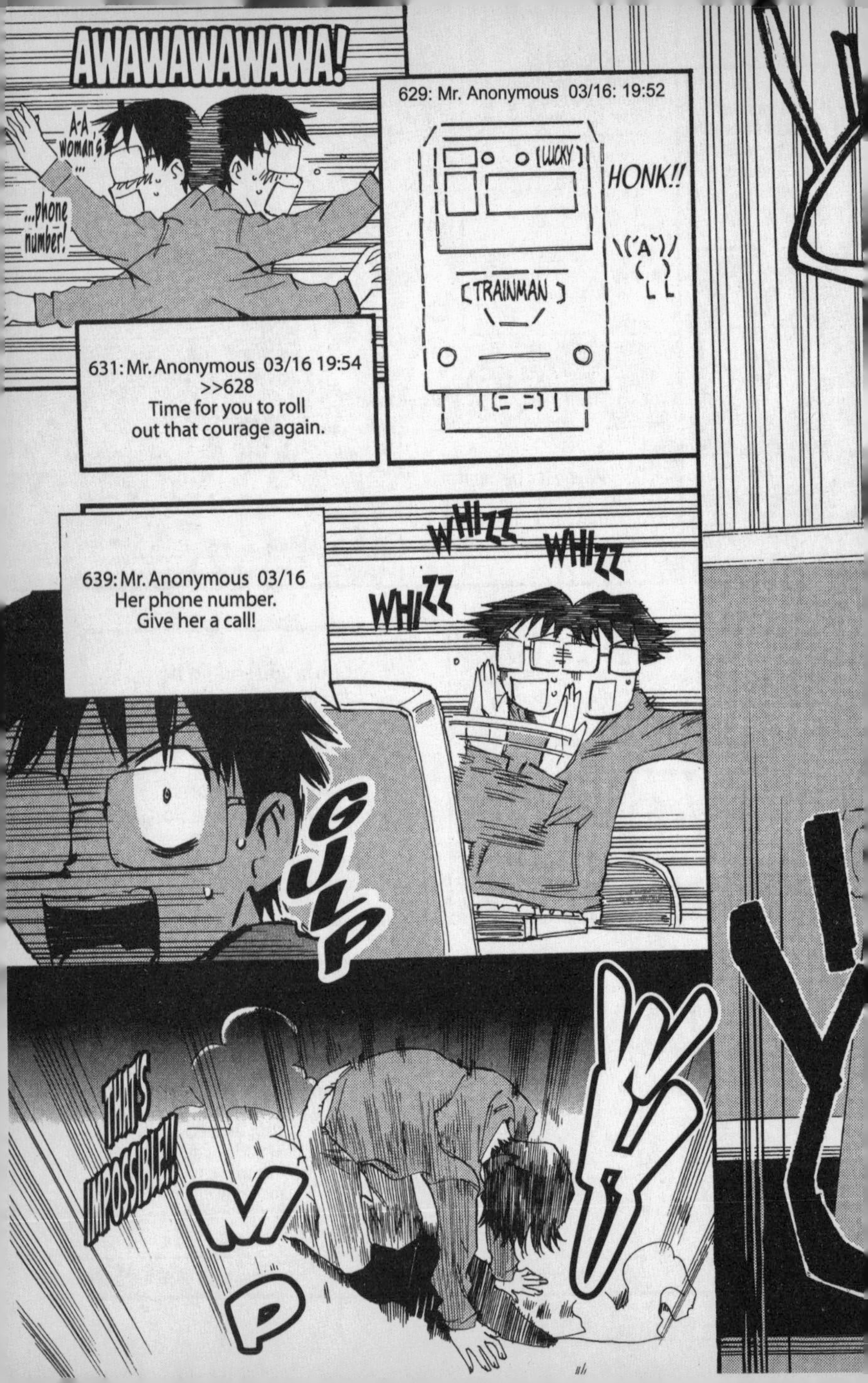
629: Mr. Anonymous 03/16: 19:52
[LUCKY]
[TRAINMAN]
HONK!!
AWAWAWAWAWA!
A-A woman's...
...phone number!
631: Mr. Anonymous 03/16 19:54
>>628
Time for you to roll out that courage again.
639: Mr. Anonymous 03/16
Her phone number.
Give her a call!
WHIZZ
WHIZZ
WHIZZ
GULP
THAT'S IMPOSSIBLE!!

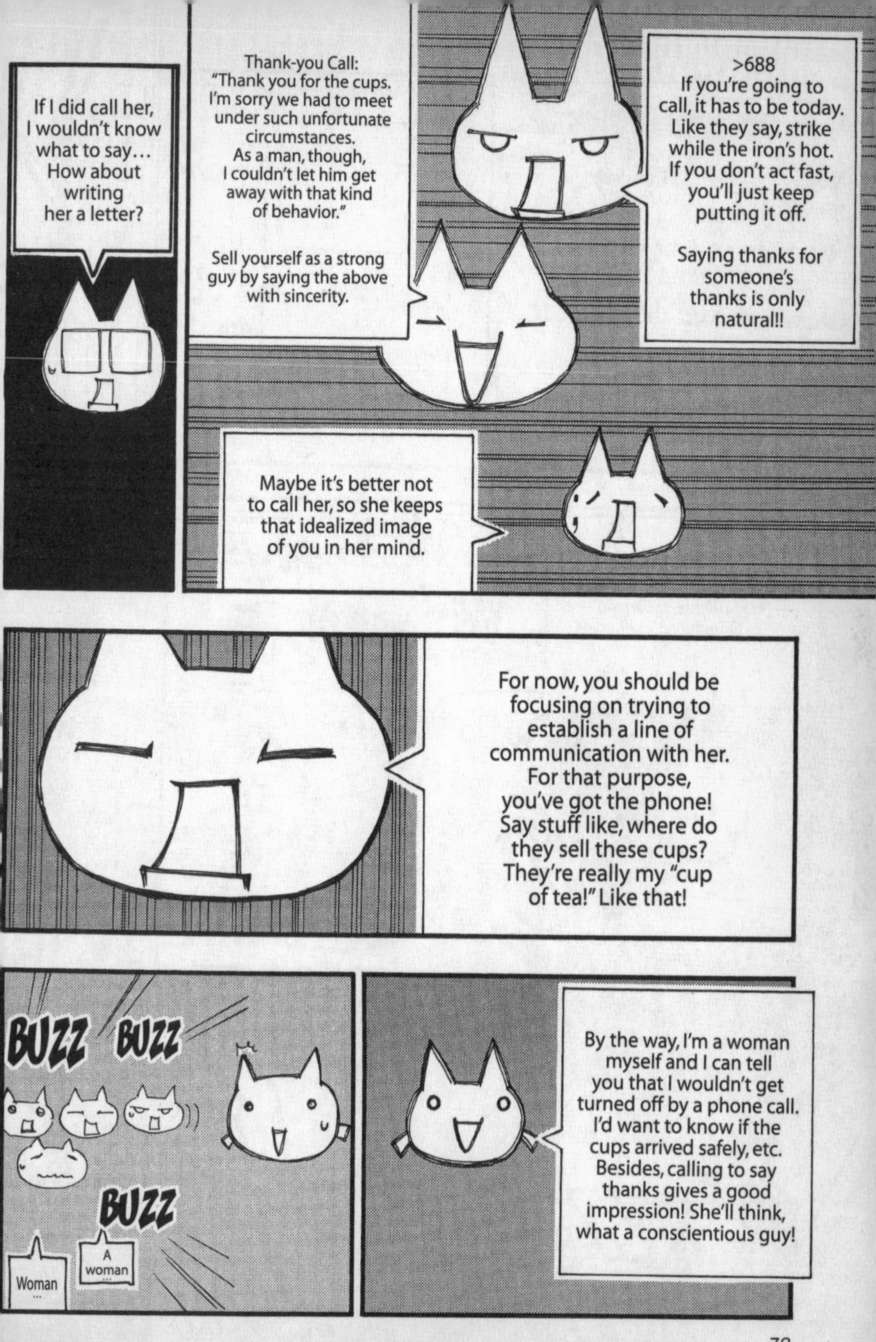
>688 If you're going to call, it has to be today. Like they say, strike while the iron's hot. If you don't act fast, you'll just keep putting it off.
Saying thanks for someone's thanks is only natural!!
Thank-you Call: "Thank you for the cups. I'm sorry we had to meet under such unfortunate circumstances. As a man, though, I couldn't let him get away with that kind of behavior."
Sell yourself as a strong guy by saying the above with sincerity.
Maybe it's better not to call her, so she keeps that idealized image of you in her mind.
If I did call her, I wouldn't know what to say… How about writing her a letter?
For now, you should be focusing on trying to establish a line of communication with her. For that purpose, you've got the phone! Say stuff like, where do they sell these cups? They're really my "cup of tea!" Like that!
By the way, I'm a woman myself and I can tell you that I wouldn't get turned off by a phone call. I'd want to know if the cups arrived safely, etc. Besides, calling to say thanks gives a good impression! She'll think, what a conscientious guy!
BUZZ
BUZZ
BUZZ
A woman …
Woman …

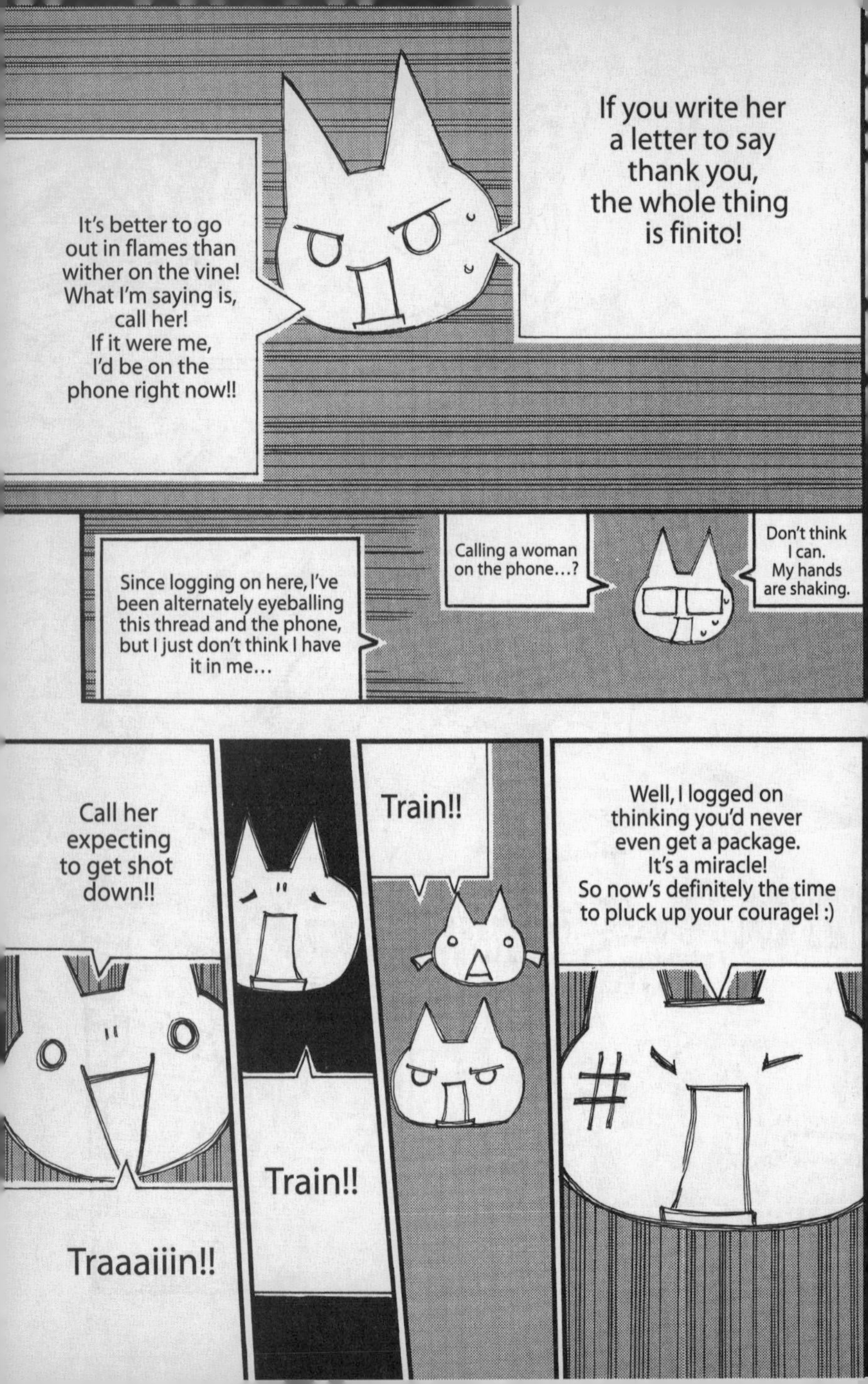
If you write her a letter to say thank you, the whole thing is finito!
It's better to go out in flames than wither on the vine! What I'm saying is, call her! If it were me, I'd be on the phone right now!!
Don't think I can. My hands are shaking.
Calling a woman on the phone…?
Since logging on here, I've been alternately eyeballing this thread and the phone, but I just don't think I have it in me…
Well, I logged on thinking you'd never even get a package. It's a miracle! So now's definitely the time to pluck up your courage! :)
Train!!
Train!!
Call her expecting to get shot down!!
Traaaiiin!!

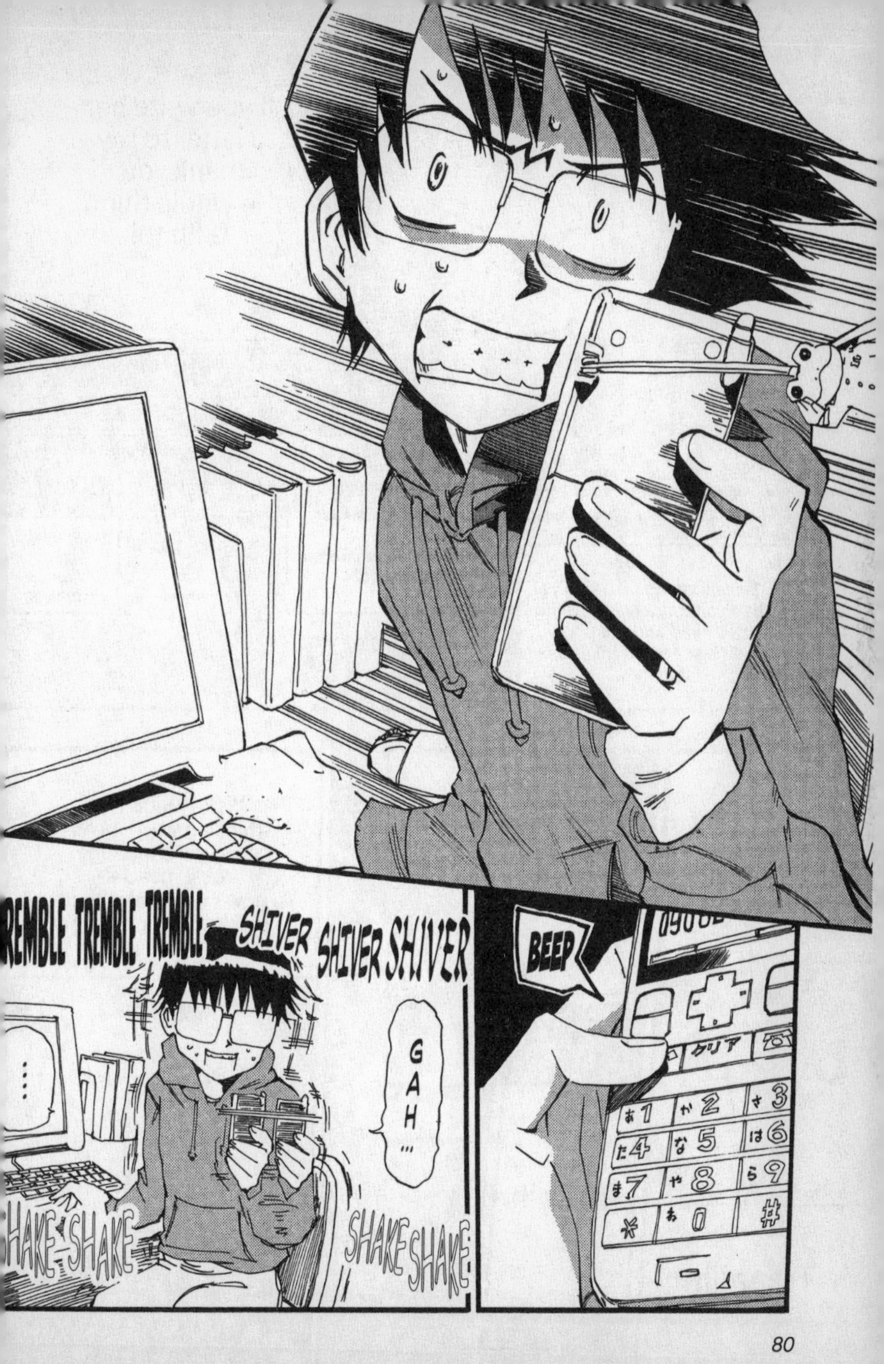
BEEP
クリア
REMBLE TREMBLE TREMBLE
SHIVER SHIVER SHIVER
GAH...
....
SHAKE SHAKE
SHAKE SHAKE

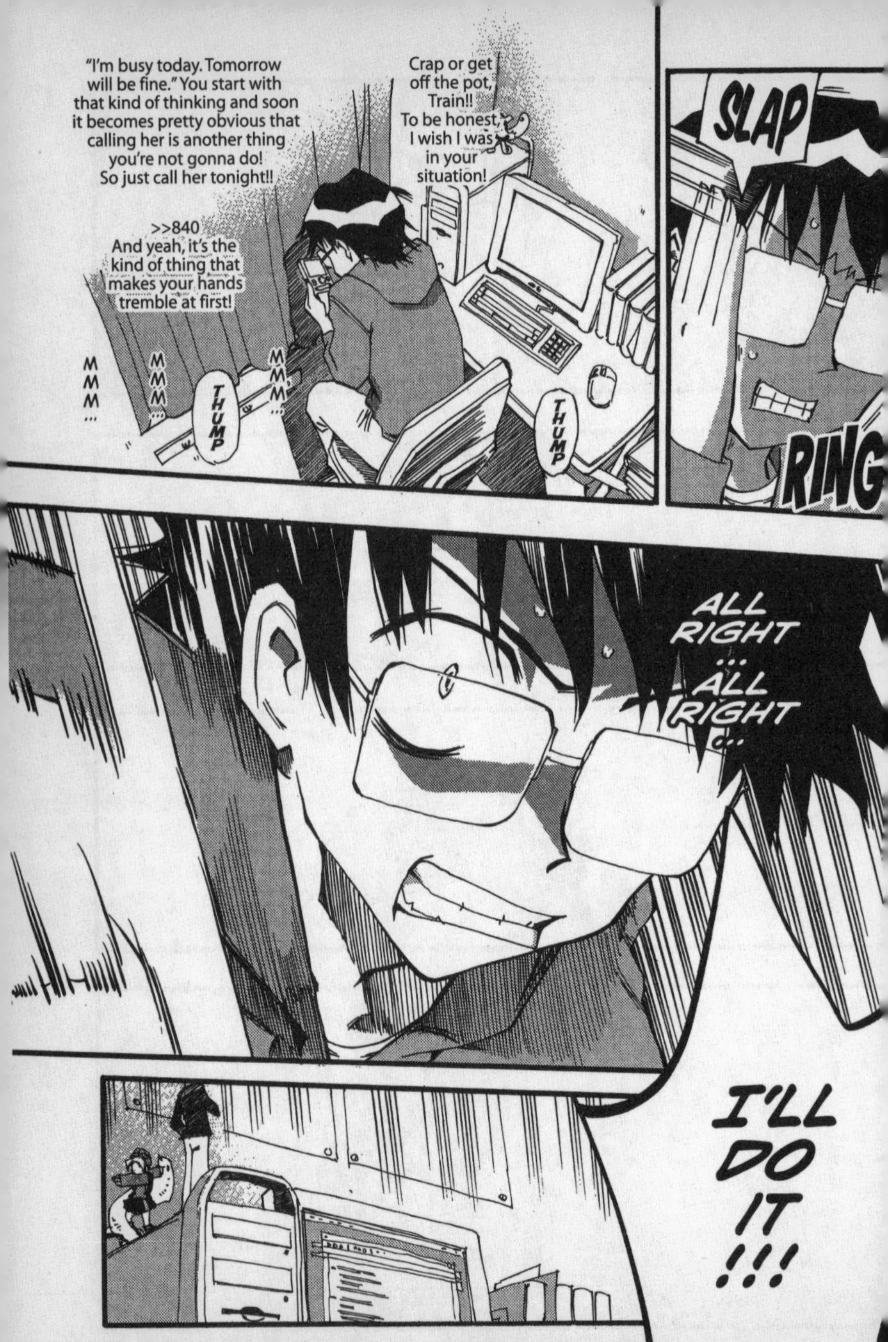
SLAP
RING
Crap or get off the pot, Train!! To be honest, I wish I was in your situation!
"I'm busy today. Tomorrow will be fine." You start with that kind of thinking and soon it becomes pretty obvious that calling her is another thing you're not gonna do! So just call her tonight!!
>>840 And yeah, it's the kind of thing that makes your hands tremble at first!
THUMP
MMM...
THUMP
MMM...
MMM...
ALL RIGHT... ALL RIGHT...
I'LL DO IT!!!

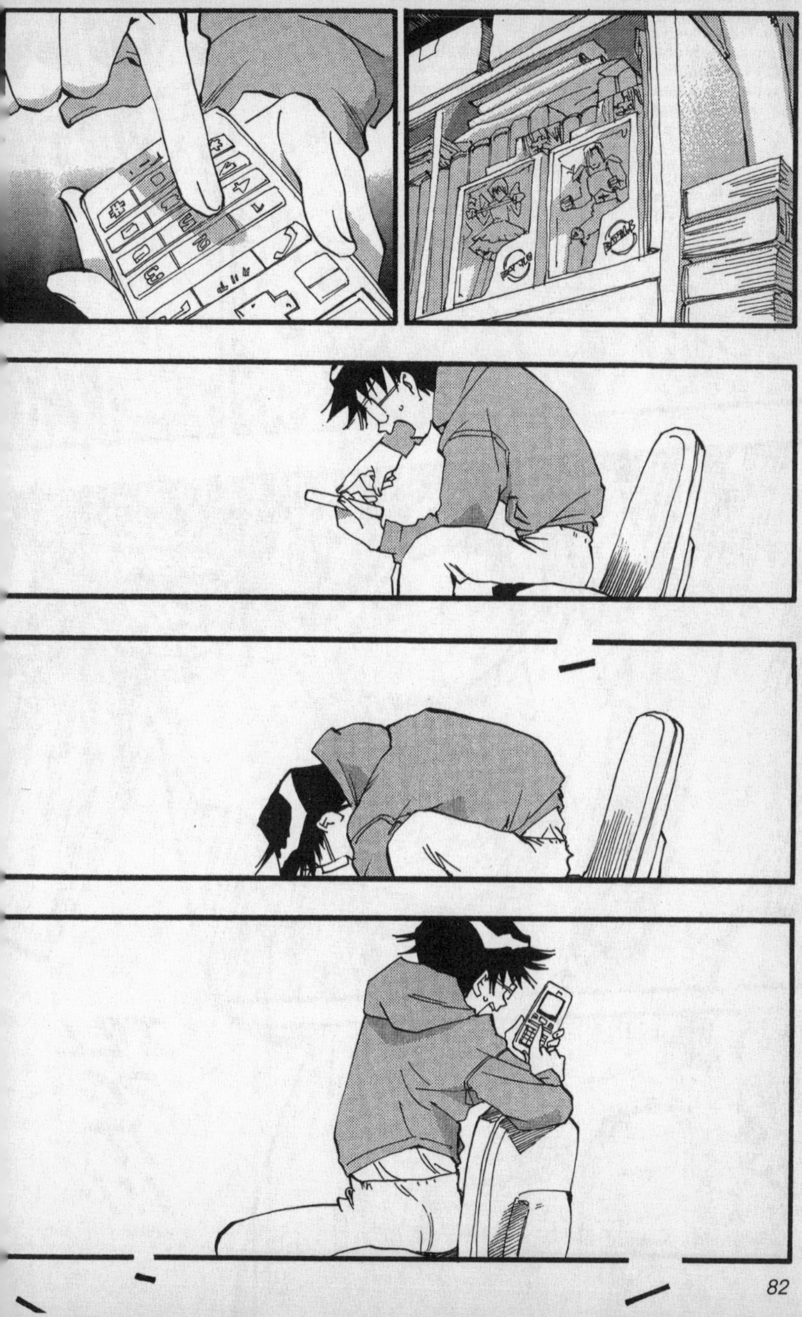

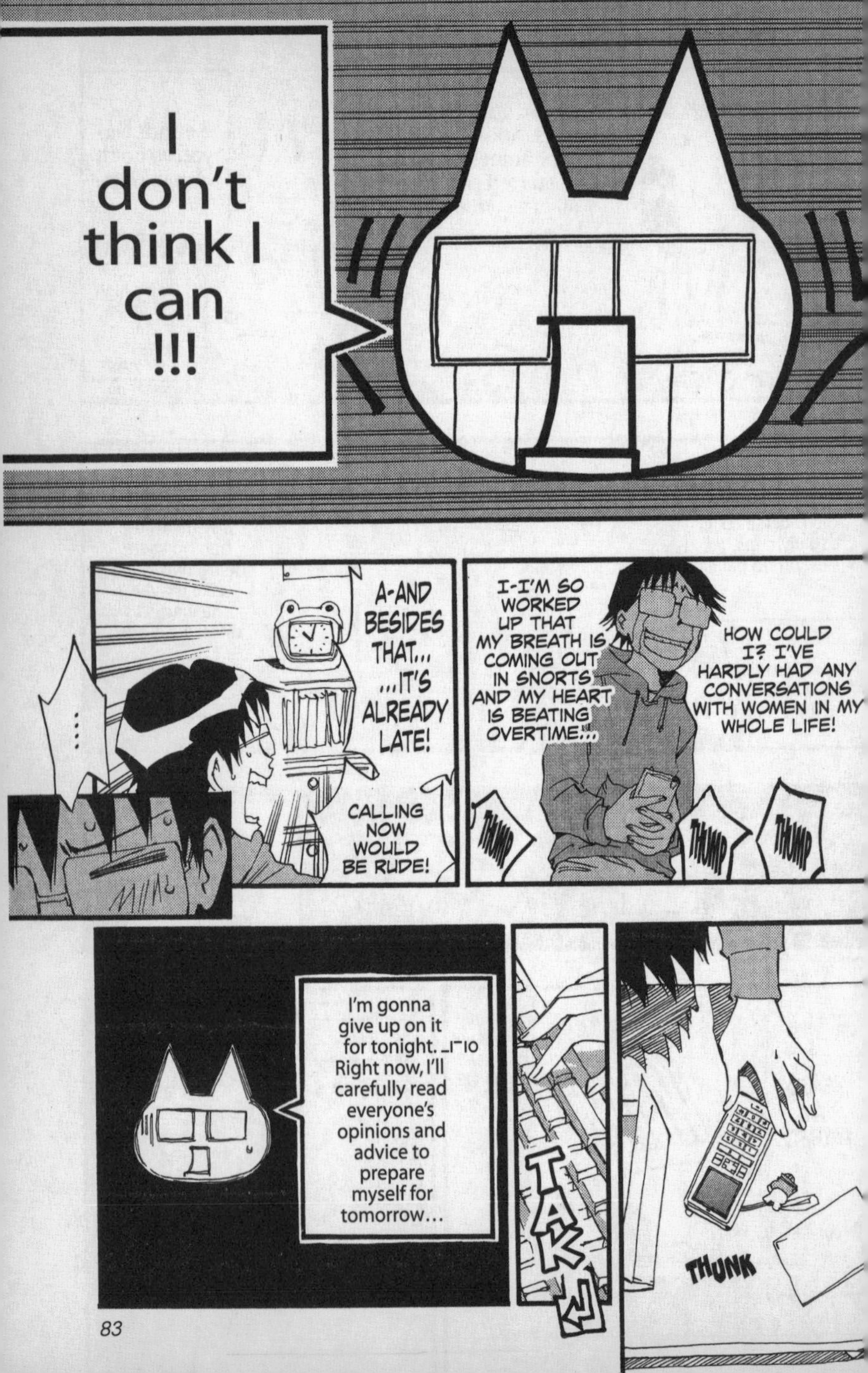

I don't think I can !!!
HOW COULD I? I'VE HARDLY HAD ANY CONVERSATIONS WITH WOMEN IN MY WHOLE LIFE!
I-I'M SO WORKED UP THAT MY BREATH IS COMING OUT IN SNORTS AND MY HEART IS BEATING OVERTIME...
THUMP
THUMP
THUMP
A-AND BESIDES THAT... ...IT'S ALREADY LATE!
CALLING NOW WOULD BE RUDE!
....
THUNK
TAK
I'm gonna give up on it for tonight. _|¯|○ Right now, I'll carefully read everyone's opinions and advice to prepare myself for tomorrow…

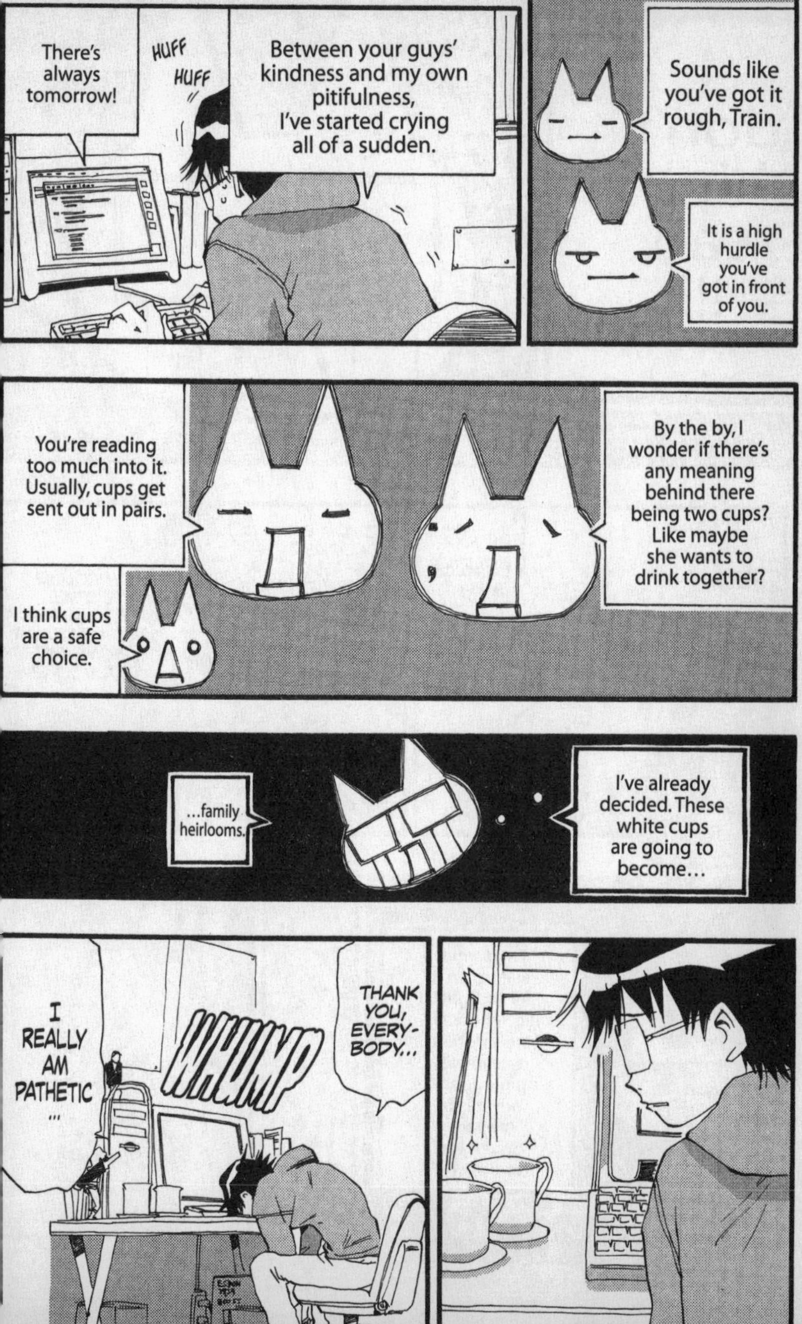
Sounds like you've got it rough, Train.
It is a high hurdle you've got in front of you.
Between your guys' kindness and my own pitifulness, I've started crying all of a sudden.
HUFF
HUFF
There's always tomorrow!
By the by, I wonder if there's any meaning behind there being two cups? Like maybe she wants to drink together?
You're reading too much into it. Usually, cups get sent out in pairs.
I think cups are a safe choice.
I've already decided. These white cups are going to become…
…family heirlooms.
THANK YOU, EVERY-BODY...
WHUMP
I REALLY AM PATHETIC ...

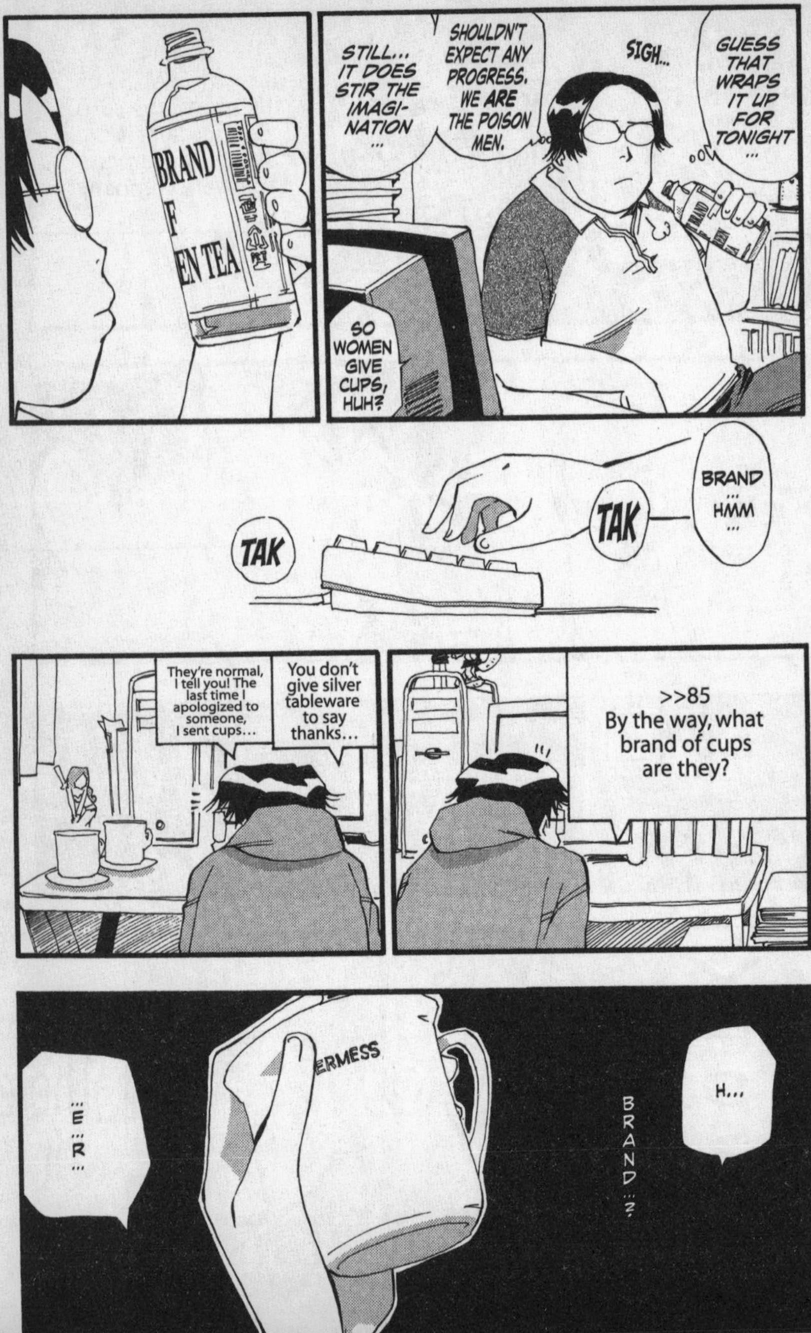
GUESS THAT WRAPS IT UP FOR TONIGHT...
SIGH...
SHOULDN'T EXPECT ANY PROGRESS. WE ARE THE POISON MEN.
STILL... IT DOES STIR THE IMAGINATION...
SO WOMEN GIVE CUPS, HUH?
BRAND... HMM...
TAK
TAK
>>85
By the way, what brand of cups are they?
You don't give silver tableware to say thanks...
They're normal, I tell you! The last time I apologized to someone, I sent cups...
H...
BRAND...?
ERMESS
...E...R...

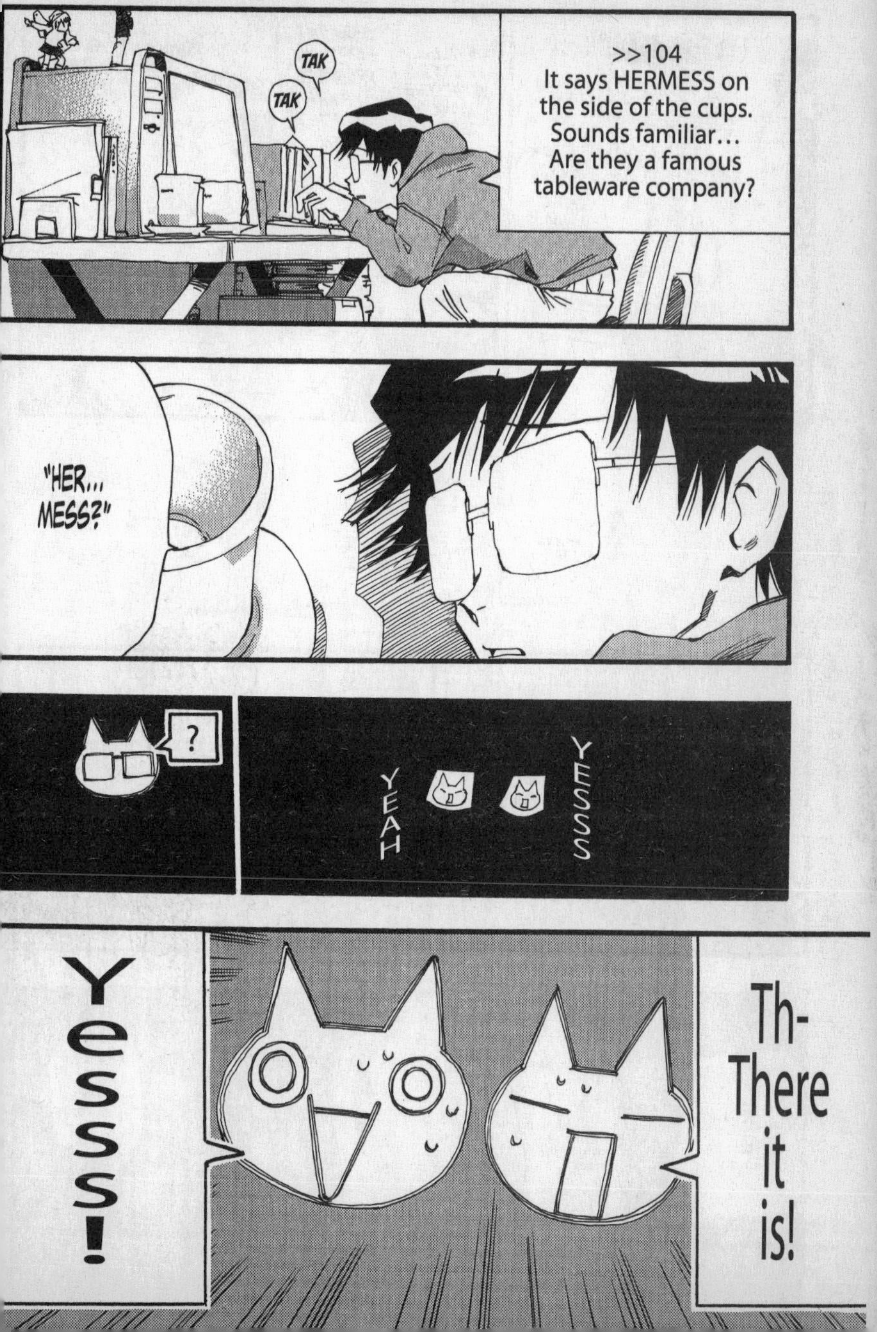
>>104
It says HERMESS on the side of the cups. Sounds familiar… Are they a famous tableware company?
TAK
TAK
"HER… MESS?"
YESSS
YEAH
?
Th- There it is!
Yess!

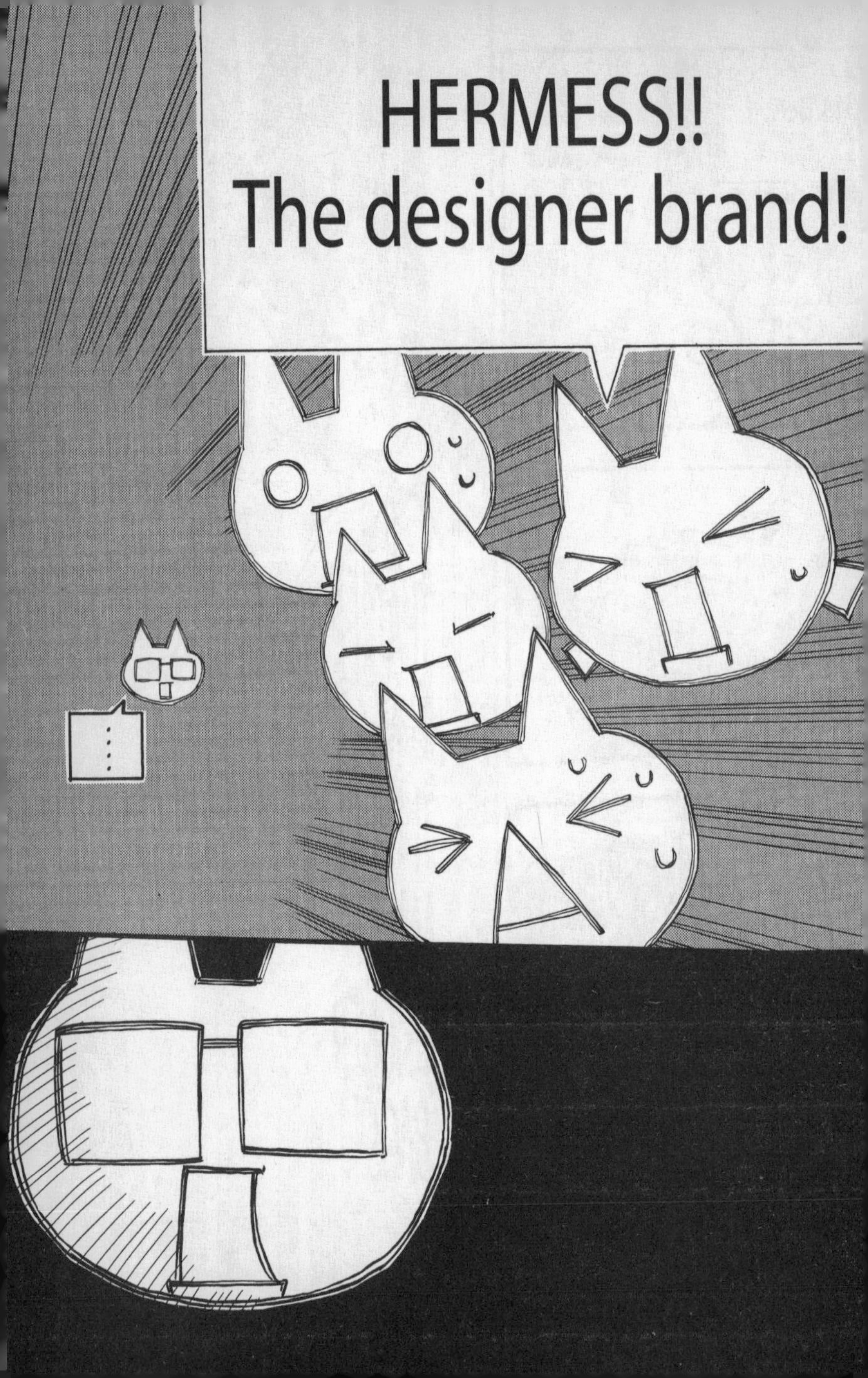
HERMESS!! The designer brand!
......

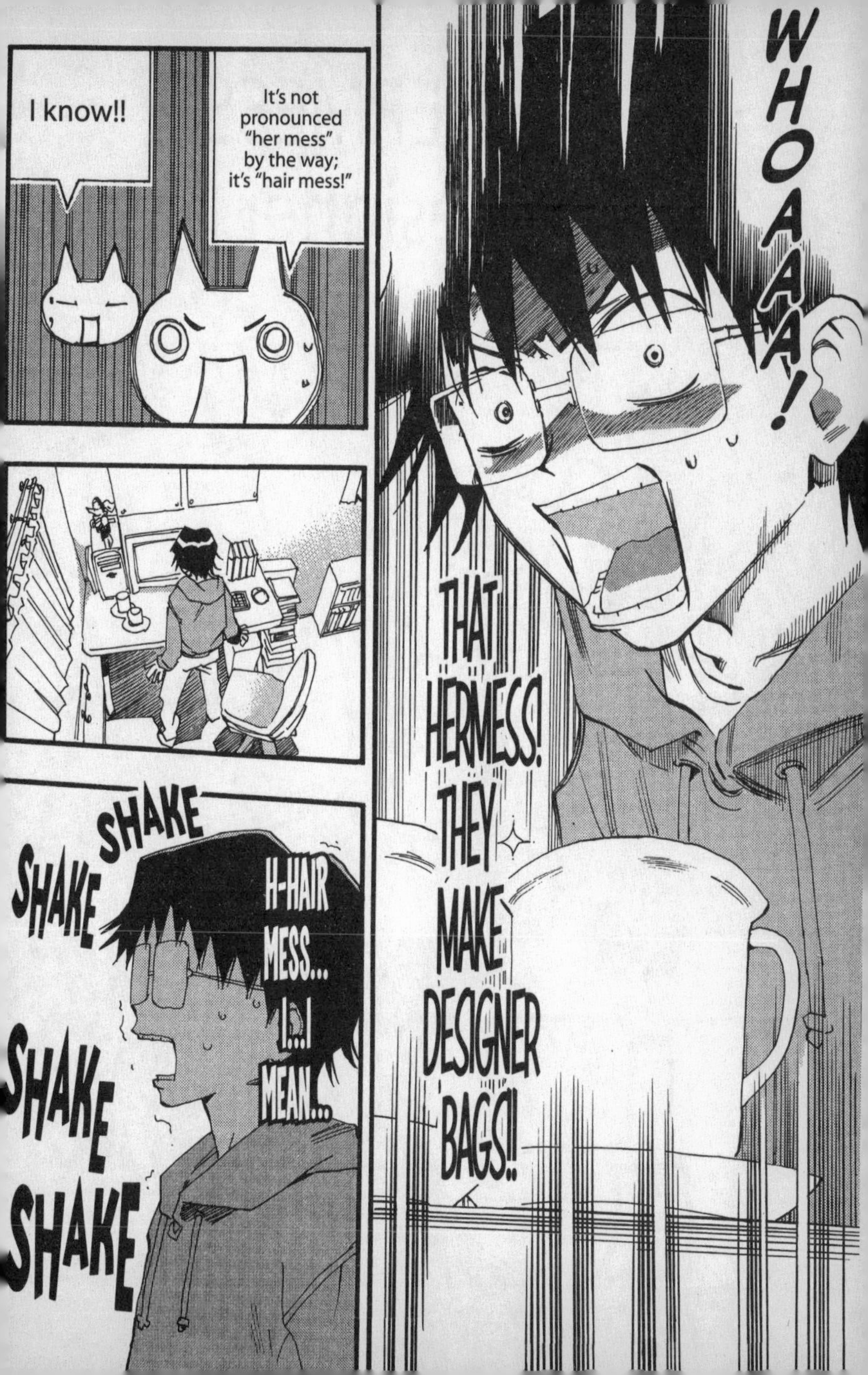
WHOAAAA!
THAT HERMESS! THEY MAKE DESIGNER BAGS!!
It's not pronounced "her mess" by the way; it's "hair mess!"
I know!!
SHAKE SHAKE
H-HAIR MESS... I...I MEAN...
SHAKE SHAKE

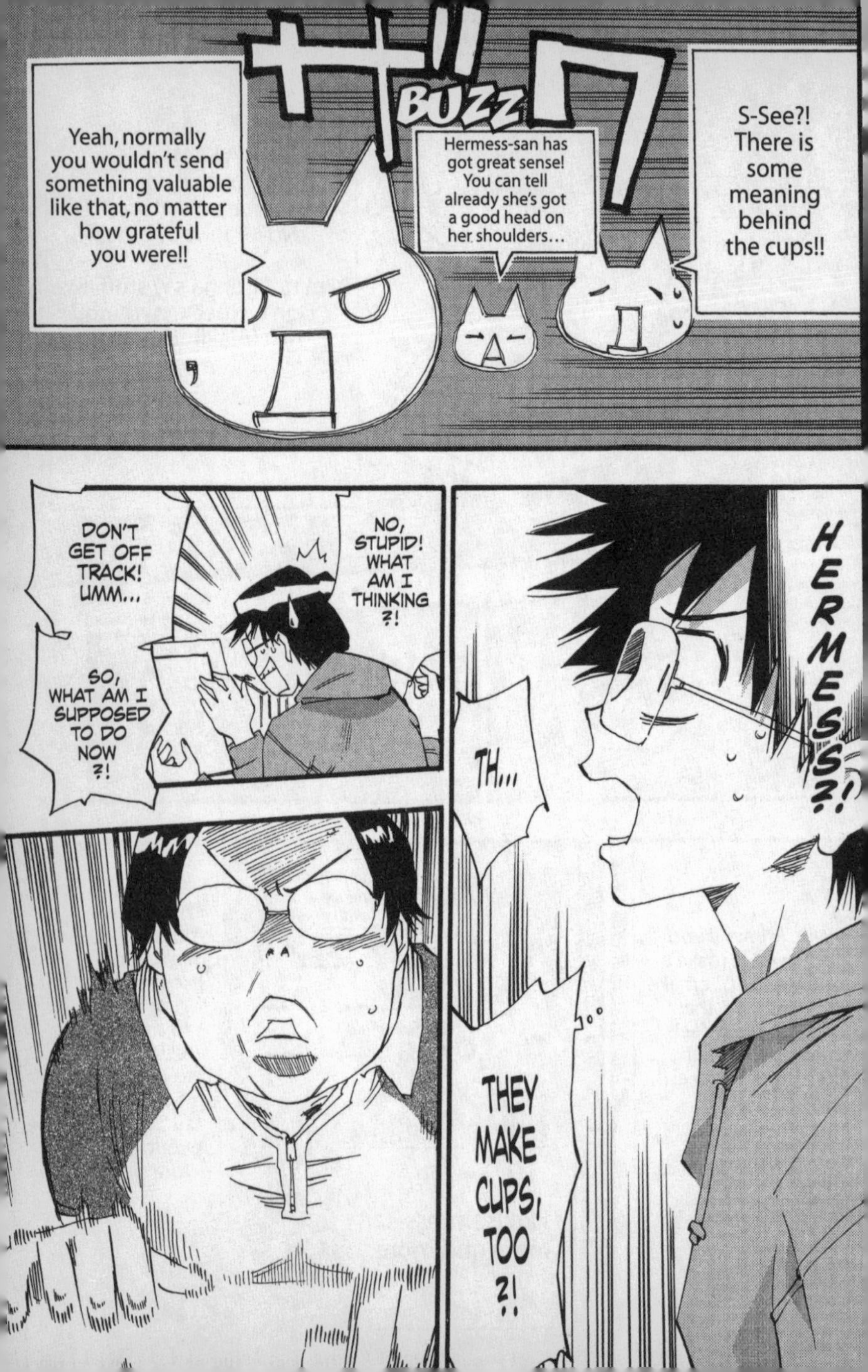
S-See?! There is some meaning behind the cups!!
BUZZ
Hermess-san has got great sense! You can tell already she's got a good head on her shoulders…
Yeah, normally you wouldn't send something valuable like that, no matter how grateful you were!!
HERMESS?!
TH…
THEY MAKE CUPS, TOO?!
NO, STUPID! WHAT AM I THINKING?!
DON'T GET OFF TRACK! UMM…
SO, WHAT AM I SUPPOSED TO DO NOW?!

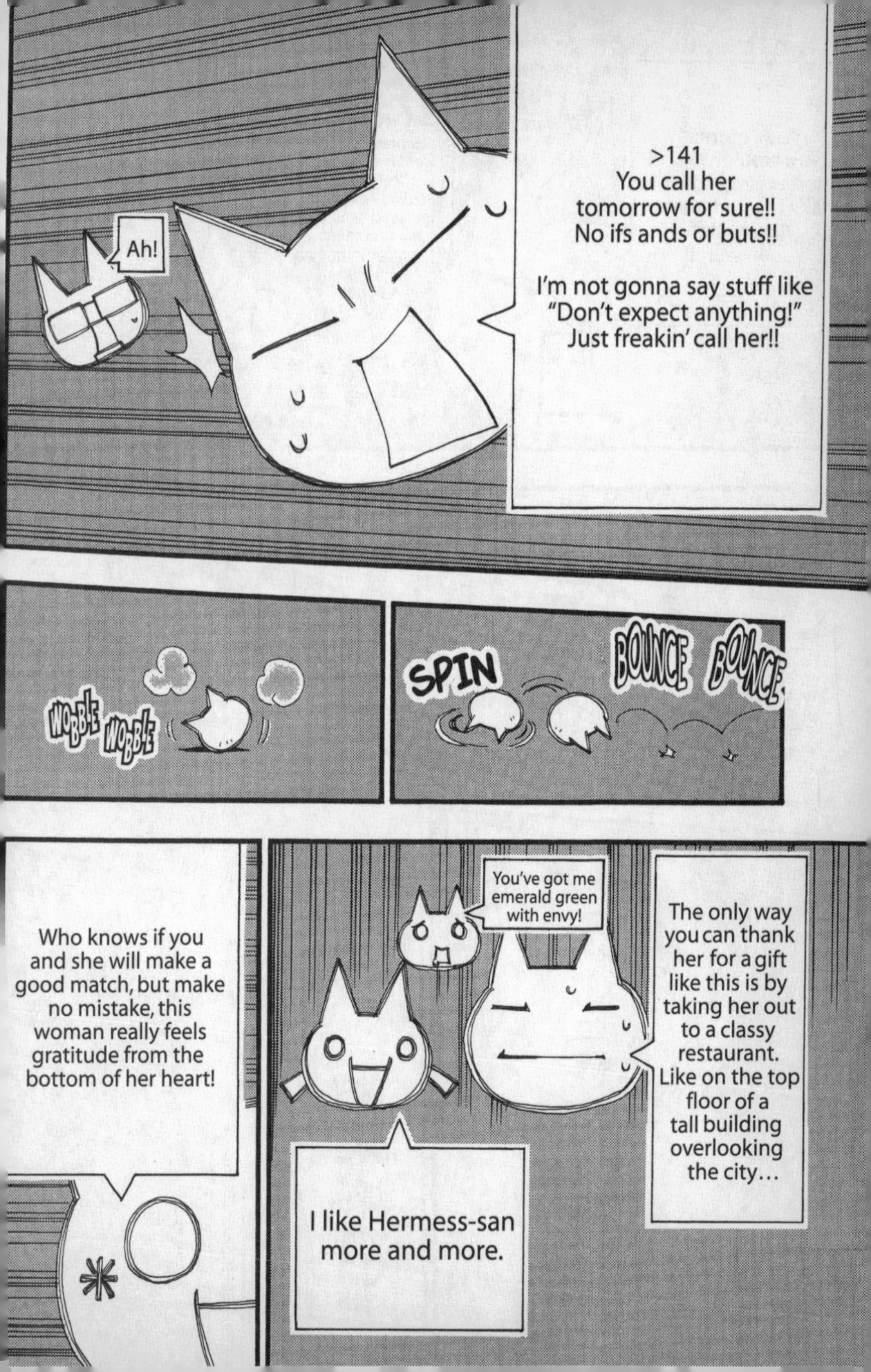
>141 You call her tomorrow for sure!! No ifs ands or buts!! I'm not gonna say stuff like "Don't expect anything!" Just freakin' call her!!
Ah!
SPIN
BOUNCE BOUNCE
WOBBLE WOBBLE
The only way you can thank her for a gift like this is by taking her out to a classy restaurant. Like on the top floor of a tall building overlooking the city…
You've got me emerald green with envy!
I like Hermess-san more and more.
Who knows if you and she will make a good match, but make no mistake, this woman really feels gratitude from the bottom of her heart!

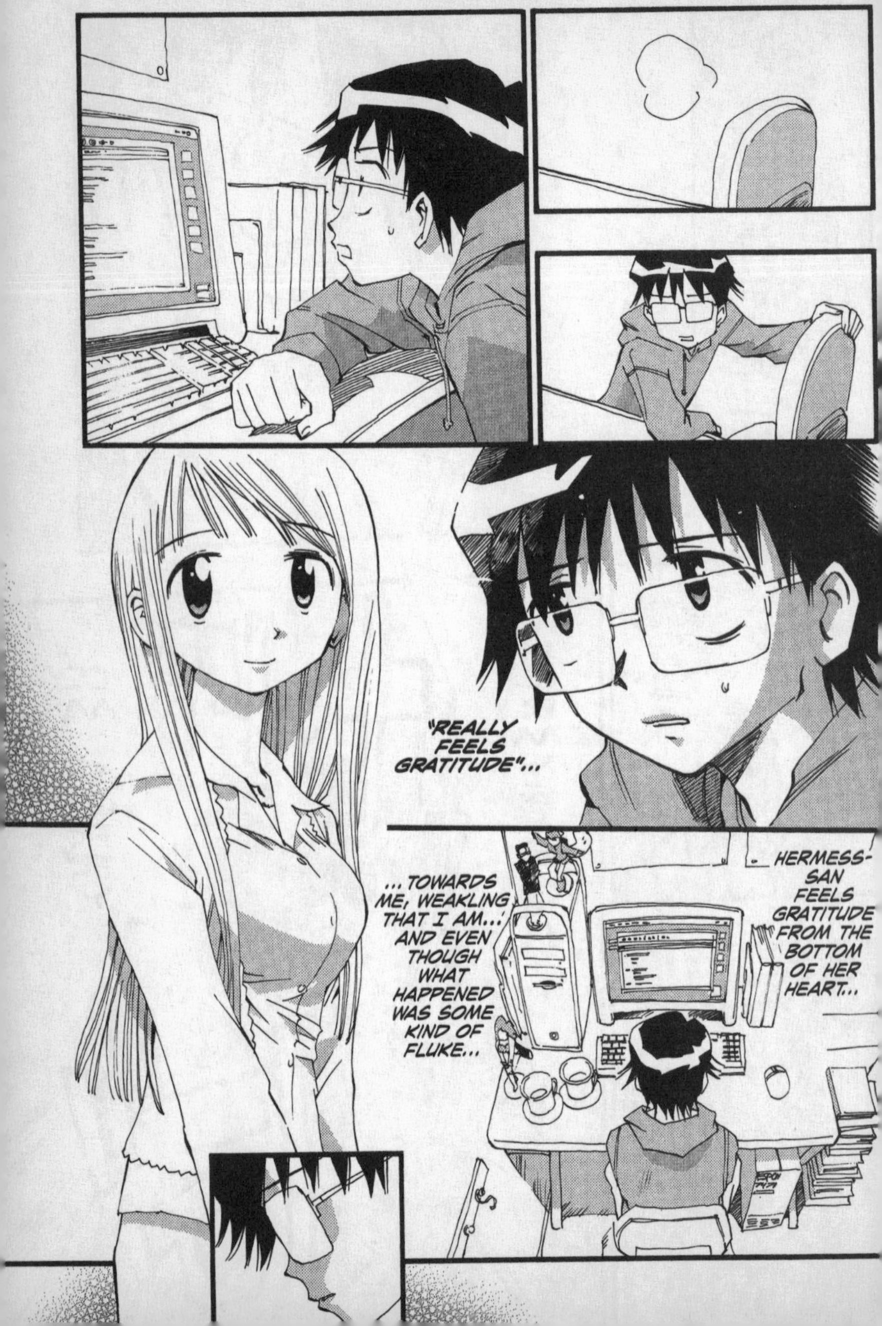
"REALLY FEELS GRATITUDE"...
HERMESS-SAN FEELS GRATITUDE FROM THE BOTTOM OF HER HEART...
...TOWARDS ME, WEAKLING THAT I AM...' AND EVEN THOUGH WHAT HAPPENED WAS SOME KIND OF FLUKE...

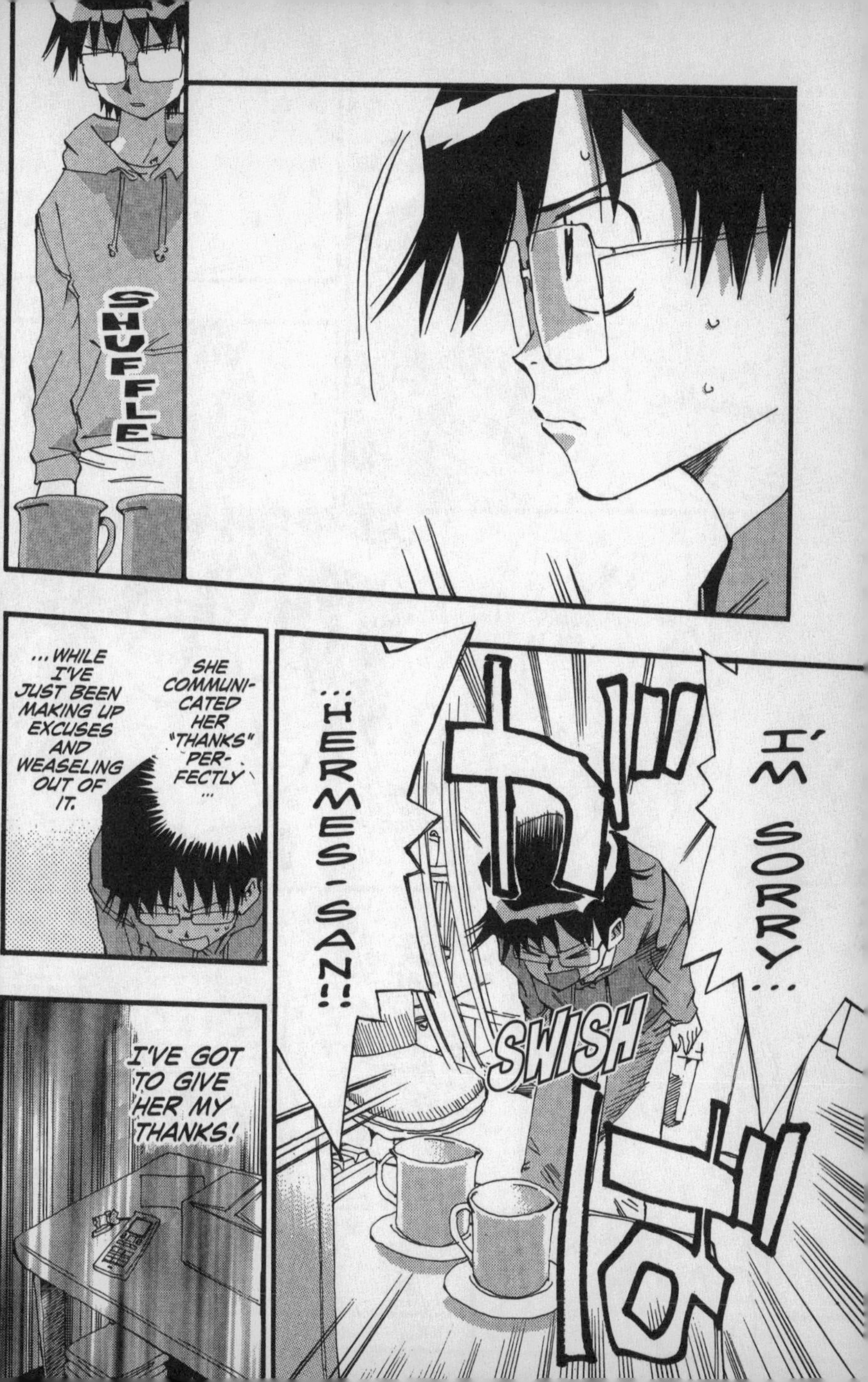
SHUFFLE
I'M SORRY...
...HERMES-SAN!!
SWISH
SHE COMMUNICATED HER "THANKS" PERFECTLY...
...WHILE I'VE JUST BEEN MAKING UP EXCUSES AND WEASELING OUT OF IT.
I'VE GOT TO GIVE HER MY THANKS!

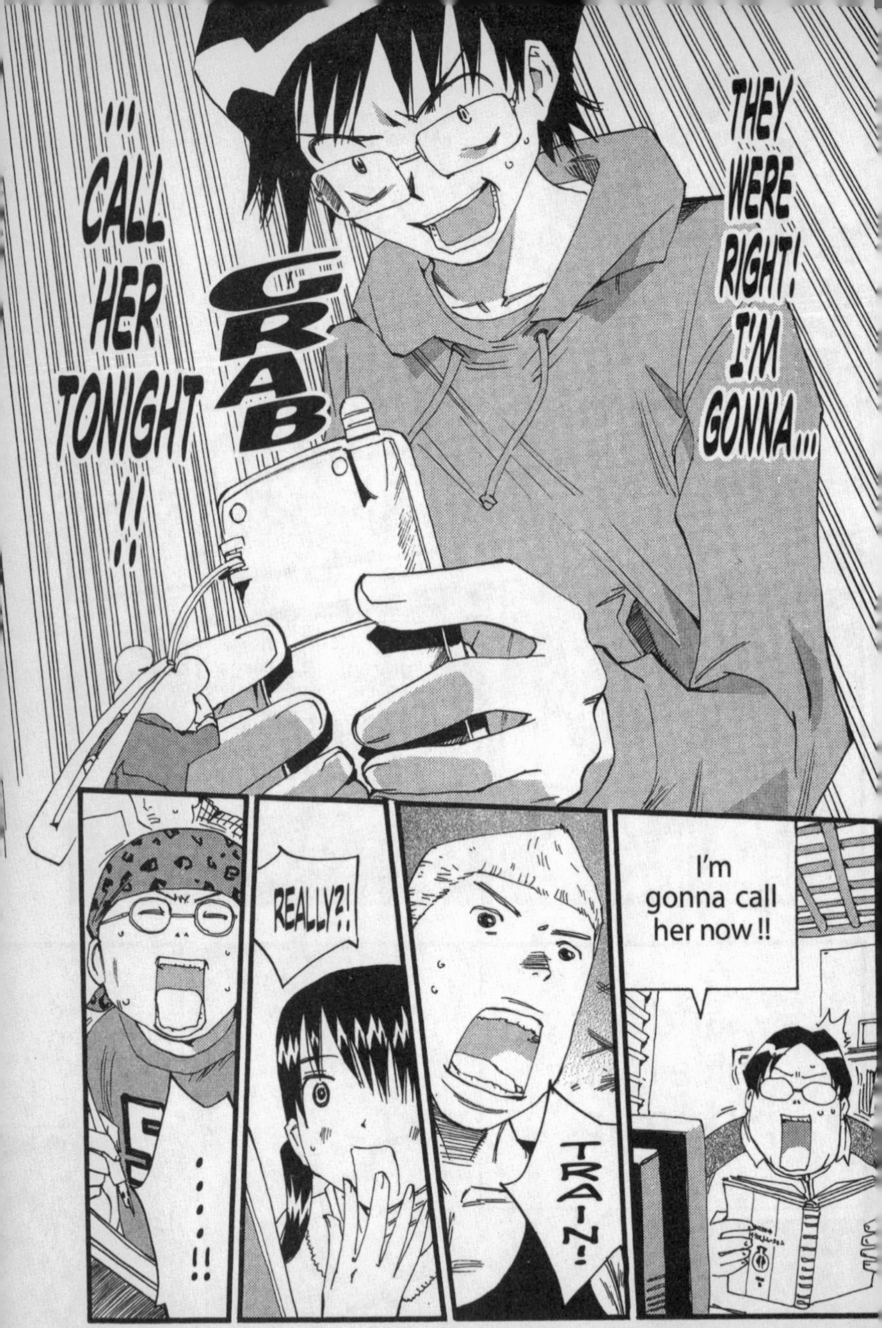
THEY WERE RIGHT! I'M GONNA...
GRAB
...CALL HER TONIGHT!!
I'm gonna call her now!!
TRAIN!
REALLY?!
......!!

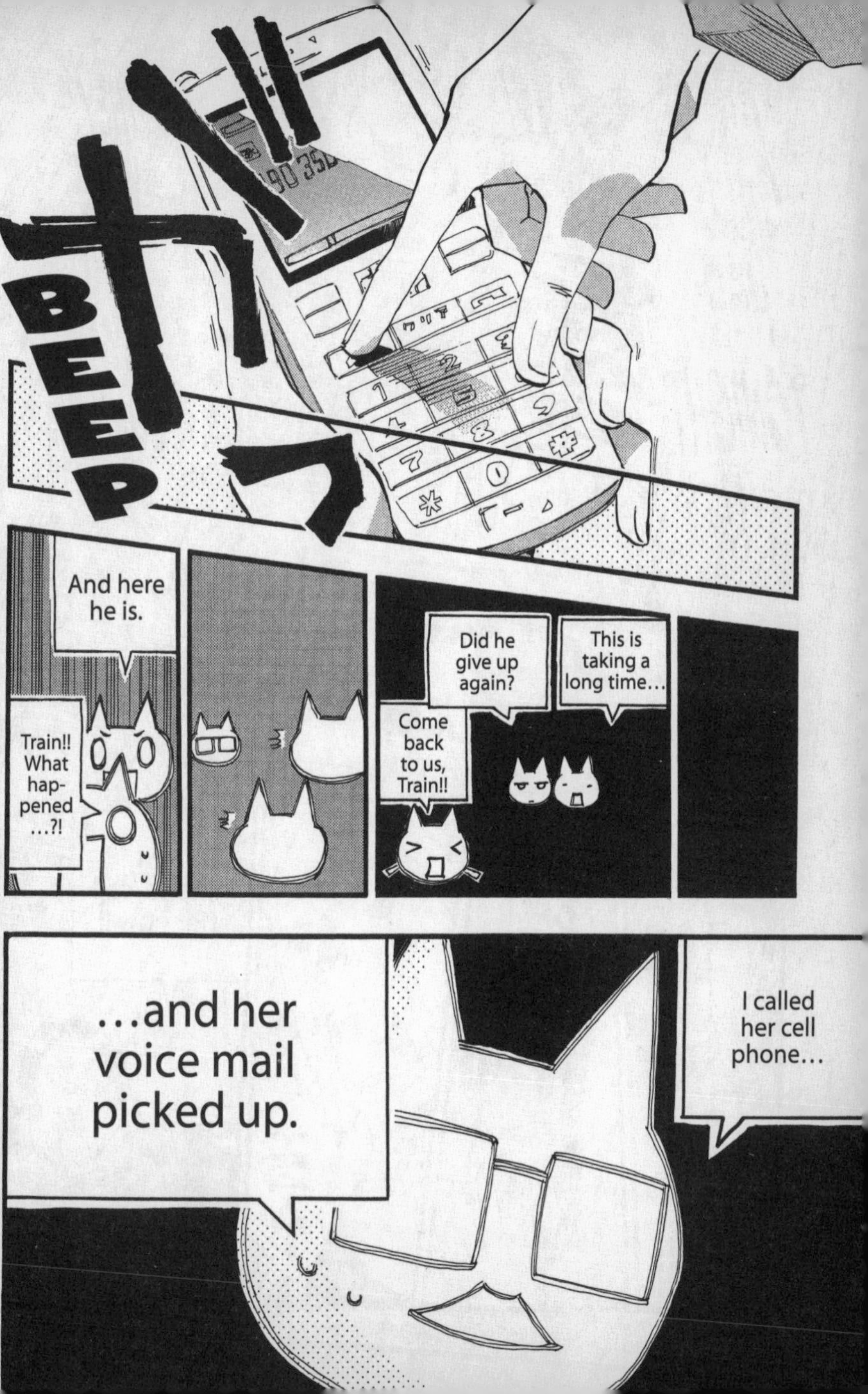
BEEP
This is taking a long time…
Did he give up again?
Come back to us, Train!!
And here he is.
Train!! What hap-pened…?!
I called her cell phone…
…and her voice mail picked up.

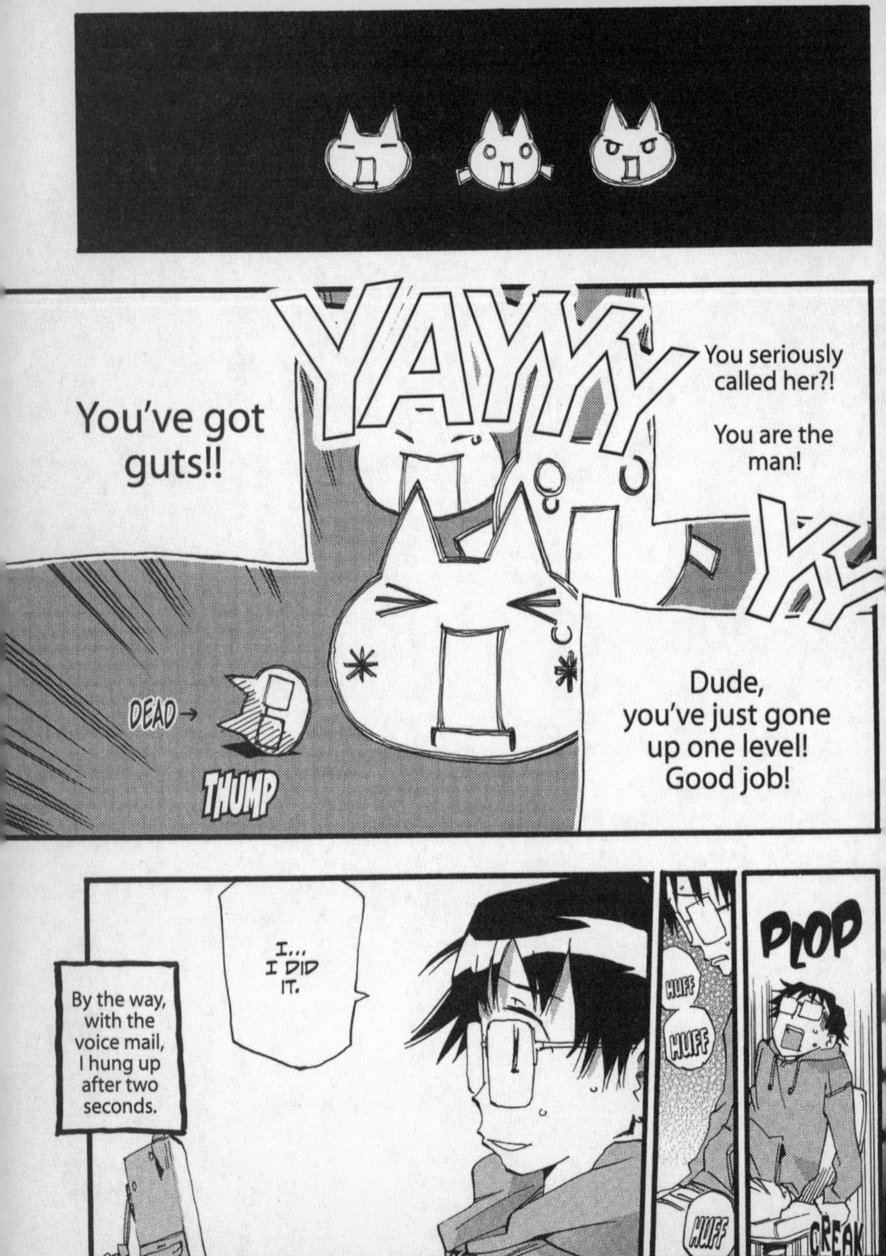
You seriously called her?!
You are the man!
YAYYY
You've got guts!!
Dude, you've just gone up one level! Good job!
DEAD→
THUMP
PLOP
CREAK
HUFF
HUFF
HUFF
I... I DID IT.
By the way, with the voice mail, I hung up after two seconds.

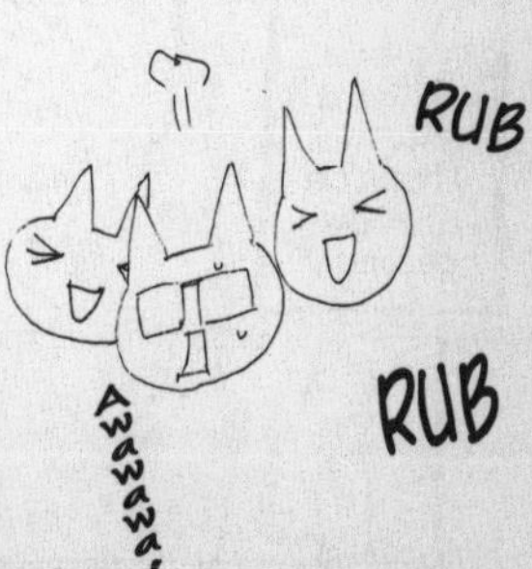
RUB
RUB
Awawawa!

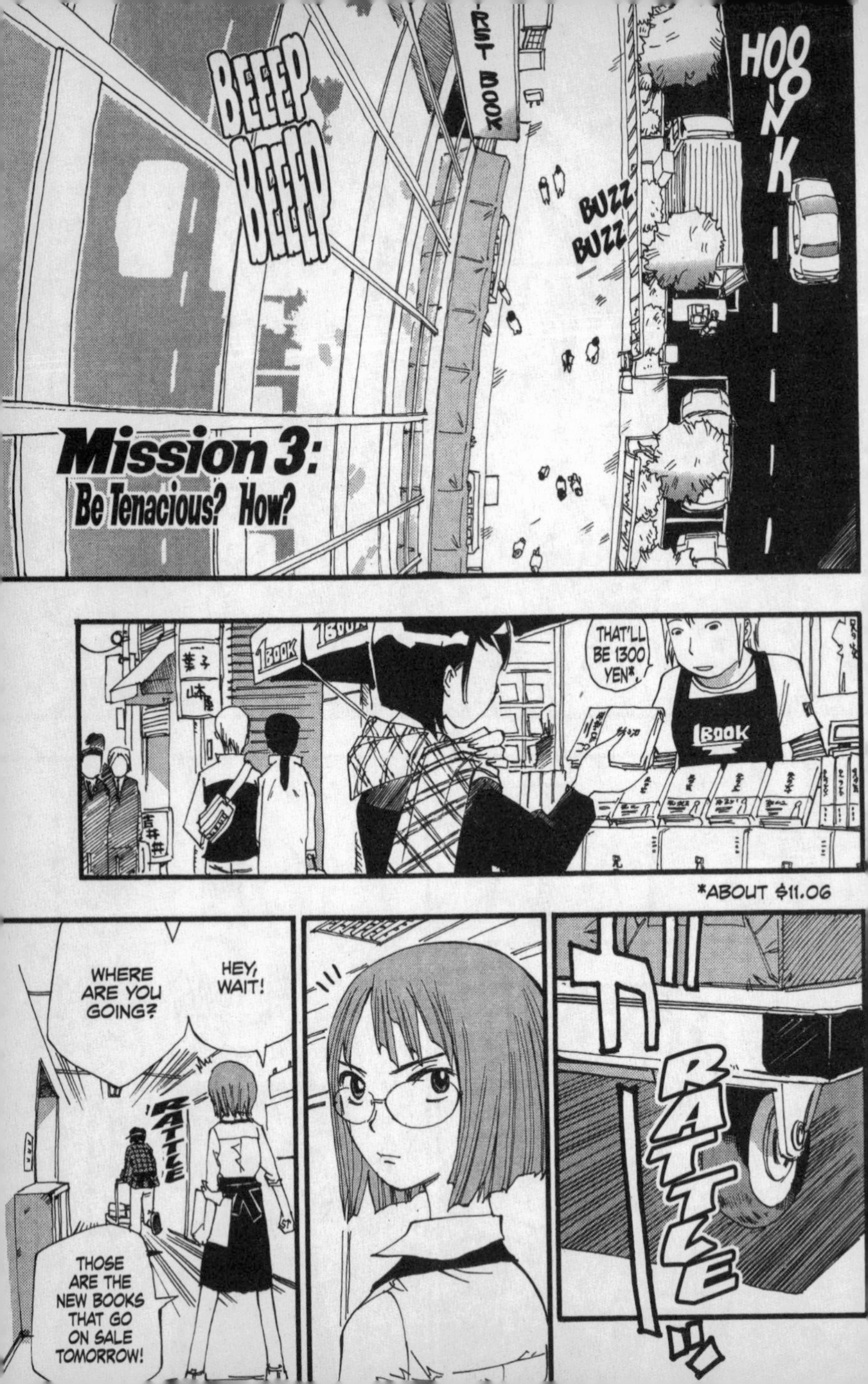
HOOONK
BUZZ BUZZ
BEEEP BEEEP
RST BOOK
Mission 3:
Be Tenacious? How?
THAT'LL BE 1300 YEN*.
1BOOK
*ABOUT $11.06
RATTLE
HEY, WAIT!
WHERE ARE YOU GOING?
RATTLE
THOSE ARE THE NEW BOOKS THAT GO ON SALE TOMORROW!

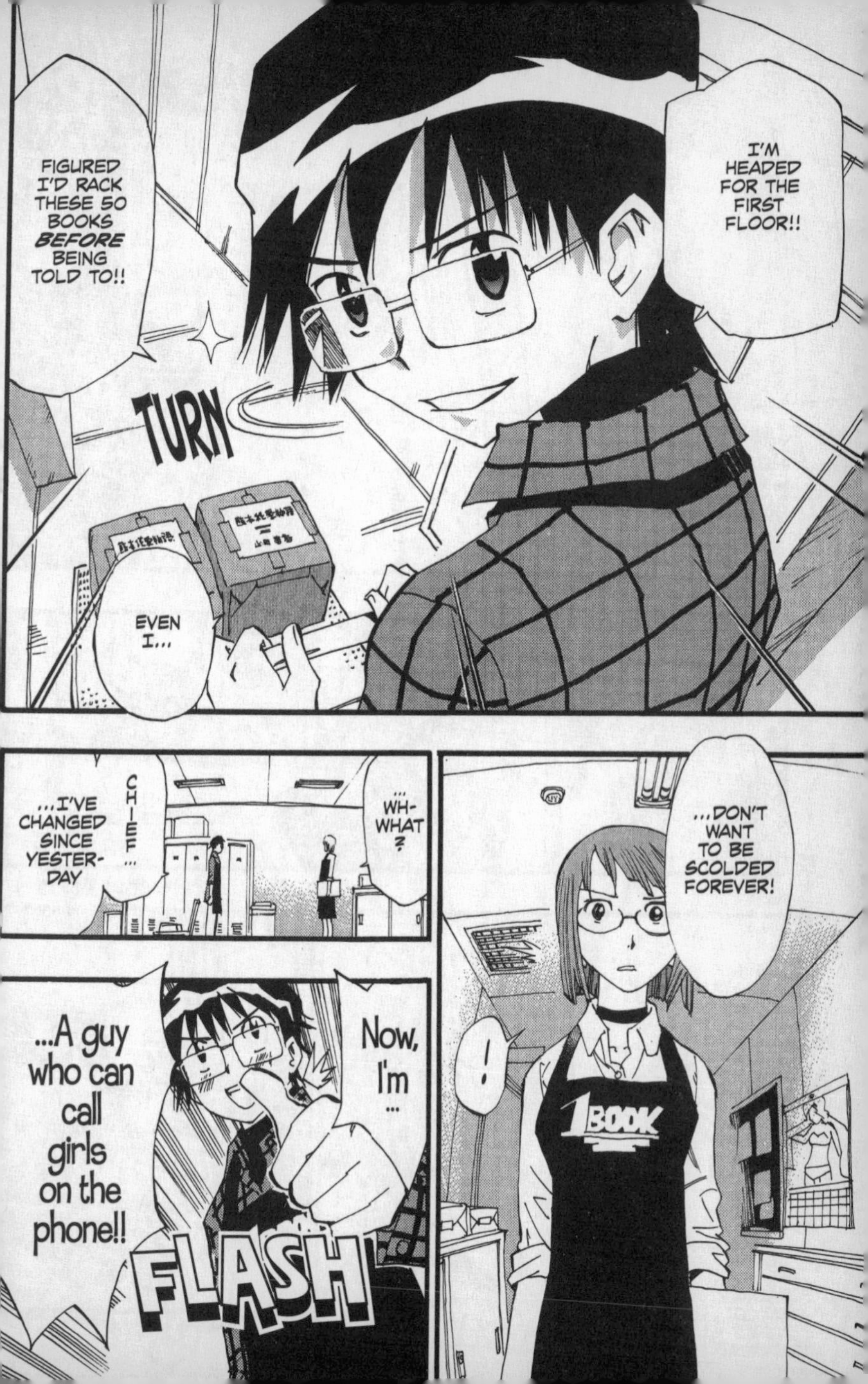
I'M HEADED FOR THE FIRST FLOOR!!
FIGURED I'D RACK THESE 50 BOOKS *BEFORE* BEING TOLD TO!!
TURN
EVEN I...
...DON'T WANT TO BE SCOLDED FOREVER!
!
...WH-WHAT?
CHIEF...
...I'VE CHANGED SINCE YESTER-DAY
Now, I'm ...
...A guy who can call girls on the phone!!
FLASH
1BOOK

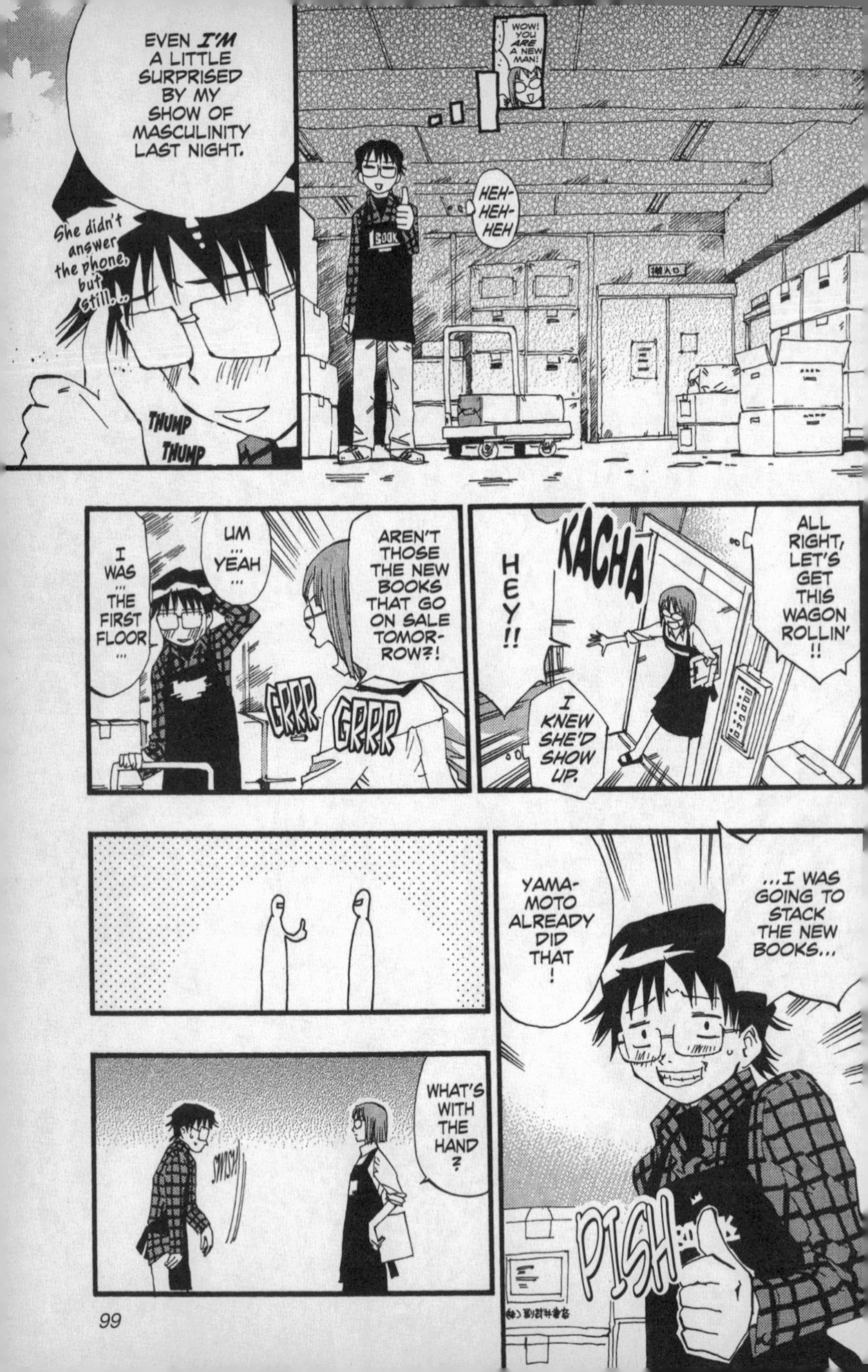
WOW! YOU ARE A NEW MAN!
HEH-HEH-HEH
EVEN I'M A LITTLE SURPRISED BY MY SHOW OF MASCULINITY LAST NIGHT.
She didn't answer the phone, but still...
THUMP THUMP
ALL RIGHT, LET'S GET THIS WAGON ROLLIN'!!
KACHA
HEY!!
I KNEW SHE'D SHOW UP.
AREN'T THOSE THE NEW BOOKS THAT GO ON SALE TOMORROW?!
UM ... YEAH ...
I WAS ... THE FIRST FLOOR ...
GRRR
GRRR
...I WAS GOING TO STACK THE NEW BOOKS...
YAMAMOTO ALREADY DID THAT!
PISH
WHAT'S WITH THE HAND?
SWISH

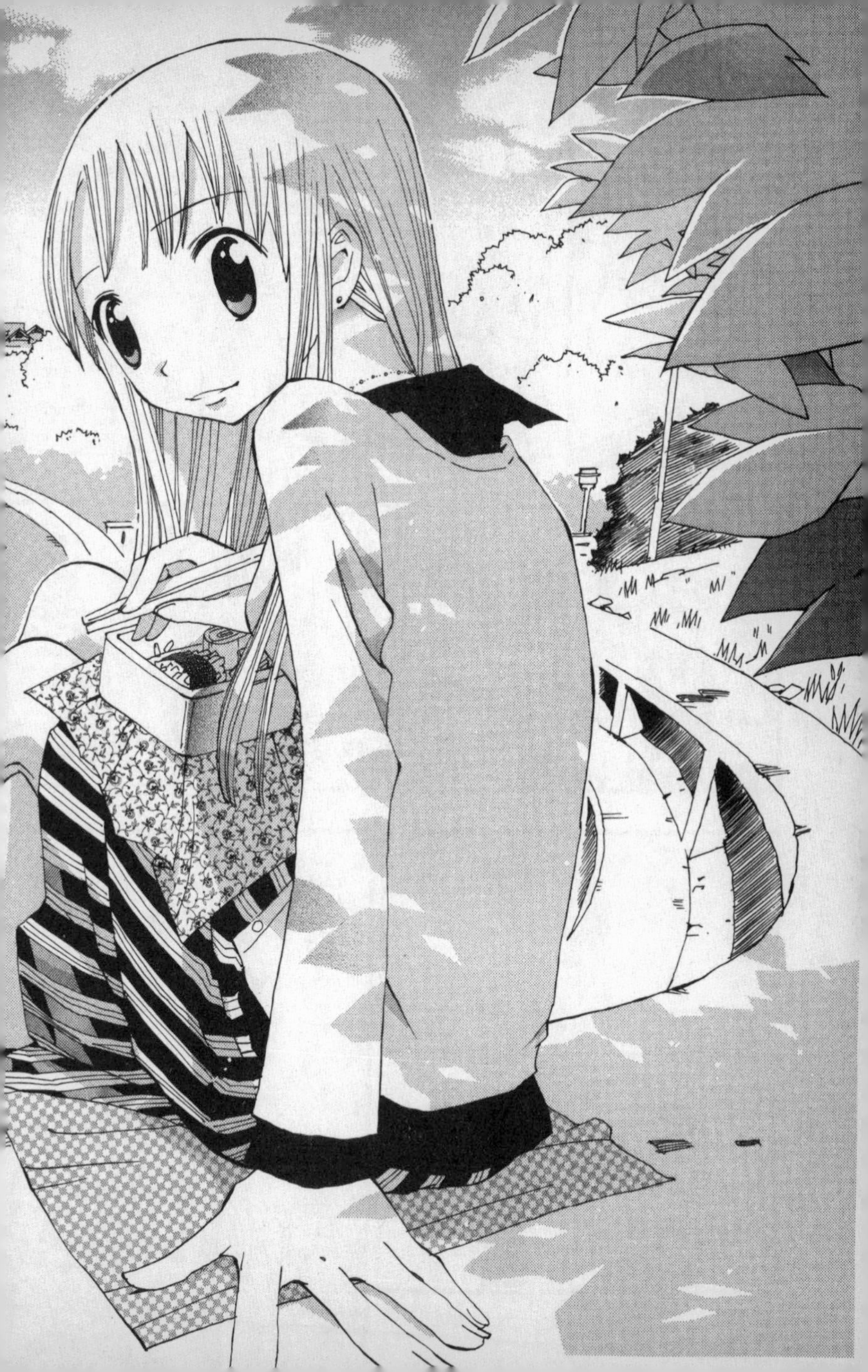

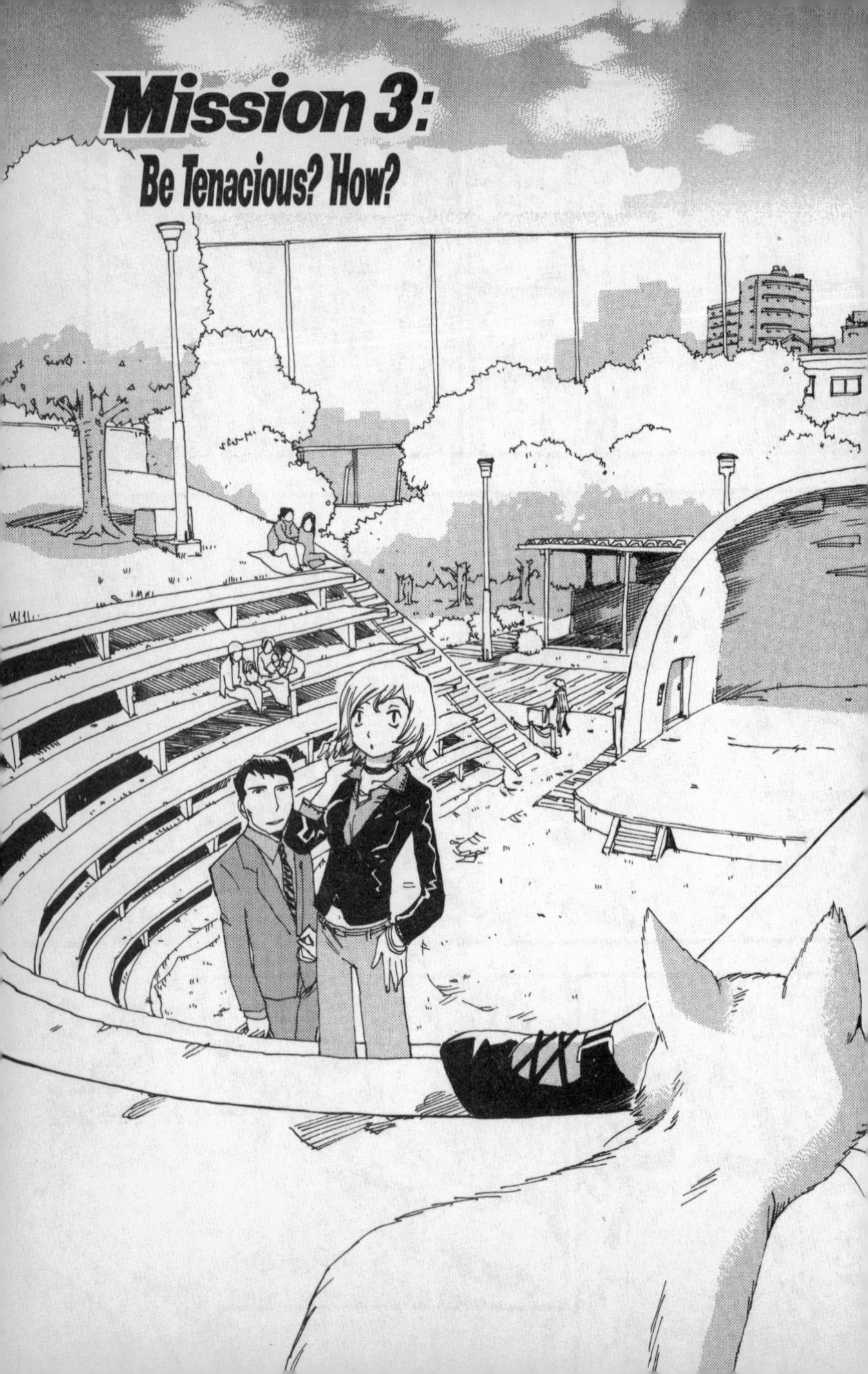
Mission 3:
Be Tenacious? How?

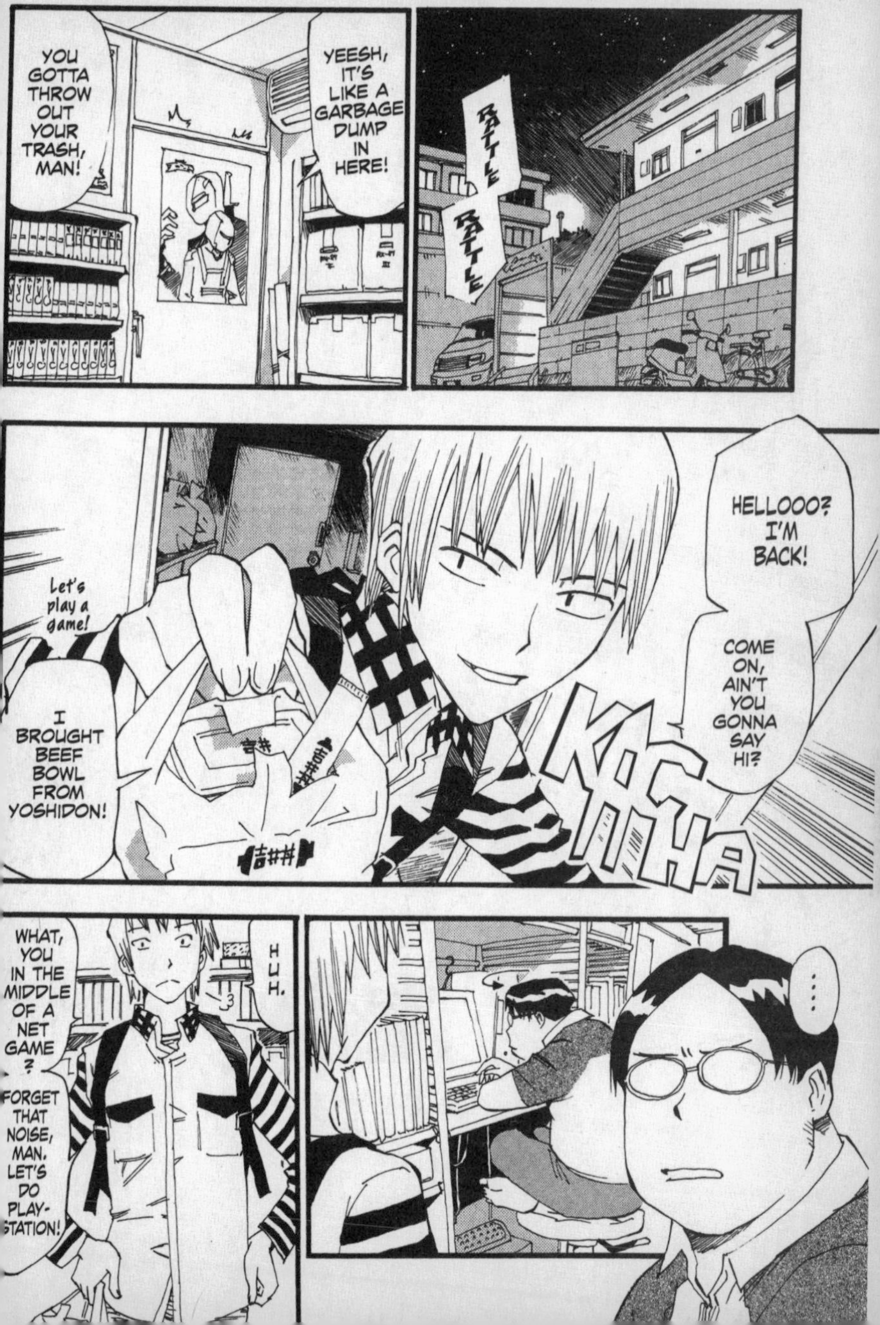
RATTLE
RATTLE
YEESH, IT'S LIKE A GARBAGE DUMP IN HERE!
YOU GOTTA THROW OUT YOUR TRASH, MAN!
HELLOOO? I'M BACK!
COME ON, AIN'T YOU GONNA SAY HI?
KACHA
Let's play a game!
I BROUGHT BEEF BOWL FROM YOSHIDON!
....
HUH.
WHAT, YOU IN THE MIDDLE OF A NET GAME?
FORGET THAT NOISE, MAN. LET'S DO PLAY-STATION!

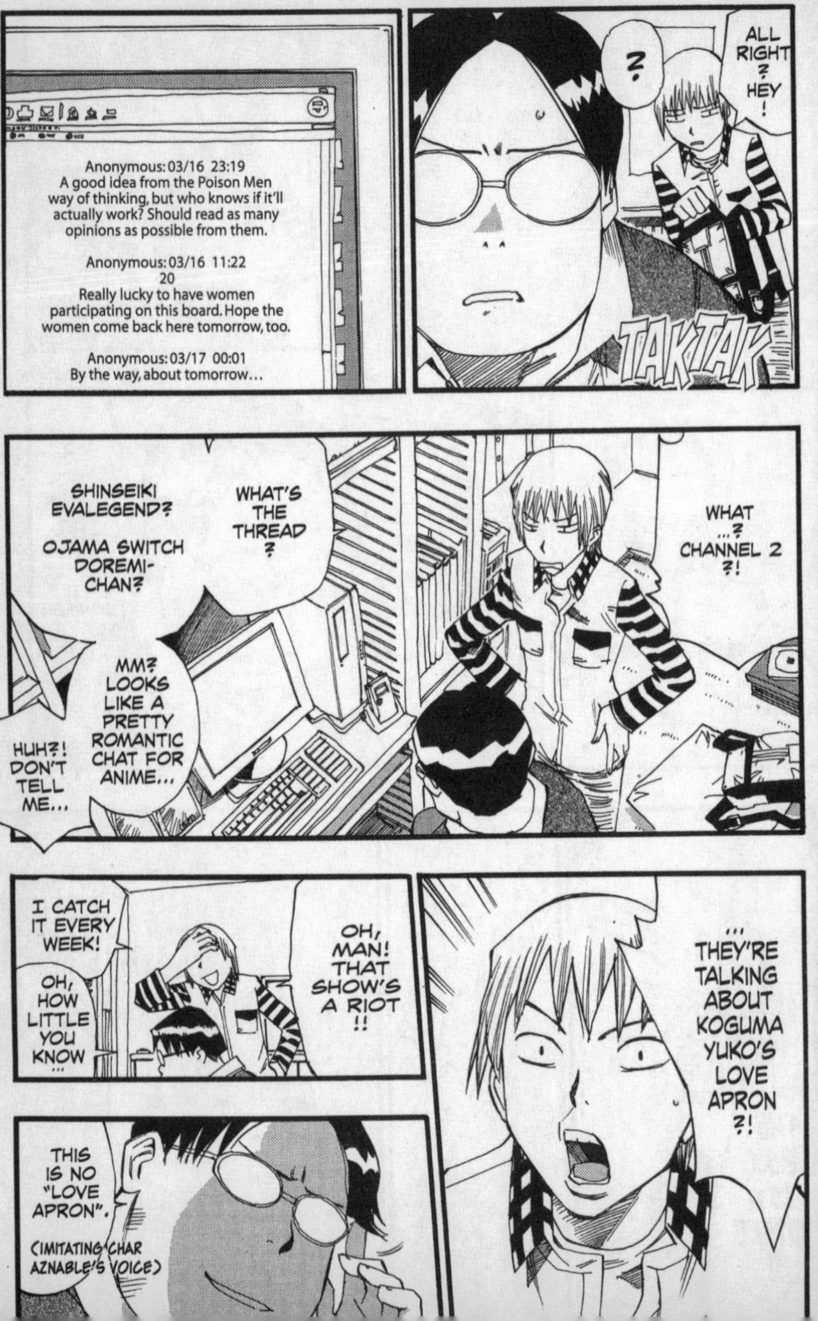
ALL RIGHT? HEY!
?
TAKTAK
Anonymous: 03/16 23:19
A good idea from the Poison Men way of thinking, but who knows if it'll actually work? Should read as many opinions as possible from them.
Anonymous: 03/16 11:22
20
Really lucky to have women participating on this board. Hope the women come back here tomorrow, too.
Anonymous: 03/17 00:01
By the way, about tomorrow...
WHAT...? CHANNEL 2?!
WHAT'S THE THREAD?
SHINSEIKI EVALEGEND? OJAMA SWITCH DOREMI-CHAN?
MM? LOOKS LIKE A PRETTY ROMANTIC CHAT FOR ANIME...
HUH?! DON'T TELL ME...
...THEY'RE TALKING ABOUT KOGUMA YUKO'S LOVE APRON?!
OH, MAN! THAT SHOW'S A RIOT!!
I CATCH IT EVERY WEEK!
OH, HOW LITTLE YOU KNOW...
THIS IS NO "LOVE APRON".
(IMITATING CHAR AZNABLE'S VOICE)

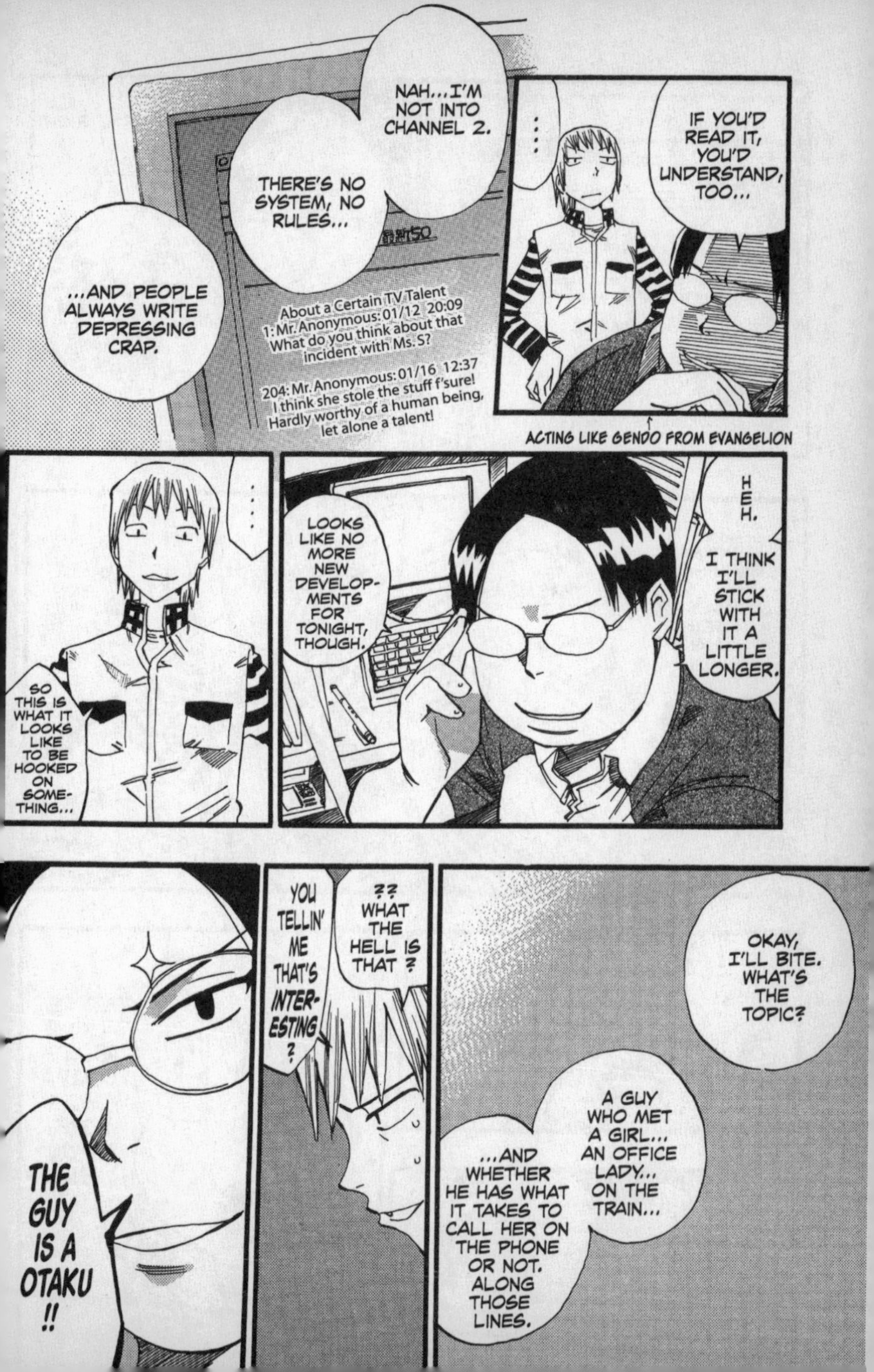
IF YOU'D READ IT, YOU'D UNDERSTAND, TOO...
....
NAH...I'M NOT INTO CHANNEL 2.
THERE'S NO SYSTEM, NO RULES...
...AND PEOPLE ALWAYS WRITE DEPRESSING CRAP.
About a Certain TV Talent
1: Mr. Anonymous: 01/12 20:09
What do you think about that incident with Ms. S?
204: Mr. Anonymous: 01/16 12:37
I think she stole the stuff f'sure! Hardly worthy of a human being, let alone a talent!
ACTING LIKE GENDO FROM EVANGELION
HEH.
I THINK I'LL STICK WITH IT A LITTLE LONGER.
LOOKS LIKE NO MORE NEW DEVELOPMENTS FOR TONIGHT, THOUGH.
....
SO THIS IS WHAT IT LOOKS LIKE TO BE HOOKED ON SOMETHING...
OKAY, I'LL BITE. WHAT'S THE TOPIC?
A GUY WHO MET A GIRL... AN OFFICE LADY... ON THE TRAIN...
...AND WHETHER HE HAS WHAT IT TAKES TO CALL HER ON THE PHONE OR NOT. ALONG THOSE LINES.
?? WHAT THE HELL IS THAT ?
YOU TELLIN' ME THAT'S INTERESTING ?
THE GUY IS A OTAKU !!

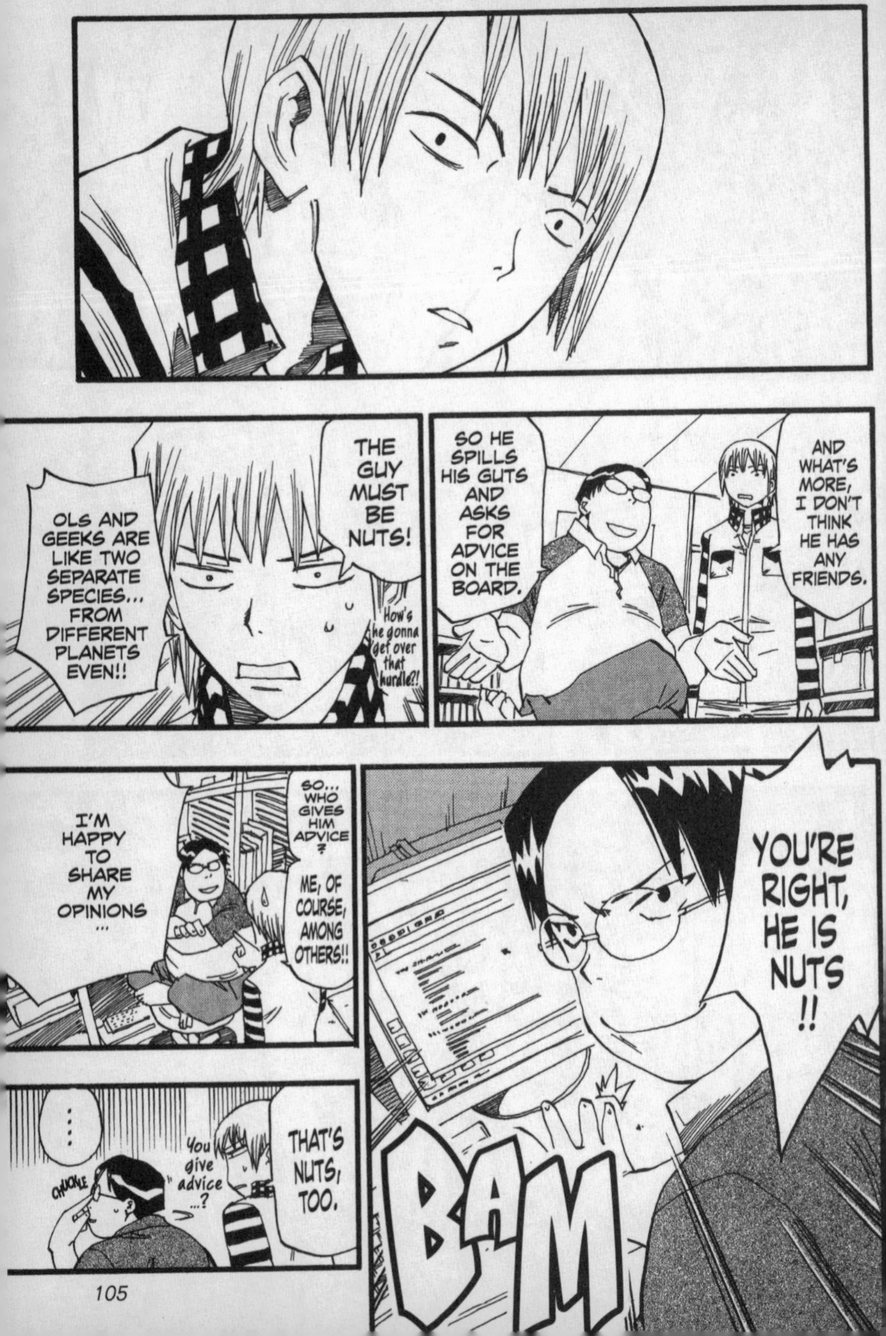
AND WHAT'S MORE, I DON'T THINK HE HAS ANY FRIENDS.
SO HE SPILLS HIS GUTS AND ASKS FOR ADVICE ON THE BOARD.
THE GUY MUST BE NUTS!
How's he gonna get over that hurdle?!
OLS AND GEEKS ARE LIKE TWO SEPARATE SPECIES... FROM DIFFERENT PLANETS EVEN!!
YOU'RE RIGHT, HE IS NUTS!!
BAM
SO... WHO GIVES HIM ADVICE?
ME, OF COURSE, AMONG OTHERS!!
I'M HAPPY TO SHARE MY OPINIONS...
THAT'S NUTS, TOO.
You give advice...?
CHUCKLE
....

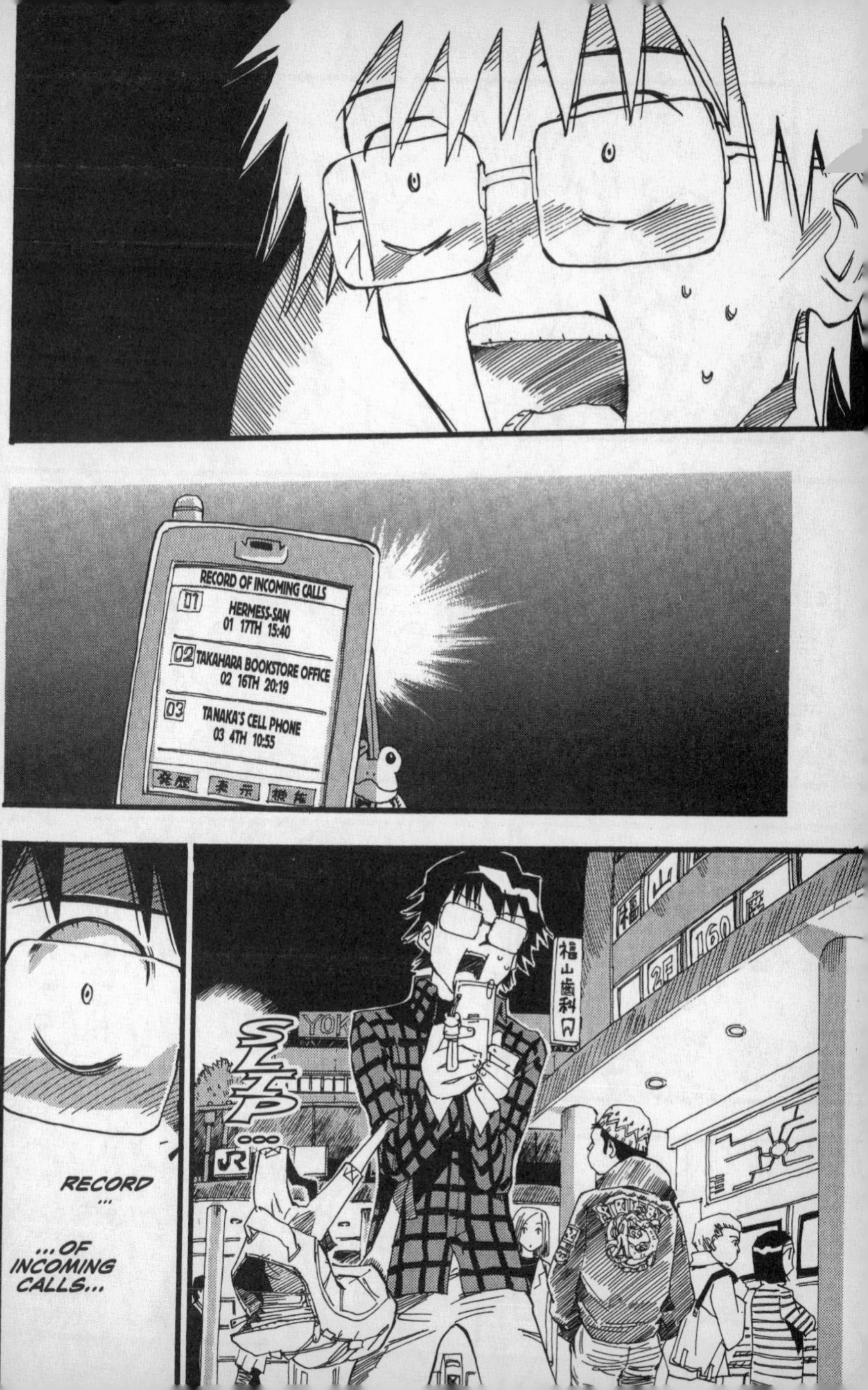

RECORD OF INCOMING CALLS
01 HERMESS-SAN
01 17TH 15:40
02 TAKAHARA BOOKSTORE OFFICE
02 16TH 20:19
03 TANAKA'S CELL PHONE
03 4TH 10:55
福山歯科
2F
160
YOK
JR
SLIP
RECORD ...
...OF INCOMING CALLS...

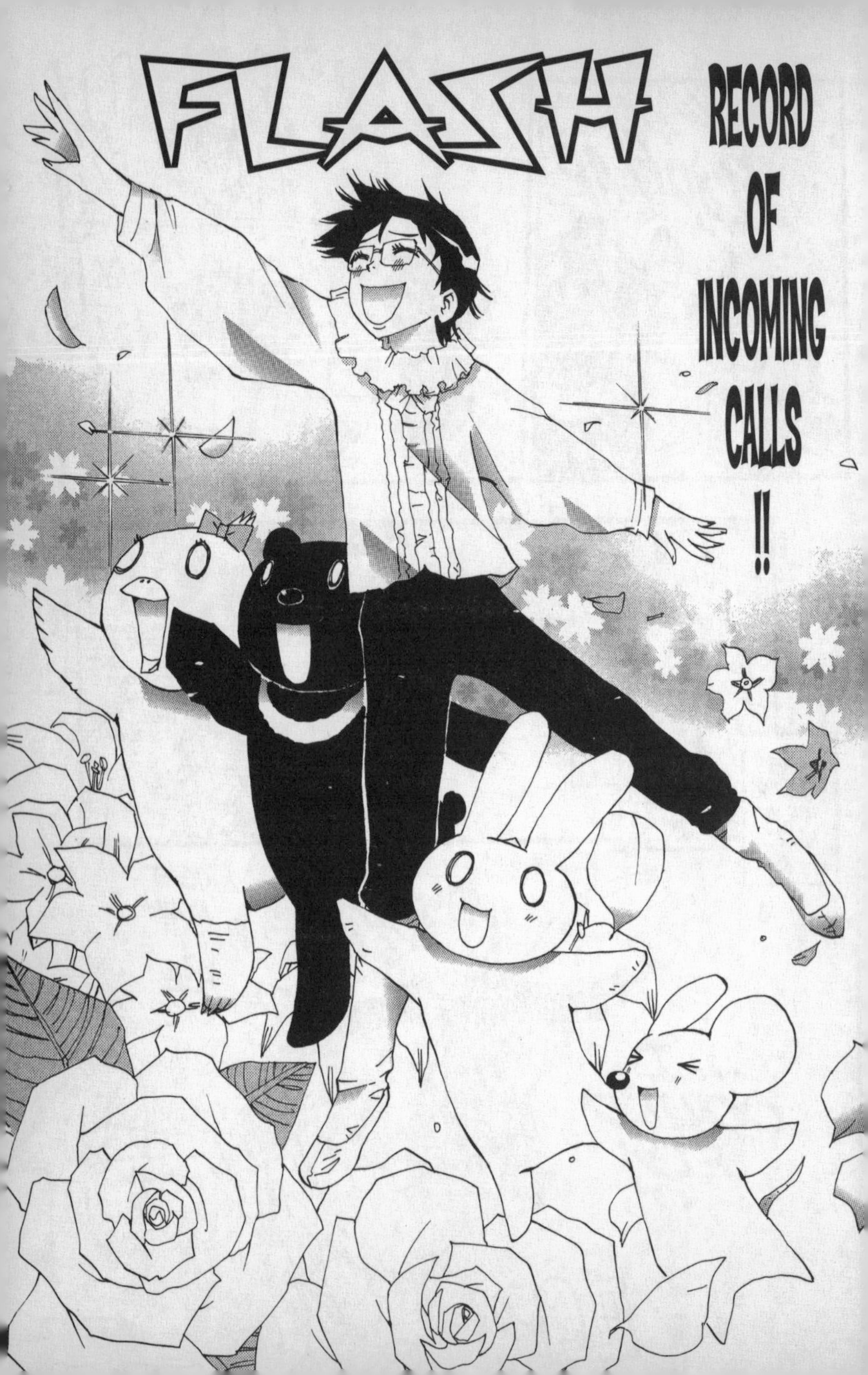
FLASH
RECORD OF INCOMING CALLS !!

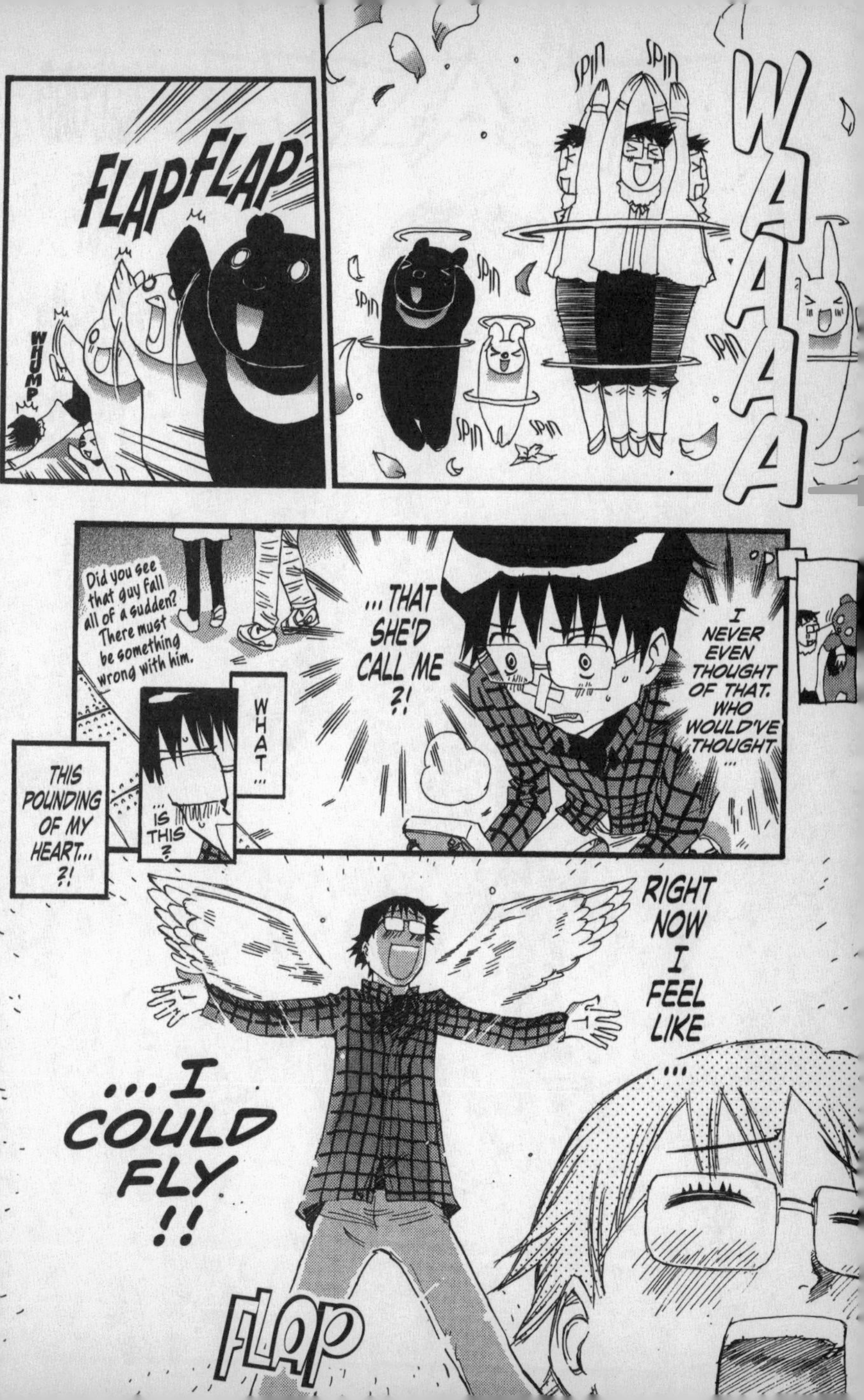
WAAAA
SPIN
SPIN
SPIN
SPIN
SPIN
SPIN
SPIN
FLAPFLAP
WHUMP
I NEVER EVEN THOUGHT OF THAT. WHO WOULD'VE THOUGHT ...
...THAT SHE'D CALL ME ?!
Did you see that guy fall all of a sudden? There must be something wrong with him.
WHAT...
...IS THIS ?
THIS POUNDING OF MY HEART... ?!
RIGHT NOW I FEEL LIKE ...
...I COULD FLY !!
FLAP

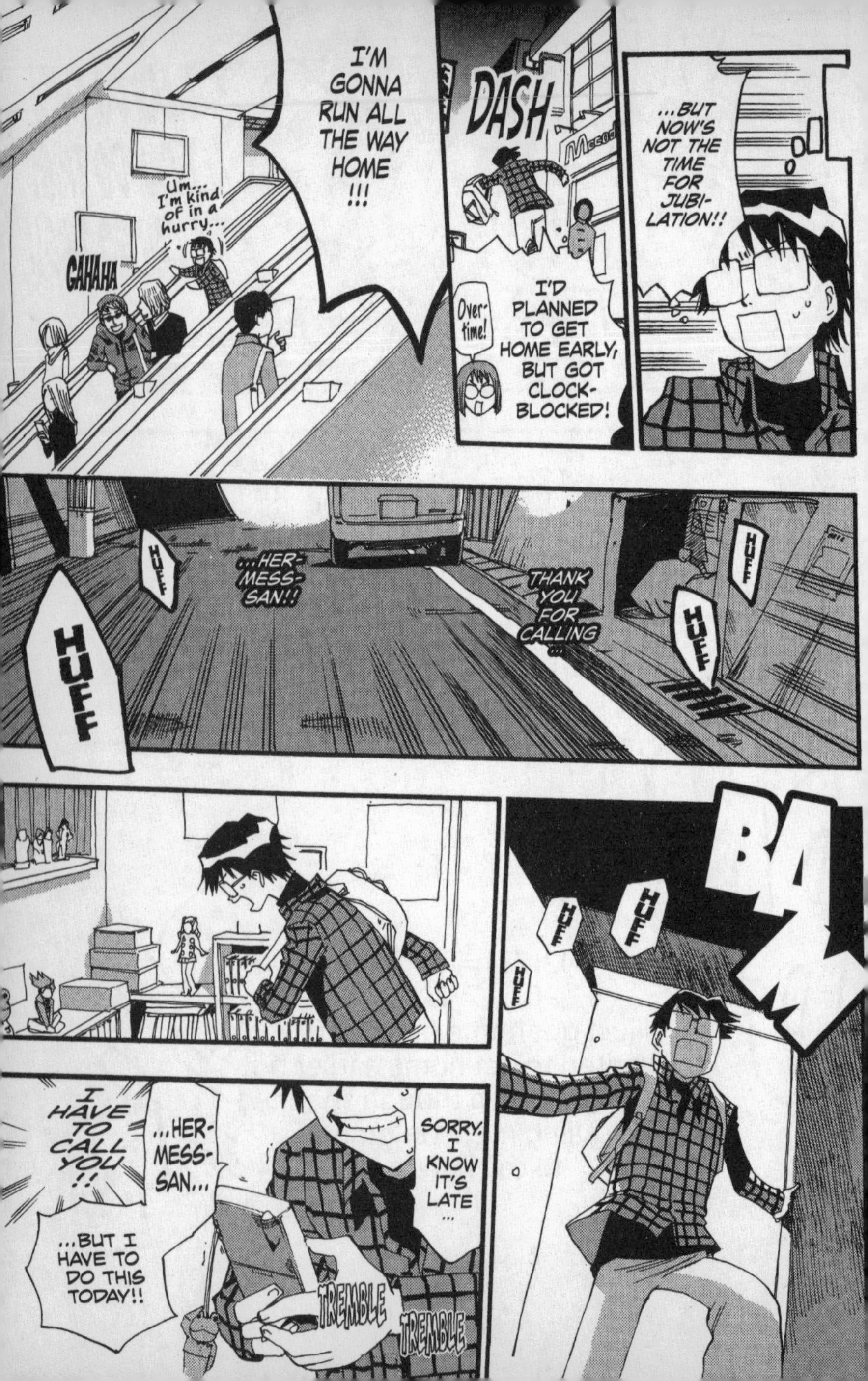
...BUT NOW'S NOT THE TIME FOR JUBILATION!!
DASH
I'D PLANNED TO GET HOME EARLY, BUT GOT CLOCK-BLOCKED!
Over-time!
I'M GONNA RUN ALL THE WAY HOME !!!
Um... I'm kind of in a hurry...
GAHAHA
HUFF
HUFF
THANK YOU FOR CALLING ...
...HER-MESS-SAN!!
HUFF
HUFF
BAM
HUFF
HUFF
HUFF
SORRY. I KNOW IT'S LATE ...
...HER-MESS-SAN...
I HAVE TO CALL YOU!!
...BUT I HAVE TO DO THIS TODAY!!
TREMBLE
TREMBLE

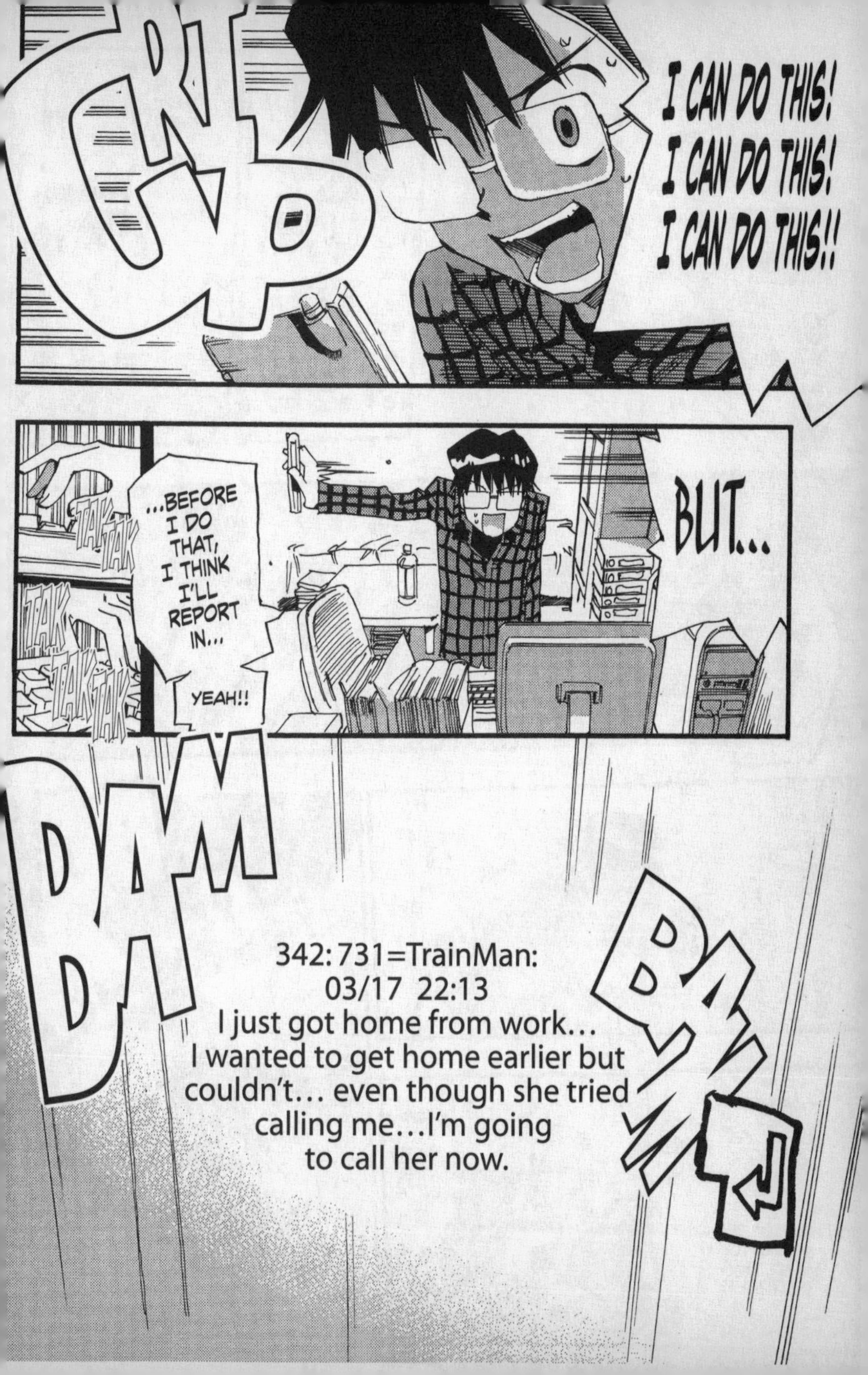

I CAN DO THIS! I CAN DO THIS! I CAN DO THIS!!
CRIP
BUT...
...BEFORE I DO THAT, I THINK I'LL REPORT IN... YEAH!!
TAK TAK
TAK TAK TAK TAK
BAM
DAM
342: 731=TrainMan:
03/17 22:13
I just got home from work…
I wanted to get home earlier but
couldn't… even though she tried
calling me…I'm going
to call her now.

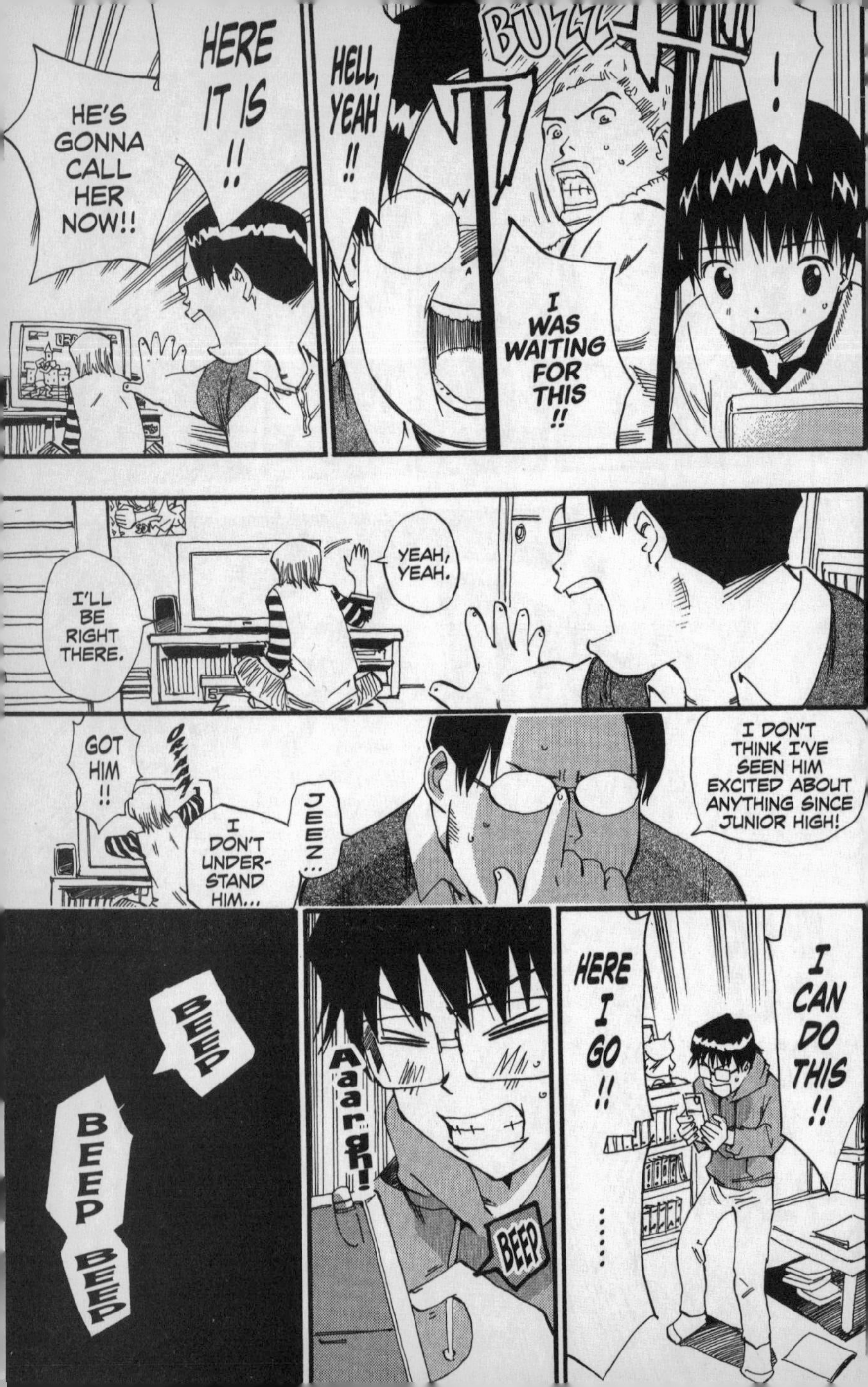
!
BUZZ
I WAS WAITING FOR THIS!!
HELL, YEAH!!
HERE IT IS!!
HE'S GONNA CALL HER NOW!!
YEAH, YEAH.
I'LL BE RIGHT THERE.
I DON'T THINK I'VE SEEN HIM EXCITED ABOUT ANYTHING SINCE JUNIOR HIGH!
JEEZ...
I DON'T UNDER-STAND HIM...
GOT HIM!!
I CAN DO THIS!!
HERE I GO!!
......
BEEP
Aaargh!
BEEP
BEEP BEEP BEEP

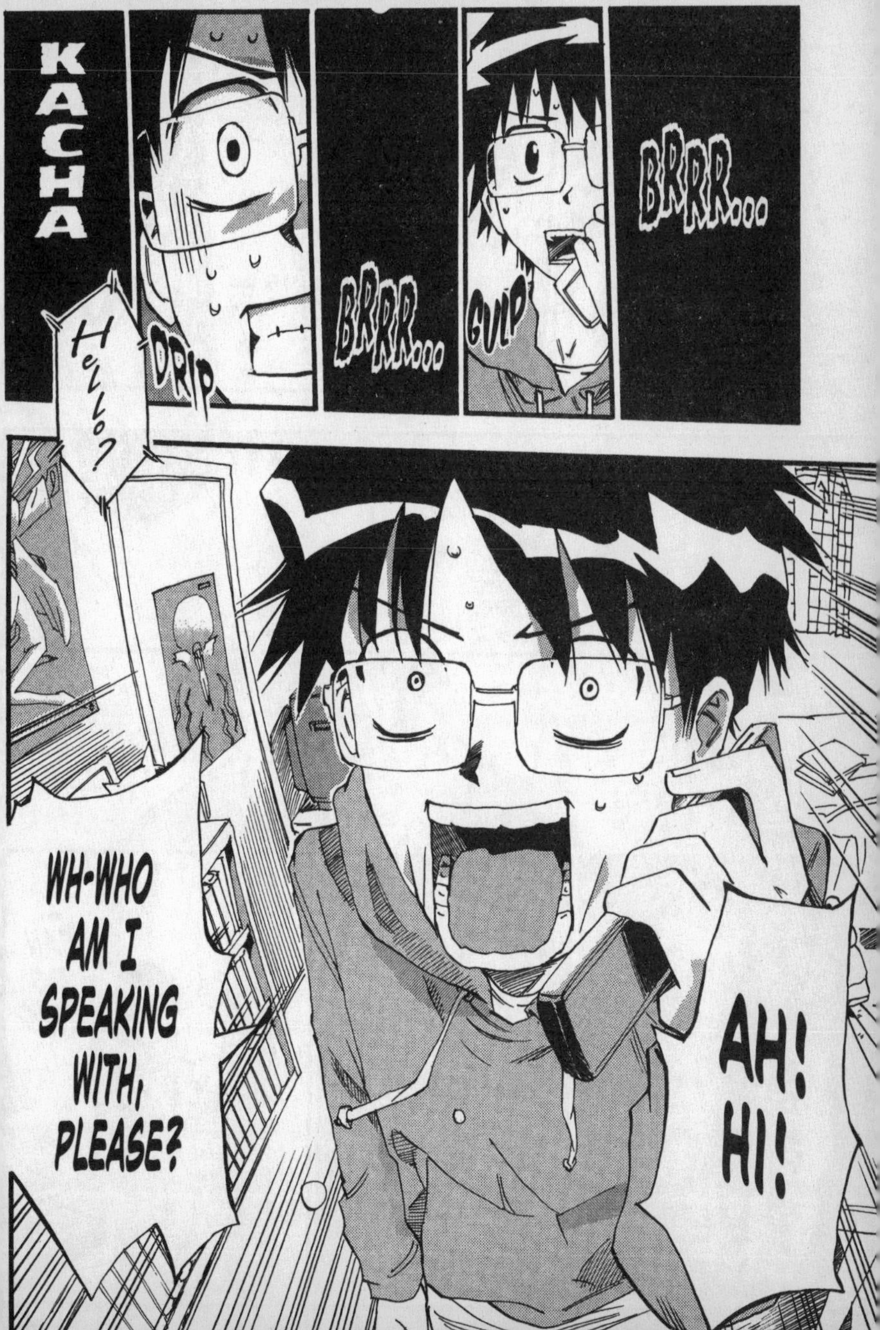
BRRR...
GULP
BRRR...
DRIP
KACHA
Hello?
AH! HI!
WH-WHO AM I SPEAKING WITH, PLEASE?

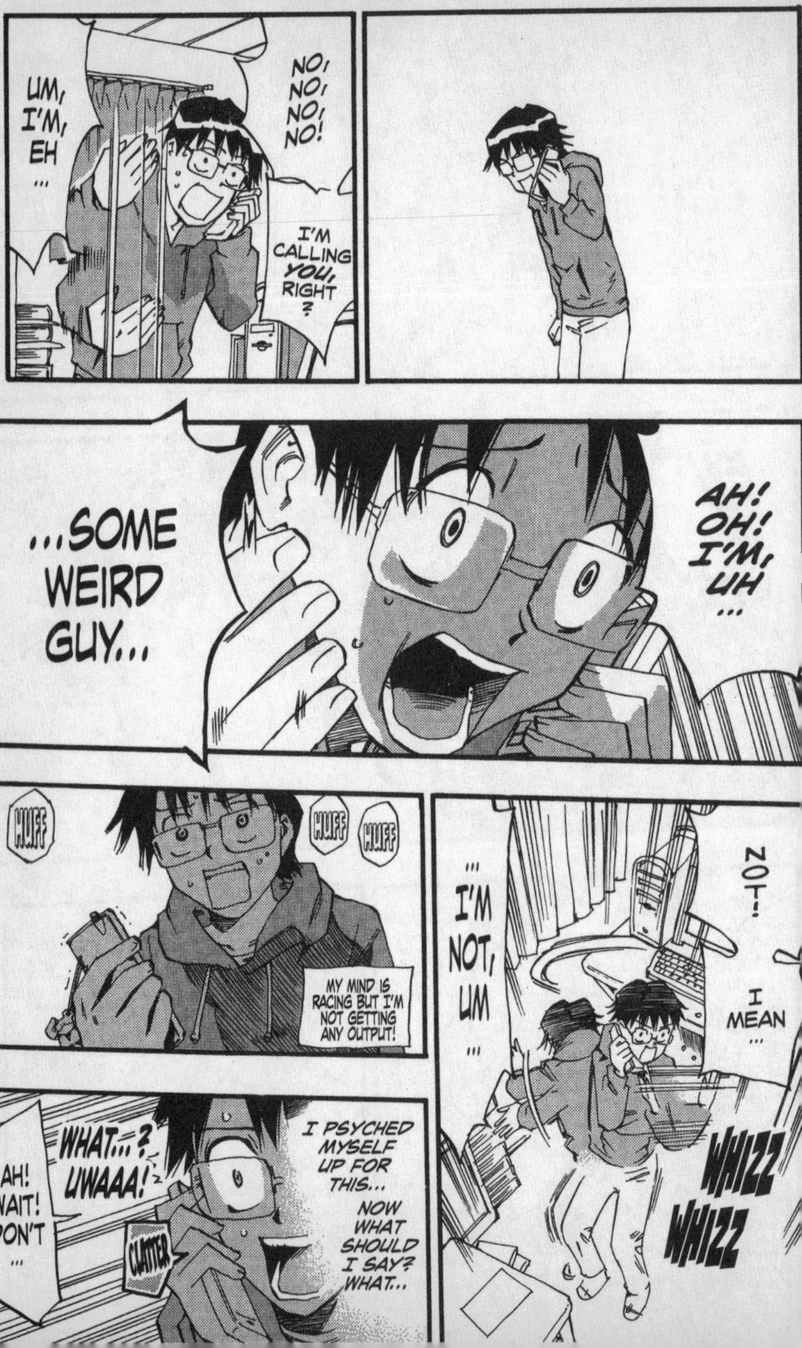
NO, NO, NO, NO!
UM, I'M, EH ...
I'M CALLING YOU, RIGHT?
AH! OH! I'M, UH ...
...SOME WEIRD GUY...
NOT!
I MEAN ...
... I'M NOT, UM ...
WHIZZ
WHIZZ
HUFF
HUFF
HUFF
MY MIND IS RACING BUT I'M NOT GETTING ANY OUTPUT!
I PSYCHED MYSELF UP FOR THIS...
NOW WHAT SHOULD I SAY? WHAT...
WHAT...?
UWAAA!
CLATTER
AH! WAIT! DON'T ...

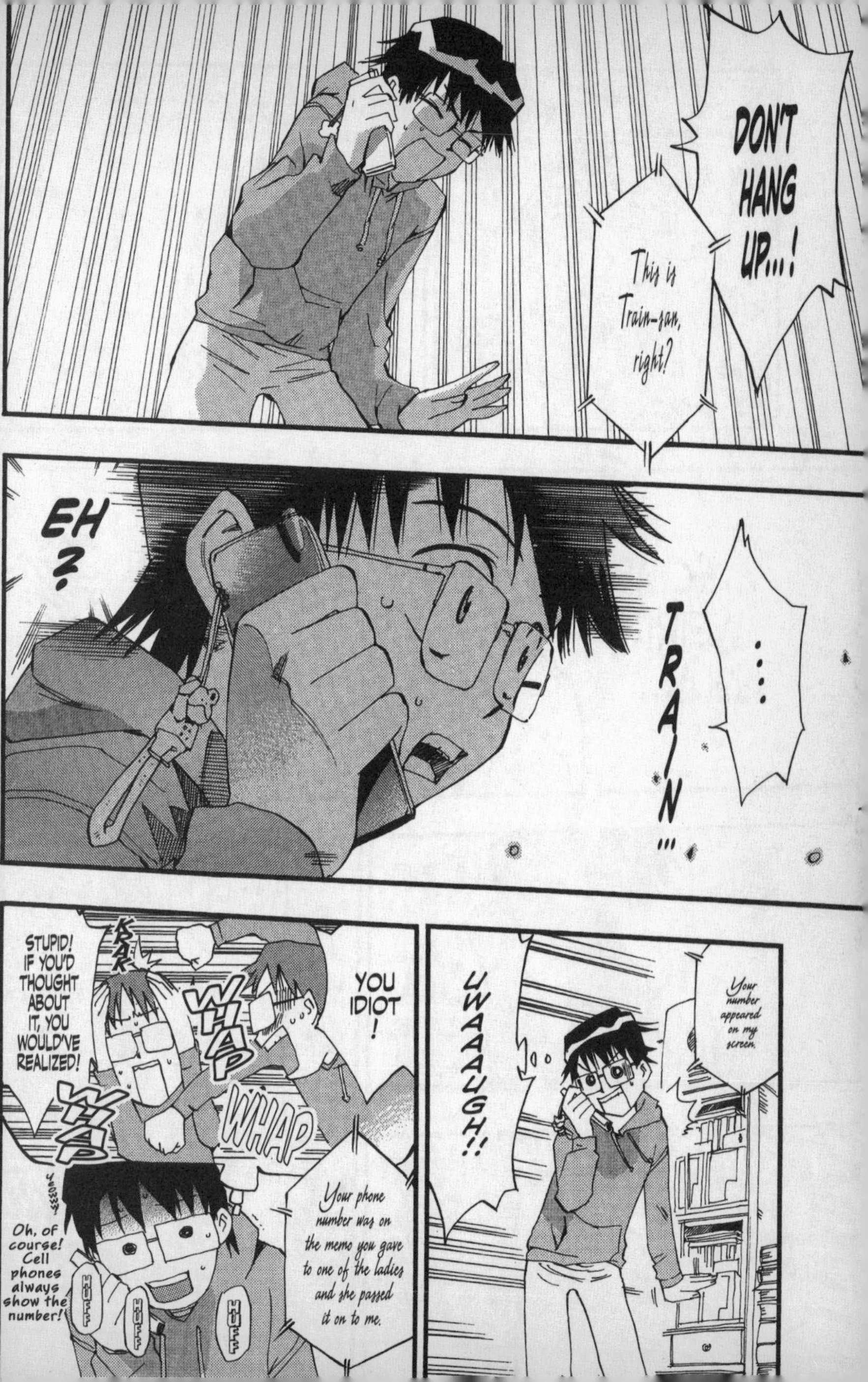
DON'T HANG UP...!
This is Train-san, right?
...
TRAIN...!
EH?
Your number appeared on my screen.
UWAAAUGH!!
Your phone number was on the memo you gave to one of the ladies and she passed it on to me.
YOU IDIOT!
WHAP
KRAK
STUPID! IF YOU'D THOUGHT ABOUT IT, YOU WOULD'VE REALIZED!
WHAP
WHAP
Oh, of course! Cell phones always show the number!
HUFF
HUFF
HUFF

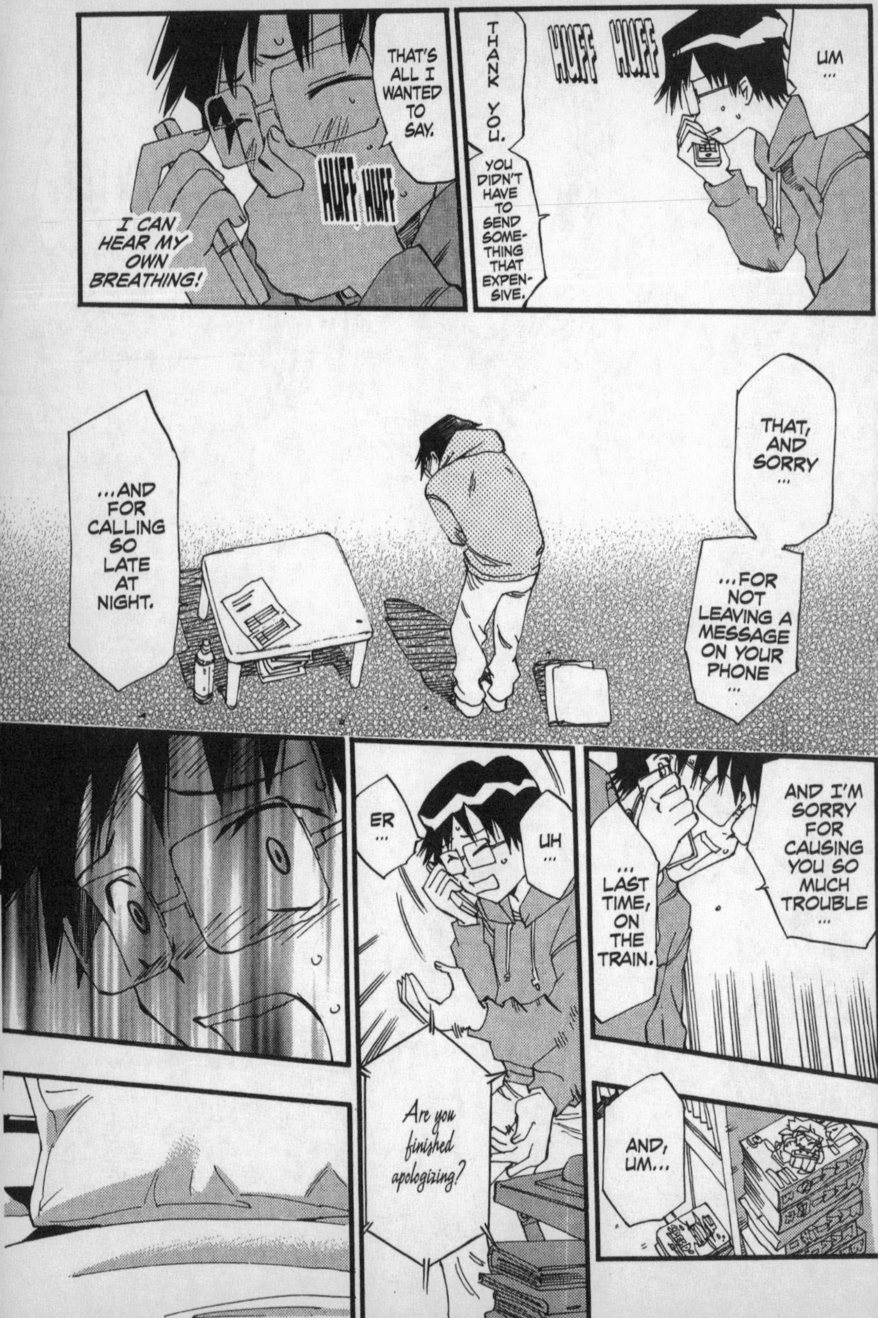
UM ...
HUFF HUFF
THANK YOU.
YOU DIDN'T HAVE TO SEND SOMETHING THAT EXPENSIVE.
THAT'S ALL I WANTED TO SAY.
HUFF HUFF
I CAN HEAR MY OWN BREATHING!
THAT, AND SORRY ...
...FOR NOT LEAVING A MESSAGE ON YOUR PHONE ...
...AND FOR CALLING SO LATE AT NIGHT.
AND I'M SORRY FOR CAUSING YOU SO MUCH TROUBLE ...
... LAST TIME, ON THE TRAIN.
AND, UM...
UH ...
ER ...
Are you finished apologizing?

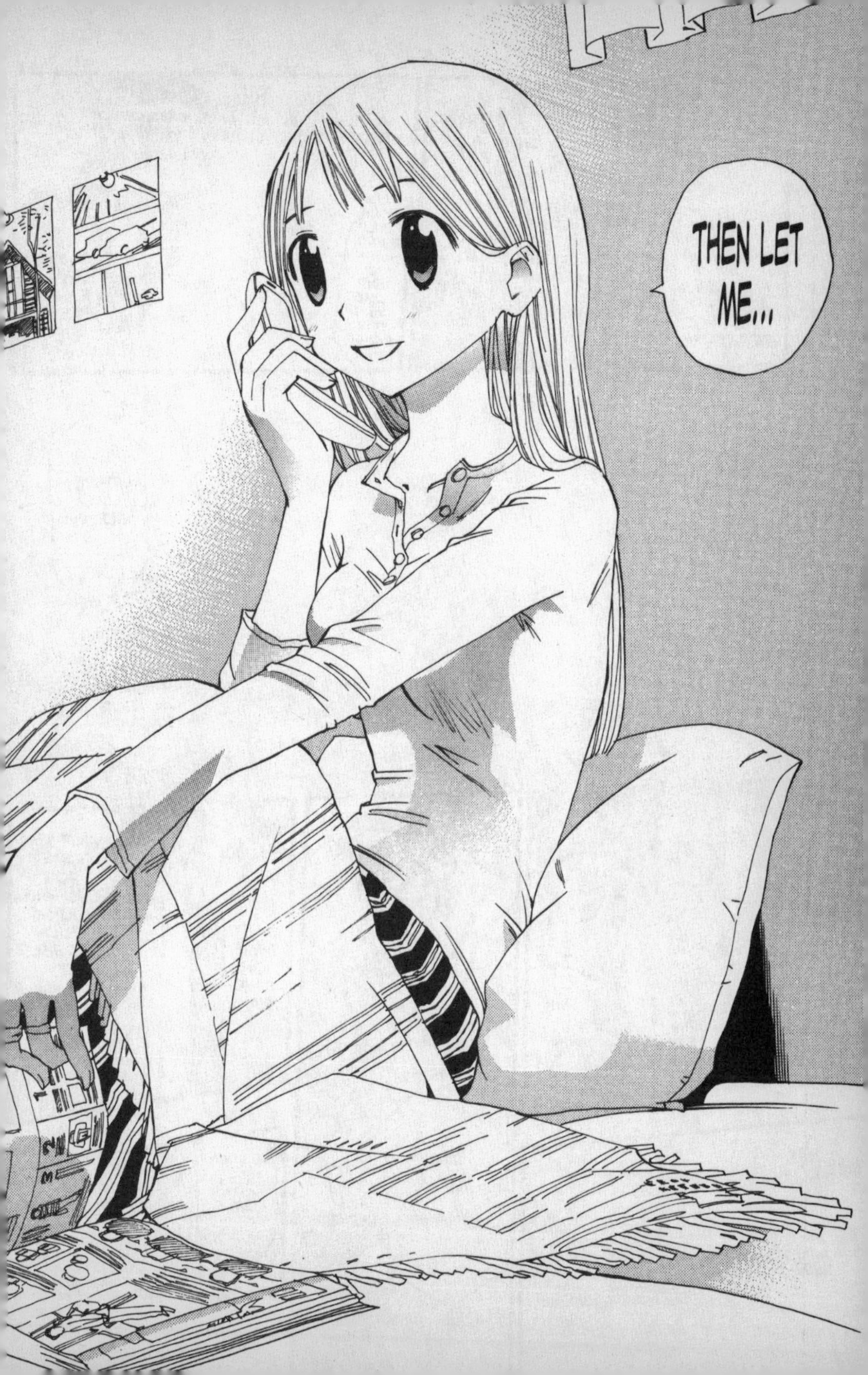
THEN LET ME...

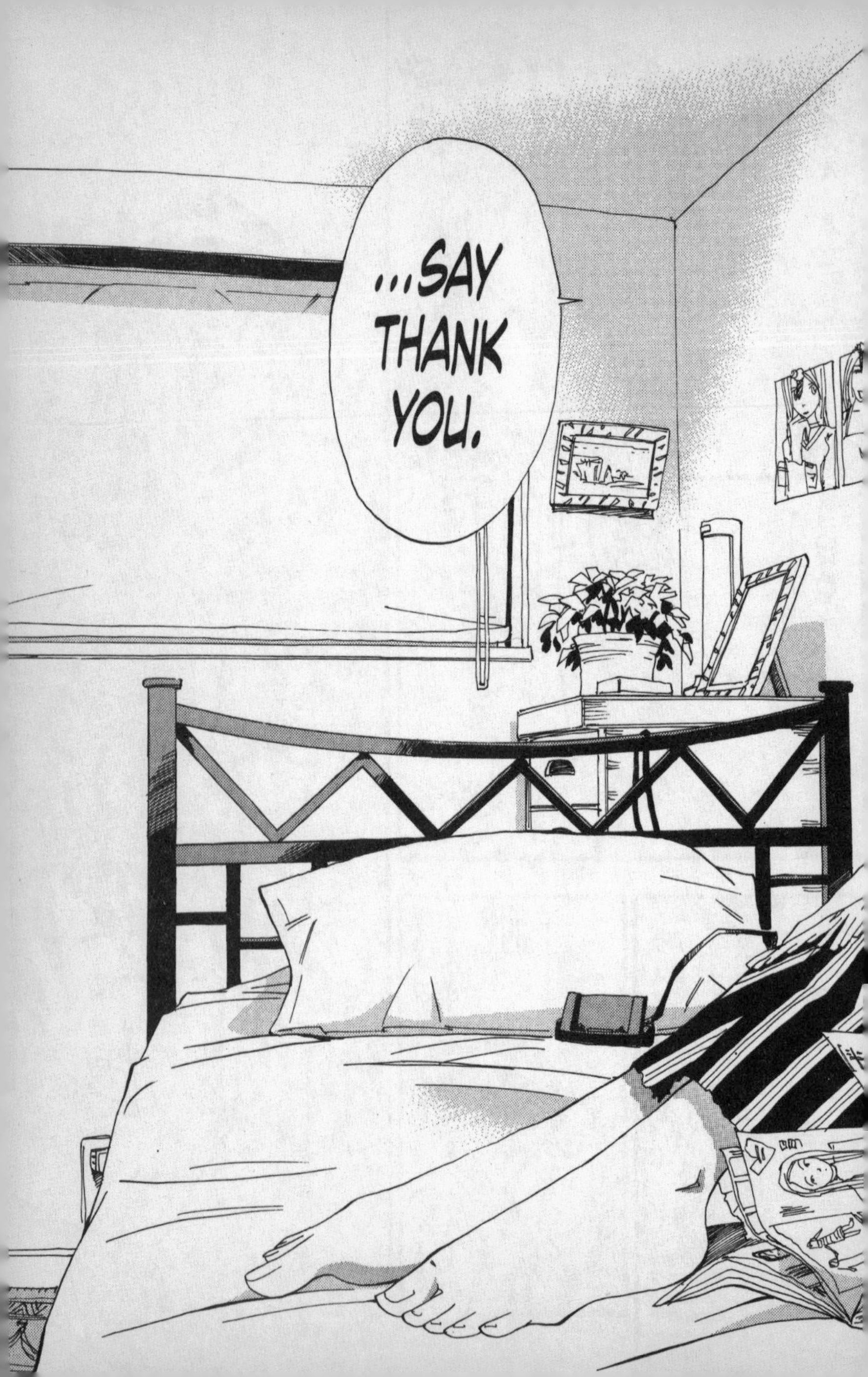
...SAY THANK YOU.

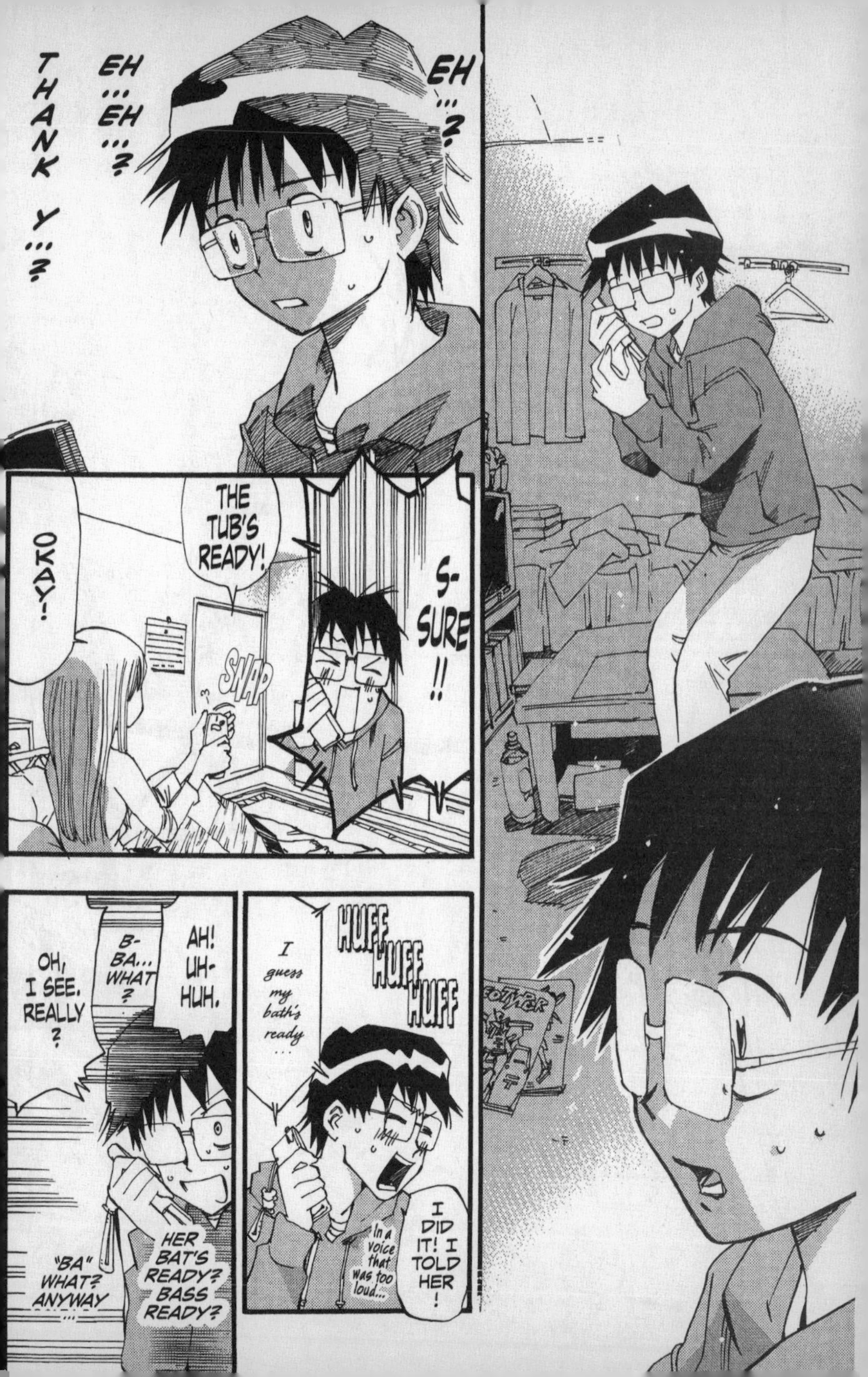
EH ...?
EH ... EH ...?
THANK Y...?
THE TUB'S READY!
S-SURE!!
OKAY!
SNAP
HUFF HUFF HUFF
I guess my bath's ready ...
I DID IT! I TOLD HER!
In a voice that was too loud...
AH! UH-HUH.
B-BA... WHAT?
OH, I SEE. REALLY?
HER BAT'S READY? BASS READY?
"BA" WHAT? ANYWAY ...

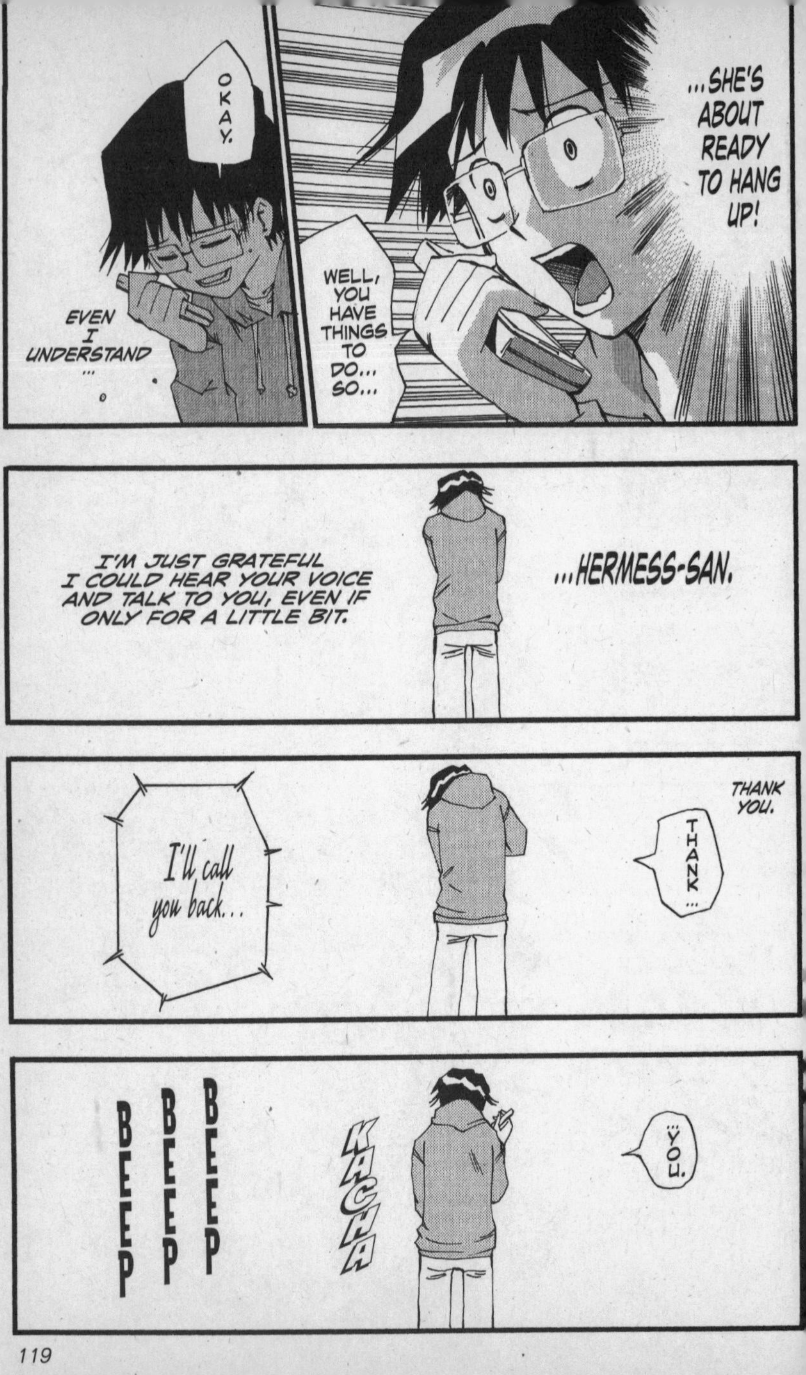
...SHE'S ABOUT READY TO HANG UP!
WELL, YOU HAVE THINGS TO DO... SO...
OKAY.
EVEN I UNDERSTAND...
...HERMESS-SAN.
I'M JUST GRATEFUL I COULD HEAR YOUR VOICE AND TALK TO YOU, EVEN IF ONLY FOR A LITTLE BIT.
THANK YOU.
THANK...
I'll call you back...
...YOU.
KACHA
BEEP
BEEP
BEEP

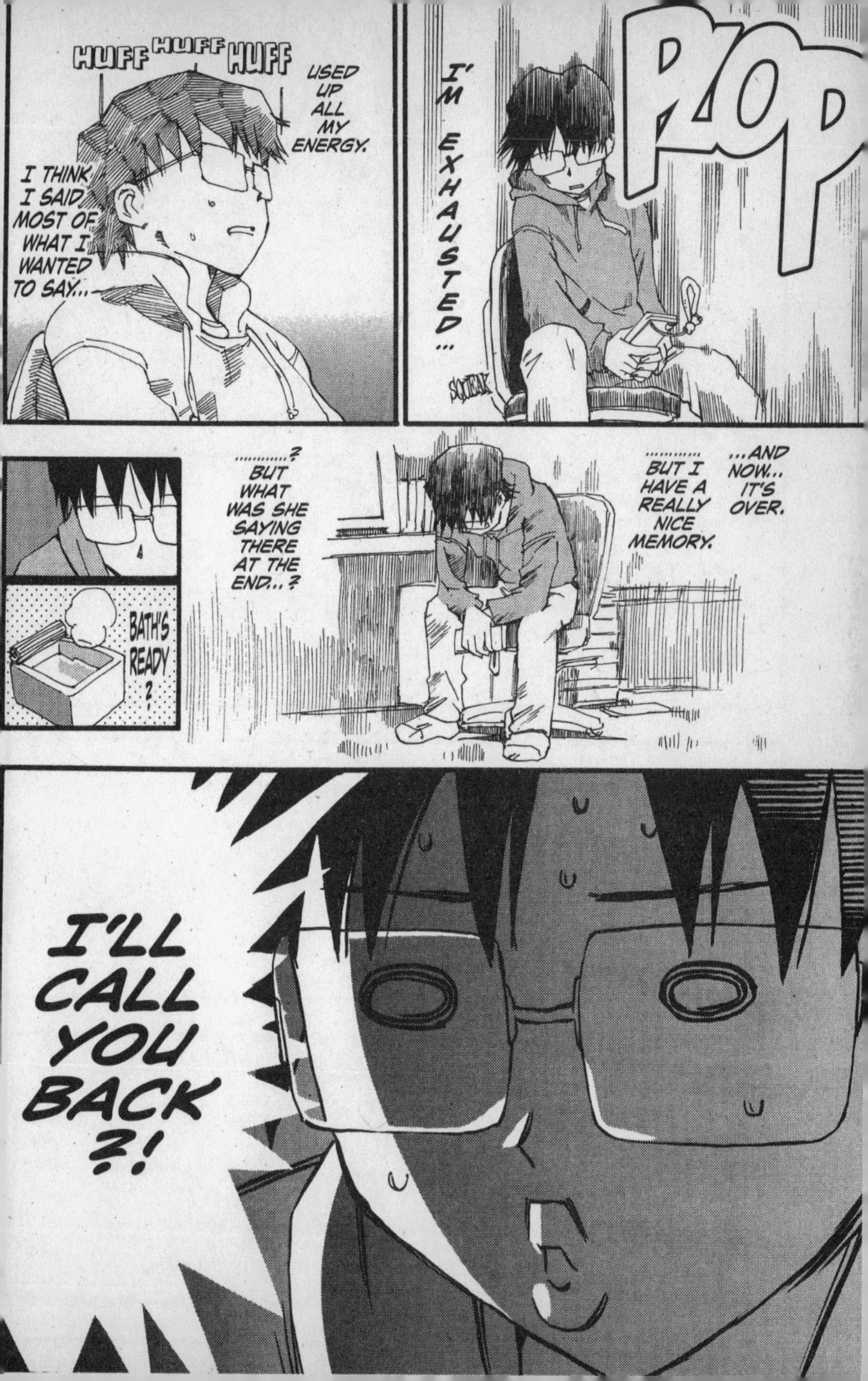
PLOP
I'M EXHAUSTED...
SQUEAK
HUFF HUFF HUFF
USED UP ALL MY ENERGY.
I THINK I SAID MOST OF WHAT I WANTED TO SAY...
...AND NOW... IT'S OVER.
..........BUT I HAVE A REALLY NICE MEMORY.
..........? BUT WHAT WAS SHE SAYING THERE AT THE END...?
BATH'S READY ♪
I'LL CALL YOU BACK ?!

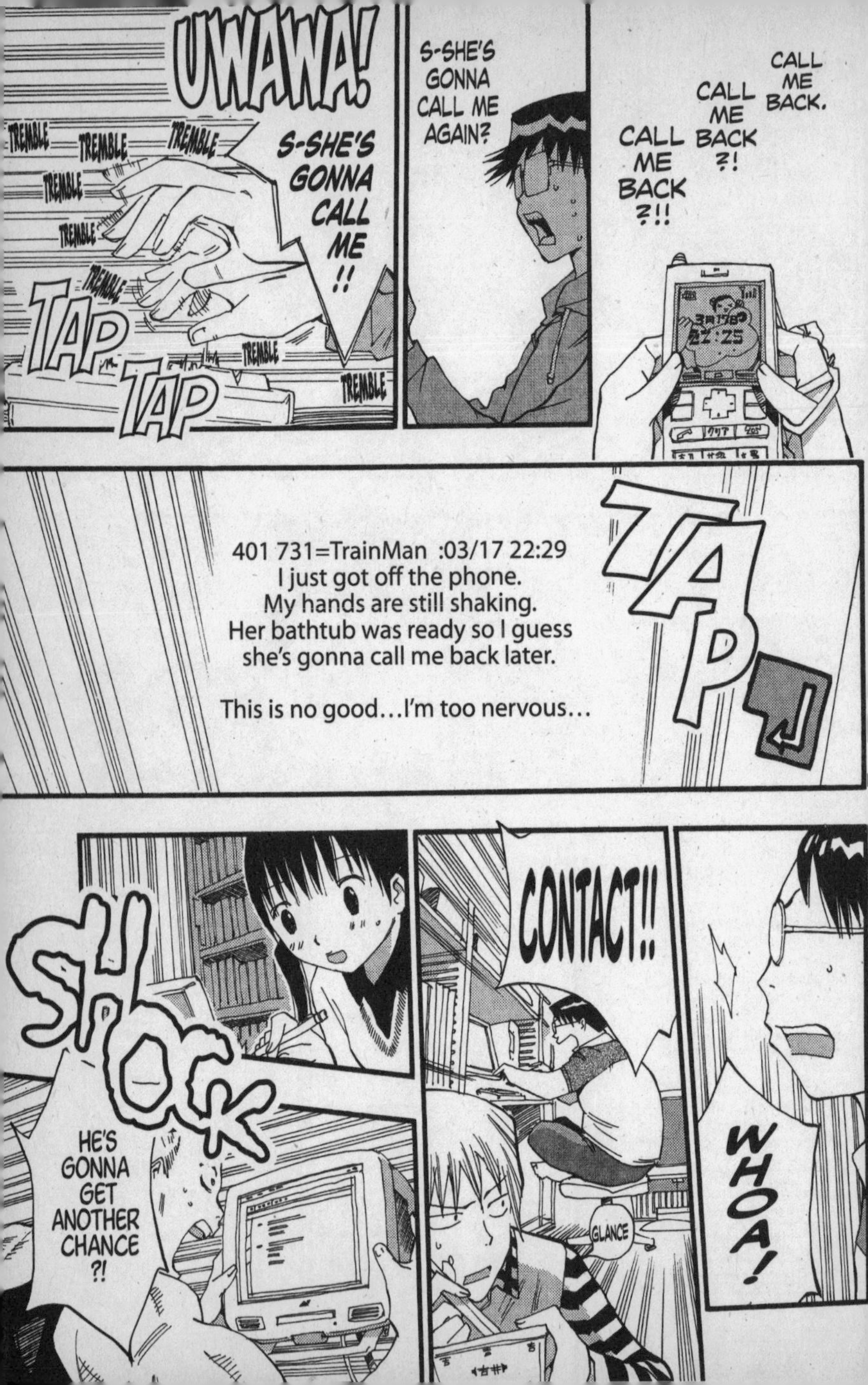
CALL ME BACK.
CALL ME BACK?!
CALL ME BACK?!!
S-SHE'S GONNA CALL ME AGAIN?
UWAWA!
S-SHE'S GONNA CALL ME!!
TREMBLE TREMBLE TREMBLE TREMBLE TREMBLE TREMBLE TREMBLE TREMBLE
TAP TAP
TAP
401 731=TrainMan :03/17 22:29
I just got off the phone.
My hands are still shaking.
Her bathtub was ready so I guess
she's gonna call me back later.
This is no good…I'm too nervous…
WHOA!
CONTACT!!
GLANCE
SHOCK
HE'S GONNA GET ANOTHER CHANCE?!

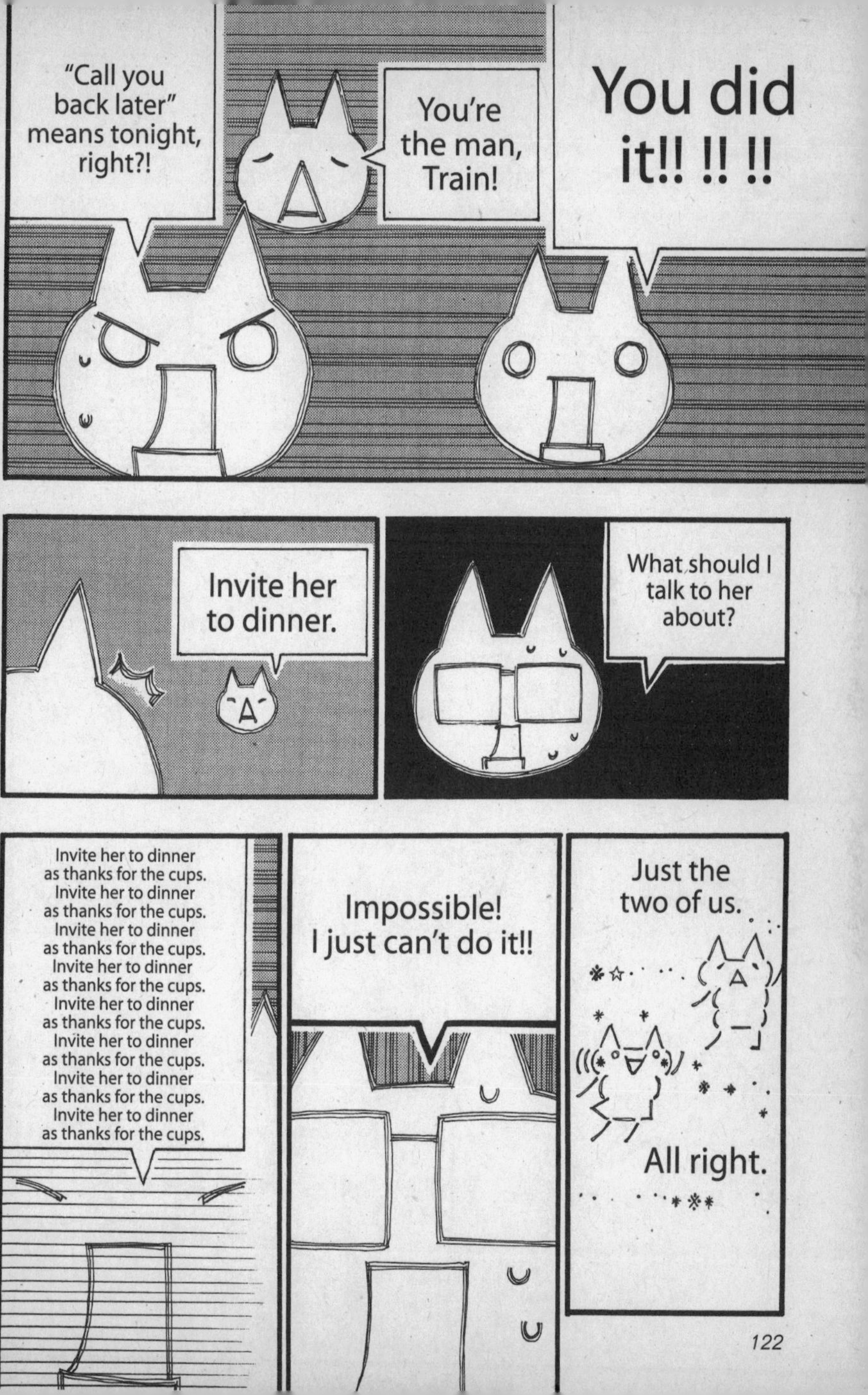
You did it!! !! !!
You're the man, Train!
"Call you back later" means tonight, right?!
What should I talk to her about?
Invite her to dinner.
Just the two of us.
All right.
Impossible! I just can't do it!!
Invite her to dinner as thanks for the cups. Invite her to dinner as thanks for the cups. Invite her to dinner as thanks for the cups. Invite her to dinner as thanks for the cups. Invite her to dinner as thanks for the cups. Invite her to dinner as thanks for the cups. Invite her to dinner as thanks for the cups. Invite her to dinner as thanks for the cups.

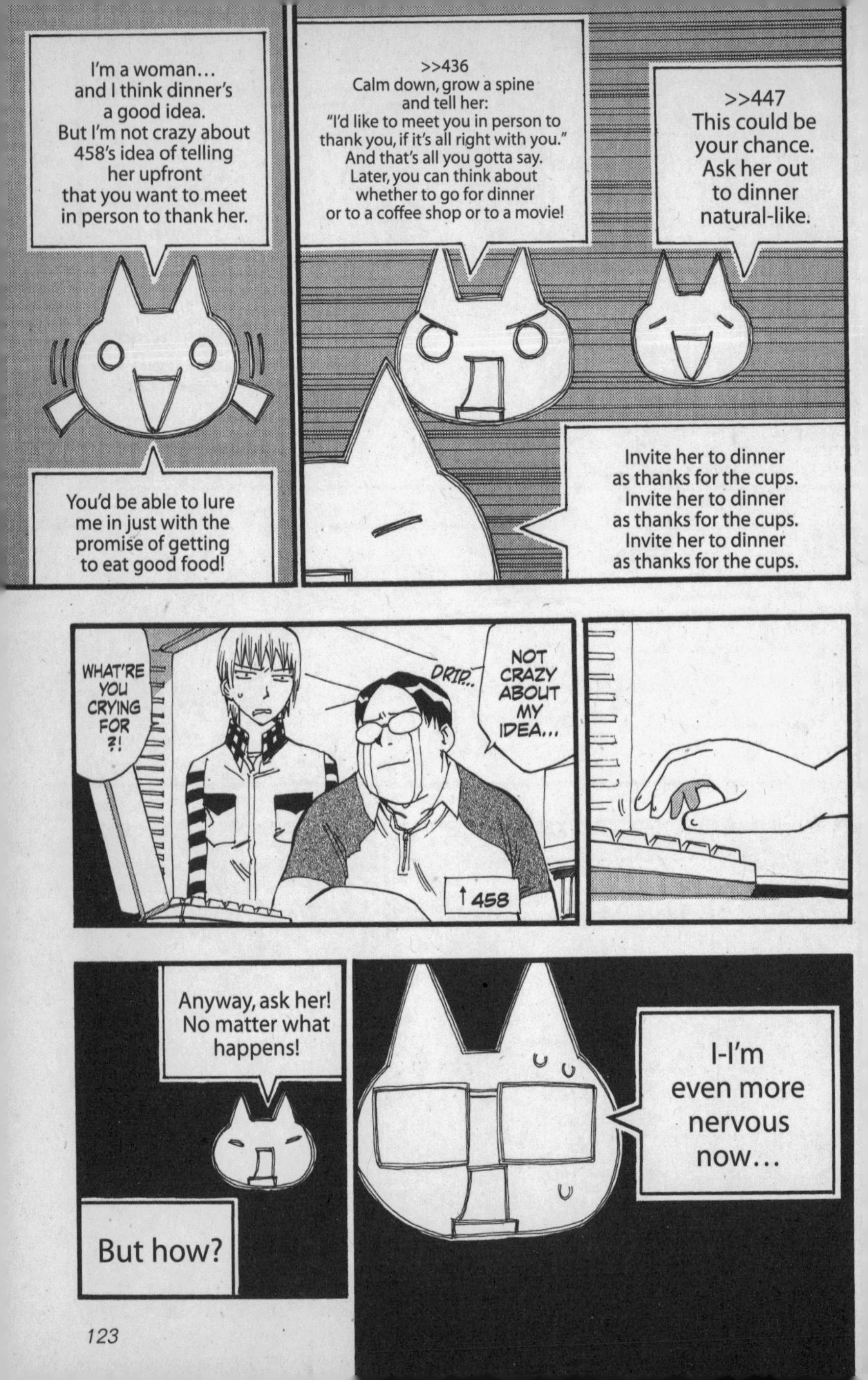
>>447 This could be your chance. Ask her out to dinner natural-like.
>>436 Calm down, grow a spine and tell her: "I'd like to meet you in person to thank you, if it's all right with you." And that's all you gotta say. Later, you can think about whether to go for dinner or to a coffee shop or to a movie!
Invite her to dinner as thanks for the cups. Invite her to dinner as thanks for the cups. Invite her to dinner as thanks for the cups.
I'm a woman… and I think dinner's a good idea. But I'm not crazy about 458's idea of telling her upfront that you want to meet in person to thank her.
You'd be able to lure me in just with the promise of getting to eat good food!
NOT CRAZY ABOUT MY IDEA...
DRIP...
WHAT'RE YOU CRYING FOR ?!
↑458
I-I'm even more nervous now…
Anyway, ask her! No matter what happens!
But how?

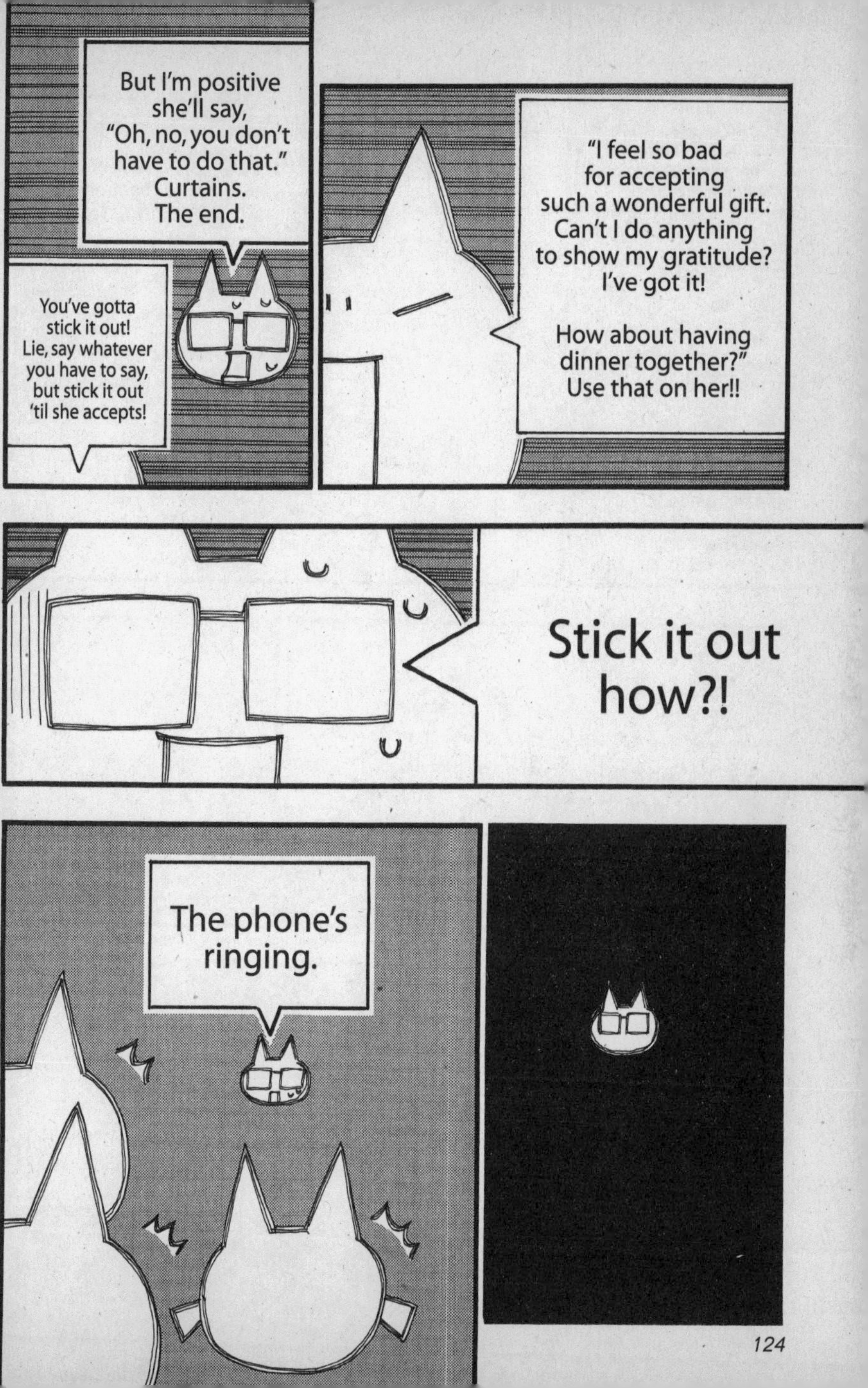
"I feel so bad for accepting such a wonderful gift. Can't I do anything to show my gratitude? I've got it!
How about having dinner together?" Use that on her!!
But I'm positive she'll say, "Oh, no, you don't have to do that." Curtains. The end.
You've gotta stick it out! Lie, say whatever you have to say, but stick it out 'til she accepts!
Stick it out how?!
The phone's ringing.

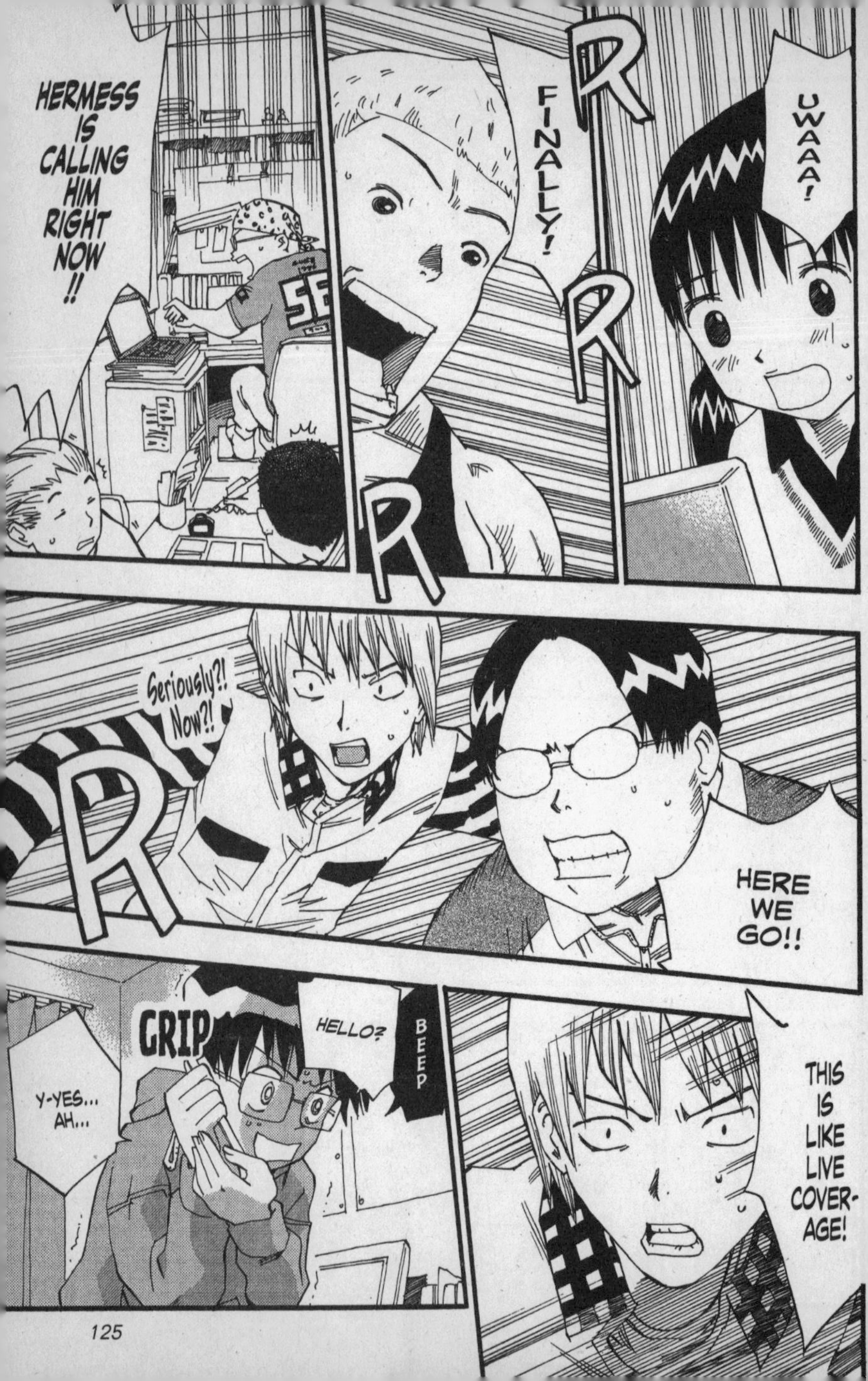
UWAAA!
R
R
FINALLY!
R
HERMESS IS CALLING HIM RIGHT NOW!!
HERE WE GO!!
Seriously?! Now?!
R
THIS IS LIKE LIVE COVER-AGE!
BEEP
HELLO?
GRIP
Y-YES... AH...

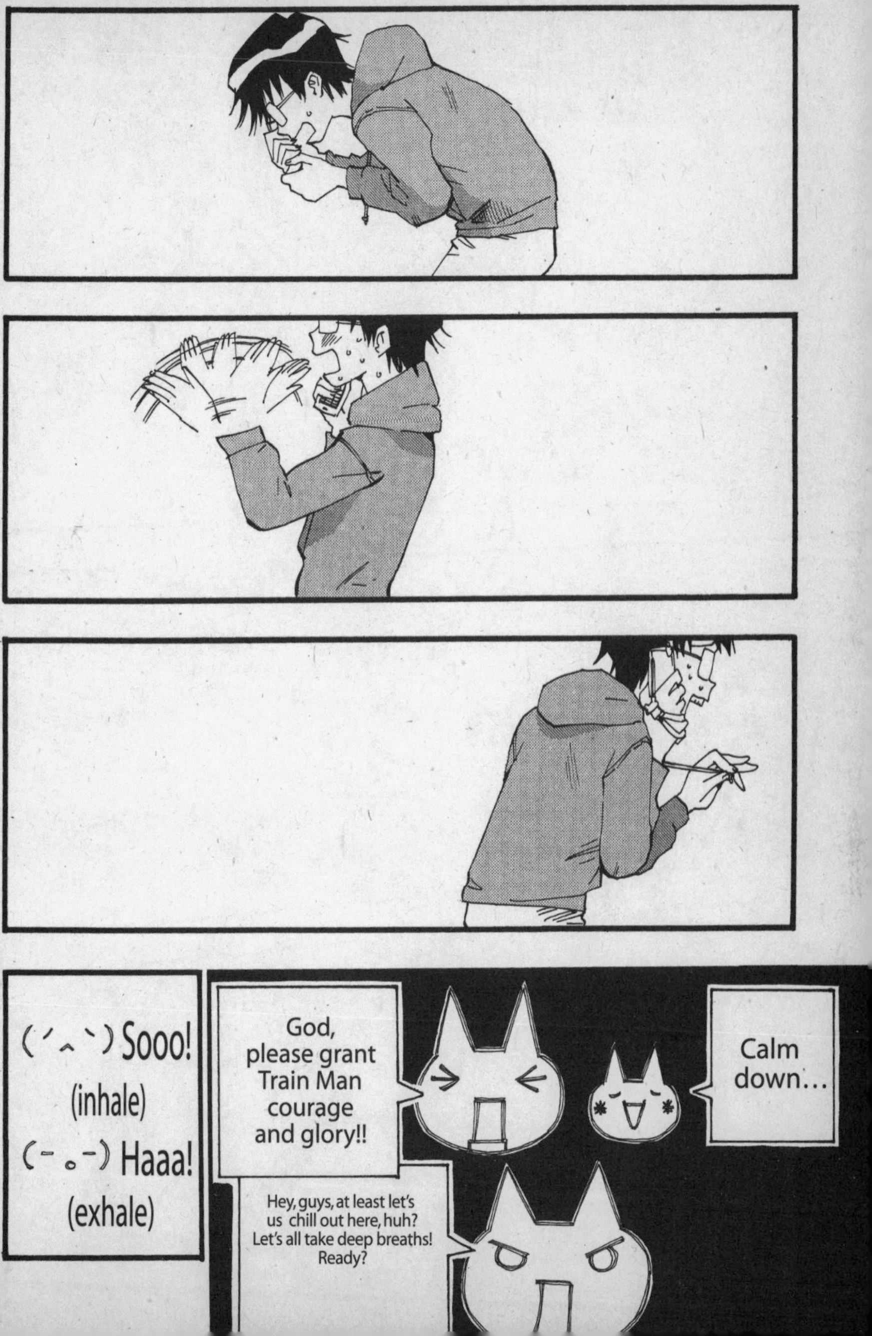
Calm down…
God, please grant Train Man courage and glory!!
Hey, guys, at least let's us chill out here, huh? Let's all take deep breaths! Ready?
(´^`) Sooo! (inhale)
(-。-) Haaa! (exhale)

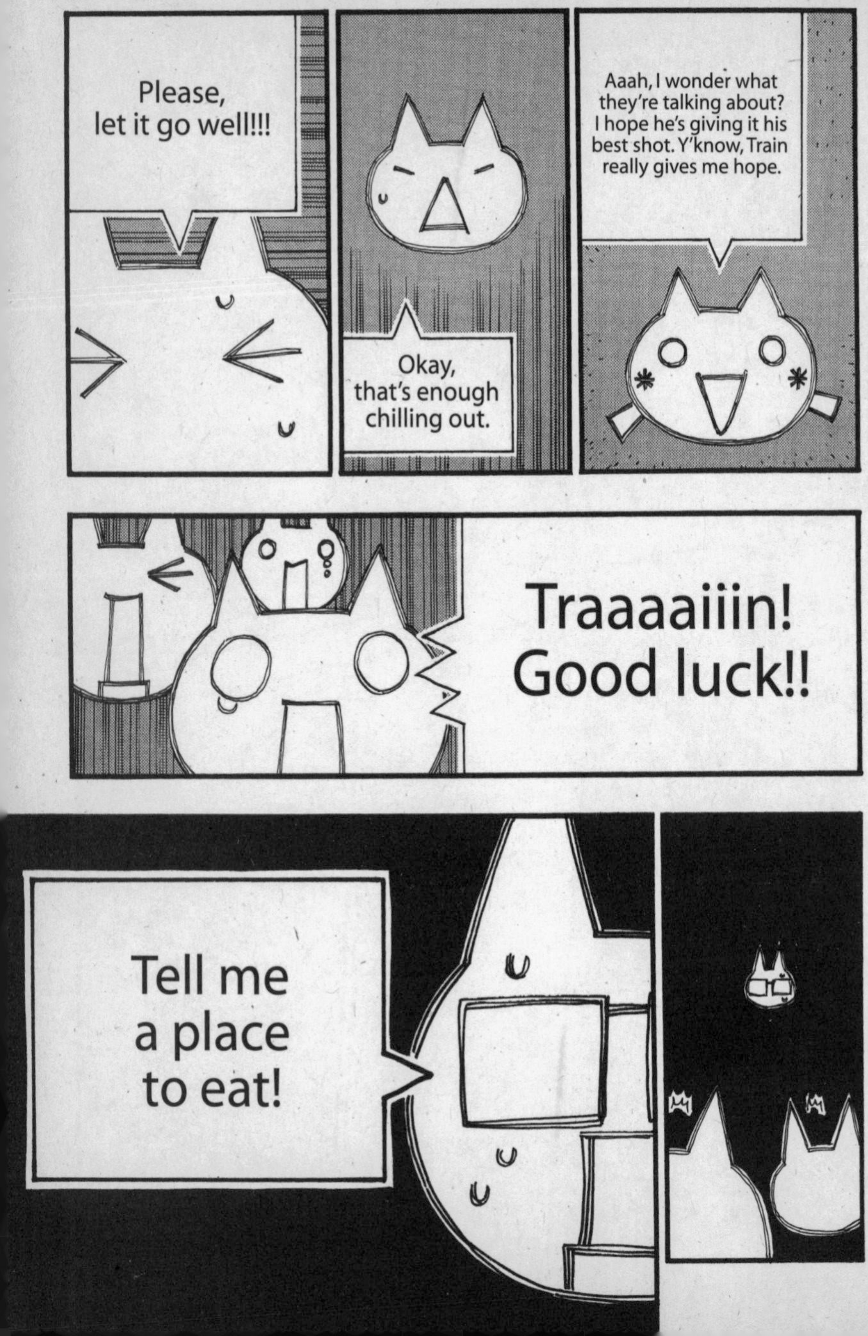
Aaah, I wonder what they're talking about? I hope he's giving it his best shot. Y'know, Train really gives me hope.
Okay, that's enough chilling out.
Please, let it go well!!!
Traaaaiiin! Good luck!!
Tell me a place to eat!

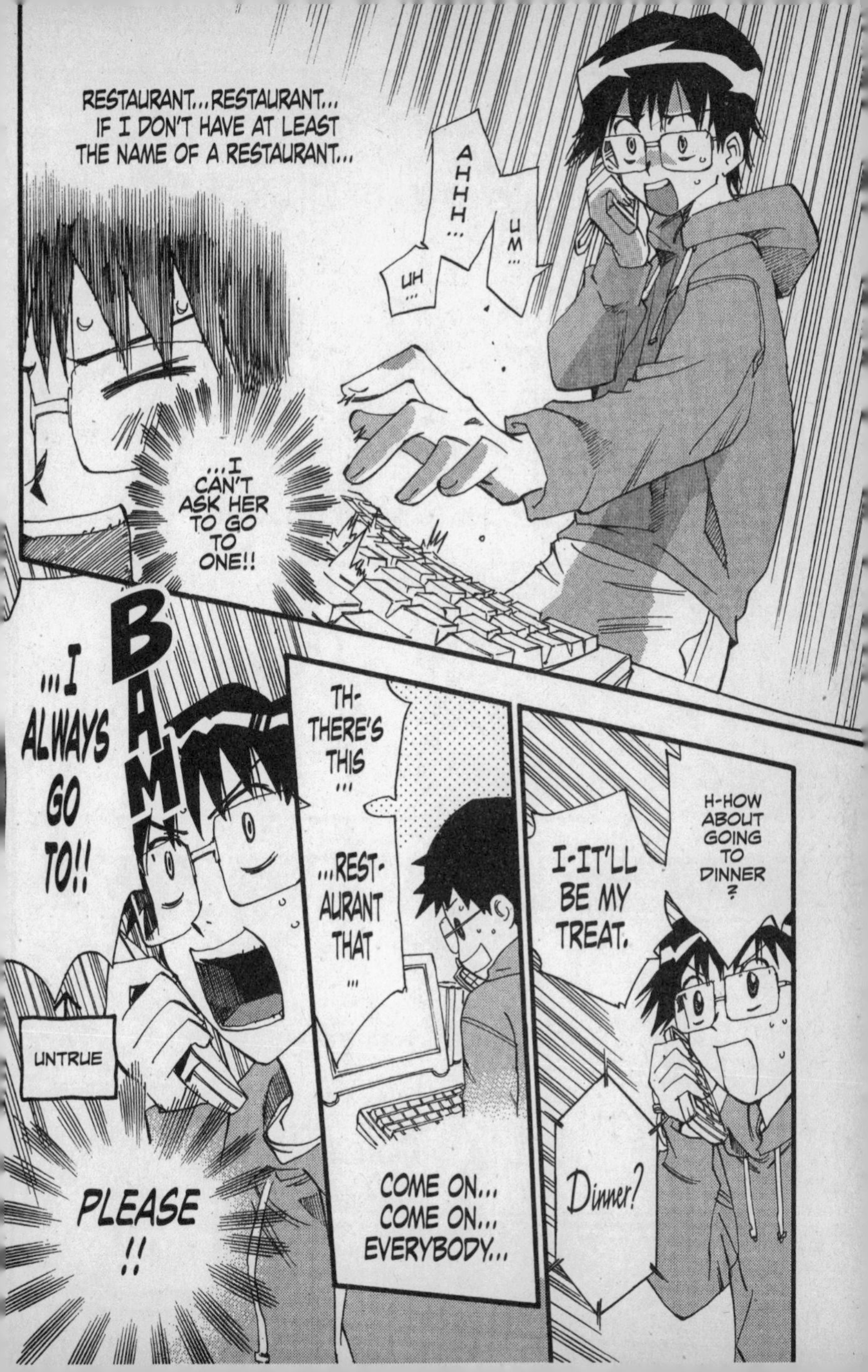
AHHH... UM...
UH...
RESTAURANT...RESTAURANT... IF I DON'T HAVE AT LEAST THE NAME OF A RESTAURANT...
...I CAN'T ASK HER TO GO TO ONE!!
H-HOW ABOUT GOING TO DINNER?
I-IT'LL BE MY TREAT.
Dinner?
TH-THERE'S THIS... ...REST-AURANT THAT...
COME ON... COME ON... EVERYBODY...
BAM
...I ALWAYS GO TO!!
UNTRUE
PLEASE!!

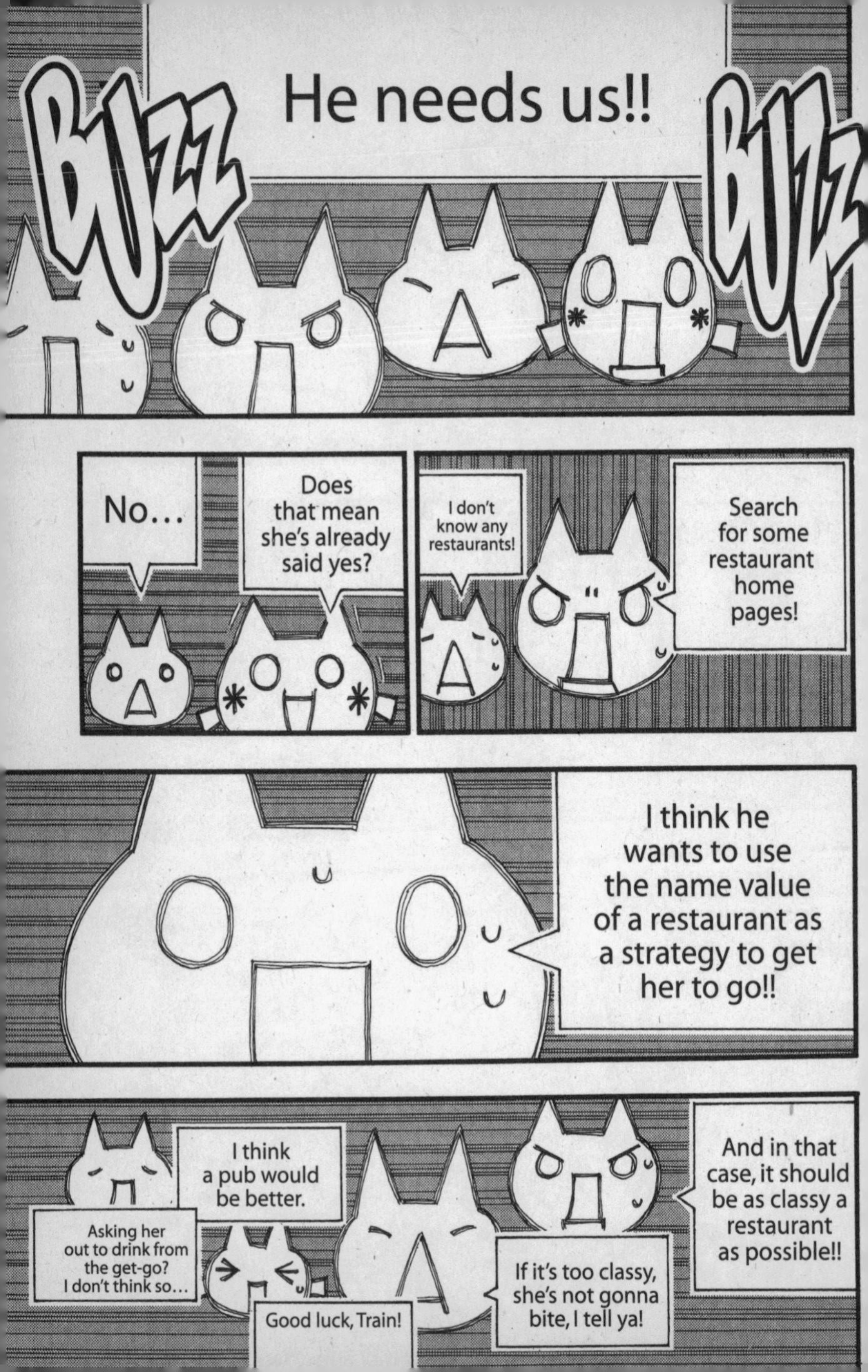
BUZZ
He needs us!!
BUZZ
Search for some restaurant home pages!
I don't know any restaurants!
Does that mean she's already said yes?
No…
I think he wants to use the name value of a restaurant as a strategy to get her to go!!
And in that case, it should be as classy a restaurant as possible!!
I think a pub would be better.
If it's too classy, she's not gonna bite, I tell ya!
Asking her out to drink from the get-go? I don't think so…
Good luck, Train!

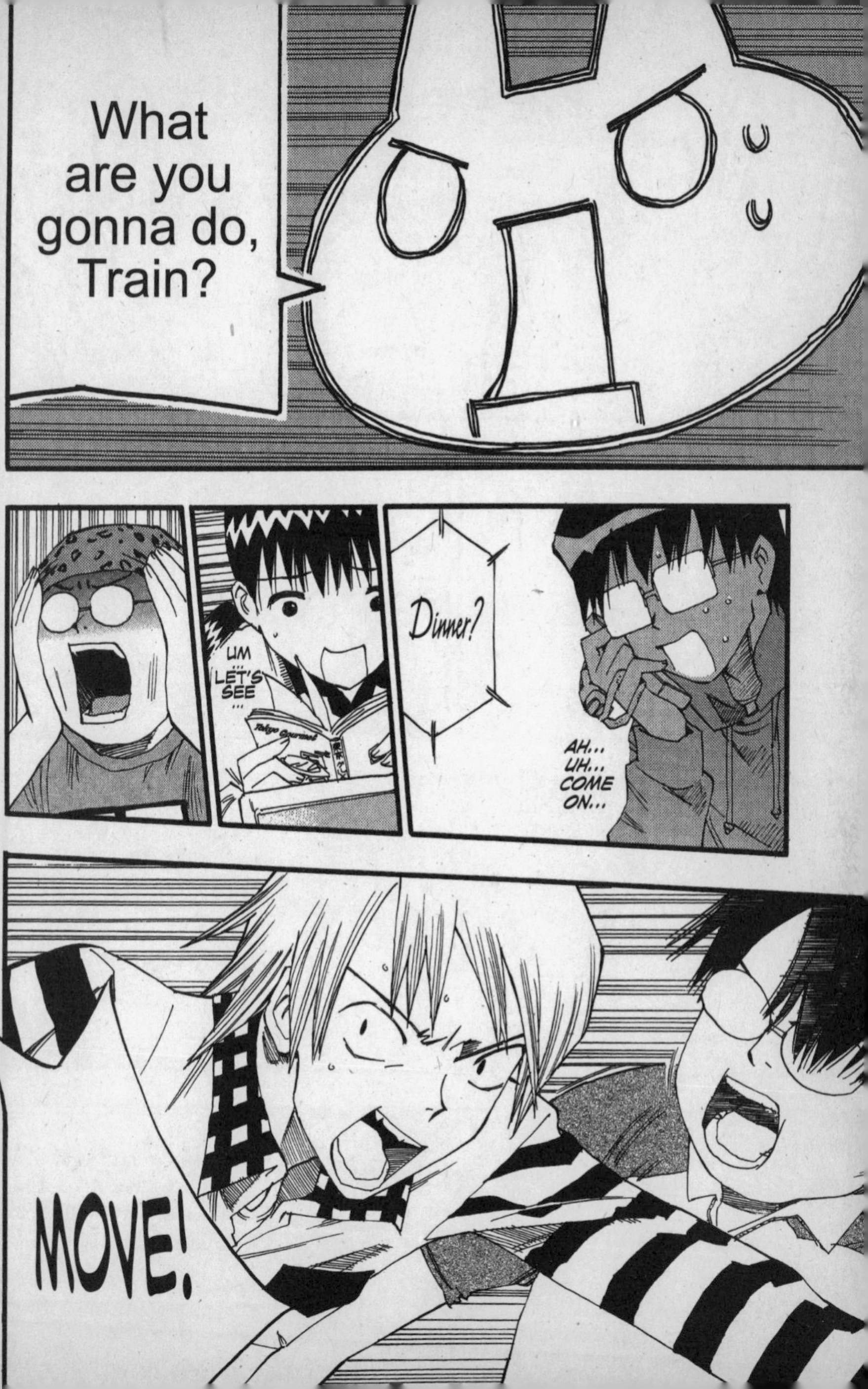
What are you gonna do, Train?
Dinner?
AH... UH... COME ON...
UM ... LET'S SEE ...
MOVE!

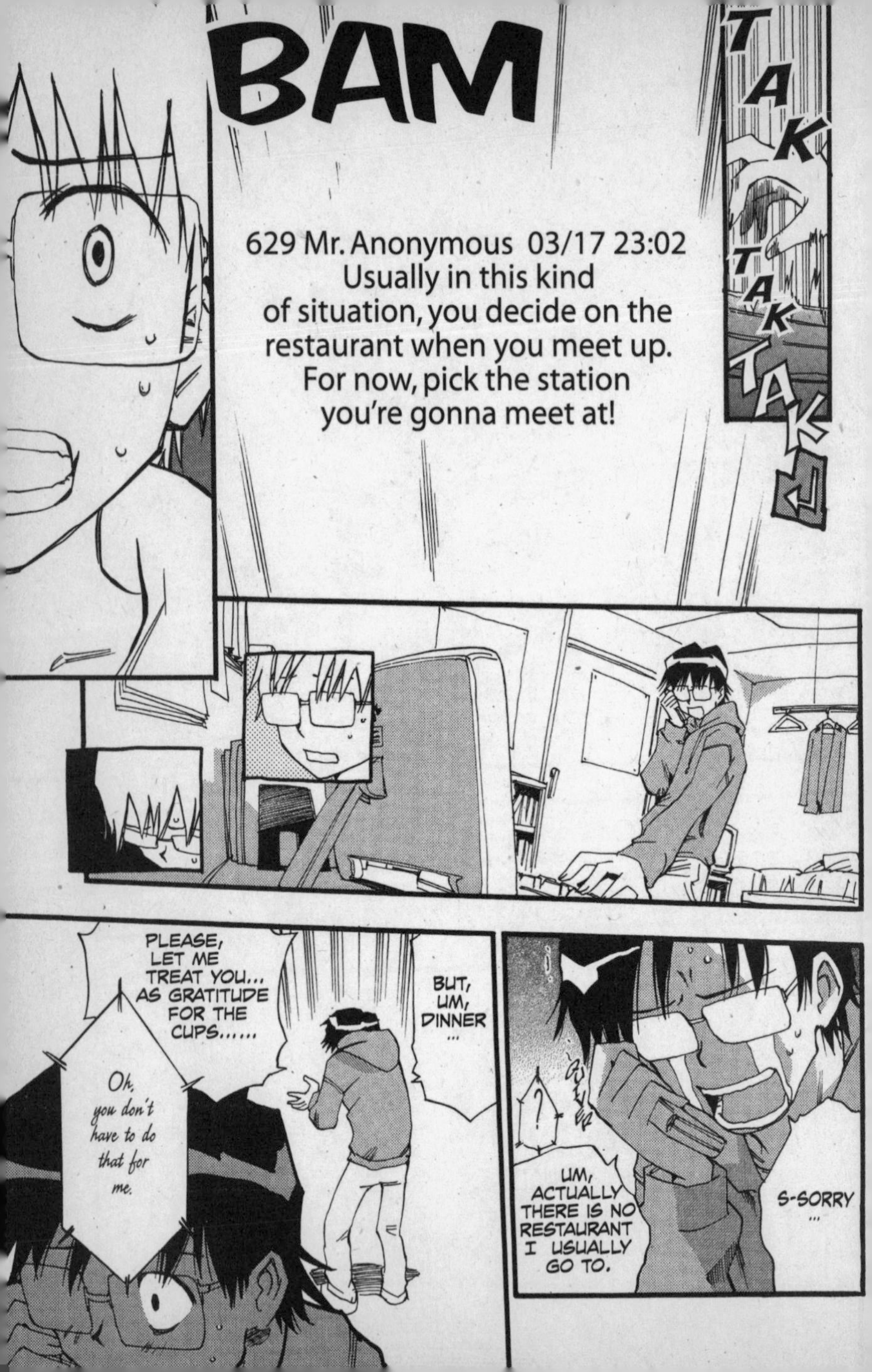
TAK TAK TAK
BAM
629 Mr. Anonymous 03/17 23:02
Usually in this kind of situation, you decide on the restaurant when you meet up. For now, pick the station you're gonna meet at!
UM, ACTUALLY THERE IS NO RESTAURANT I USUALLY GO TO.
S-SORRY ...
BUT, UM, DINNER ...
PLEASE, LET ME TREAT YOU... AS GRATITUDE FOR THE CUPS......
Oh, you don't have to do that for me.

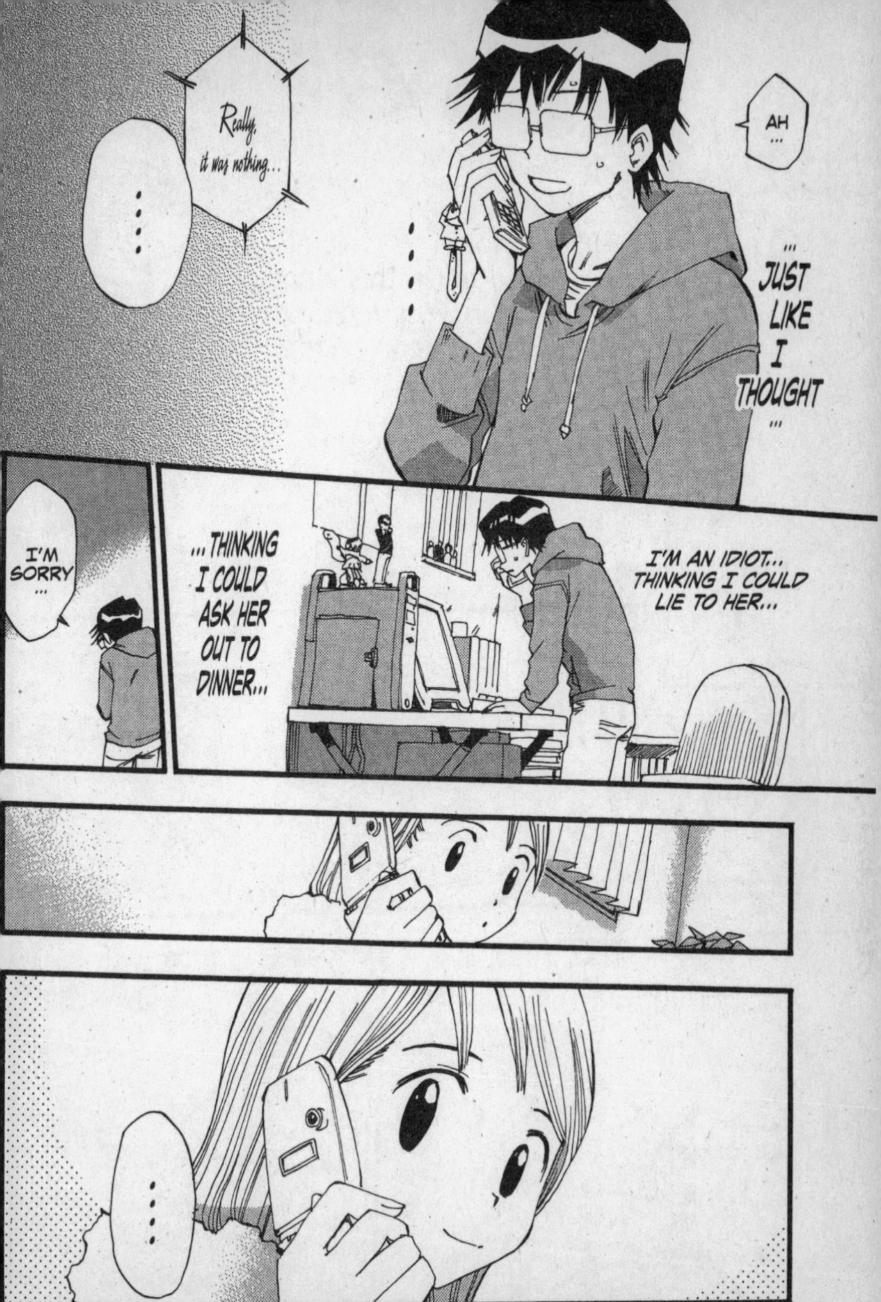
AH ...
... JUST LIKE I THOUGHT ...
....
Really, it was nothing...
....
I'M AN IDIOT... THINKING I COULD LIE TO HER...
...THINKING I COULD ASK HER OUT TO DINNER...
I'M SORRY ...
....

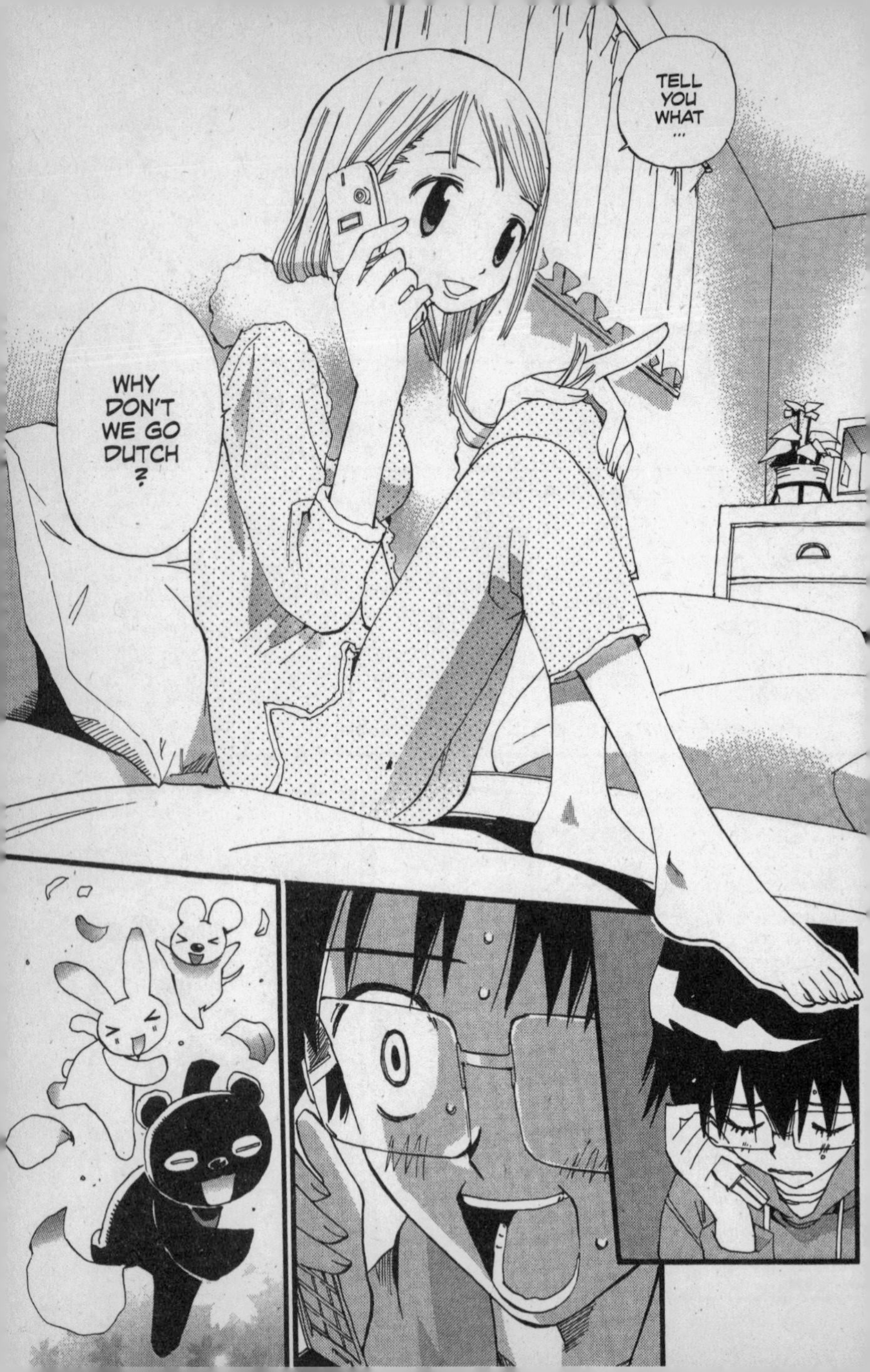

TELL YOU WHAT ...
WHY DON'T WE GO DUTCH ?

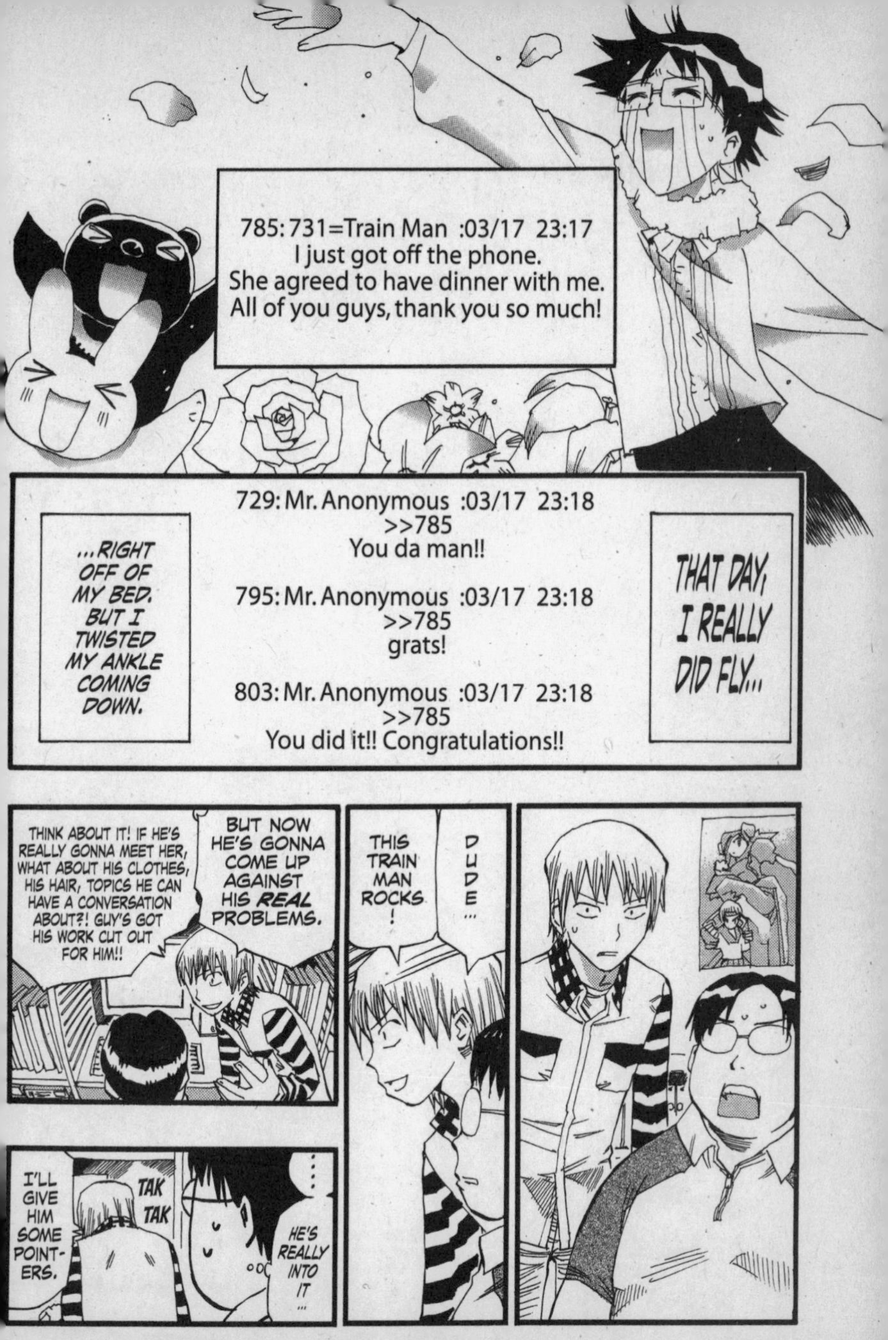
785: 731=Train Man :03/17 23:17
I just got off the phone.
She agreed to have dinner with me.
All of you guys, thank you so much!
THAT DAY, I REALLY DID FLY...
729: Mr. Anonymous :03/17 23:18
>>785
You da man!!
795: Mr. Anonymous :03/17 23:18
>>785
grats!
803: Mr. Anonymous :03/17 23:18
>>785
You did it!! Congratulations!!
...RIGHT OFF OF MY BED. BUT I TWISTED MY ANKLE COMING DOWN.
DUDE...
THIS TRAIN MAN ROCKS!
BUT NOW HE'S GONNA COME UP AGAINST HIS REAL PROBLEMS.
THINK ABOUT IT! IF HE'S REALLY GONNA MEET HER, WHAT ABOUT HIS CLOTHES, HIS HAIR, TOPICS HE CAN HAVE A CONVERSATION ABOUT?! GUY'S GOT HIS WORK CUT OUT FOR HIM!!
....
TAK TAK
HE'S REALLY INTO IT...
I'LL GIVE HIM SOME POINTERS.

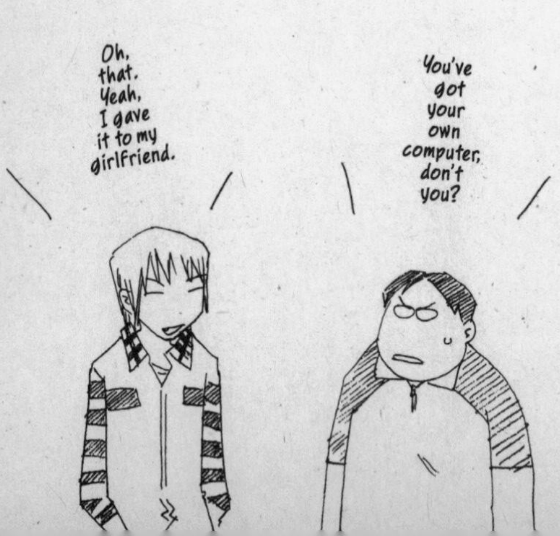

You've got your own computer, don't you?
Oh, that. Yeah, I gave it to my girlfriend.

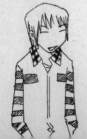

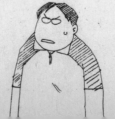

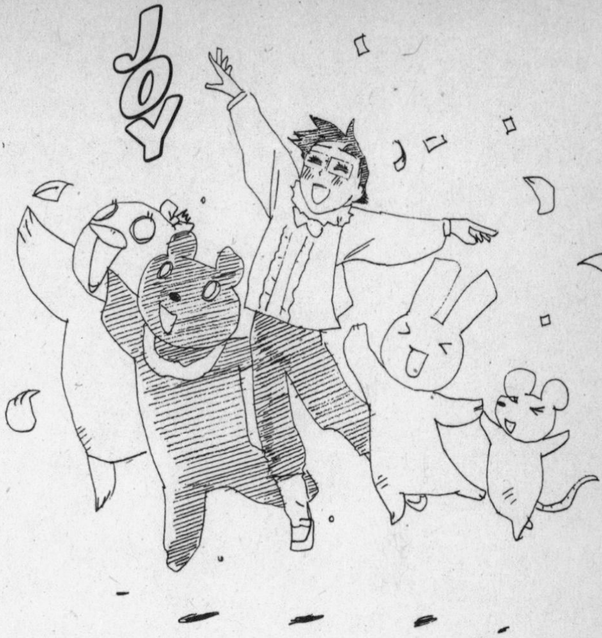
JOY

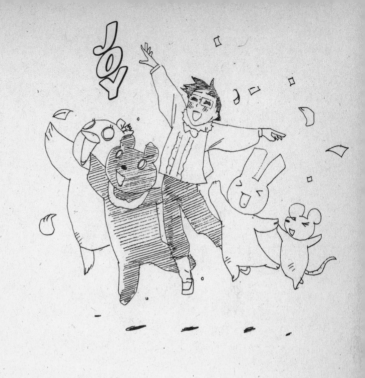

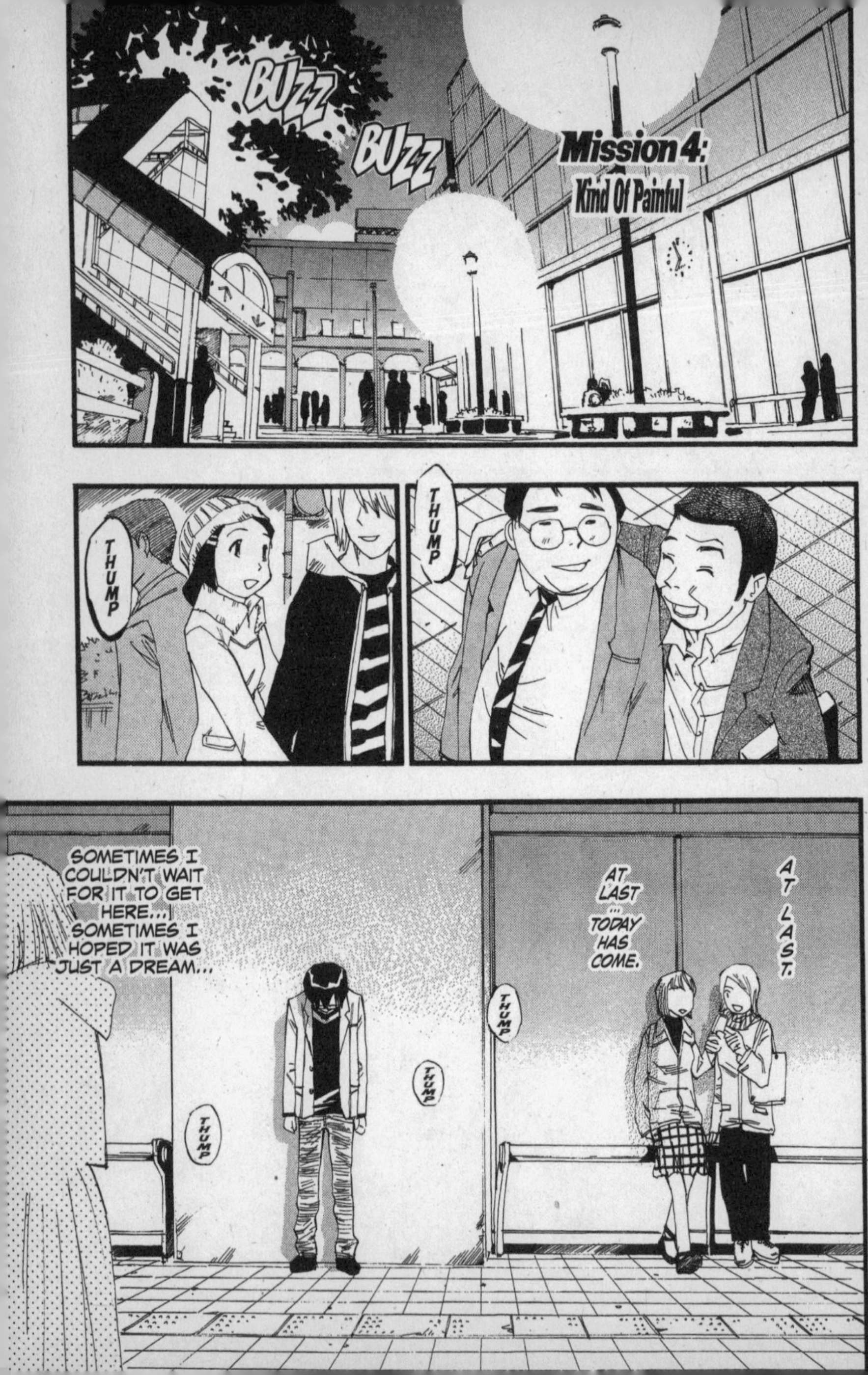
Mission 4:
Kind Of Painful
BUZZ
BUZZ
THUMP
THUMP
AT LAST.
AT LAST ... TODAY HAS COME.
THUMP
THUMP
SOMETIMES I COULDN'T WAIT FOR IT TO GET HERE... SOMETIMES I HOPED IT WAS JUST A DREAM...
THUMP

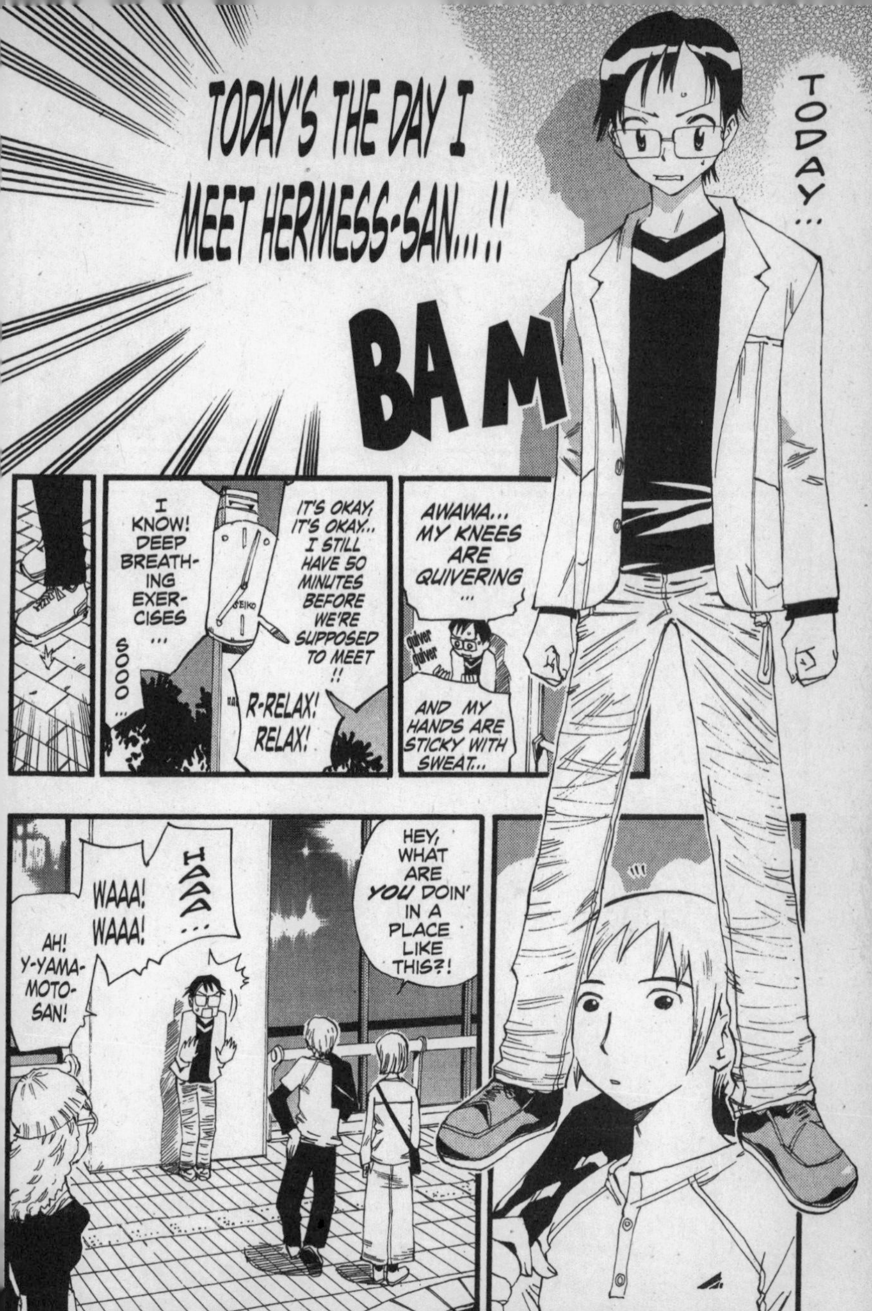
TODAY...
TODAY'S THE DAY I MEET HERMESS-SAN...!!
BAM
AWAWA... MY KNEES ARE QUIVERING...
quiver quiver
AND MY HANDS ARE STICKY WITH SWEAT...
IT'S OKAY, IT'S OKAY... I STILL HAVE 50 MINUTES BEFORE WE'RE SUPPOSED TO MEET!!
R-RELAX! RELAX!
I KNOW! DEEP BREATHING EXERCISES...
SOOO...
!!!
HEY, WHAT ARE YOU DOIN' IN A PLACE LIKE THIS?!
HAAA...
WAAA! WAAA!
AH! Y-YAMAMOTO-SAN!

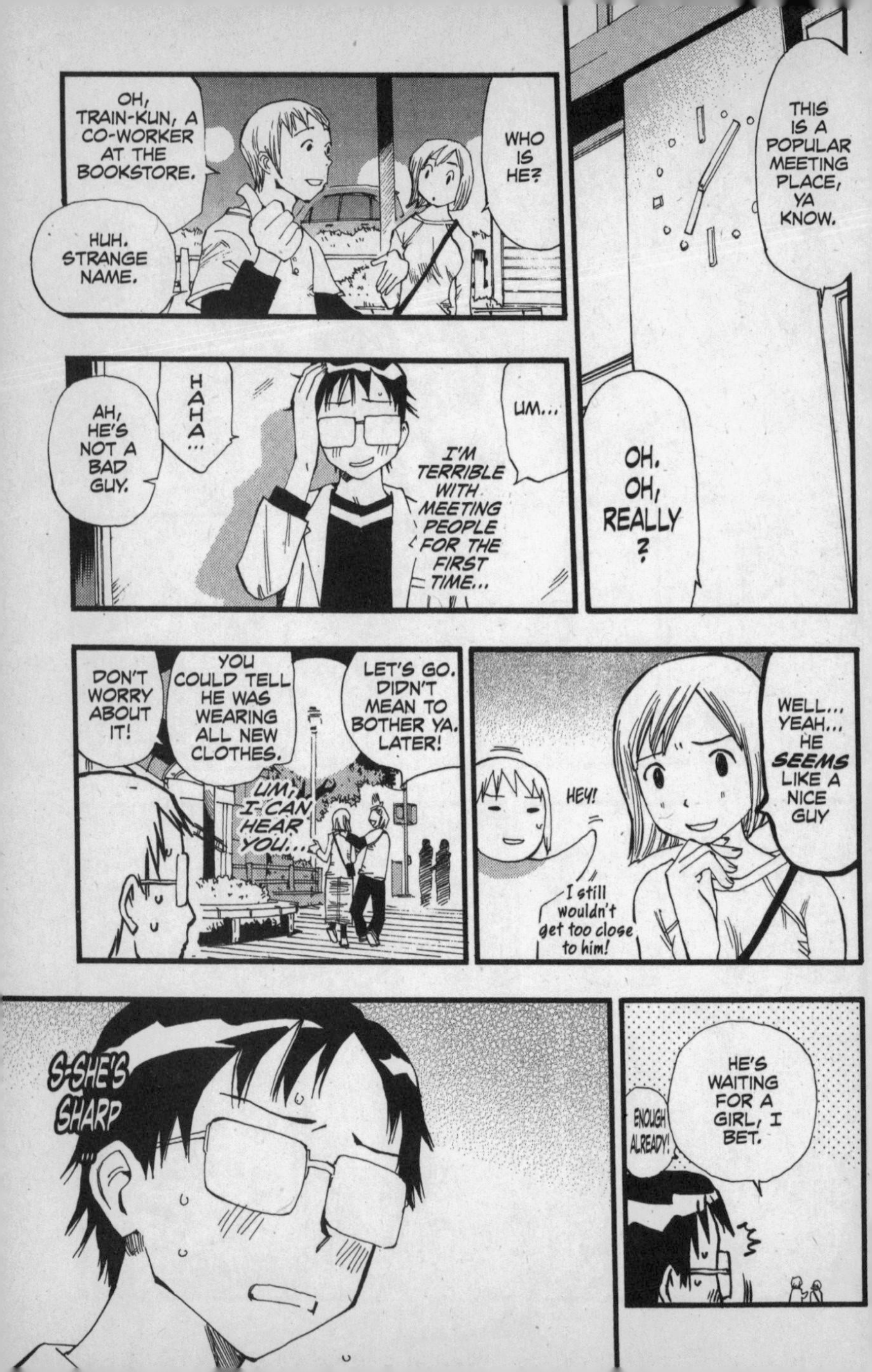
THIS IS A POPULAR MEETING PLACE, YA KNOW.
OH. OH, REALLY?
WHO IS HE?
OH, TRAIN-KUN, A CO-WORKER AT THE BOOKSTORE.
HUH. STRANGE NAME.
UM...
I'M TERRIBLE WITH MEETING PEOPLE FOR THE FIRST TIME...
HAHA...
AH, HE'S NOT A BAD GUY.
WELL... YEAH... HE *SEEMS* LIKE A NICE GUY
HEY!
I still wouldn't get too close to him!
LET'S GO. DIDN'T MEAN TO BOTHER YA. LATER!
UM, I CAN HEAR YOU...
YOU COULD TELL HE WAS WEARING ALL NEW CLOTHES.
DON'T WORRY ABOUT IT!
HE'S WAITING FOR A GIRL, I BET.
ENOUGH ALREADY!
S-SHE'S SHARP

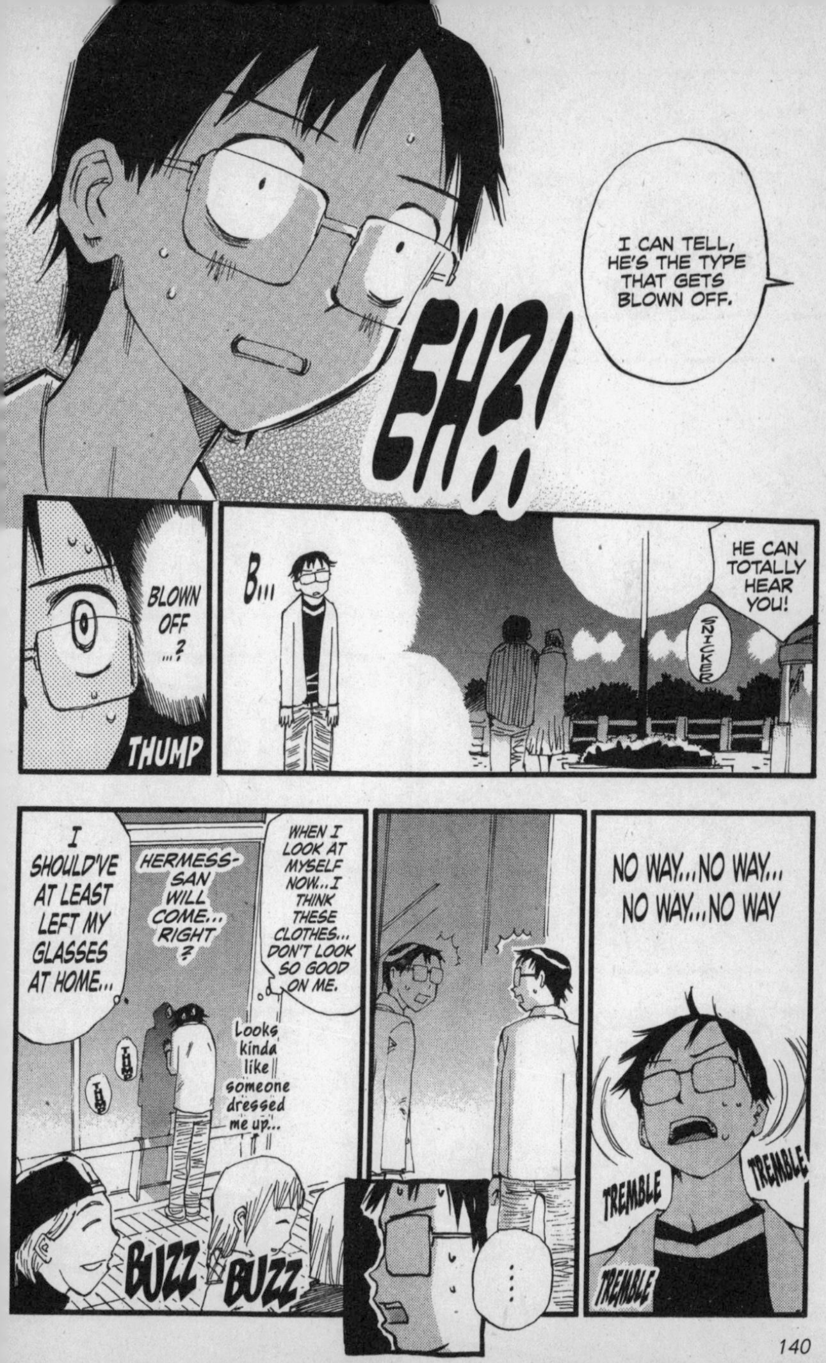
I CAN TELL, HE'S THE TYPE THAT GETS BLOWN OFF.
EH?!
HE CAN TOTALLY HEAR YOU!
SNICKER
B...
BLOWN OFF ...?
THUMP
NO WAY...NO WAY... NO WAY...NO WAY
TREMBLE
TREMBLE
TREMBLE
....
WHEN I LOOK AT MYSELF NOW...I THINK THESE CLOTHES... DON'T LOOK SO GOOD ON ME.
HERMESS-SAN WILL COME... RIGHT?
I SHOULD'VE AT LEAST LEFT MY GLASSES AT HOME...
Looks kinda like someone dressed me up...
THUMP
THUMP
BUZZ
BUZZ

Mission 4:
Kind Of Painful...

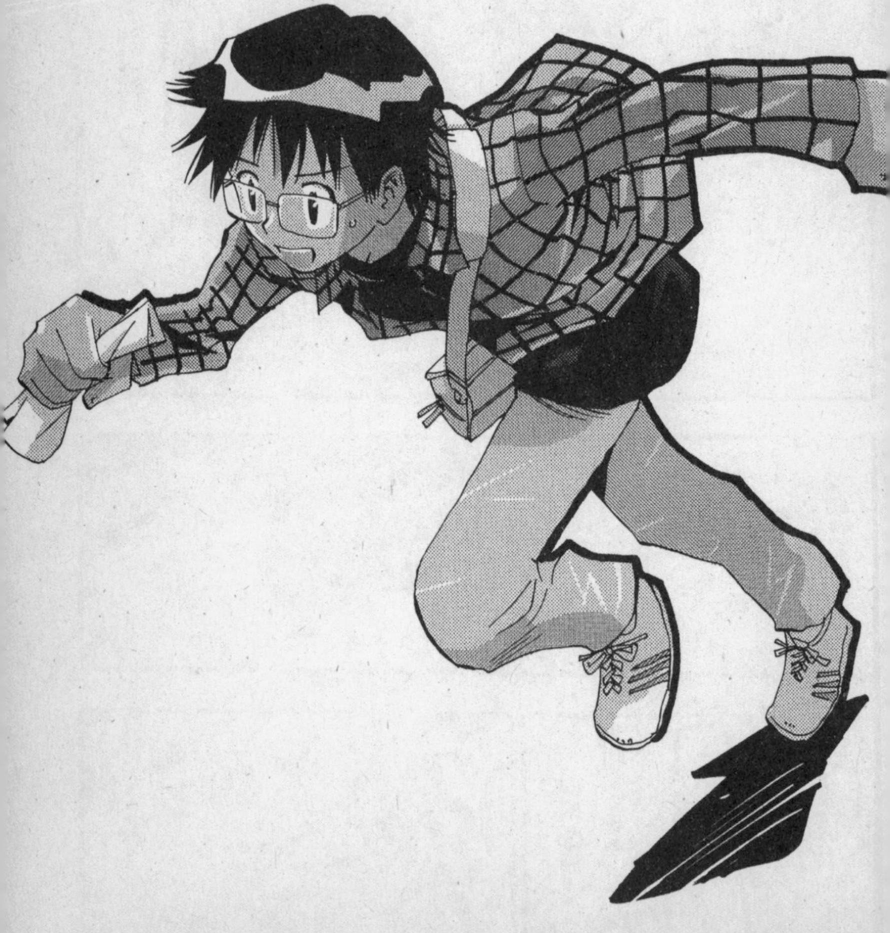

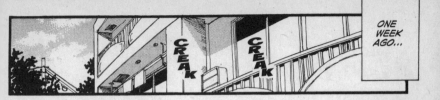

ONE WEEK AGO...

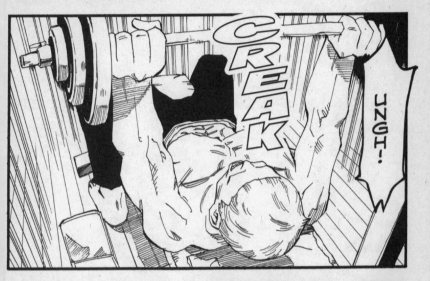

CREAK CREAK

CREAK

UNGH!

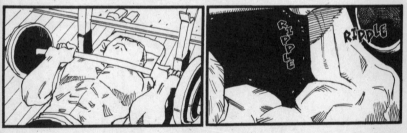

RIPPLE

RIPPLE

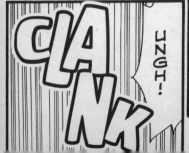

CLANK

UNGH!

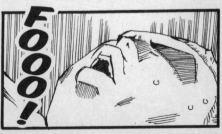

FOOO!

142

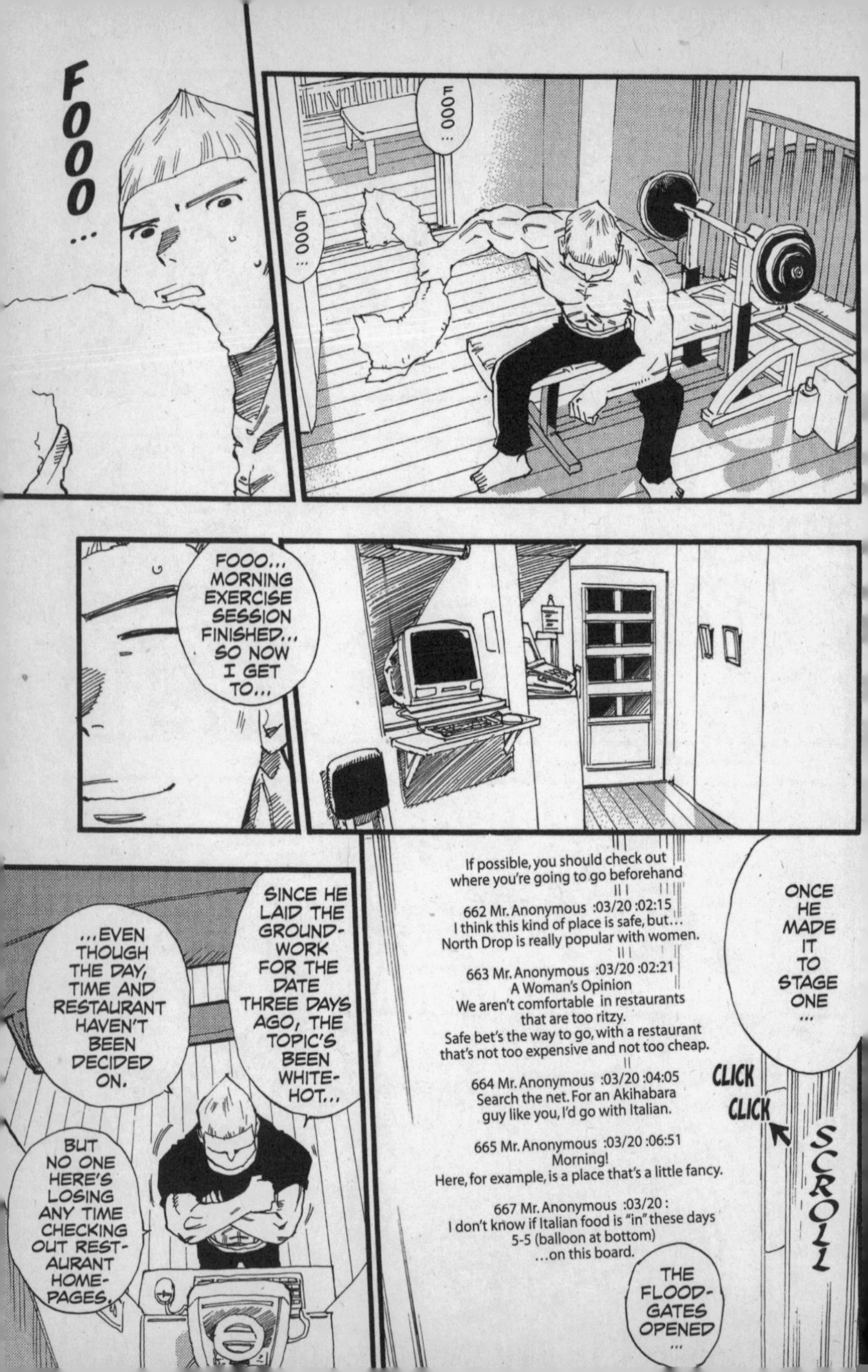
FOOO...
FOOO...
FOOO...
FOOO... MORNING EXERCISE SESSION FINISHED... SO NOW I GET TO...
ONCE HE MADE IT TO STAGE ONE...
If possible, you should check out where you're going to go beforehand
662 Mr. Anonymous :03/20 :02:15
I think this kind of place is safe, but...
North Drop is really popular with women.
663 Mr. Anonymous :03/20 :02:21
A Woman's Opinion
We aren't comfortable in restaurants that are too ritzy.
Safe bet's the way to go, with a restaurant that's not too expensive and not too cheap.
664 Mr. Anonymous :03/20 :04:05
Search the net. For an Akihabara guy like you, I'd go with Italian.
665 Mr. Anonymous :03/20 :06:51
Morning!
Here, for example, is a place that's a little fancy.
667 Mr. Anonymous :03/20 :
I don't know if Italian food is "in" these days
5-5 (balloon at bottom)
...on this board.
CLICK
CLICK
SCROLL
THE FLOODGATES OPENED...
SINCE HE LAID THE GROUNDWORK FOR THE DATE THREE DAYS AGO, THE TOPIC'S BEEN WHITE-HOT...
...EVEN THOUGH THE DAY, TIME AND RESTAURANT HAVEN'T BEEN DECIDED ON.
BUT NO ONE HERE'S LOSING ANY TIME CHECKING OUT RESTAURANT HOMEPAGES.

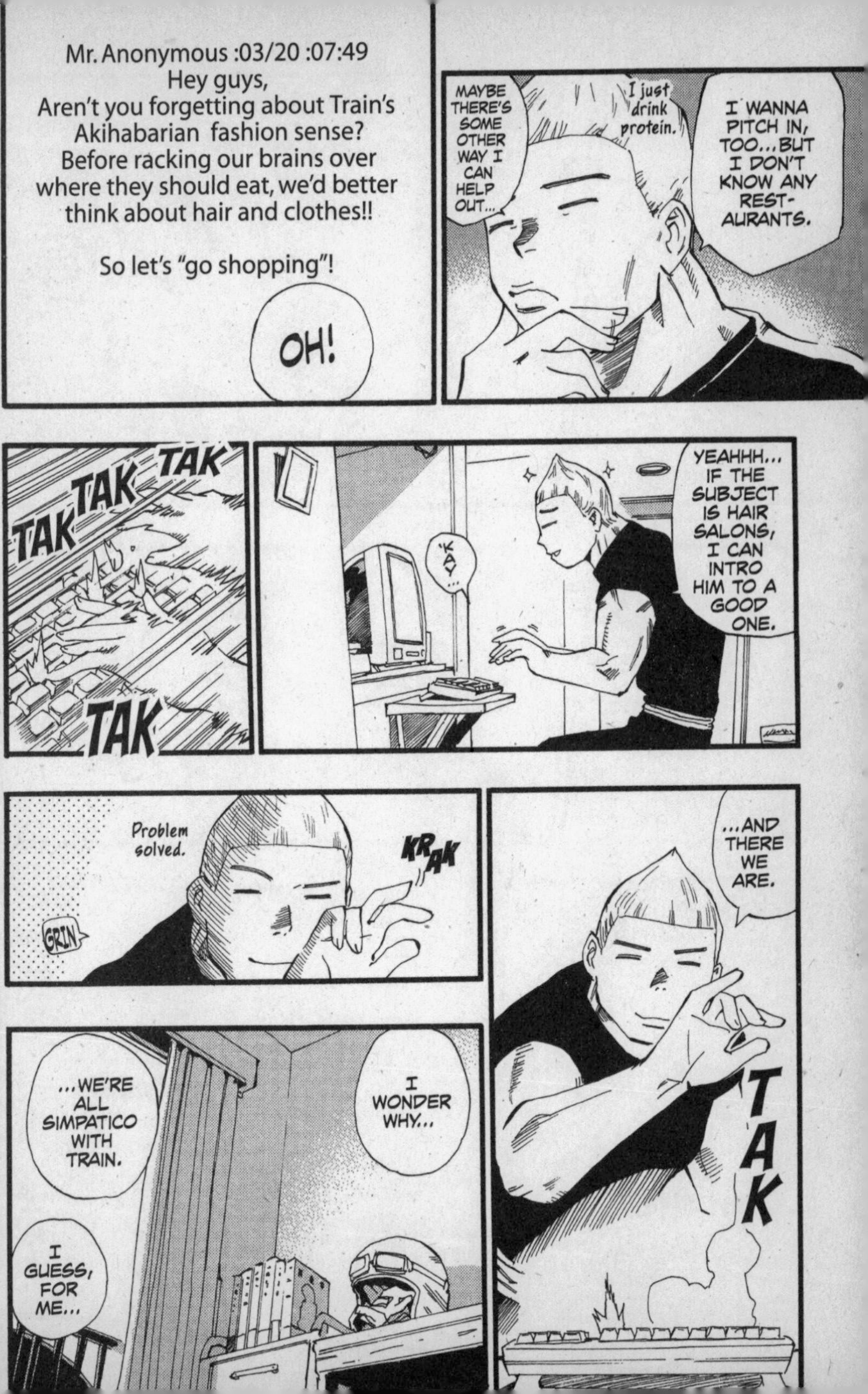
I WANNA PITCH IN, TOO...BUT I DON'T KNOW ANY REST-AURANTS.
I just drink protein.
MAYBE THERE'S SOME OTHER WAY I CAN HELP OUT...
Mr. Anonymous :03/20 :07:49
Hey guys,
Aren't you forgetting about Train's Akihabarian fashion sense?
Before racking our brains over where they should eat, we'd better think about hair and clothes!!
So let's "go shopping"!
OH!
YEAHHH... IF THE SUBJECT IS HAIR SALONS, I CAN INTRO HIM TO A GOOD ONE.
'KAY...
TAK TAK TAK
TAK
...AND THERE WE ARE.
TAK TAK
Problem solved.
KRAK
GRIN
I WONDER WHY...
...WE'RE ALL SIMPATICO WITH TRAIN.
I GUESS, FOR ME...

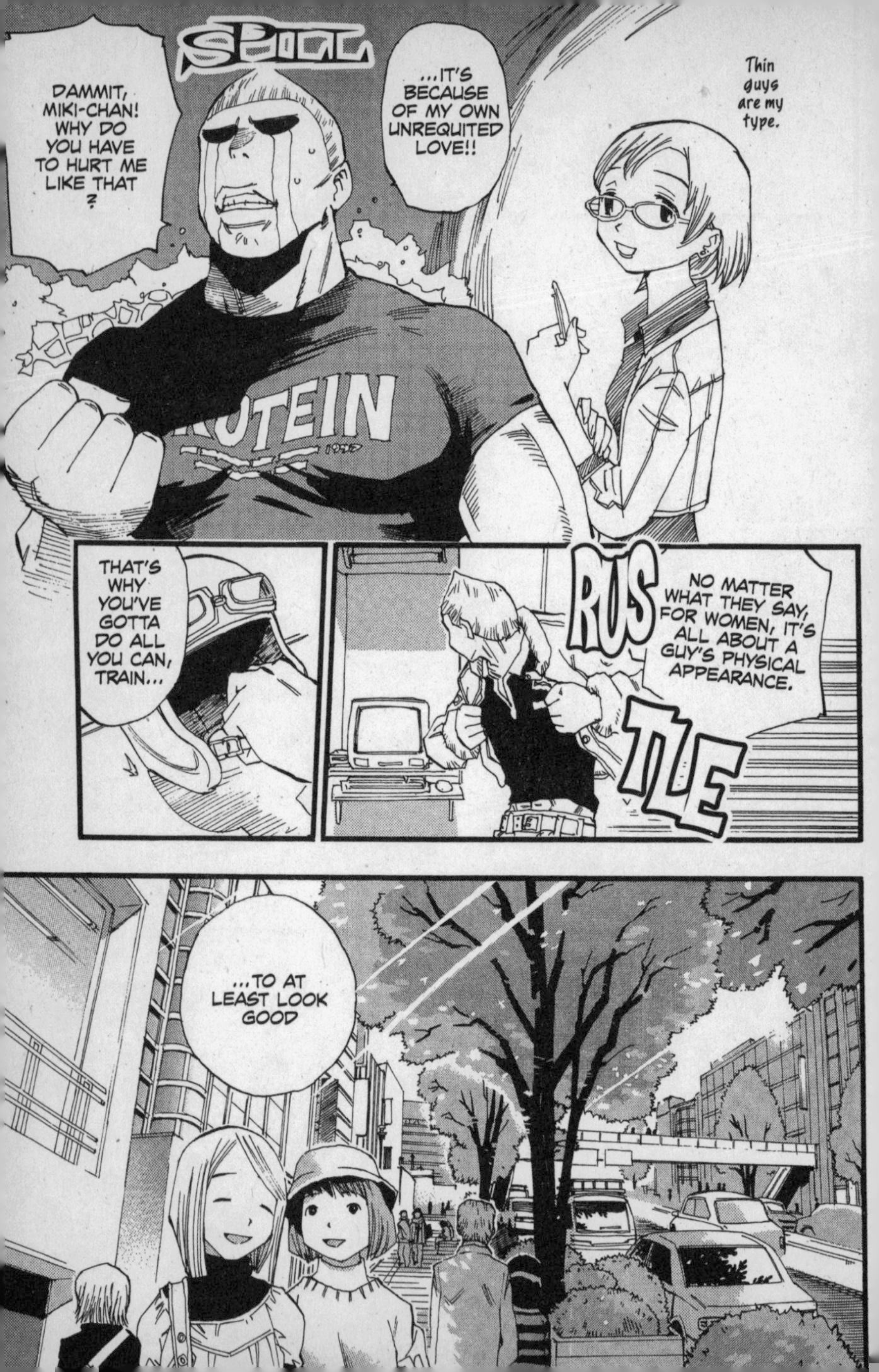
Thin guys are my type.
...IT'S BECAUSE OF MY OWN UNREQUITED LOVE!!
DAMMIT, MIKI-CHAN! WHY DO YOU HAVE TO HURT ME LIKE THAT?
RUSTLE
NO MATTER WHAT THEY SAY, FOR WOMEN, IT'S ALL ABOUT A GUY'S PHYSICAL APPEARANCE.
THAT'S WHY YOU'VE GOTTA DO ALL YOU CAN, TRAIN...
...TO AT LEAST LOOK GOOD

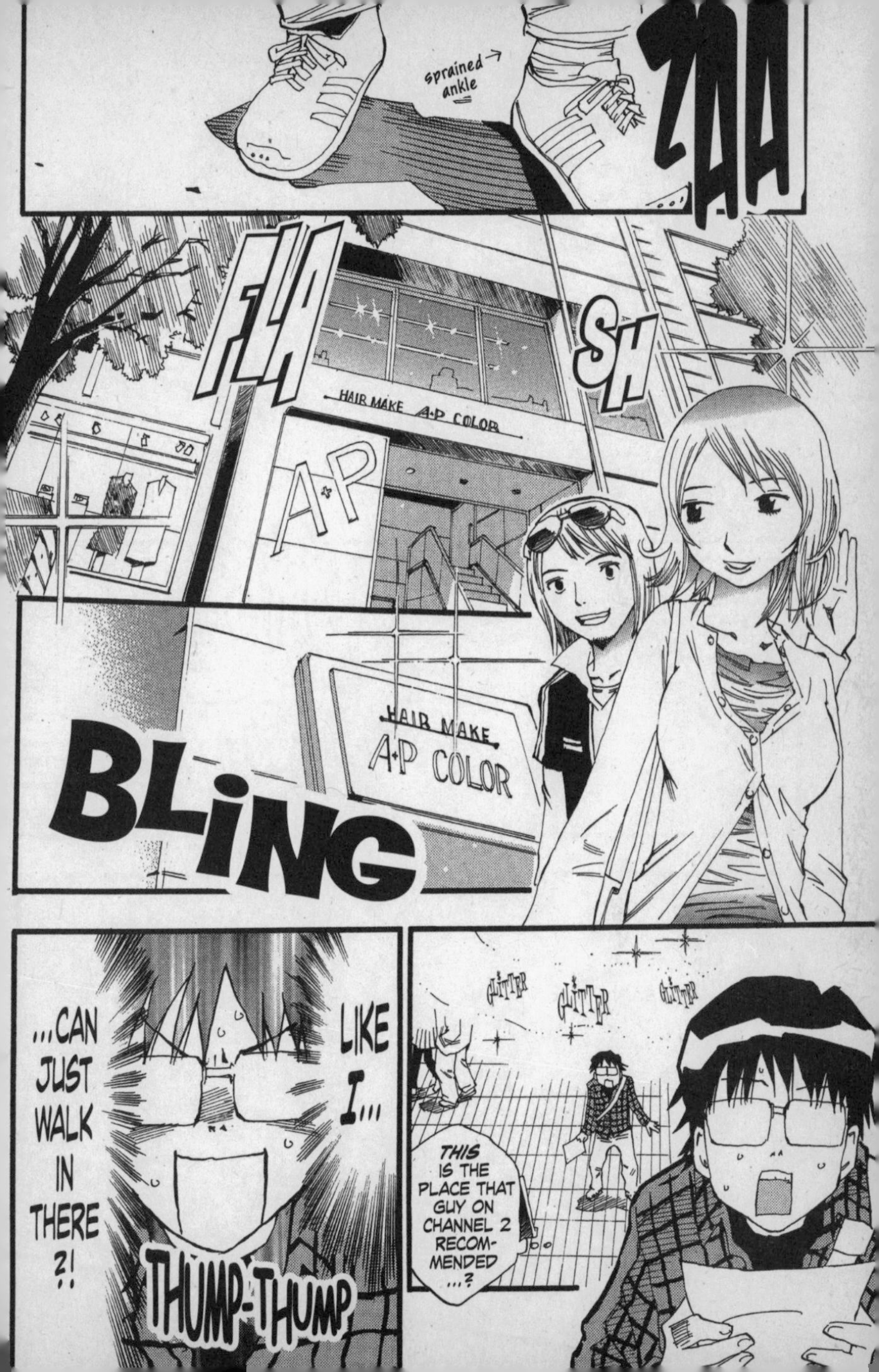
ZAA
sprained ankle
FLA
SH
HAIR MAKE A·P COLOR
A·P
HAIR MAKE
A·P COLOR
BLING
GLITTER
GLITTER
GLITTER
THIS IS THE PLACE THAT GUY ON CHANNEL 2 RECOMMENDED ...?
LIKE I...
...CAN JUST WALK IN THERE ?!
THUMP-THUMP

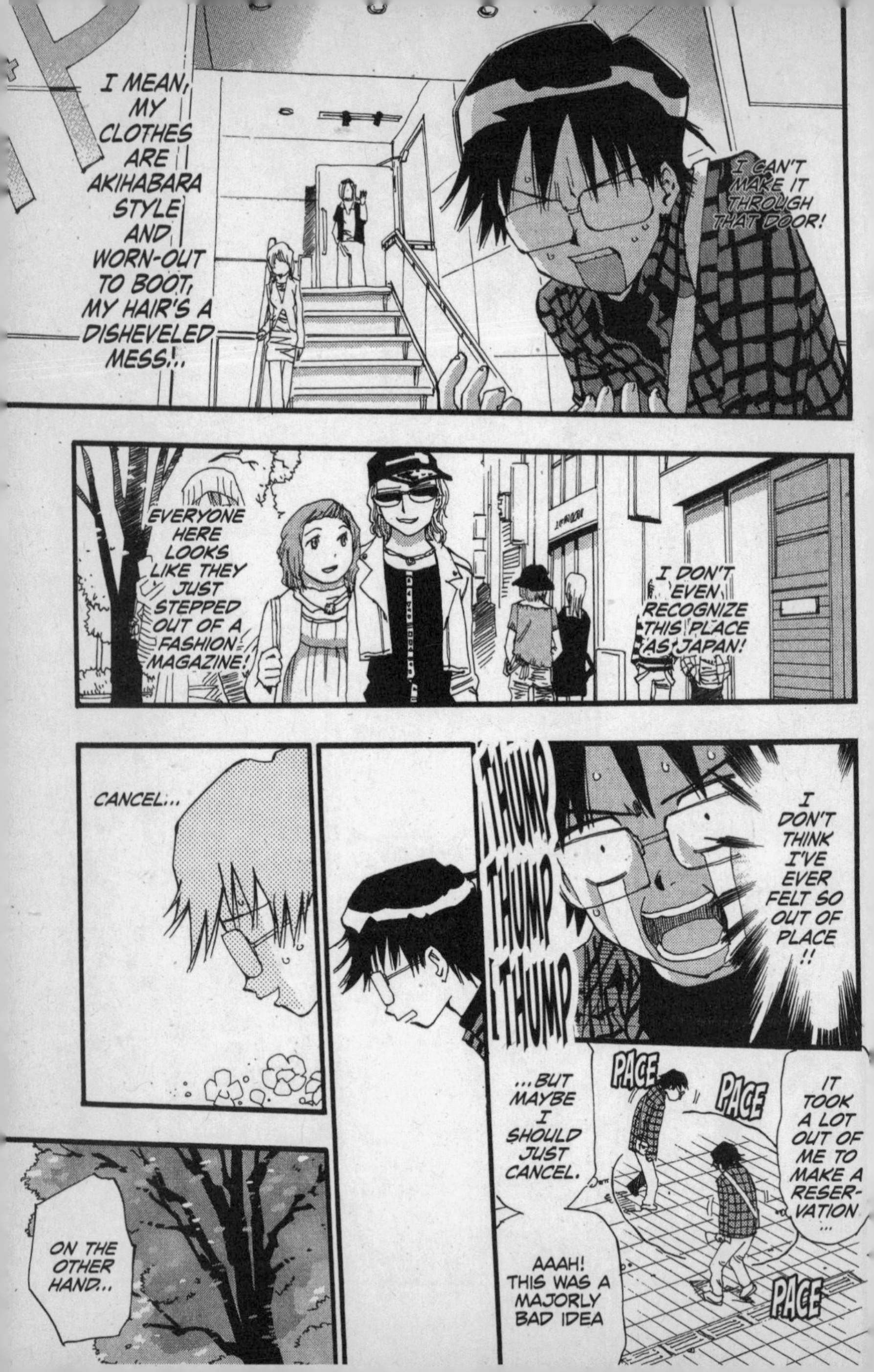

I CAN'T MAKE IT THROUGH THAT DOOR!
I MEAN, MY CLOTHES ARE AKIHABARA STYLE AND WORN-OUT TO BOOT, MY HAIR'S A DISHEVELED MESS!...
I DON'T EVEN RECOGNIZE THIS PLACE AS JAPAN!
EVERYONE HERE LOOKS LIKE THEY JUST STEPPED OUT OF A FASHION MAGAZINE!
THUMP
THUMP
THUMP
I DON'T THINK I'VE EVER FELT SO OUT OF PLACE !!
IT TOOK A LOT OUT OF ME TO MAKE A RESERVATION ...
PACE
PACE
...BUT MAYBE I SHOULD JUST CANCEL.
PACE
AAAH! THIS WAS A MAJORLY BAD IDEA
CANCEL...
ON THE OTHER HAND...

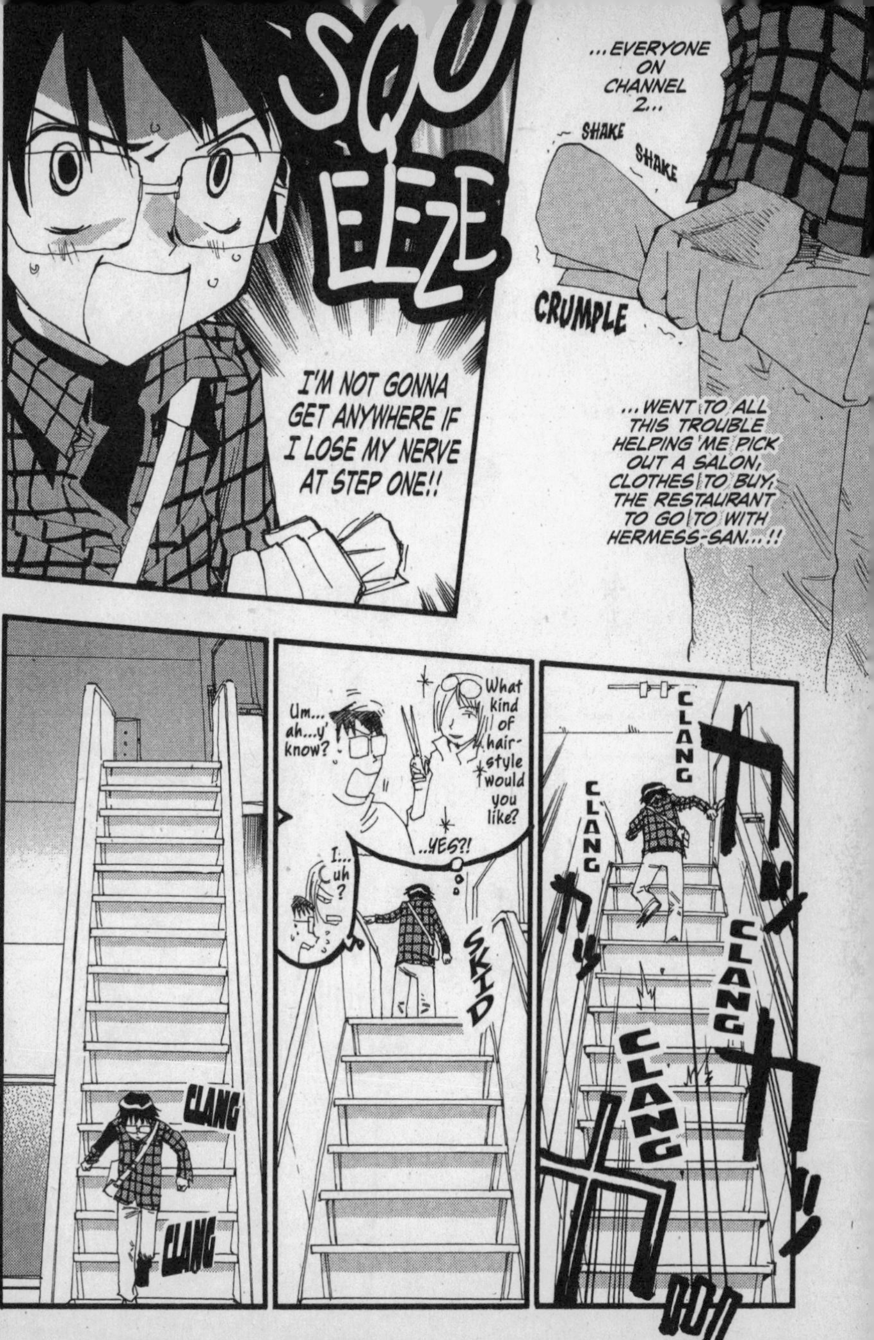
...EVERYONE ON CHANNEL 2...
SHAKE
SHAKE
CRUMPLE
...WENT TO ALL THIS TROUBLE HELPING ME PICK OUT A SALON, CLOTHES TO BUY, THE RESTAURANT TO GO TO WITH HERMESS-SAN...!!
SQUEEZE
I'M NOT GONNA GET ANYWHERE IF I LOSE MY NERVE AT STEP ONE!!
CLANG
CLANG
CLANG
CLANG
CLANG
What kind of hair-style would you like?
Um... ah...y' know?
...YES?!
I... uh?
SKID
CLANG
CLANG

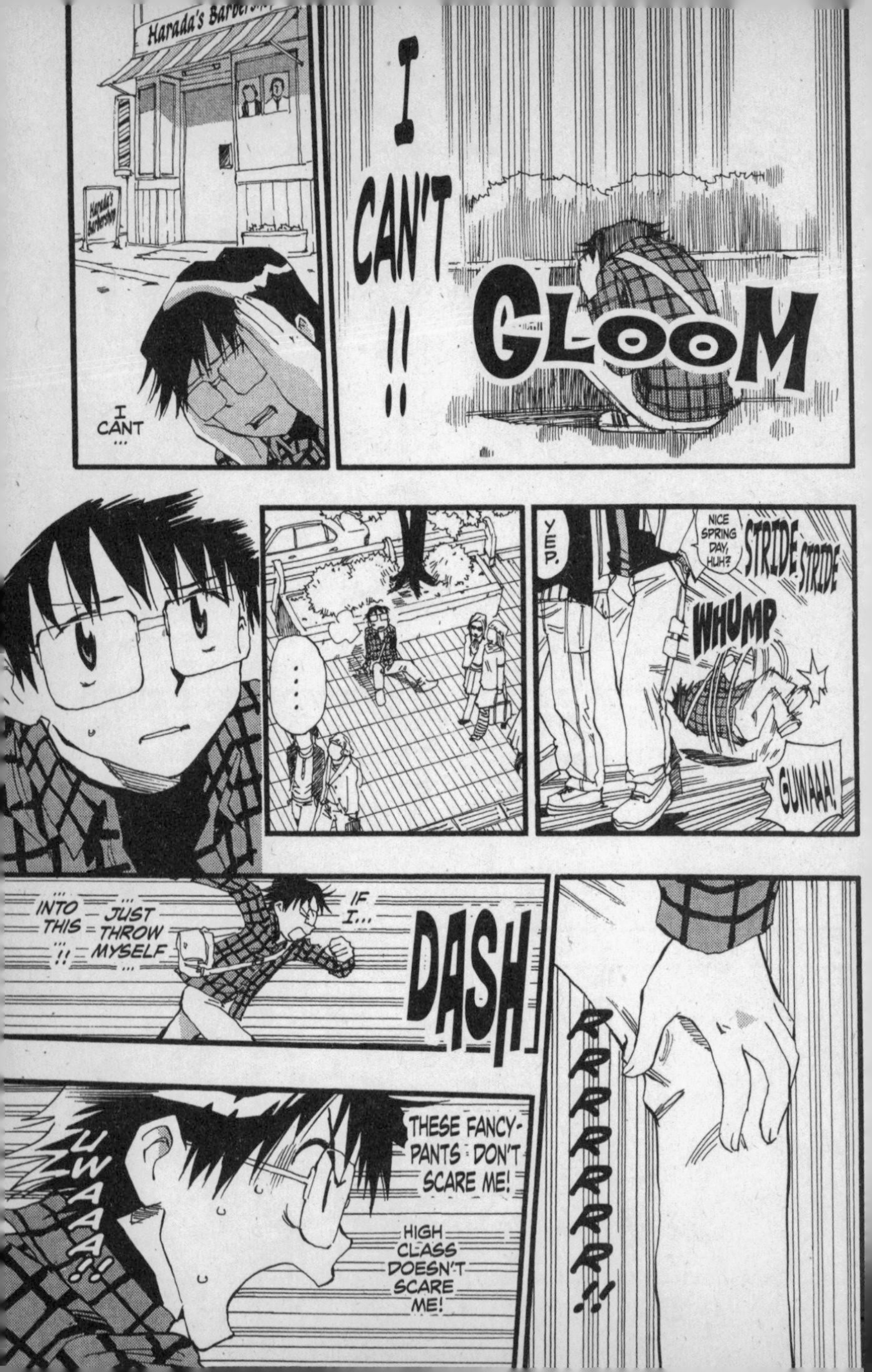
I CAN'T !!
GLOOM
Harada's Barbershop
I CANT ...
YEP.
NICE SPRING DAY, HUH?
STRIDE STRIDE
WHUMP
GUWAAA!
....
RRRRRRRR!!
IF I...
JUST THROW MYSELF ...
... INTO THIS ...!!
DASH
THESE FANCY-PANTS DON'T SCARE ME!
HIGH CLASS DOESN'T SCARE ME!
UWAAA!!

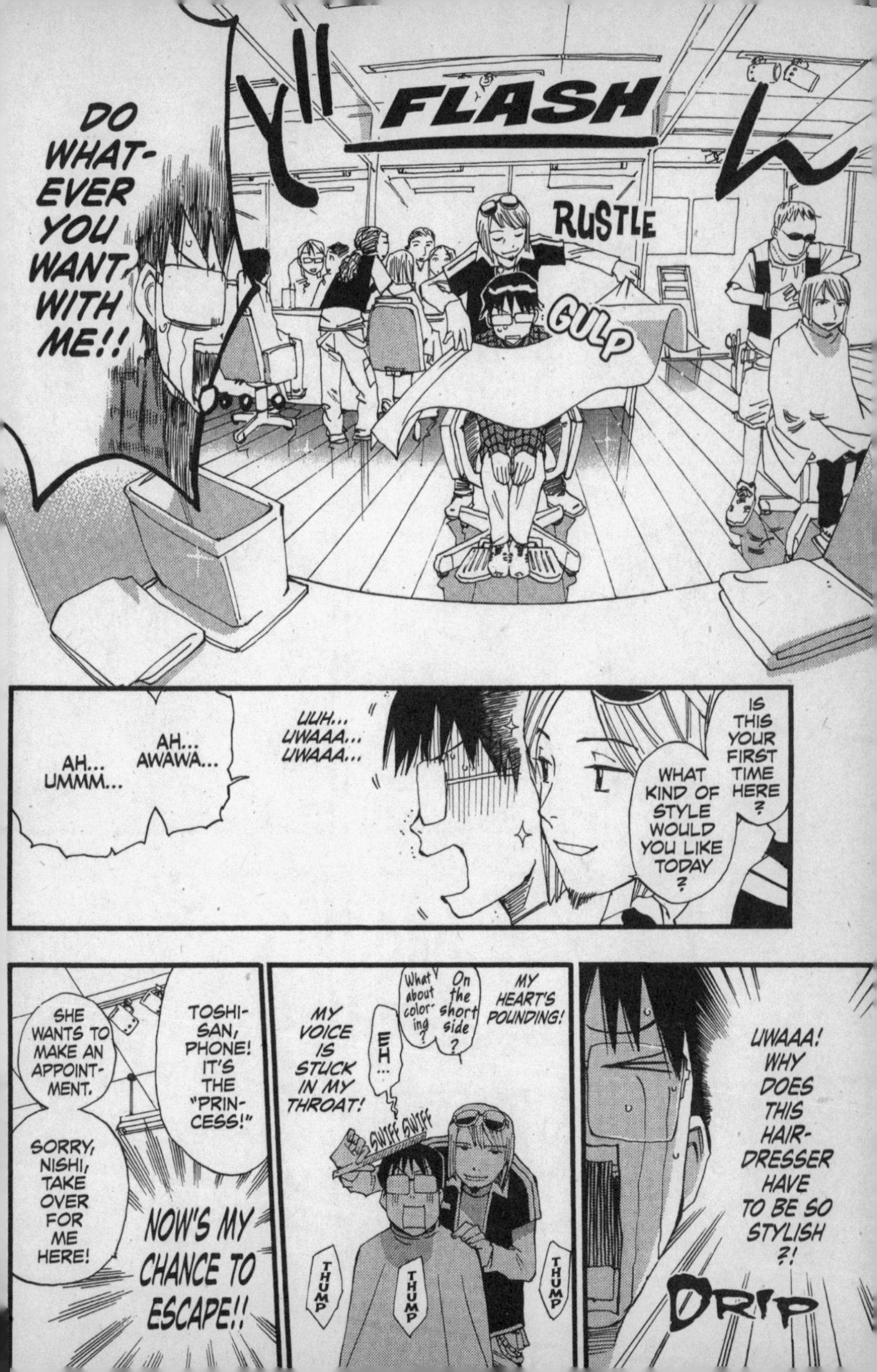
FLASH
RUSTLE
GULP
DO WHATEVER YOU WANT WITH ME!!
IS THIS YOUR FIRST TIME HERE?
WHAT KIND OF STYLE WOULD YOU LIKE TODAY?
UUH... UWAAA... UWAAA...
AH... AWAWA...
AH... UMMM...
UWAAA! WHY DOES THIS HAIRDRESSER HAVE TO BE SO STYLISH?!
DRIP
MY HEART'S POUNDING!
On the short side?
What about coloring?
EH...
MY VOICE IS STUCK IN MY THROAT!
SWIFF SWIFF
THUMP
THUMP
THUMP
TOSHI-SAN, PHONE! IT'S THE "PRINCESS!"
SHE WANTS TO MAKE AN APPOINTMENT.
SORRY, NISHI, TAKE OVER FOR ME HERE!
NOW'S MY CHANCE TO ESCAPE!!

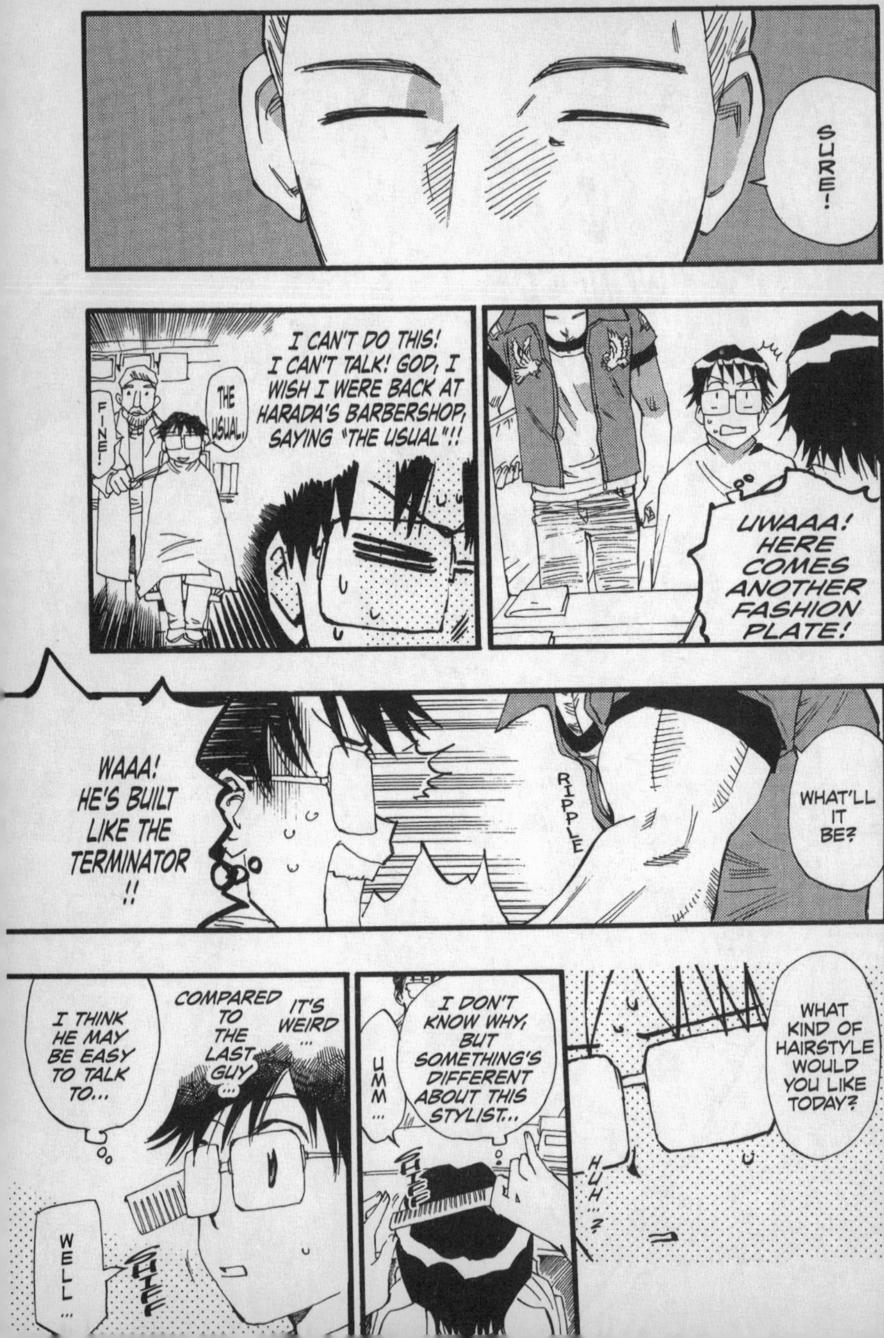
SURE!
UWAAA! HERE COMES ANOTHER FASHION PLATE!
I CAN'T DO THIS! I CAN'T TALK! GOD, I WISH I WERE BACK AT HARADA'S BARBERSHOP, SAYING "THE USUAL"!!
THE USUAL.
FINE!
WHAT'LL IT BE?
RIPPLE
WAAA! HE'S BUILT LIKE THE TERMINATOR!!
WHAT KIND OF HAIRSTYLE WOULD YOU LIKE TODAY?
HUH...?
I DON'T KNOW WHY, BUT SOMETHING'S DIFFERENT ABOUT THIS STYLIST...
UMM...
SHIFF
IT'S WEIRD...
COMPARED TO THE LAST GUY...
I THINK HE MAY BE EASY TO TALK TO...
SHIFF
WELL...

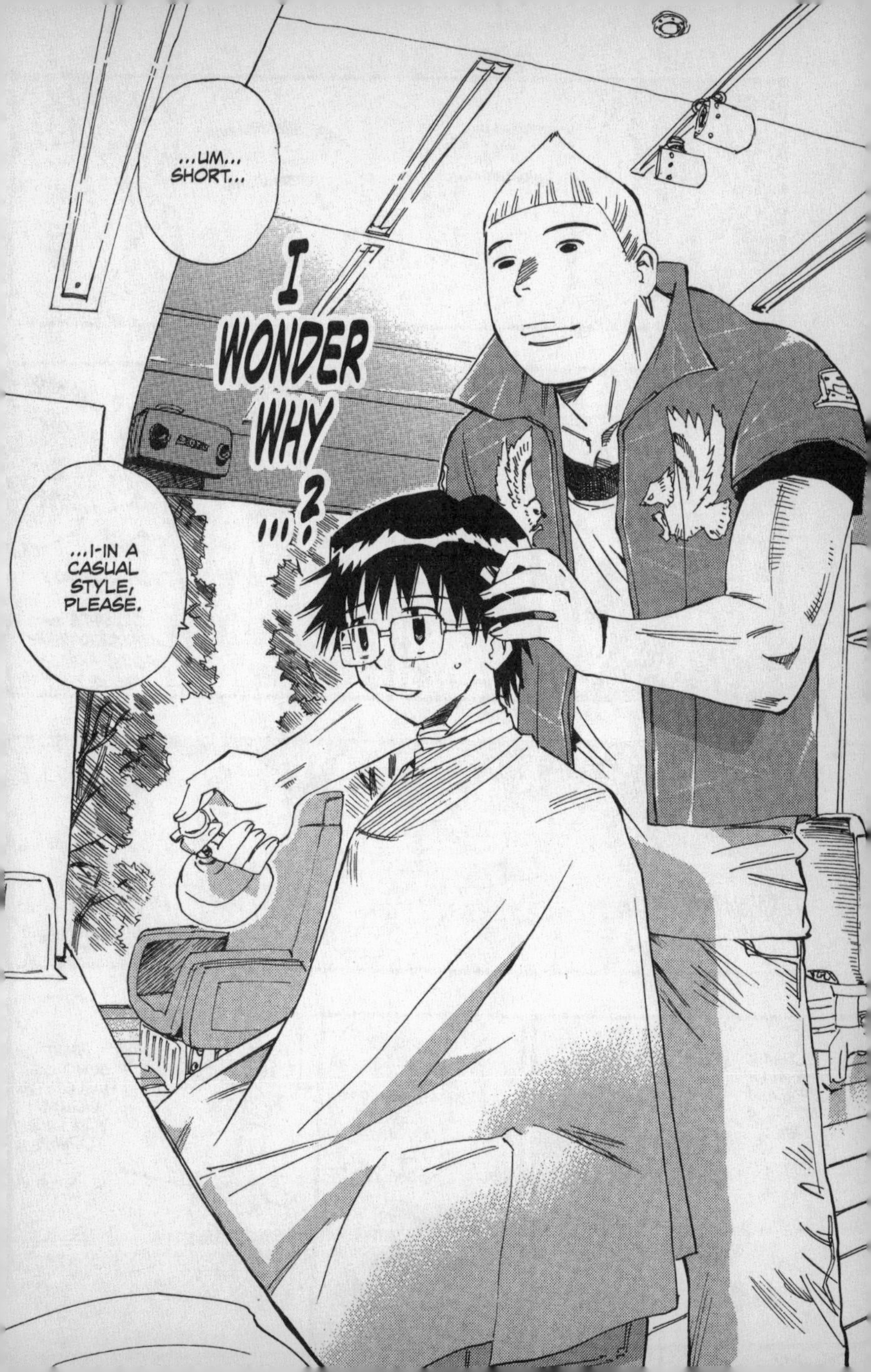
...UM... SHORT...
I WONDER WHY...?
...I-IN A CASUAL STYLE, PLEASE.

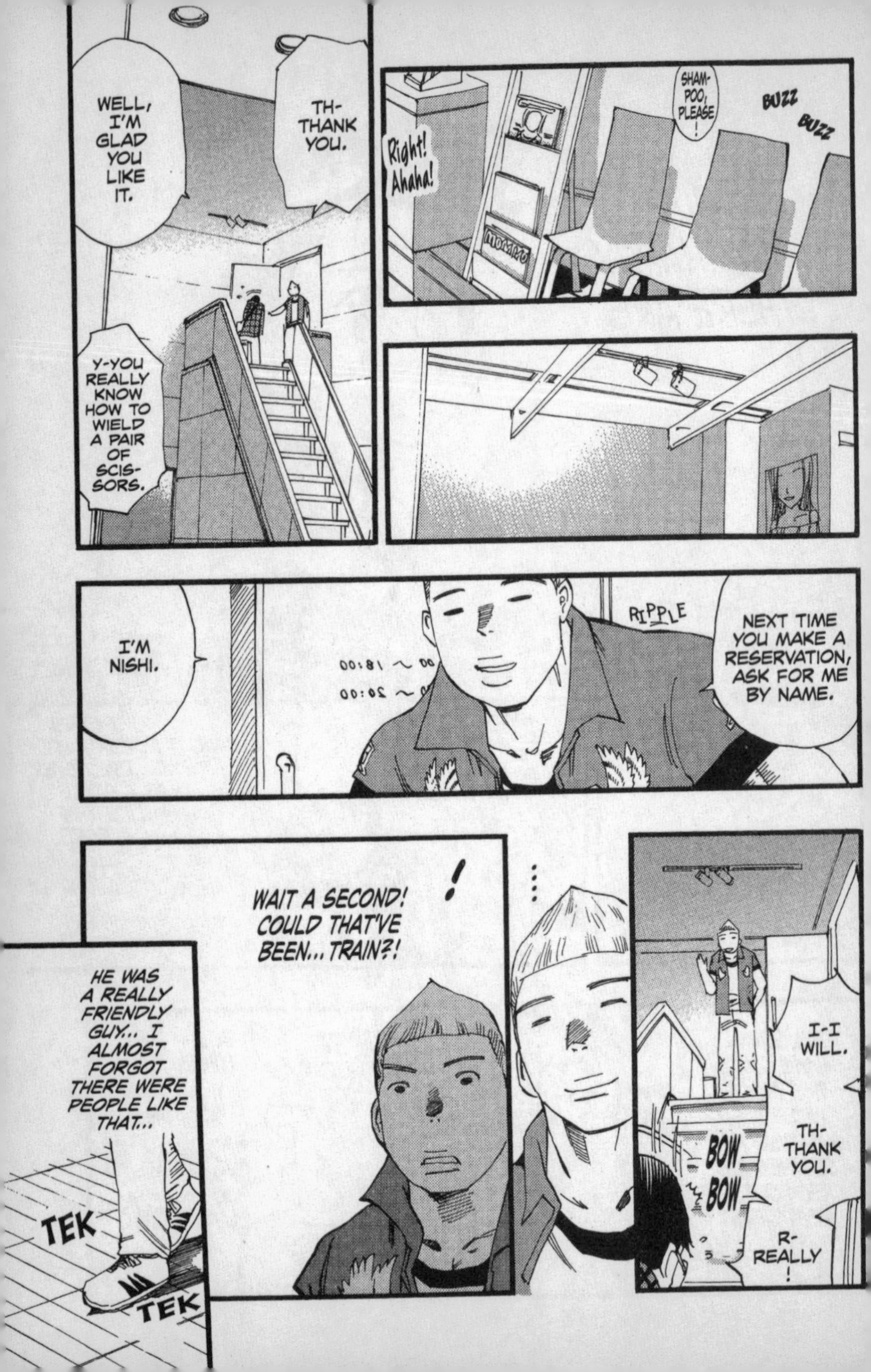

BUZZ BUZZ
SHAM-POO, PLEASE!
Right! Ahaha!
TH-THANK YOU.
WELL, I'M GLAD YOU LIKE IT.
Y-YOU REALLY KNOW HOW TO WIELD A PAIR OF SCIS-SORS.
RIPPLE
NEXT TIME YOU MAKE A RESERVATION, ASK FOR ME BY NAME.
I'M NISHI.
I-I WILL.
TH-THANK YOU.
BOW BOW
R-REALLY!
....
!
WAIT A SECOND! COULD THAT'VE BEEN... TRAIN?!
HE WAS A REALLY FRIENDLY GUY... I ALMOST FORGOT THERE WERE PEOPLE LIKE THAT...
TEK
TEK

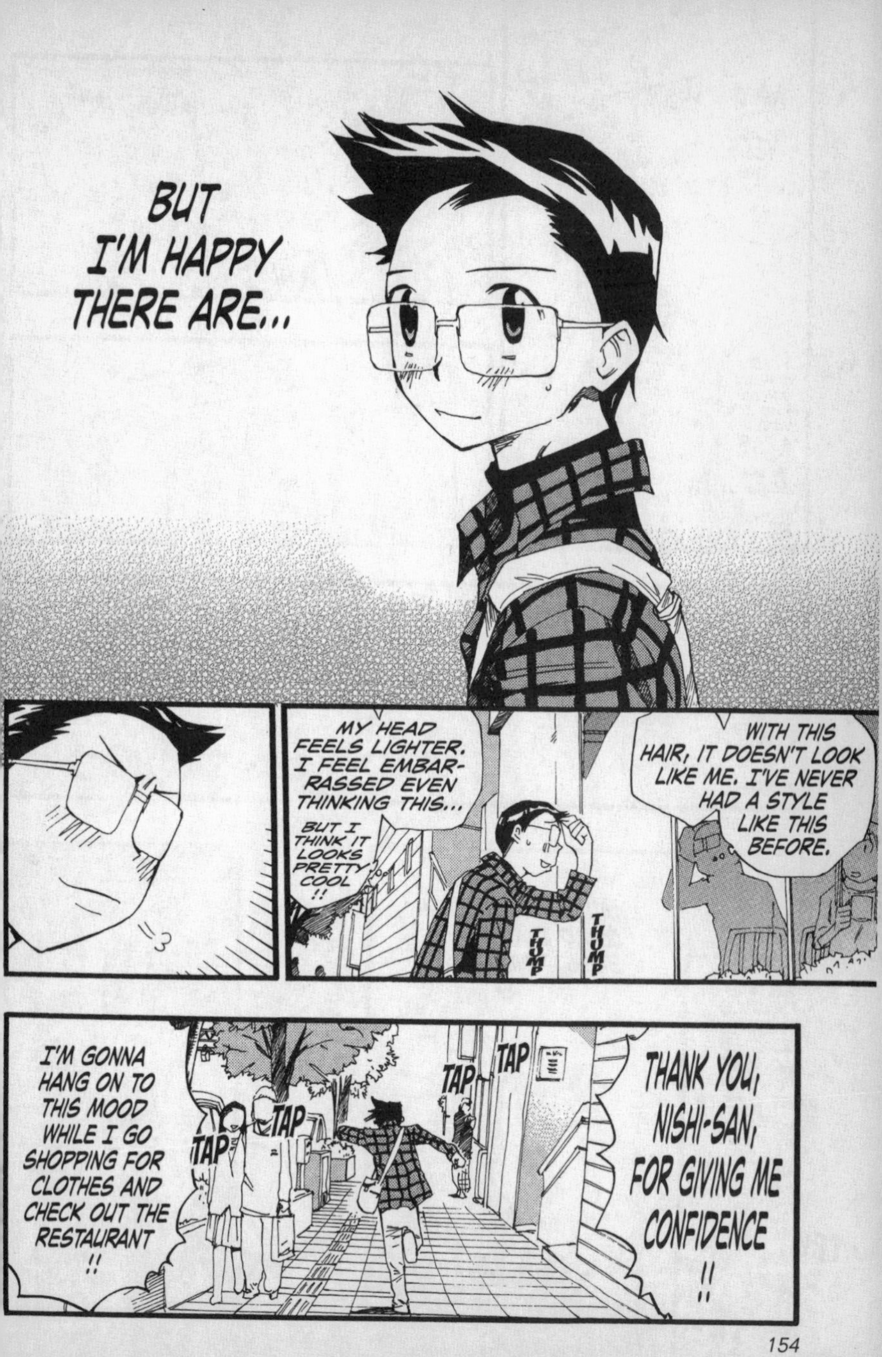
BUT I'M HAPPY THERE ARE...
WITH THIS HAIR, IT DOESN'T LOOK LIKE ME. I'VE NEVER HAD A STYLE LIKE THIS BEFORE.
MY HEAD FEELS LIGHTER. I FEEL EMBAR-RASSED EVEN THINKING THIS...
BUT I THINK IT LOOKS PRETTY COOL !!
THUMP
THUMP
THANK YOU, NISHI-SAN, FOR GIVING ME CONFIDENCE !!
TAP
TAP
TAP
TAP
I'M GONNA HANG ON TO THIS MOOD WHILE I GO SHOPPING FOR CLOTHES AND CHECK OUT THE RESTAURANT !!

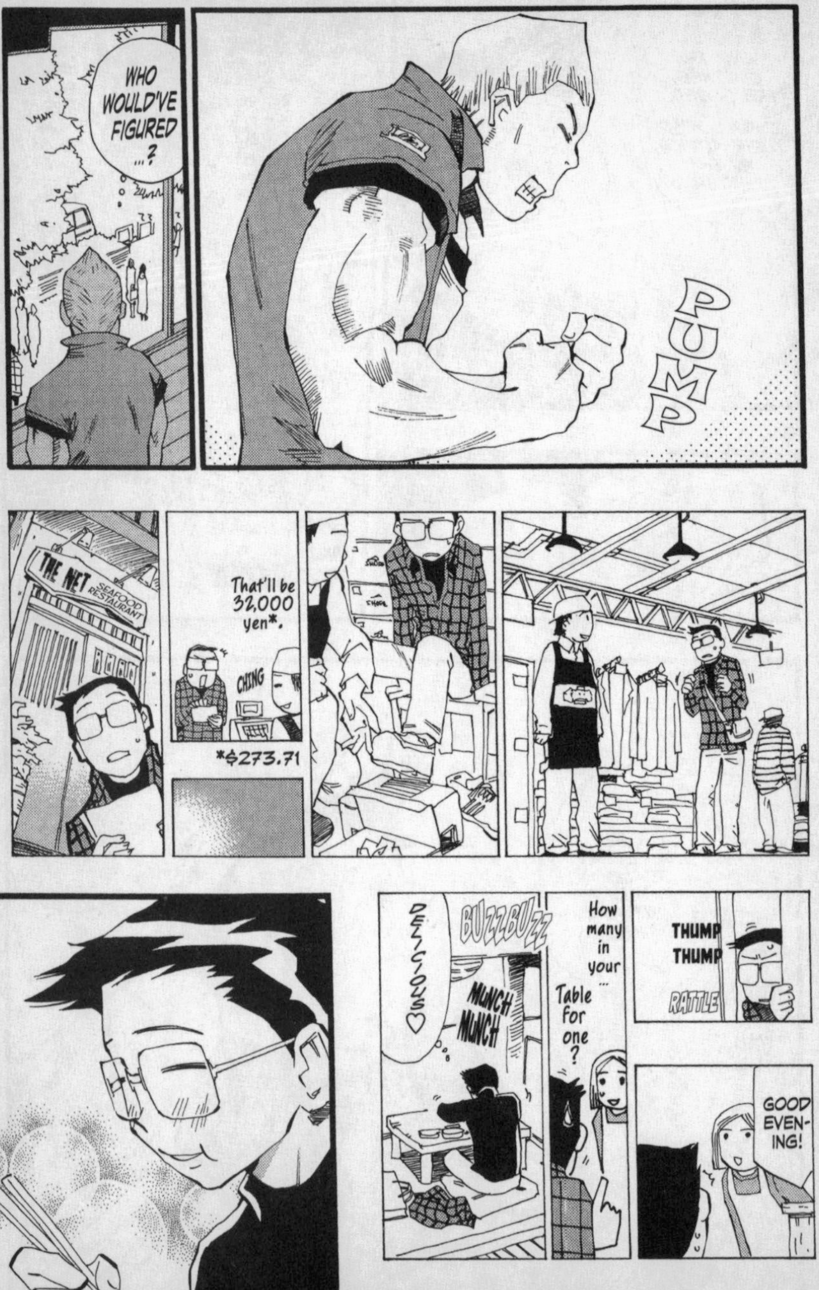
PUMP
WHO WOULD'VE FIGURED ...?
That'll be 32,000 yen*.
CHING
*$273.71
THE NET SEAFOOD RESTAURANT
THUMP THUMP
RATTLE
GOOD EVEN-ING!
How many in your ...
Table for one?
BUZZBUZZ
DELICIOUS♥
MUNCH MUNCH

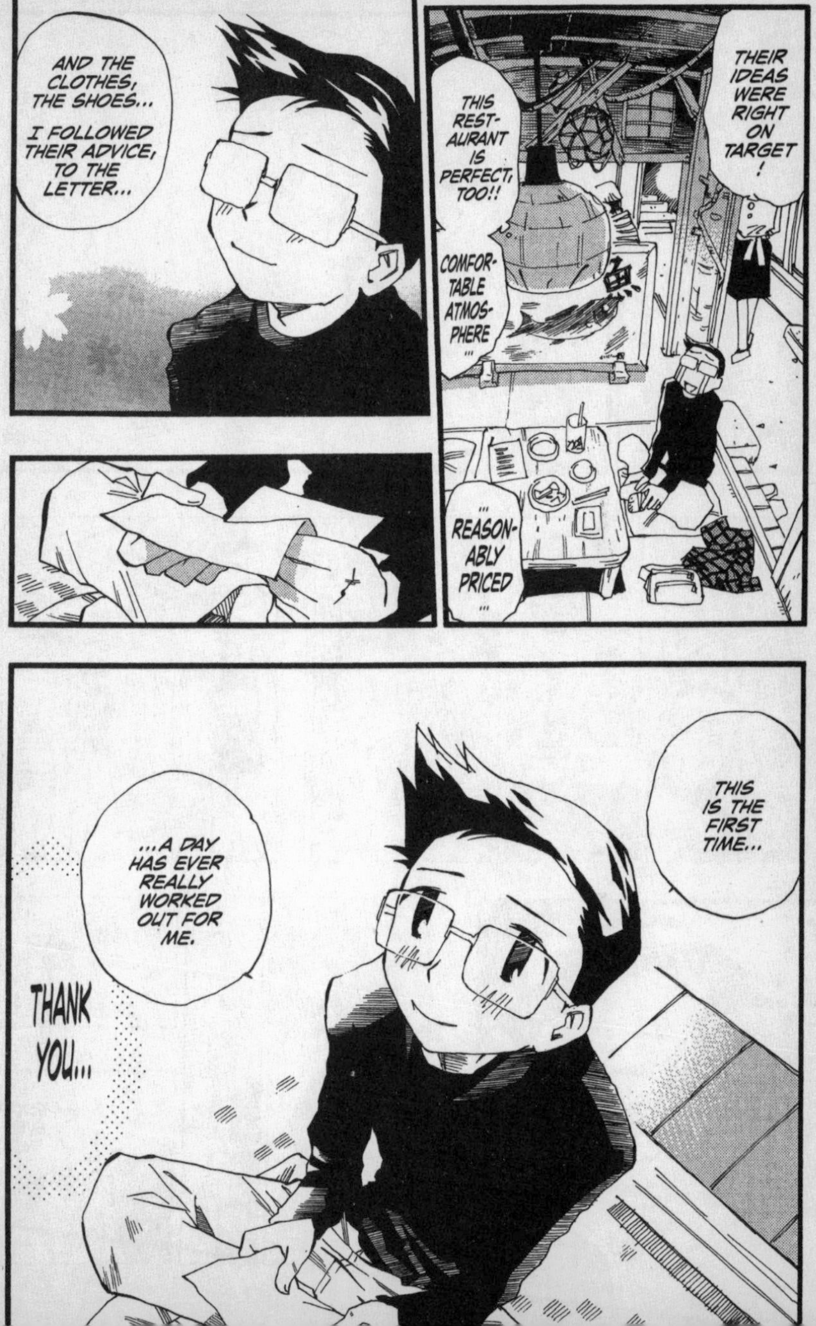
THEIR IDEAS WERE RIGHT ON TARGET!
THIS REST-AURANT IS PERFECT, TOO!!
COMFOR-TABLE ATMOS-PHERE...
...REASON-ABLY PRICED...
AND THE CLOTHES, THE SHOES...
I FOLLOWED THEIR ADVICE, TO THE LETTER...
THIS IS THE FIRST TIME...
...A DAY HAS EVER REALLY WORKED OUT FOR ME.
THANK YOU...

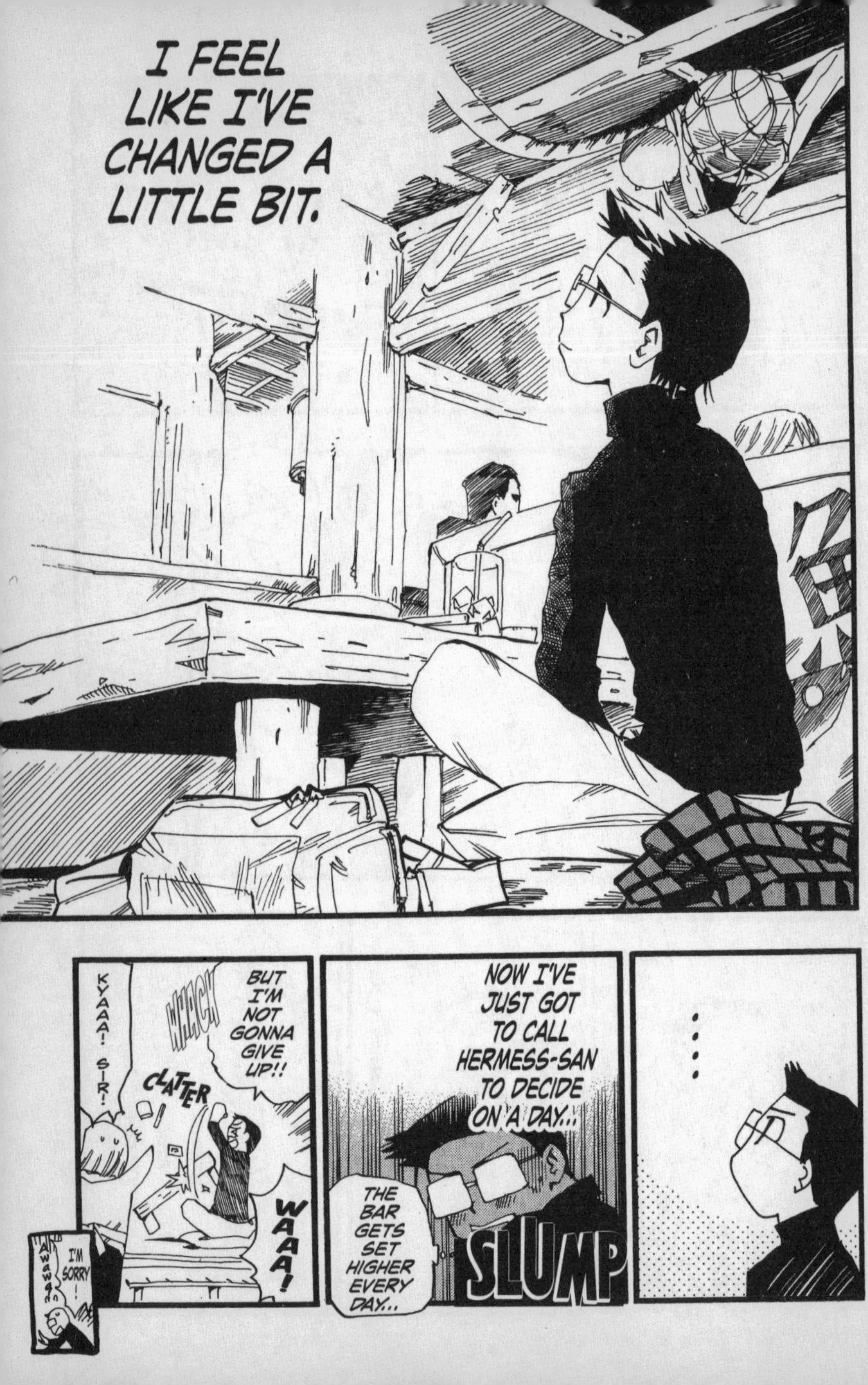
I FEEL LIKE I'VE CHANGED A LITTLE BIT.
....
NOW I'VE JUST GOT TO CALL HERMESS-SAN TO DECIDE ON A DAY...
SLUMP
THE BAR GETS SET HIGHER EVERY DAY...
BUT I'M NOT GONNA GIVE UP!!
WHACK
KYAAA! SIR!
CLATTER
WAAAA!
I'M SORRY!

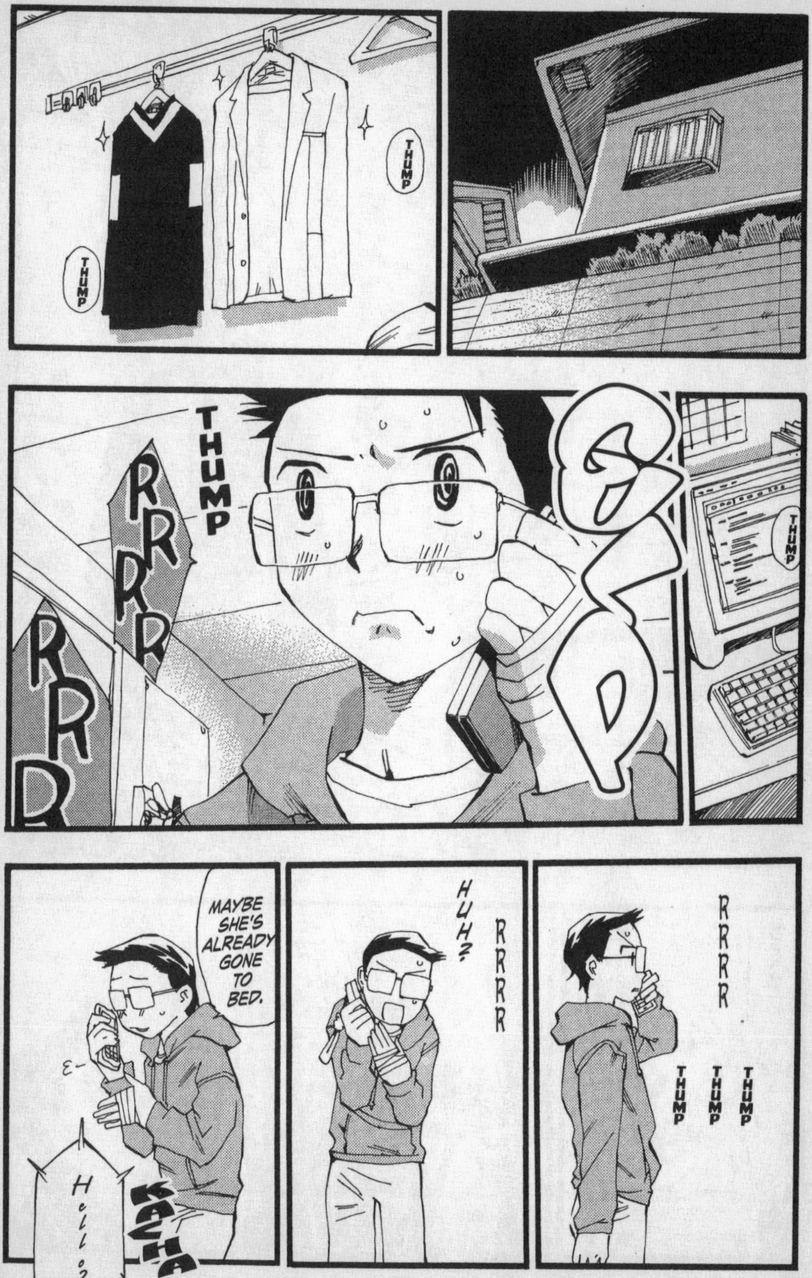
THUMP
THUMP
THUMP
THUMP
RRRRRRR
RRRR
THUMP THUMP THUMP
HUH?
RRRR
MAYBE SHE'S ALREADY GONE TO BED.
KACHA
Hello...?

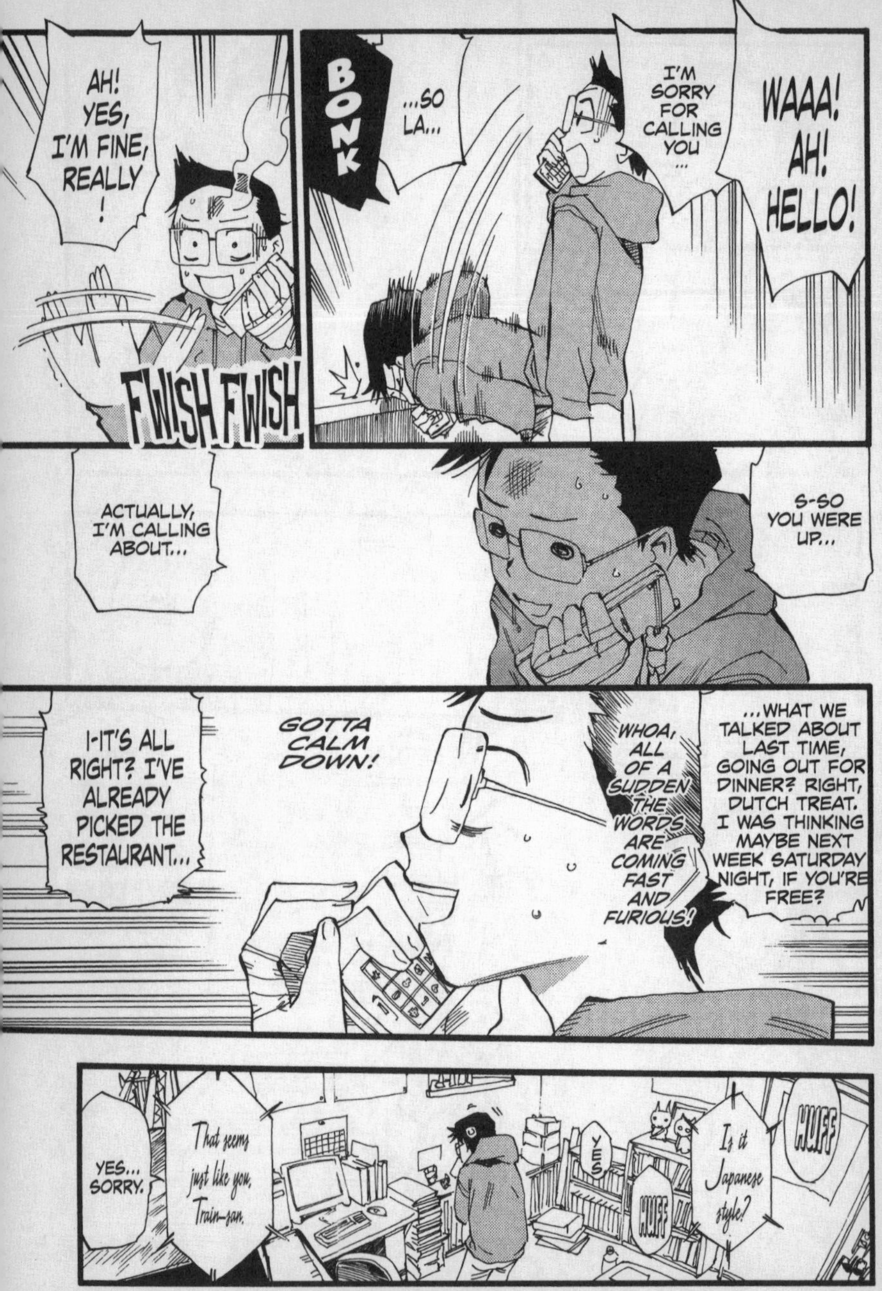
WAAA! AH! HELLO!
I'M SORRY FOR CALLING YOU ...
...SO LA...
BONK
AH! YES, I'M FINE, REALLY!
FWISH FWISH
S-SO YOU WERE UP...
ACTUALLY, I'M CALLING ABOUT...
...WHAT WE TALKED ABOUT LAST TIME, GOING OUT FOR DINNER? RIGHT, DUTCH TREAT. I WAS THINKING MAYBE NEXT WEEK SATURDAY NIGHT, IF YOU'RE FREE?
WHOA, ALL OF A SUDDEN THE WORDS ARE COMING FAST AND FURIOUS!
GOTTA CALM DOWN!
I-IT'S ALL RIGHT? I'VE ALREADY PICKED THE RESTAURANT...
HUFF
Is it Japanese style?
HUFF
YES
That seems just like you, Train-san.
YES... SORRY.

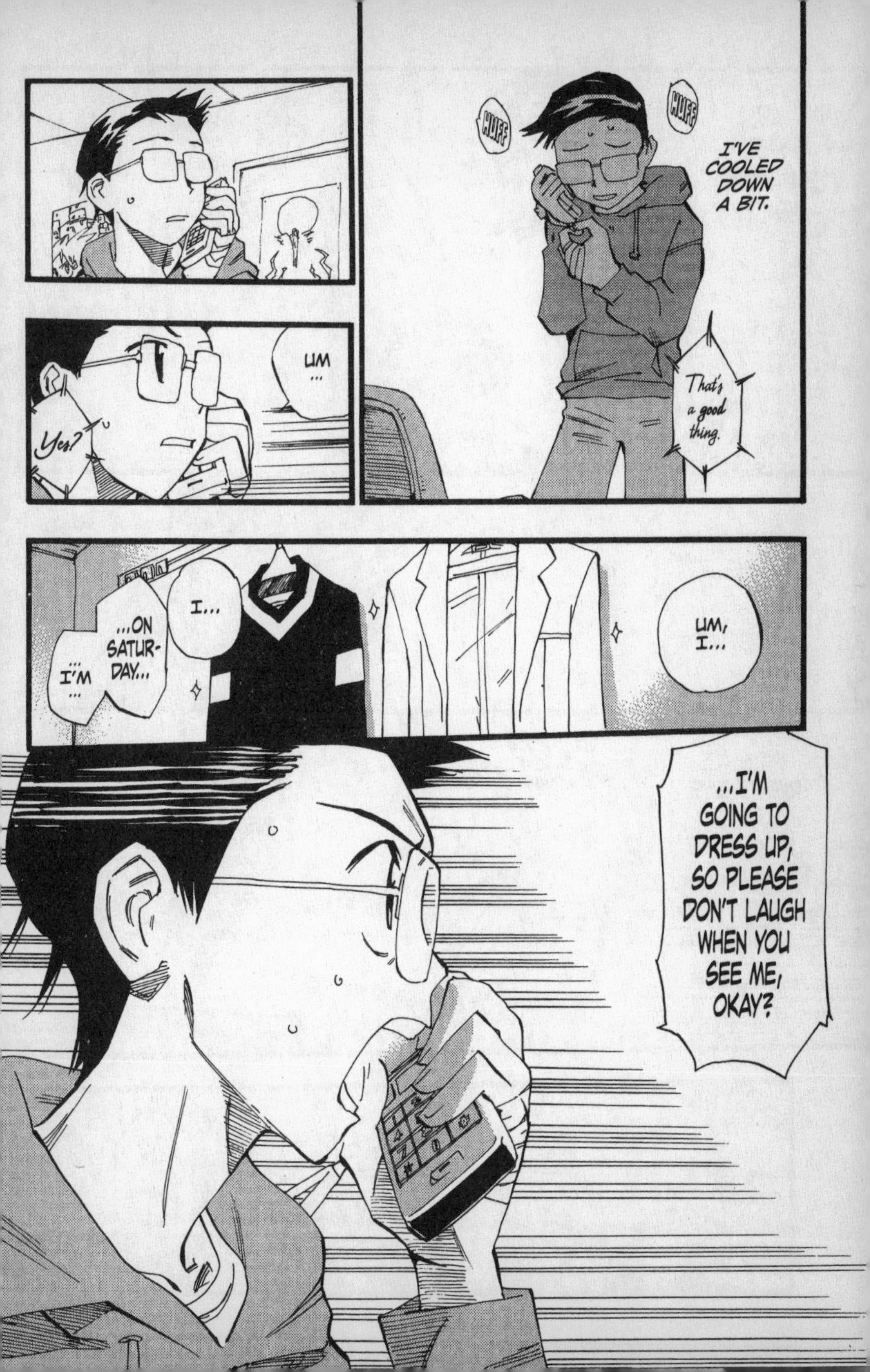
HUFF
HUFF
I'VE COOLED DOWN A BIT.
That's a good thing.
UM ...
Yes?
UM, I...
I...
...ON SATURDAY...
... I'M ...
...I'M GOING TO DRESS UP, SO PLEASE DON'T LAUGH WHEN YOU SEE ME, OKAY?

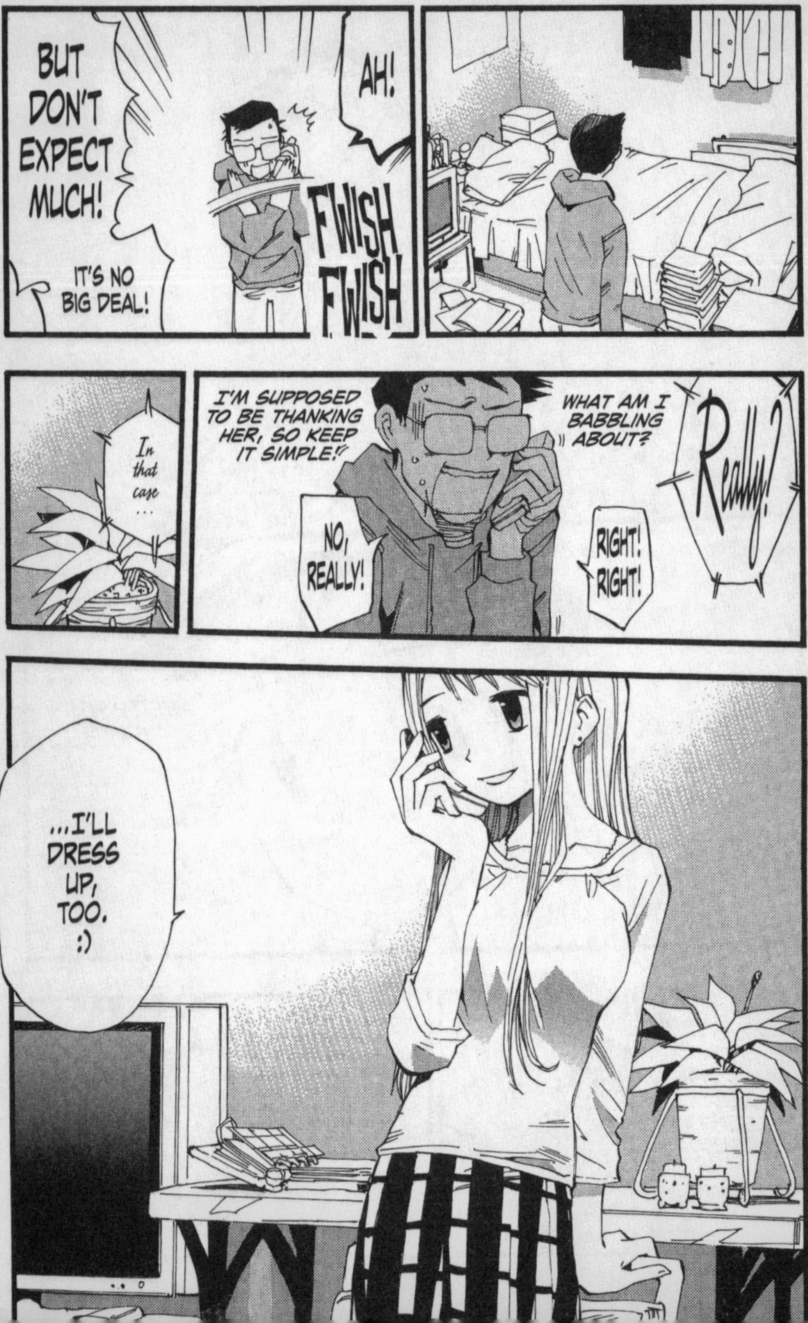
AH!
FWISH FWISH
BUT DON'T EXPECT MUCH!
IT'S NO BIG DEAL!
Really?
WHAT AM I BABBLING ABOUT?
RIGHT! RIGHT!
I'M SUPPOSED TO BE THANKING HER, SO KEEP IT SIMPLE!
NO, REALLY!
In that case...
...I'LL DRESS UP, TOO. :)

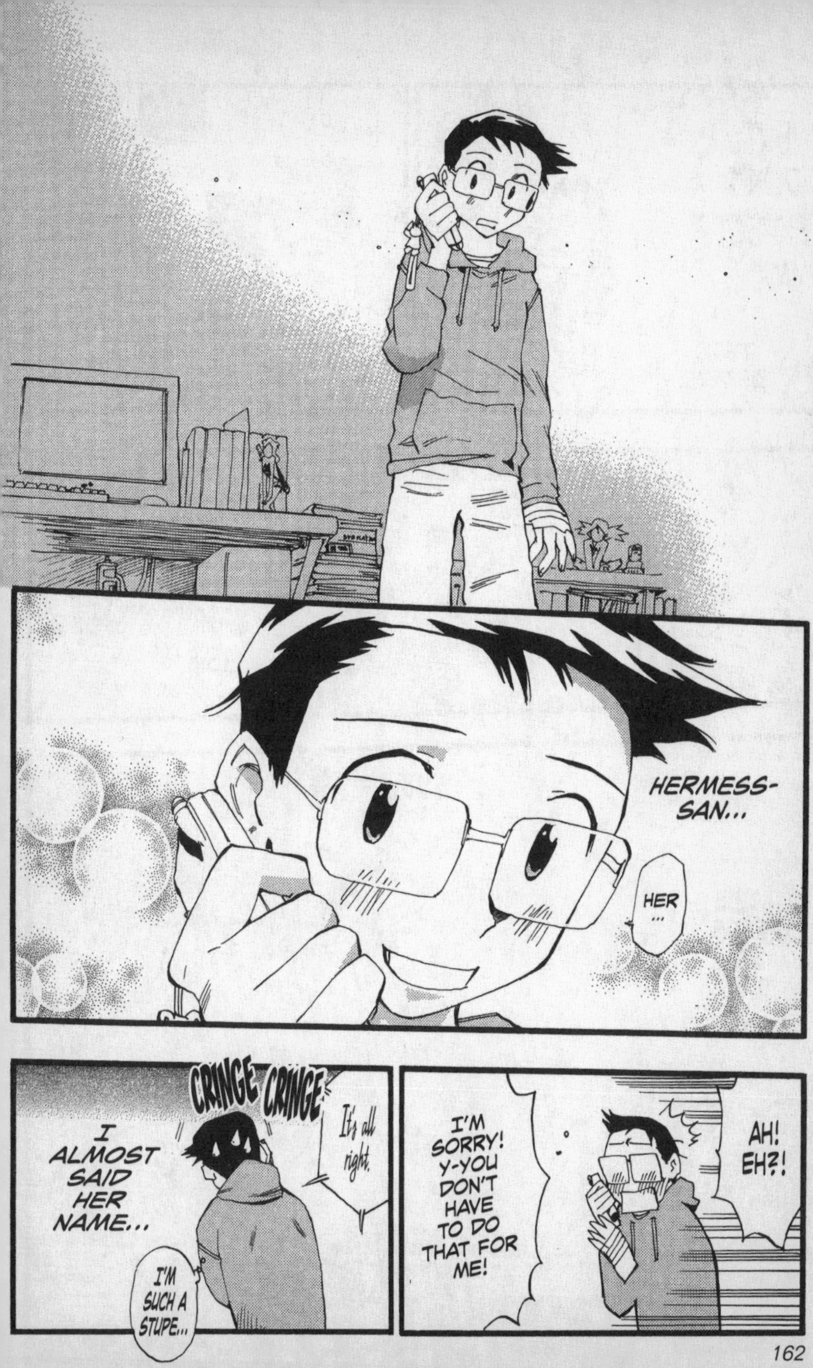
HERMESS-SAN...
HER ...
AH! EH?!
I'M SORRY! Y-YOU DON'T HAVE TO DO THAT FOR ME!
It's all right.
CRINGE CRINGE
I ALMOST SAID HER NAME...
I'M SUCH A STUPE...

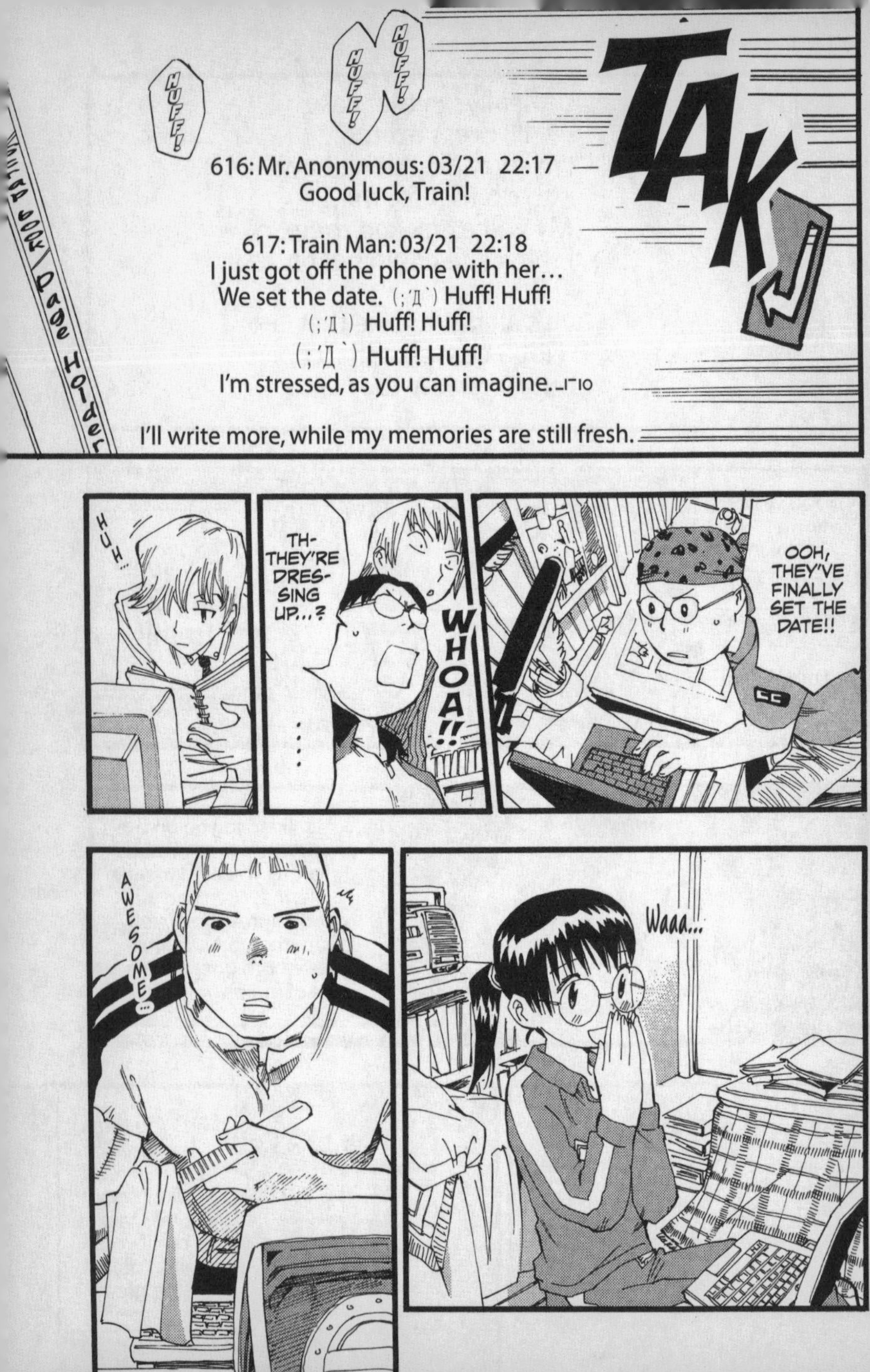
TAK
HUFF! HUFF!
HUFF!
616: Mr. Anonymous: 03/21 22:17
Good luck, Train!
617: Train Man: 03/21 22:18
I just got off the phone with her…
We set the date. (;´Д`) Huff! Huff!
(;´Д`) Huff! Huff!
(;´Д`) Huff! Huff!
I'm stressed, as you can imagine._|￣|○
I'll write more, while my memories are still fresh.
Page Holder
OOH, THEY'VE FINALLY SET THE DATE!!
WHOA!!
TH- THEY'RE DRES-SING UP…?
HUH…
Waaa…
AWESOME…

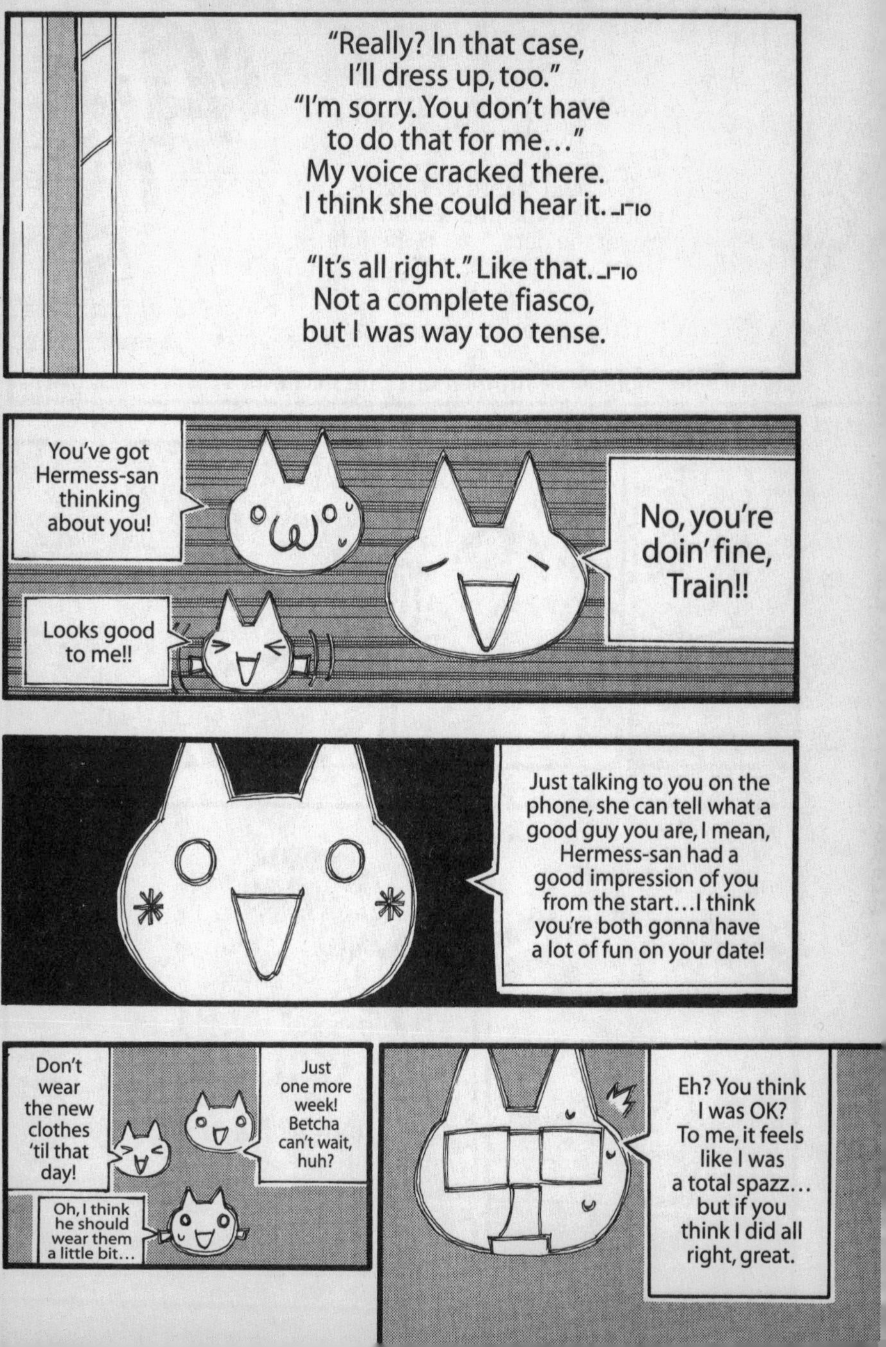
"Really? In that case, I'll dress up, too." "I'm sorry. You don't have to do that for me…" My voice cracked there. I think she could hear it. _|¯|o
"It's all right." Like that. _|¯|o Not a complete fiasco, but I was way too tense.
No, you're doin' fine, Train!!
You've got Hermess-san thinking about you!
Looks good to me!!
Just talking to you on the phone, she can tell what a good guy you are, I mean, Hermess-san had a good impression of you from the start…I think you're both gonna have a lot of fun on your date!
Eh? You think I was OK? To me, it feels like I was a total spazz… but if you think I did all right, great.
Just one more week! Betcha can't wait, huh?
Don't wear the new clothes 'til that day!
Oh, I think he should wear them a little bit…

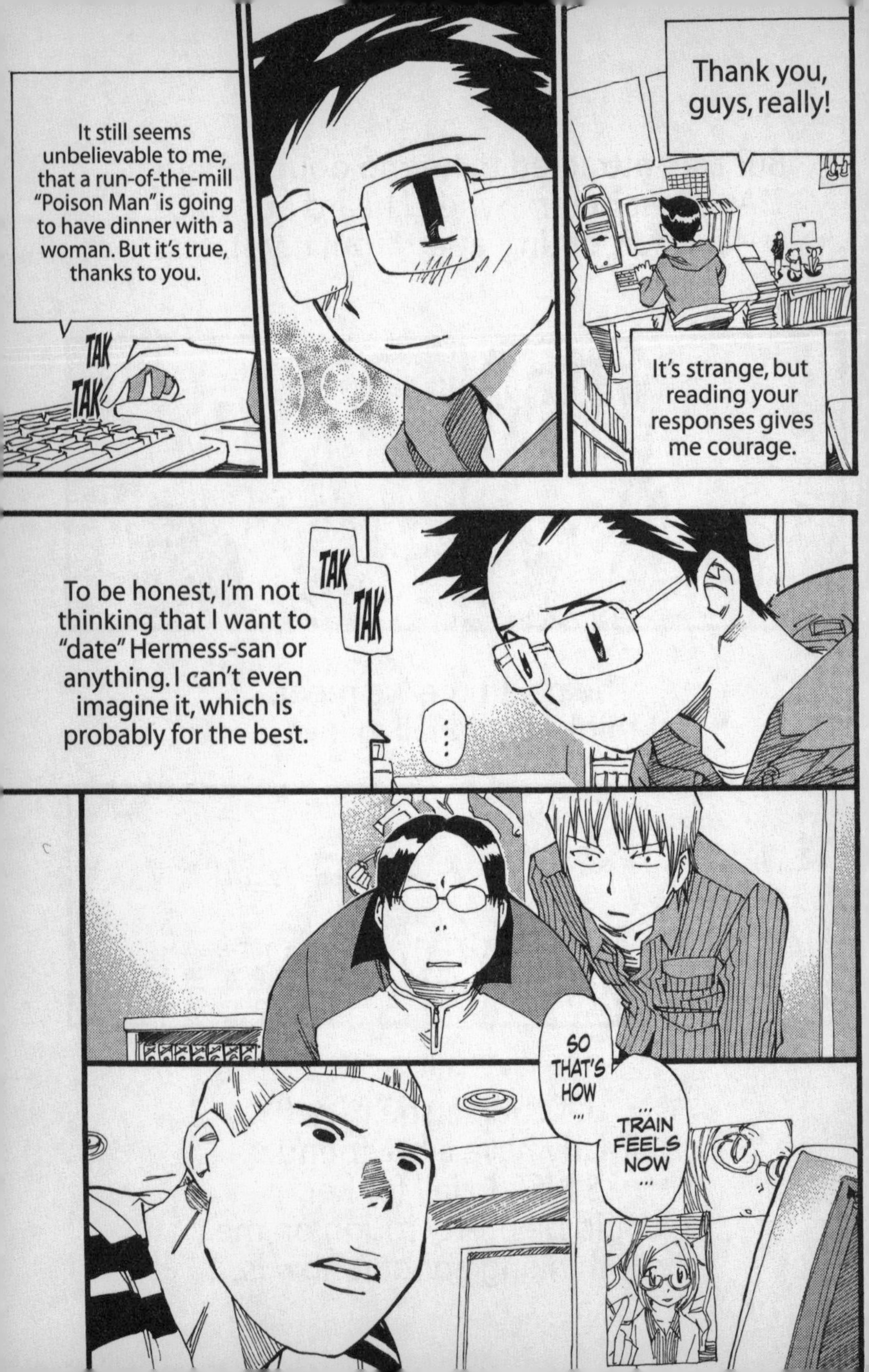
Thank you, guys, really!
It's strange, but reading your responses gives me courage.
It still seems unbelievable to me, that a run-of-the-mill "Poison Man" is going to have dinner with a woman. But it's true, thanks to you.
TAK TAK
TAK TAK
To be honest, I'm not thinking that I want to "date" Hermess-san or anything. I can't even imagine it, which is probably for the best.
.....
SO THAT'S HOW ...
... TRAIN FEELS NOW ...

But I am attracted to her, no doubt about it.
And just before, when I heard her voice,
I felt something, apart from my stress.

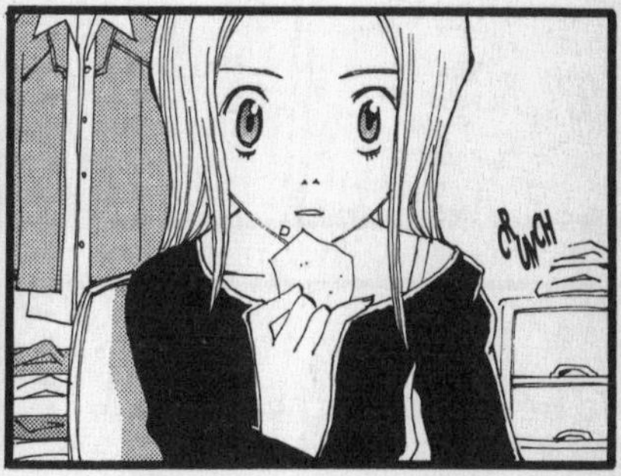
CRUNCH
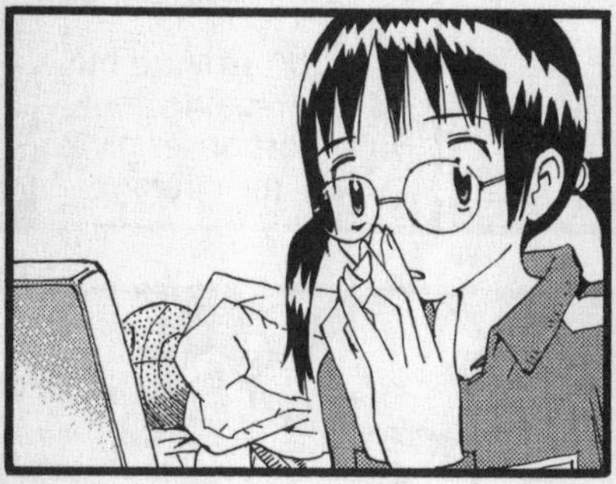

The next time we meet,
I think I could fall in love…

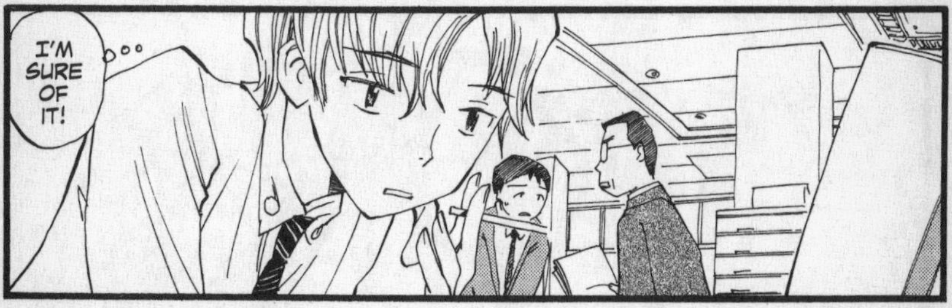
I'M SURE OF IT!

Of course, she may
already have a boyfriend…
So if I do fall for her,
it could be pretty rough on me.
Even thinking about it now is…

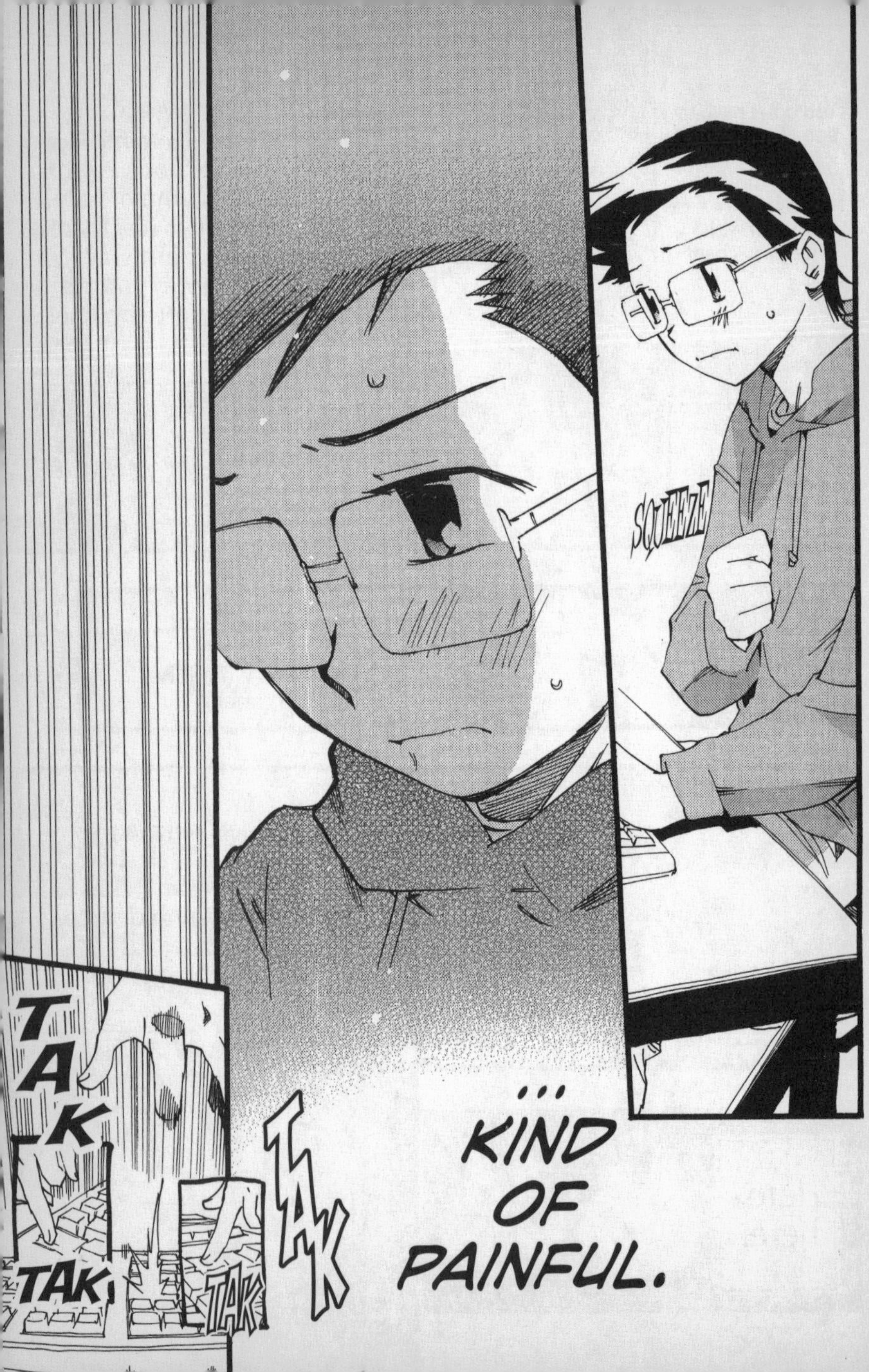
SQUEEZE
... KIND OF PAINFUL.
TAK
TAK
TAK
TAK

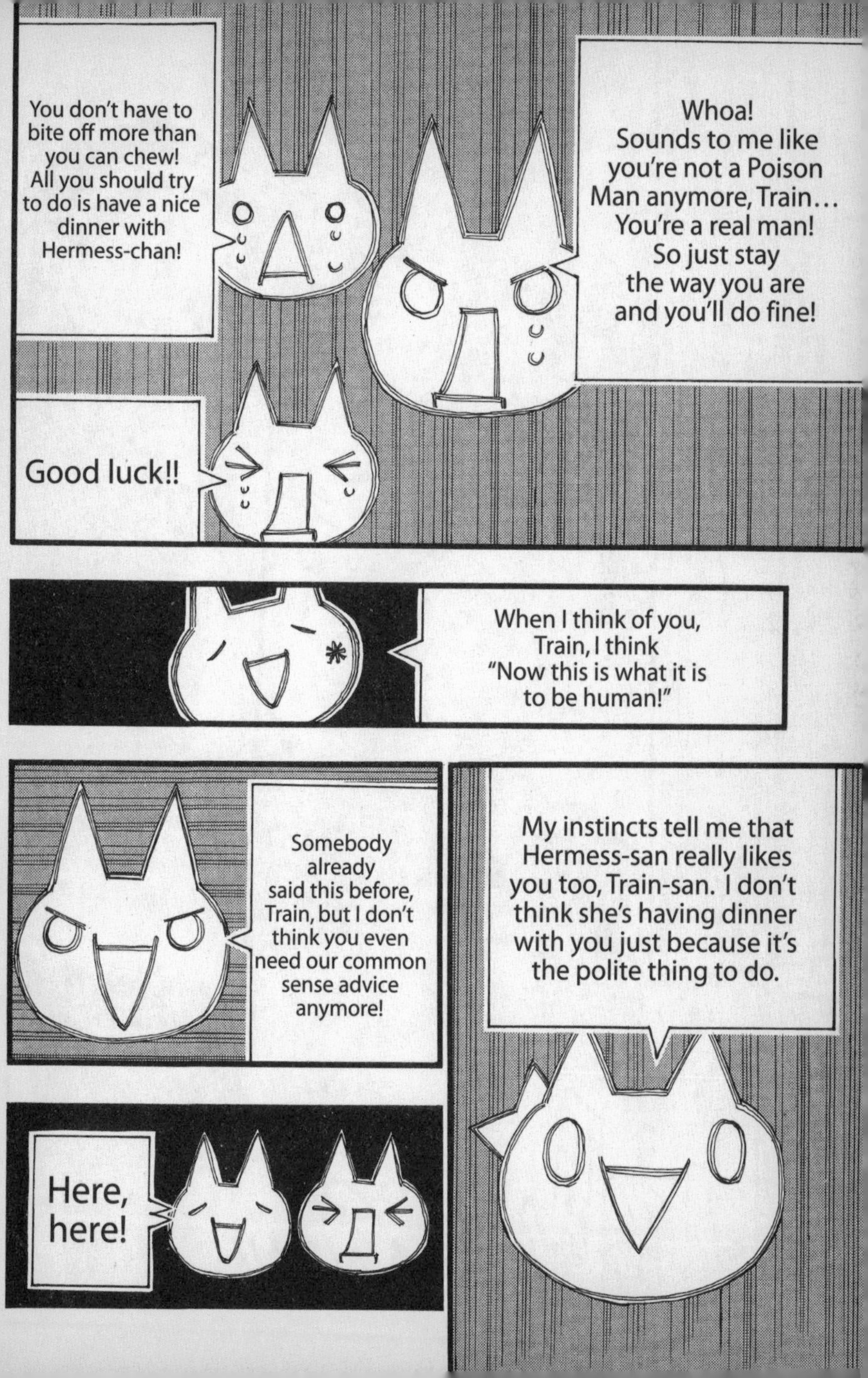
Whoa! Sounds to me like you're not a Poison Man anymore, Train… You're a real man! So just stay the way you are and you'll do fine!
You don't have to bite off more than you can chew! All you should try to do is have a nice dinner with Hermess-chan!
Good luck!!
When I think of you, Train, I think "Now this is what it is to be human!"
My instincts tell me that Hermess-san really likes you too, Train-san. I don't think she's having dinner with you just because it's the polite thing to do.
Somebody already said this before, Train, but I don't think you even need our common sense advice anymore!
Here, here!

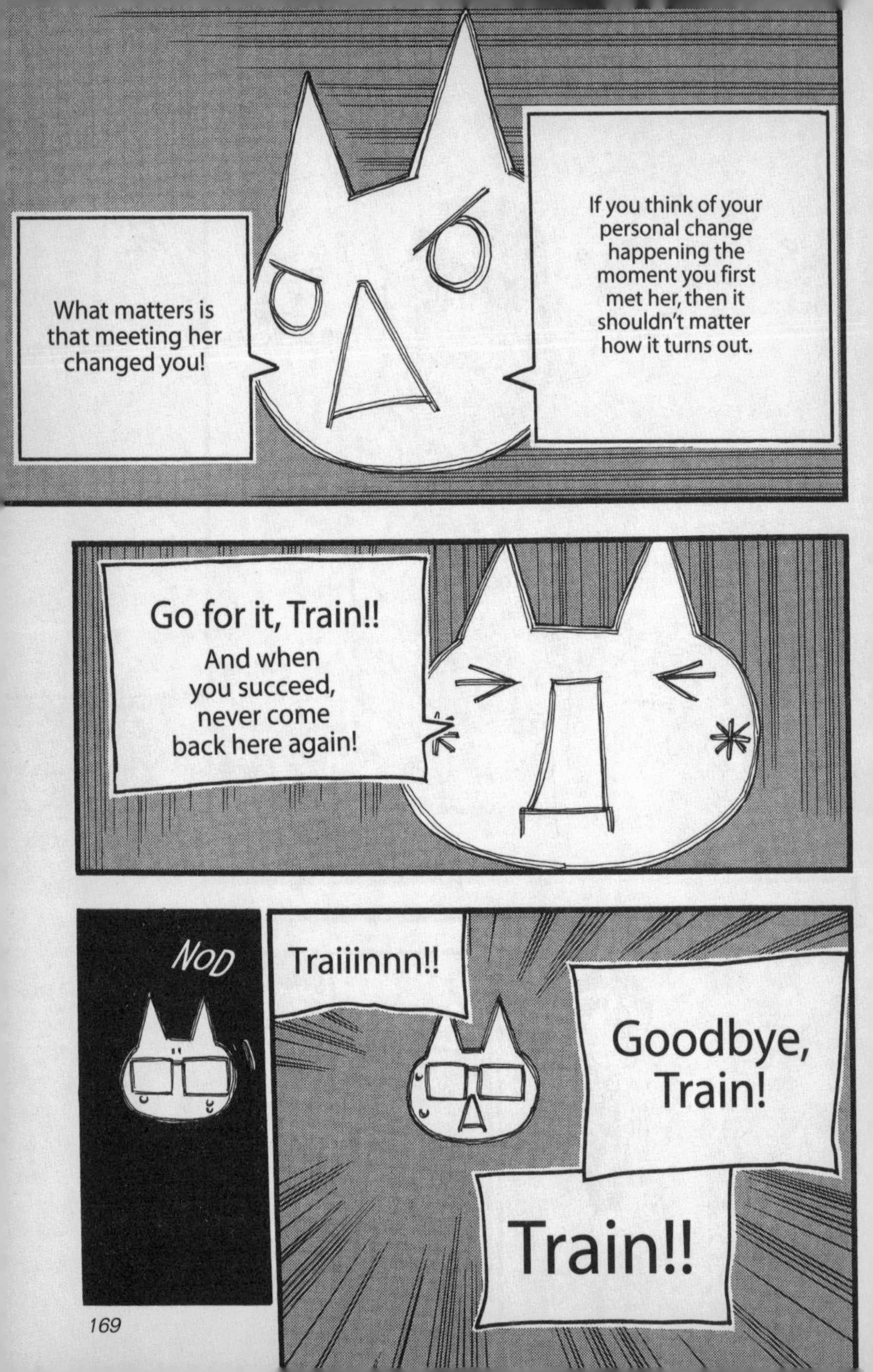
If you think of your personal change happening the moment you first met her, then it shouldn't matter how it turns out.
What matters is that meeting her changed you!
Go for it, Train!! And when you succeed, never come back here again!
Goodbye, Train!
Traiiinnn!!
Train!!
NOD

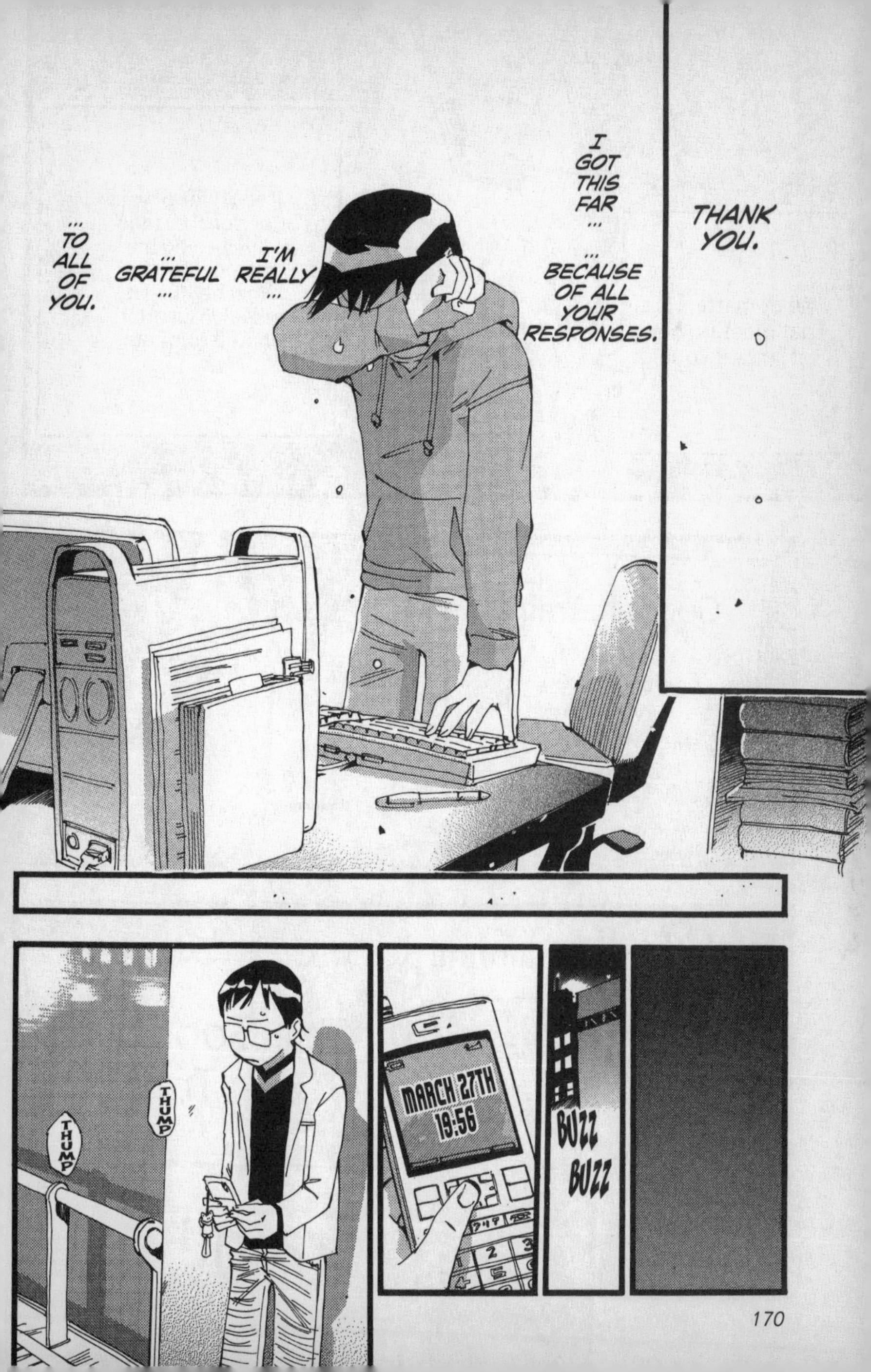
THANK YOU.
I GOT THIS FAR ...
... BECAUSE OF ALL YOUR RESPONSES.
I'M REALLY ...
... GRATEFUL ...
... TO ALL OF YOU.
BUZZ BUZZ
MARCH 27TH 19:56
THUMP
THUMP

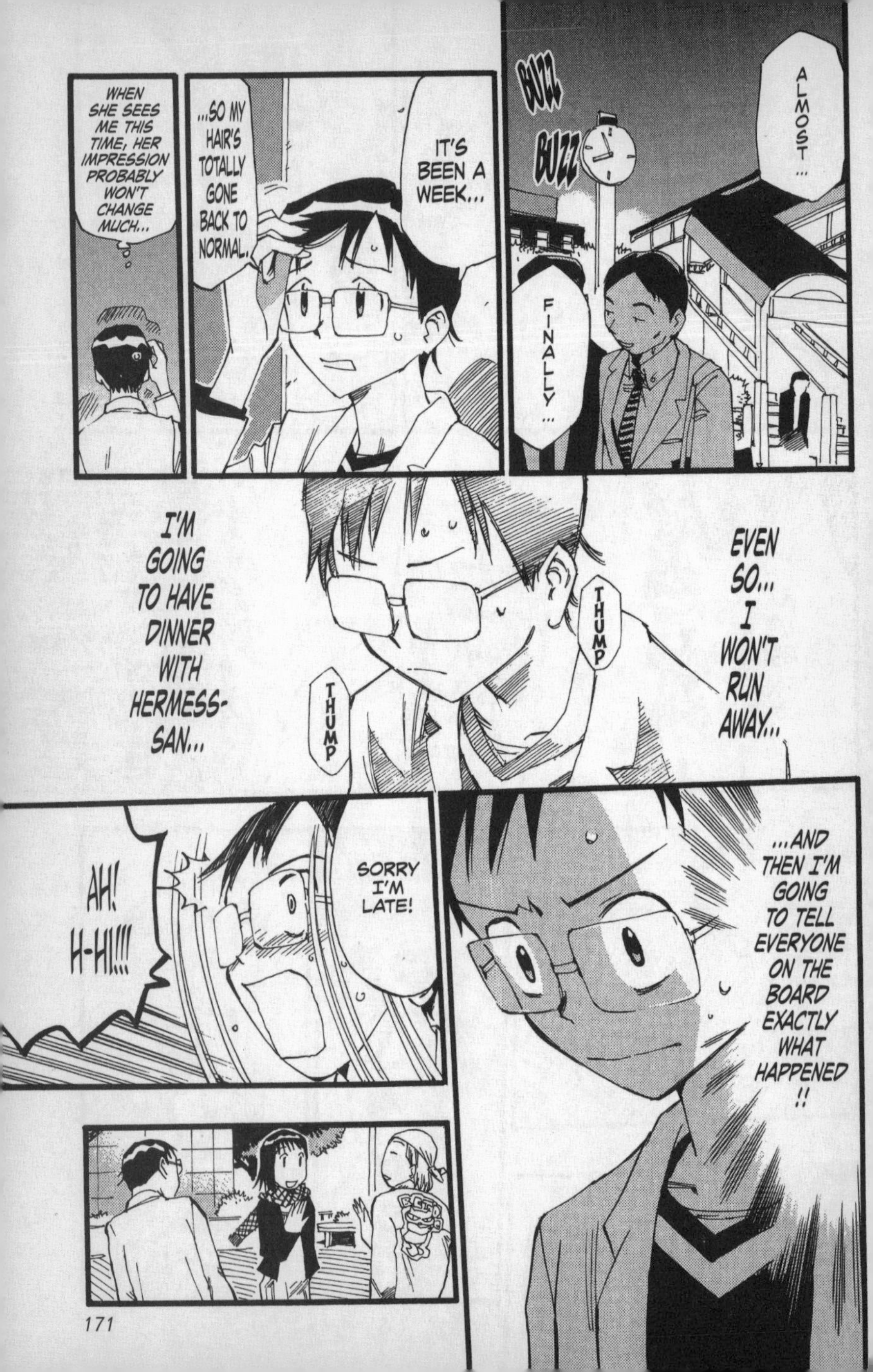
ALMOST...
BUZZ
BUZZ
FINALLY...
IT'S BEEN A WEEK...
...SO MY HAIR'S TOTALLY GONE BACK TO NORMAL.
WHEN SHE SEES ME THIS TIME, HER IMPRESSION PROBABLY WON'T CHANGE MUCH...
EVEN SO... I WON'T RUN AWAY...
THUMP
THUMP
I'M GOING TO HAVE DINNER WITH HERMESS-SAN...
...AND THEN I'M GOING TO TELL EVERYONE ON THE BOARD EXACTLY WHAT HAPPENED!!
SORRY I'M LATE!
AH! H-HI!!!

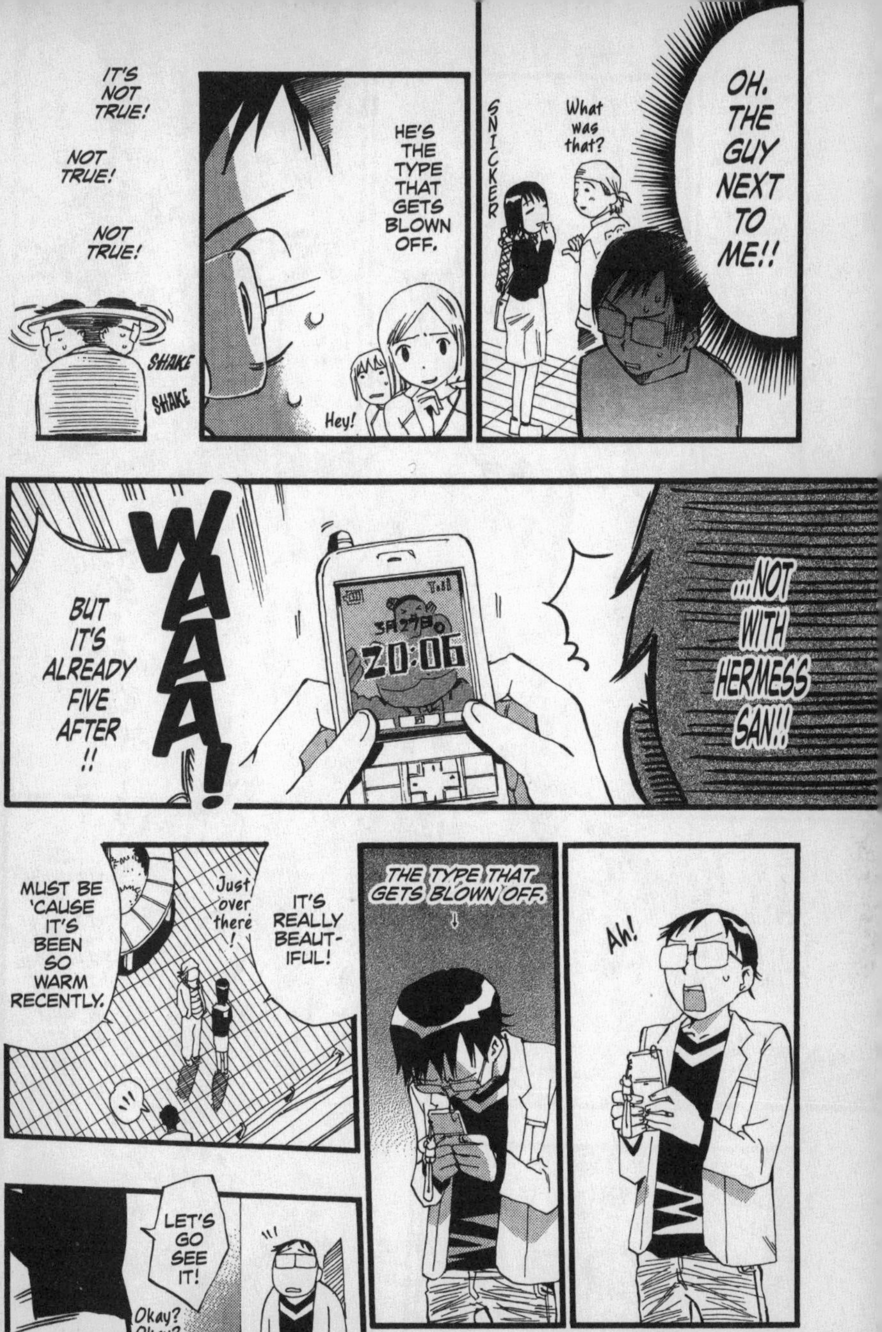
OH. THE GUY NEXT TO ME!!
What was that?
SNICKER
HE'S THE TYPE THAT GETS BLOWN OFF.
Hey!
IT'S NOT TRUE!
NOT TRUE!
NOT TRUE!
SHAKE
SHAKE
...NOT WITH HERMESS SAN!!
WAAA!
BUT IT'S ALREADY FIVE AFTER!!
20:06
Ah!
THE TYPE THAT GETS BLOWN OFF.
IT'S REALLY BEAUTIFUL!
Just over there!
MUST BE 'CAUSE IT'S BEEN SO WARM RECENTLY.
LET'S GO SEE IT!
Okay? Okay?

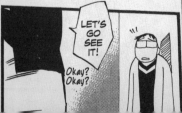

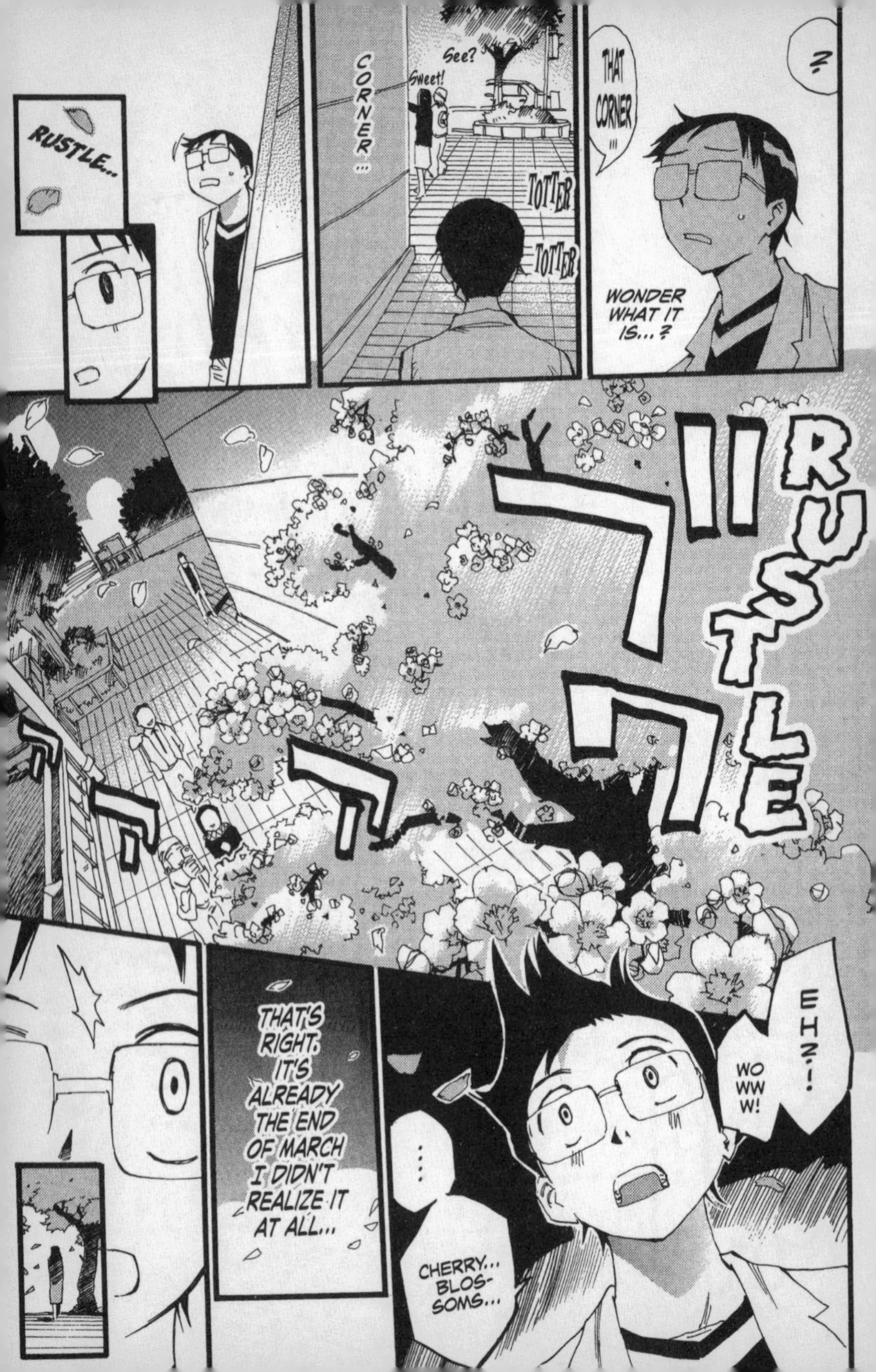
?
THAT CORNER ...
WONDER WHAT IT IS...?
CORNER ...
See?
Sweet!
TOTTER
TOTTER
RUSTLE...
RUSTLE
EH?!
WOWWW!
...
CHERRY... BLOSSOMS...
THAT'S RIGHT. IT'S ALREADY THE END OF MARCH
I DIDN'T REALIZE IT AT ALL...

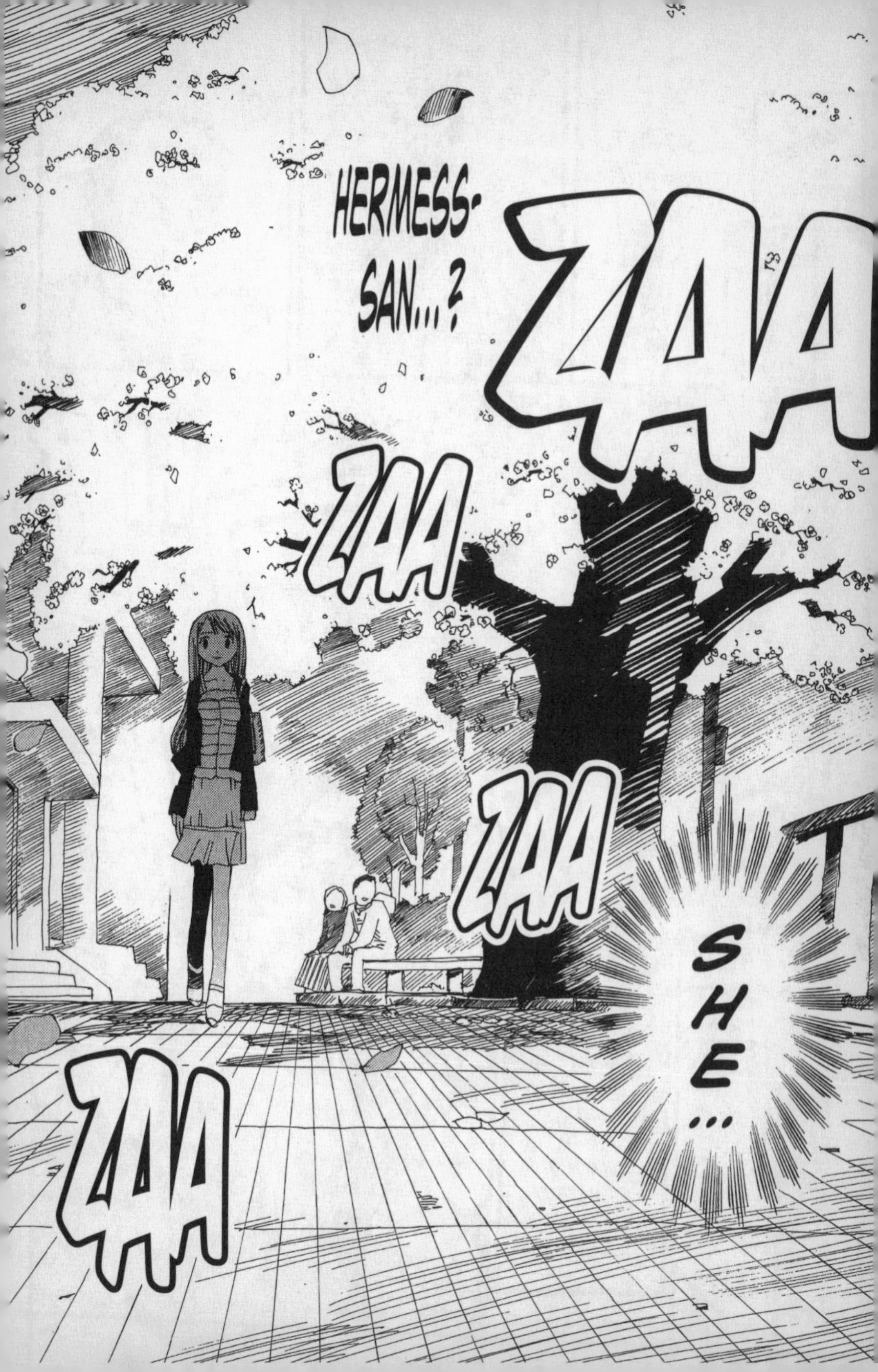
ZAA
HERMESS-SAN...?
ZAA
ZAA
SHE...
ZAA

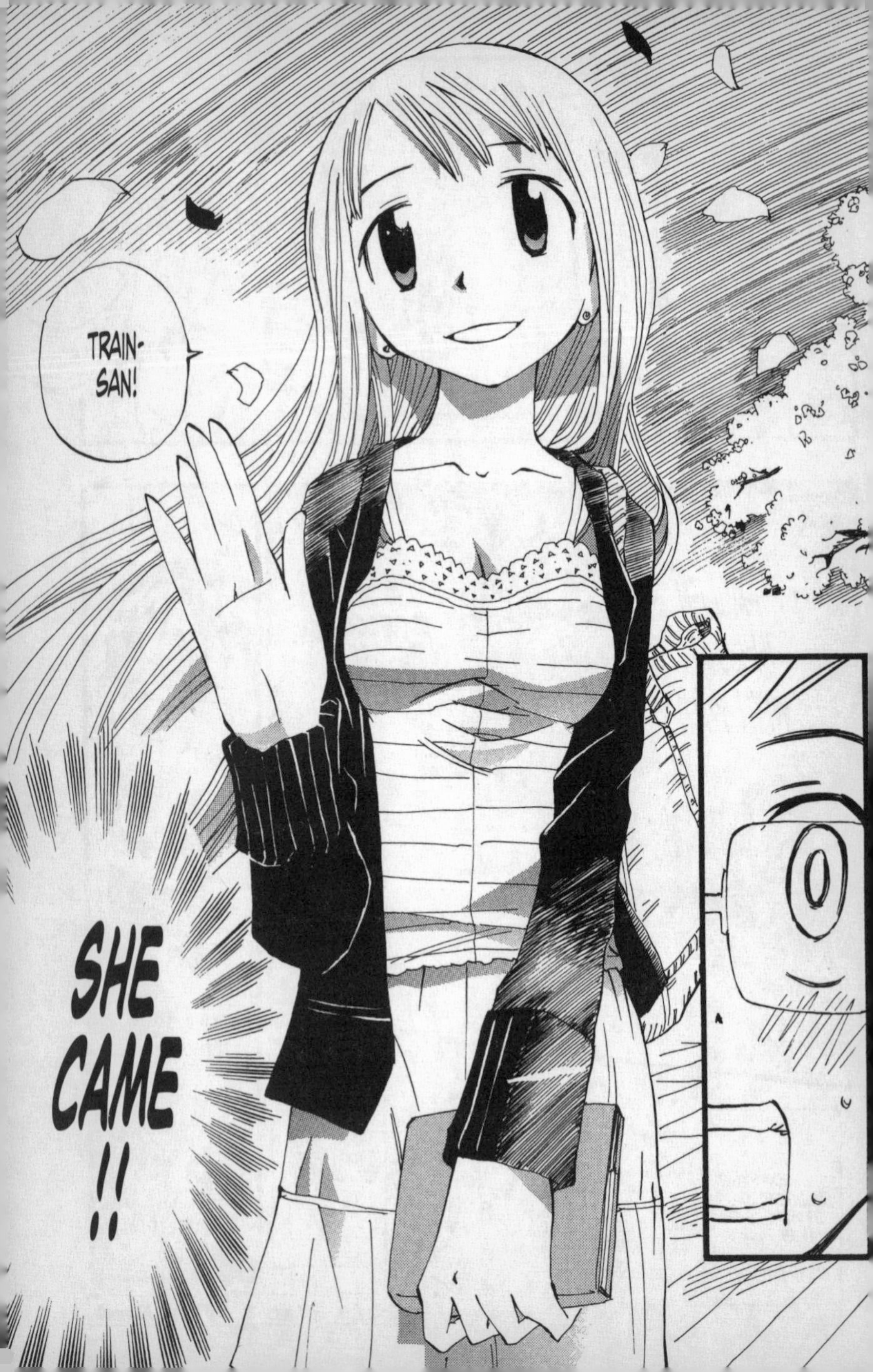
TRAIN-SAN!
SHE CAME !!

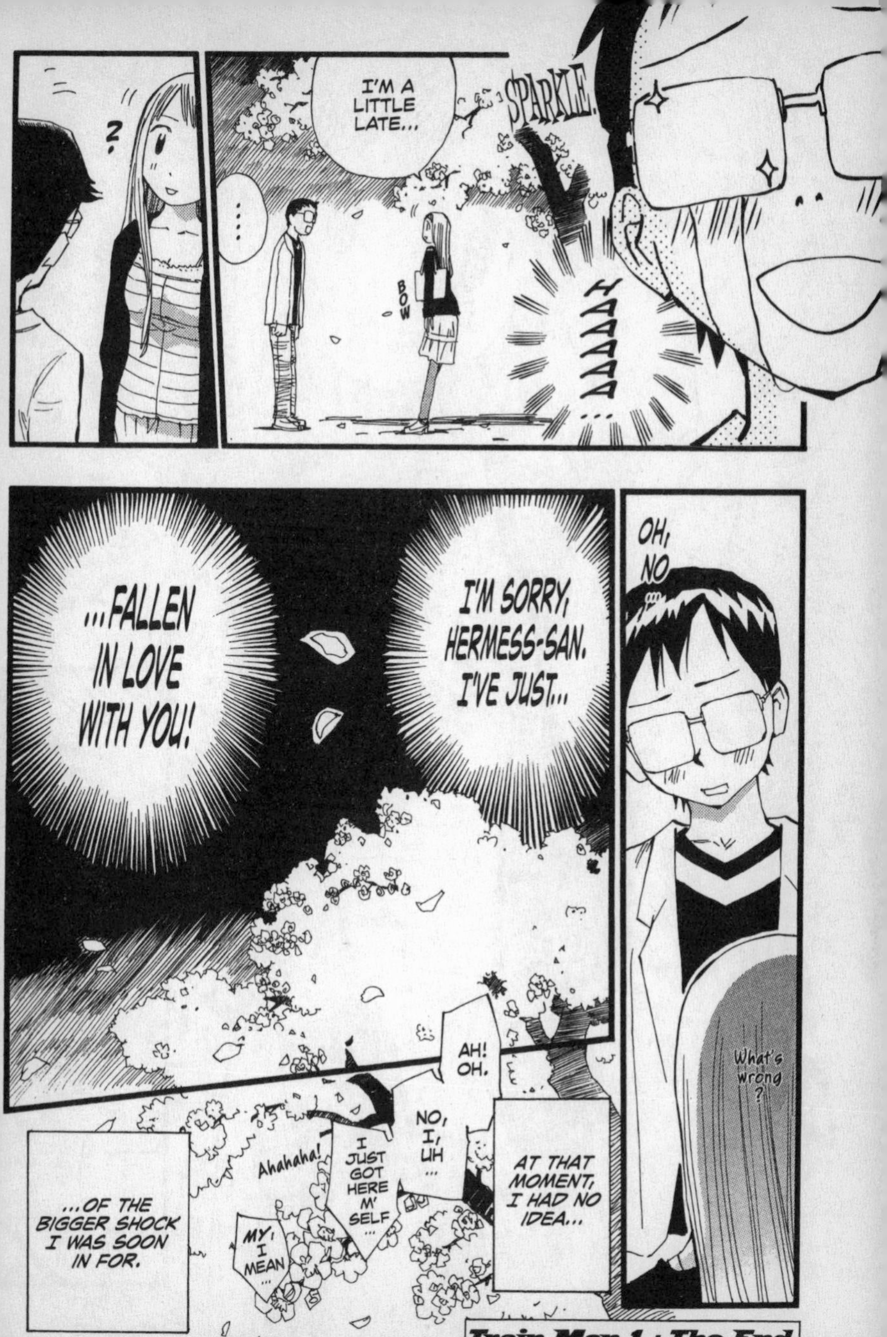
SPARKLE
HAAAAAA...
I'M A LITTLE LATE...
BOW
....
?
OH, NO...
What's wrong?
I'M SORRY, HERMESS-SAN. I'VE JUST...
...FALLEN IN LOVE WITH YOU!
AT THAT MOMENT, I HAD NO IDEA...
AH! OH.
NO, I, UH...
I JUST GOT HERE M' SELF...
Ahahaha!
MY, I MEAN...
...OF THE BIGGER SHOCK I WAS SOON IN FOR.

Train Man 1 : The End

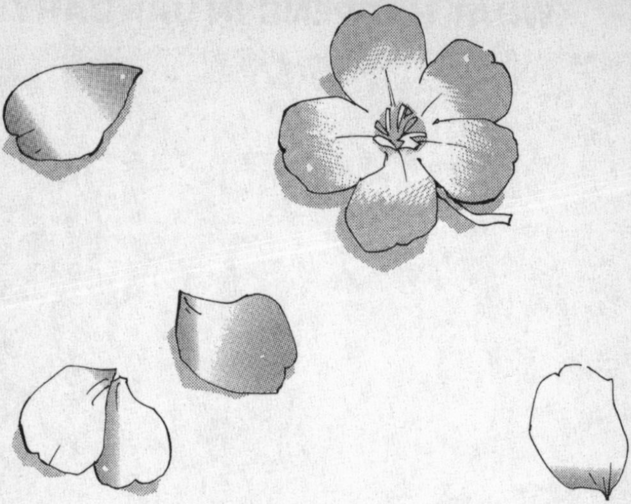

THANK YOU.

REJECTED COVER PROPOSALS

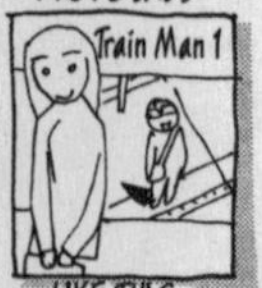
Train Man 1

LIKE THIS...

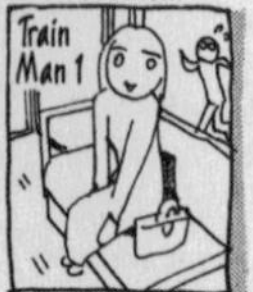
Train Man 1

...AND THIS...

Nice to meet you. I'm Watanabe. Hello to those of you who already know me. Well, after one thing and another, DENSHA OTOKO ("Train Man") volume 1 is out. I hope you have a good time reading it…! I believe the story will continue for one or two more volumes, so I also hope you don't get tired of it. A lot of stuff in here is original with me, so maybe you'll have a good time comparing it with the original book. By the way, about the cover: Through a previous arrangement, I produced ten different drawings as potential covers. Most of them were some form of Train-kun and Hermess-san together with a trainin the background, but in the end, the drawing I thought was the roughest was chosen. At the time of drawing it, my simple idea was, "A train and Hermess… Hey, I'll have her ride on top of it!"

Hope you come back for volume 2!
Watanabe Wataru 3/31/05

05.3.31

IT'S TOO MUCH TO BEAR! FIND OUT WHAT HAPPENS IN JANUARY!

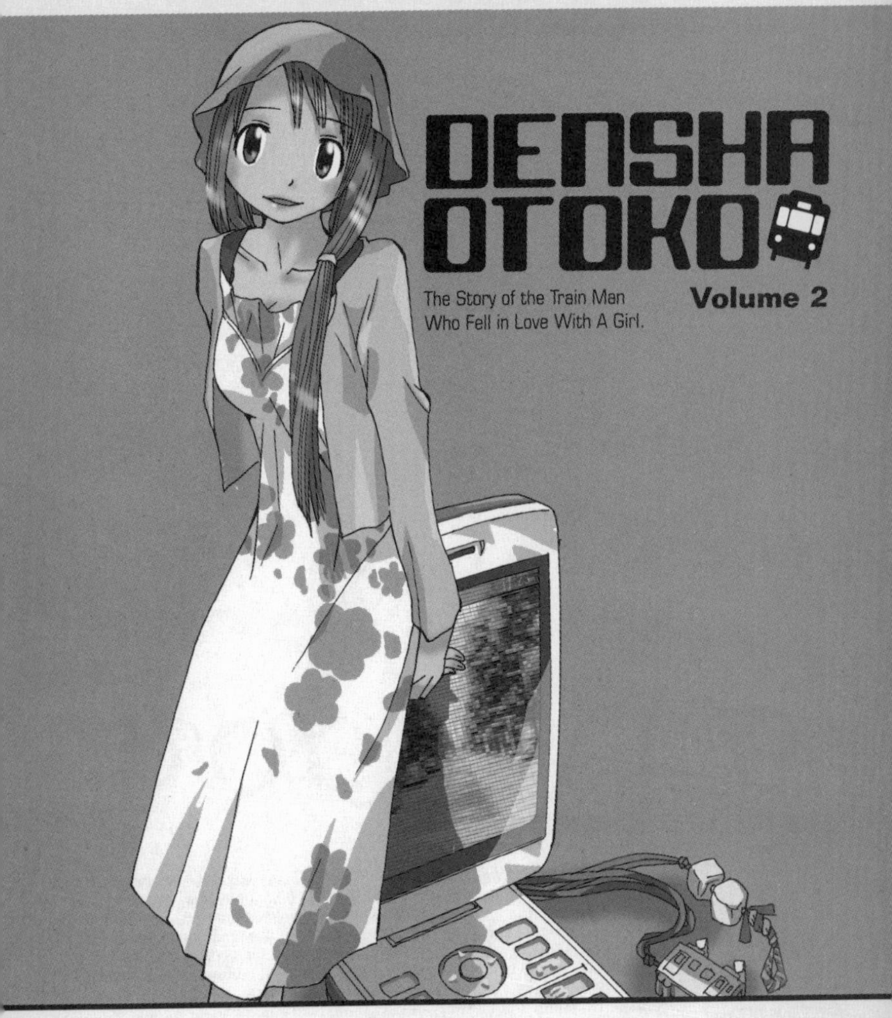
DENSHA OTOKO
The Story of the Train Man Who Fell in Love With A Girl.
Volume 2

By Hitori Nakano & Wataru Watanabe. The big day has come! "Train" is out on his date with "Hermess"! But now what? What does he say? What does he do? He's on his own and doesn't have his online support group to guide him through the event. You can be sure that he'll be back on the keyboard to recap it afterwards...and try to figure out what to do next. But will his anonymous "friends" still be able to relate to him?

The Story of The Train Man Who Fell in Love With A Girl.

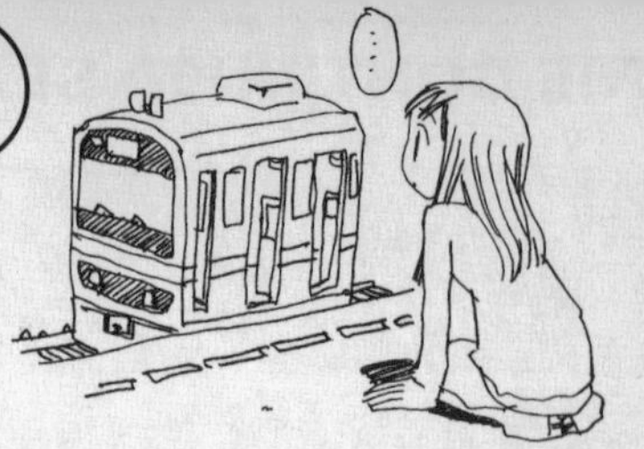

Truth or Fiction?
There's some debate over whether or not the original story this manga is based on ever actually happened. Supposedly a shy young Japanese man did meet a girl as a result of coming to her aid on a train, she did send him a gift of designer tea cups, and he did go online and ask visitors to a popular chat room for advice on how to win her over. This alleged online correspondence was collected into book form, the book became a best seller, and the story of "The Train Man"—true or not—went on to become a cultural phenomenon in Japan. It spawned a television series, a movie, and several manga, one of which became the English adaptation you now hold in your hands.

The debate continues as to whether or not the compiled material was real or made up and merely presented as reality. Whatever the case, it seems to be irrelevant. The story obviously struck a very deep chord and you could say that even if it didn't happen, it's easy enough to believe it might have happened.

What is an Otaku?
Part of the reason why the story found such wide acceptance is the fact that its lead character is an obvious "otaku." In America, perhaps the closest thing we might have to an otaku would be a geek or a nerd. Those terms are used to describe someone (usually a guy, but not always) with limited social skills and a set of obsessive interests in one or more of the following areas: comic books, anime, movies, science fiction, fantasy, video games, etc.

But in Japan, these types of individuals are perhaps even more hardcore and almost everyone seems to know at least one person who fits in this category. The term can have slightly more negative connotations as well. Otaku can be regarded as individuals whose entire lives revolve around their dedicated interests, almost to the exclusion of having normal, healthy lives. But many otaku have adapted the term as almost a badge of honor.

Densha Otoko or Otaku
Those of you who do not speak Japanese may be a bit confused about the title. DENSHA OTOKO literally translates to "Train Man." But a person in Japan could have an obsessive interest in trains, and then be called a Densha Otaku. I personally suspect that the play on words in this story's title might very well be deliberate.

Become an "OTOKO" Otaku
You can find a lot of information online about DENSHA OTOKO and otaku in general. But I warn you that it could be addicting and then you might become an otaku yourself. If you do, at least be sure to come back here for the rest of the series and let us know what you think.
You can write us at:

DENSHA OTOKO
c/o CMX
888 Prospect Street, Suite 240
La Jolla CA 92037

Or post your comments on the message boards at: cmxmanga.com

Jim Chadwick
Editor

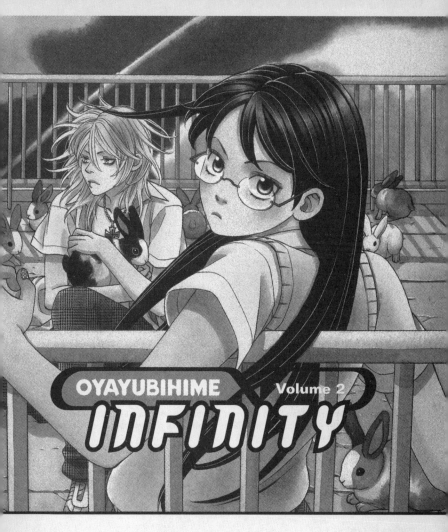

OYAYUBIHIME

INFINITY

Volume 2

By Toru Fujieda. Kanoko and friends have begun searching for a person with a butterfly-shaped birthmark on her thumb — the sign of a time-spanning connection from a past life — to find Tsubame's supposed true love. Who was this person, and what's she like now? But Tsubame might not be ready to give up on Kanoko just yet. He's got to persuade her that love is more important than fate.

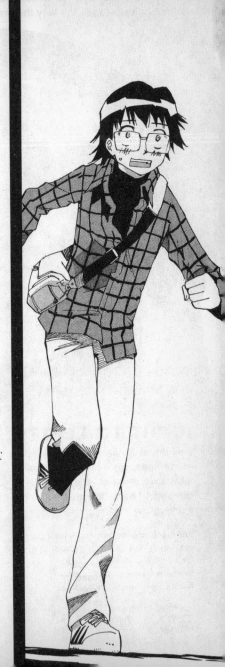

DENSHA OTOKO - DEMO ORE, TABIDATSUYO. - Vol.1 ©
2005 Wataru Watanabe, Hitori Nakano. All rights reserved.
First published in Japan in 2005 by Akita Publishing Co.,
Ltd., Tokyo.

DENSHA OTOKO - THE STORY OF THE TRAIN MAN WHO
FELL IN LOVE WITH A GIRL Volume 1, published by
WildStorm Productions, an imprint of DC Comics, 888
Prospect St. #240, La Jolla, CA 92037. English Translation
© 2006. All Rights Reserved. English translation rights in
U.S.A. And Canada arranged with Akita Publishing Co., Ltd.,
through Tuttle-Mori Agency, Inc., Tokyo. The stories, charac-
ters, and incidents mentioned in this magazine are entirely
fictional. Printed on recyclable paper. WildStorm does not
read or accept unsolicited submissions of ideas, stories or
artwork. Printed in Canada.

DC Comics, a Warner Bros. Entertainment Company.

Sheldon Drzka – Translation and Adaptation
Art Monkeys' Melanie Olsen – Lettering
Larry Berry – Design
Jim Chadwick – Editor

ISBN:1-4012-1141-0
ISBN-13: 978-1-4012-1141-7

All the pages in this book were created—and are printed in RIGHT-to-LEFT format. No ar... can read the stories the wa...

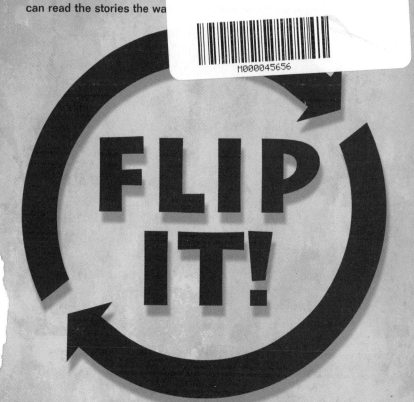

FLIP IT!

RIGHT TO LEFT?!

Traditional Japanese manga starts at the upper right-hand corner, and moves right-to-left as it goes down the page. Follow this guide for an easy understanding.

For more information and sneak previews, visit cmxmanga.com. Call 1-800-COMIC BOOK for the nearest comics shop or head to your local book store.

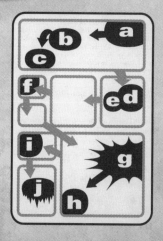